ENCYCLOPEDIA OF
REGIONAL
AMERICAN
GARDENING

ENCYCLOPEDIA OF REGIONAL AMERICAN GARDENING

Edited by Judith Lindquist
with a foreword by Alan Titchmarsh

Arch Cape Press
New York

This 1988 edition published by Arch Cape Press,
distributed by Crown Publishers, Inc., 225 Park
Avenue South, New York, New York 10003

© Octopus Books Limited 1988
Michelin House
81 Fulham Road
London SW3 6RB

ISBN 0-517-65345-1

h g f e d c b a

Editor: Marilyn Inglis
Art Editor: Bob Gordon
Picture Research: Angela Grant
Production Controller: Garry Lewis
Index: Hilary Bird

Typeset by J&L Composition Ltd,
Filey, North Yorkshire, England

Printed by Mandarin Offset in Hong Kong

CONTENTS

FOREWORD

Gardening is a funny thing. Some folks like it and some folks don't, but sooner or later the bug bites nearly everybody simply because there's nothing nicer than sitting out in the sun surrounded by flowers, fruits and vegetables that are home-grown.

I started early, being crazy about gardening at the age of 12, when I'd sow packets of seeds straight into the soil of our suburban garden. Sometimes they'd grow, and the thrill of seeing flowers that I'd never set eyes on before is one that's never faded. In a corner of the tiny garden I built a polythene greenhouse just 3 ft x 6 ft (90 x 180 cm) and packed it with potted plants. When other youngsters were playing football, I was pinching back petunias.

At last I got a job in the local nursery. That first day, when the foreman ushered me into a cathedral-like greenhouse and told me it was mine, was one of the happiest days of my life. I stood in the doorway gazing down the 75 ft (23 m) pathway with banks of flowering pot plants on either side. All was silent, except for the gentle dripping of water from the benches into the underground water tanks. Red and yellow plumes of celosia sprouted up among coleus and silk-barked oaks; primulas rubbed shoulders with geraniums and asparagus ferns. All I had to do was to keep them alive! From that day onward, growing plants has been an obsession.

There's an endless list of things to try, whether you have a patio or stately acres, a doorstep or a windowbox, a windowsill or a bottle garden. But one thing that gardening shouldn't be is boring. If it strikes you that a garden is simply something that must be kept tidy so that the neighbors don't complain, then you're missing out. It's not something to fit in between washing the car and doing the shopping on a Saturday morning; get the other jobs out of the way so that you can enjoy the gardening and take a bit of time over it.

The fact that things don't happen instantaneously in the garden is a positive advantage in a jet-set age. Mind you, the weeds can come through with seemingly jet-set speed even if your seedlings don't! And that's another point to remember, for even the most experienced gardeners have their failures. There are those who try once and then give up if they don't succeed – but they are the types who would never have scaled Everest, broken the World Land Speed Record or crossed the Atlantic in record time. Oh yes, gardening can be exciting stuff!

It's often very difficult to persuade new gardeners that there's more common sense to be found in this craft than there is muck and mystery. There is much to learn and many mistakes to be made, but with a book like *The Encyclopedia of Regional American Gardening* on your shelf you'll always have somewhere to turn for the answers. Treat your plants as individuals; observe them and you'll soon notice when they are not happy. The book will help you to pinpoint the cause of the problem and put it right, but your plants will still need a bit of tender loving care on your part.

Be original. Many a gardener is a stick-in-the-mud when it comes to devising a garden scheme and plant groupings. I don't believe it's for lack of imagination but because fear prevents them from trying anything different. A long time ago, one gardener decided to plant a summer bedding scheme with those pretty annual flowers. He liked the look of lobelia and alyssum along the front edge of the border to make a blue and yellow line. Behind these he put orange French marigolds, and behind the marigolds he planted scarlet salvias. To break the monotony he put 'dot plants' of gray-leaved cinerarias every yard or so. It made a bright scheme, but for some reason or other thousands of gardeners now copy this design as though there were no other. Where annuals are concerned, it's much more fun to think up a new color scheme for a bed or border as though you were decorating a room. Use shades of pink and pale blue, or oranges and yellows. Your garden will be far more varied as a result.

Don't be afraid of failure. Sometimes a group of plants that you thought would look tremendous looks just plain silly. But every now and again you'll get lucky and the result will look stunning.

There are a few rules in gardening that it's as well to observe, but hundreds of others are crying out to be bent.

What you must do above all is to make a garden that fits your needs. *You* are the person who must tend it. *You* are the person who must enjoy it. So, to hell with what the neighbors say – just get out there and have fun!

What about the plants that just won't grow? The chances are that it's your fault. You've probably put them in the wrong spot, or not given them the kind of treatment they need to do well. Generally speaking, most plants will thrive in good light and in well-drained soil that's been laced with manure or garden compost. Most gardeners, though, are faced with a plot that has rotten soil, more than its fair share of shade and otherwise far from ideal growing conditions. Don't worry.

This fat book contains plenty of plants that are adapted to thrive in such inhospitable spots. Choose the right plant for the right place and your problems will become a thing of the past – unless they are caused by pests and diseases, that is. Bugs, beasts and blights cause more worry in the garden than anything else. The tables on pages 228–232 will help you become a weekend expert at recognizing the most common ailments that are likely to assail your plants.

Have I made gardening sound like a minefield? It isn't really. It's one of the most rewarding, frustrating, fulfilling and irritating pursuits on earth – and it's much safer than trying to break the World Land Speed Record!

BACK TO BASICS

I f you have little or no gardening experience at all a new garden can be a daunting prospect, especially if it is wildly overgrown, littered with builders' debris or completely stripped of its topsoil during building operations. Whatever the state of your plot, and whatever you would like to make of it, it is a great advantage to acquire some basic knowledge of local climate, soil and situation before setting to work.

Climate
Climate is the single most important factor in deciding what plants to choose for the garden and in how successfully they will grow. Climate includes many variables – rainfall, humidity, temperature, wind, intensity of light and type of soil. Successful gardening requires familiarity with all of the variables specific to the gardener's locale. The regional guide, which begins on page 214, deals specifically with the various zones and regional influences in North America and lists the plants that thrive in each major section of the continent.

While regional guides are essential for selecting the right plants, they do not indicate the critical temperature variations that exist with differences in altitude and proximity to areas of water. Thermal belts and fog belts are always at work, and each small variation cannot be cited. There are areas in the United States where specific conditions exist in only a 5–10 mile (8–16 km) radius.

There are also variations from the general climate of the region within each garden. These may span a few yards (meters) or a few hundred acres (hectares). For example, a south-facing wall will store heat while a slope away from the protection of a building will be cooler. Warm air rises and cool air sinks, so gardens in hilly areas encompass several microclimates where tempera-

ture and humidity vary. Where there is protection from the wind – such as houses, a barrier of trees or a wall – heat will radiate from the structures, and a mass of warmer air can raise the existing temperatures.

Large areas of water considerably affect the climate within a zone. They can raise the temperature as much as one full zone from inland regions, so that sites close to the coast will have a lower hardiness zone than neighboring sites further inland.

These factors are specifically addressed in the regional section on pages 214–227 but it is important to note that everyone should consult with their state agricultural station, local garden suppliers and neighborhood green thumbs to determine specific regional climatic influences.

Soil
A fertile soil is the key to good plant growth, so it is worthwhile finding out what sort you have.

Soil is composed of inorganic matter (minute rock particles), organic matter (from decayed plants and animals), bacteria and other micro-organisms, water and air. It is the varying proportions of these ingredients that create the various soil types.

The final breakdown of organic matter results in the colloid known as humus. This coats all the rock particles and, being of a jelly-like nature, holds moisture and dissolved minerals, which are essential plant foods.

Soils composed largely of very fine particles (clay and silt) are heavy and have very small air spaces. They dry out slowly and are poorly aerated. On the other hand, such soils also have a high mineral content and are rich in plant food. For most plants, however, these soils need to be broken up with a fork and to have organic matter and/or coarse

mineral particles, such as sand, added to make them better drained. Soils with a high clay content can be readily hand-molded when moist, and this is the easiest identification test to apply.

Soils composed of larger particles (sand) are the opposite of clay, being very loose, free-draining and aerated but with very poor supplies of plant food.

Loam is the name given to a blend of clay and sand. It is a very variable soil, depending on the amounts of clay and sand present. The best loams have more clay than sand, plus a good organic matter content.

Soils composed largely of organic matter are those known as peat or mull. Peat is formed in bogs or fens and is composed mostly of dead plant remains in a state of arrested decay owing to lack of oxygen in waterlogged conditions. Bog or moss peat is largely formed of sphagnum moss; sedge or fen peat of the roots and leaves of sedges. They are low in plant food but are excellent humus-providers and conditioners to add to clay and sandy soils. Mixed with mineral plant foods, they form the basis of modern potting mixes. Mull is the top layer of partially decayed soil in woodland and is better known as leaf mold. It is best used in the same way as peat.

Acidity and alkalinity
In addition to all other factors, soil is either acid, alkaline (limy) or neutral in reaction. All plants need lime for healthy growth, but usually in small quantities. Most plants do best under neutral conditions; that is, halfway between acid and alkaline. Some plants thrive where there is plenty of lime, for example members of the cabbage family, while others must have acid conditions, for example rhododendrons and their allies. For those reasons it is worthwhile testing your soil for its lime content. There are several very simple

testing kits on the market that use the chemical pH scale; this is numbered from 0–14. Zero indicates maximum acidity, 14 maximum alkalinity, and 7 is neutral. The kits use an indicator chart: red = acid, blue = alkaline, green = neutral.

Soil minerals

For satisfactory growth, plants need certain basic minerals. These fall into two groups: the major nutrient elements and the minor or trace elements. The first group contains nitrogen, phosphorus, potassium, magnesium and sulphur, all of which are needed in relatively large amounts. Trace elements are needed in minute amounts, but their deficiency can cause serious disorders to certain plants; they are calcium, iron, manganese, copper, zinc, boron, molybdenum and chlorine. Some of these occur as impurities in the major elements, and they seldom need to be added separately. All the best general fertilizers now contain the most important of them.

Major elements

These are essential for all plants and each one fulfills a need in the plant tissue.

Nitrogen is essential for the formation of proteins which, in turn, are constituents of protoplasm, the life-stuff of all plants. It is in short supply in most soils, especially in the vegetable garden where crops are continually being harvested. It can easily be added by dressing the soil with a nitrogenous fertilizer; for example, sulphate of ammonia, nitrate of lime, urea.

Phosphorus enters into the complex process of photosynthesis and is a constituent of protoplasm. It can be added to the soil by dressing with fertilizers known as phosphates; for example, superphosphate or bonemeal.

Potassium is an essential constituent of the plant cell nucleus. It is also needed for the functioning of several enzymes, which result in the formation of starches, sugars and fibrous tissue. It is added as a potash fertilizer; for example, sulphate of potash. (Contrary to popular belief there is very little potassium in pure wood ash.)

Magnesium is essential for certain enzymes involved in the movement of phosphates within the plant and is a constituent of chlorophyll. It is added as magnesium sulphate (Epsom Salts) at $1\frac{1}{4}$ oz (30 g) per sq yd (m) in spring.

Sulphur, an essential constituent of proteins, also enters into the make-up of protoplasm. In the soil it is usually combined with other minerals as a sulphate and is applied as a fertilizer in this form; for example, sulphate of potash.

Compost is built up in layers of soil, vegetable matter and an activator. Appropriate containers are available or you can make your own.

Preparation

Before one can improve the soil and make it ready for planting, the site must be cleared. This may mean removing builders' rubble or clearing overgrown shrubs and deep-seated perennial weeds. There is now a range of substances called herbicides (weedkillers), stocked by every garden center, which can be used to kill woody and deep-rooted perennial weeds. Used according to instructions, these can be a boon to the gardener. Once the site is cleared, work on improving the soil can begin. Although most soils will readily support plant life, most benefit from soil amendments.

Drainage

Soils that quickly become waterlogged after rain require the most improvement. Few plants thrive in soil that is wet for most of the year, and some sort of drainage system should be installed. The most efficient method is to lay land drainage pipes, which involves a herringbone pattern of trenches leading to an outlet ditch. This needs professional advice and is seldom practical in the small garden. An alternative is to create raised beds, either by digging out paths and placing the soil on the bed sites or mixing in well-drained topsoil. Although often expensive, the latter alternative is to be recommended. Indeed, it is the only really effective solution if the garden site has been denuded of its topsoil during building operations. Subsoil can be rendered fertile with organic matter, but this is likely to be at least as expensive as soil.

If the soil is of a clay type and only lies wet after heavy rain, there are several less drastic measures one can take. Acid clays benefit from an application of hydrated lime. This has the effect of clumping the tiny clay particles into larger ones, creating air spaces between them and allowing freer passage of water. Both acid and limy clays benefit greatly from doses of organic matter (humus) provided by such substances as rotted farmyard manure, garden compost, spent hops (hop manure) or peat. Humus, by coating the clay particles, opens them up. Another method of opening up a clay soil is to add generous quantities of coarse sand or grit, digging it well into the clay.

Making compost

Well-made compost is an invaluable component that helps the soil maintain its fertility. Any refuse which will rot is suitable but it is best to exclude diseased material and weeds that have gone to seed. Too many grass cuttings should not be put into the heap at one time as they will turn into a soggy mess.

Put a 5–6 inch (13–15 cm) layer of vegetable matter directly on to the soil base. Add a sprinkling of garden soil and then another layer of vegetable matter. Top with a sprinkling of garden lime or suitable activator. Repeat these layers until the container is full. Cover the container with plastic sheeting with ventilation holes in it and top with an insulating layer of soil.

The quality of the compost will be improved and decomposition hastened if the sides of the heap, which will be less rotted, are turned in to the middle after 2–3 weeks. The compost will generally be ready for use after about 6 months but may take longer.

Digging

Forking and turning the top layer of soil over is necessary for the working in of humus and sand. Digging by itself also opens up the soil and provides temporary drainage channels. An additional benefit is gained if the soil is dug in autumn and the surface left in a very rough or irregular state. In cold climates, frost will penetrate, expanding the accumulated water and separating the particles. All soils benefit from an initial digging and the working in of organic matter – especially if they are sandy, chalky or otherwise very free-draining, or clay, as we have already seen above. In the past soils were deeply dug, often twice or three times the depth of a fork. Nobody wants to do that sort of thing nowadays and, happily, it is not essential. One fork's depth or even a bit less is enough – about 6–9 inches (15–23 cm) deep.

No digging

There is a school of thought which says, not without justification, that it is unnecessary and wrong to dig and invert the upper soil layers. Non-diggers apply organic matter as a top dressing (layer) to allow worms and other soil organisms to work it in naturally. This system works well if the soil has no persistent perennial weeds, there is a plentiful supply of organic matter (it must be applied annually on the vegetable plot), and the site is not waterlogged.

The no-digging approach has much to commend it for perennials, shrubs or mixed beds or for planting trees. Use a hormone weedkiller to remove weeds or grass if the site was a field or lawn. Dig holes at the tree or shrub sites and incorporate organic matter as each plant is set in position. For a perennials bed or border, spread organic matter in a layer not less than 2–3 inches (5–7.5 cm) deep and work it in around the roots.

If you favor a digging system, incorporate the organic matter before planting. Weedkillers can still be used initially, or perennial weed roots must be picked out during the digging operation.

Tools
A wide range of tools is available from garden centers, horticultural suppliers, supermarkets, etc. Some are basic and essential, others have a very limited use or are downright gimmicky. With all tools, go for the best. Choose a reputable maker who uses quality steel. It is also essential to handle each tool you think of buying to see if it feels comfortable to use. Good tools of this sort should last for many years if you look after them. Although it may seem a chore, always clean tools after use and, ideally, wipe them over with an oily rag. For the novice gardener, the following tools will prove indispensable:

Spade for digging, and making trenches and planting holes. A full-sized one is best, but smaller so-called ladies' spades are also available for those who are not used to manual labor.

Fork (the same size as the spade but with five tines instead of the blade) for digging, loosening the soil surface and using as a rake for rough leveling. Smaller versions are available.

Trowel for planting and lifting young plants and bulbs. A model that has the blade on an L-shaped shaft so that it sits below the level of the handle is best.

Handfork as a companion to the trowel, preferably with at least four tines. It is ideal for weeding, loosening compacted surface soil around young plants, and lifting and separating larger plants.

Hoe for weeding and loosening the soil surface and for taking out seed furrows. There are several kinds of hoeing tools available. The conventional hoe is most widely used, but there are three-tined hoes and English scuffle hoes that cut weeds as they are pulled and pushed. Ideally you should experiment with several different kinds of hoe depending on your particular needs.

Rake for leveling the soil, especially prior to making furrows and sowing grass seed. A rake is also invaluable if you have a lot of trees in your garden and need to clear fallen leaves off the ground in the autumn.

Pruning shears and a garden line are also well worth acquiring. A garden line is essential for drawing out straight seed furrows and for marking out beds and borders. Pruning shears are necessary for pruning trees and shrubs and even for removing light scrub from an overgrown garden. Always keep shears sharpened, or they will be useless for the job.

Digging with the correct weight spade (far left) and using a long-handled cultivator.

Preparing the seed bed with a rake (far left) and weeding with one variety of hoe.

THE LAWN

Despite the chore of mowing, there is no doubt that a lawn can add an air of peace and maturity to a garden and provides a splendid foil for the flowers. At the other extreme, a lawn can be an important recreation area for children's and adults' games and barbecues. In general, the larger the lawn the more effective and useful it is, provided there are flower and/or shrub beds of sufficient depth and substance to enclose it. Not enough consideration is given to the shape of a lawn. It is usually thought of as a square or oblong carpet when an irregular curving shape would be more effective. To be both useful and aesthetically pleasing, a lawn must not be too small. Anything less than 10 ft x 10 ft (3 m x 3 m) usually looks rather paltry and is really not worth the cost of a mower. In such a situation a paved area would be more sensible, especially with a few tough but pleasing rock plants erupting from the crevices.

Preparing the site
As the lawn is likely to occupy more than half of your flower garden, it is seldom possible to choose a site that is suitable overall for the grasses that will compose it. Ideally, the best site is open to the sky with no large trees nearby. At least it should not be shaded for more than half the day in summer. Grass does, of course, grow in shade and there are some special mixtures for growing under trees, but they form loose turf which does not stand up to hard wear.

The soil should be reasonably well drained; waterlogged land is no good for a lawn and must be drained first. Laying tile drains (earthenware pipes) is the usual solution. A herringbone pattern of trenches at least 1 ft (30 cm) deep is dug across the lawn area with the bottom of the main (central) trench at the lowest point. The tile drains, 2–3 inches (5–7.5 cm) in diameter, are laid, butted end to end and just covered with gravel. The trenches are then filled and secured. For the less wet site, stones or coarse gravel alone can be used about 5–6 inches (13–15 cm) deep. At the lowest point there must be a ditch or drain to take surplus water.

Horizontal lawns are the norm, but sloping ones can be very effective. Whichever you choose to create, the surface must be level enough for a mower to negotiate it easily. This is the primary consideration when preparing the site. If it is a new one remove any builders' rubbish, making sure there are no half-buried lumps of concrete or bricks. At this point, if the soil is thin, chalky or sandy, apply a dressing (at least 2 inches [5 cm] thick) of peat, garden compost or decayed manure. Afterwards, turn over at least the top 9 inches (23 cm) or use a rotary tiller. Level any bumps and hollows, and tread the surface to finish. Rake thoroughly down the plot then across, removing all the larger stones. Ideally, allow the soil to settle for at least a month, preferably twice as long. Any weeds that appear during this period must be hoed out or treated with a short-term commercial herbicide.

Sowing
Grasses are categorized as either cool-season or warm-season varieties. The cool-season grasses, including bentgrass, fescue, Kennedy bluegrass and ryegrass, are used mainly in the north. Warm-season grasses, including Bermuda grass, centipede grass, St Augustine grass and zoysia, are especially adapted to southern climates. Cool-season grasses are usually seeded in early spring or autumn while warm-season grasses should be started in late spring or early summer.

Grass seed is light and not easily sown evenly by hand, so if possible borrow or rent a spreader. If you do sow by hand, mark out the lawn in 1 yd (1 m) wide strips with string and stakes (see illustration on page 14. If the soil is very fertile and has been weeded once or twice beforehand, allow $\frac{1}{2}$ oz (15 g) of seed per sq yd (m). If the soil is less rich and has not been weeded before sowing, double this quantity. As much as 2 oz (60 g) per sq yd (m) is sometimes recommended, but this is very wasteful of seed and can lead to such troubles as damping-off disease. Mark off a sq yd (m), weigh the appropriate amount of seed and do a trial sowing to see what the density looks like. Thereafter, it should be possible to continue at that rate along each strip. When the entire lawn has been sown, gently rake the surface with long, steady strokes first down and then across to cover as much of the seed as possible. Cover the area with netting or black cotton raised up on short sticks if birds are troublesome. (It is important to use cotton rather than nylon, which can trap birds by their legs.) Nothing need be done until the seedlings are well grown if the soil is moist. If the surface dries out before germination, use a fine spray or lawn sprinkler.

Maintenance: When the seedling grasses are about 1 inch (2.5 cm) high, give them a light rolling. This helps to firm the little plants and encourages branching from the base. A week later, mow the lawn, setting the cutting blade at $\frac{3}{4}$–1 inch (2–2.5 cm). About two months after germination, or in the spring following an autumn sowing, you can apply a light top dressing of sandy soil, though it is not essential. Use a dressing of compost or 50–50 garden soil and sand, making it about $\frac{1}{2}$ inch (12 mm) deep. If you did not do it previously, spread a commercial fertilizer over the area according to the label

directions. Water regularly during dry spells and remove any broad-leaved weeds by hand.

Thereafter, feed at least annually in spring and, ideally, in early autumn also. Apply weed and moss killers as required, always following the makers' directions. It is advisable to apply a top dressing of fine compost, soil or sand and peat at least every other year. Prior to this, work over the grass with a wire-tined rake to remove dead grass and moss. If the soil surface becomes compacted, go over it with a spiked roller or a handfork to aerate. Fallen leaves should be raked regularly in autumn to prevent the grass yellowing and even browning.

Sodding

Starting a lawn from sod is more expensive than seed, especially if you buy a good-quality product. Sod is lawn grass that has been seeded and grown on a sod farm, cut loose from the soil and rolled or stacked. About ¾ inch (2 cm) of soil is attached. It achieves an instant lawn and prevents erosion on slopes.

Prepare the site as for seed; early autumn and spring are the best times for laying. Apply a lawn fertilizer before laying and rake it in. Stand to one side of the lawn site and lay a row of sods along one edge, butting them end to end. Now place a plank across the laid sods and put down the next row, staggering them like rows of bricks in a wall. Move the plank over and lay the next row and so on until the job is complete. If the lawn has curving edges, shape the sod by trimming with a sharp serrated knife. Don't worry about odd points or edges of sod protruding over the lawn outline as these can be trimmed with an edging tool when the laying is completed. Walking along the plank will firm the sod as it is laid (any that misses the plank should be tapped down with the back of a

spade). You can give it a light rolling but this should not be necessary. If there are any cracks between the strips of sod, fill them with fine soil and sand and work it in with the back edge of a rake.

Maintenance: Autumn-laid sod will not need mowing until the following spring. Spring-laid sod will need to be cut about 3–4 weeks later. Make the first cut a high one, about 1 inch (2.5 cm), but thereafter mow as required. The procedures for feeding, watering and weeding are the same as for a seeded lawn.

Neglected lawns

If you move into an older property with an established garden, you might be faced with a lawn that has been neg-

An impeccable lawn is an ideal foil for lavishly planted beds and borders.

lected and looks unkempt and weedy. It will be quite easy to renovate if you carry out the following procedure. First, mow it, setting the blade of the mower as high as is necessary to prevent it being fouled by over-thick grass. A rotary mower is best or for very long thick grass, a power clipper may be needed. After mowing, work the lawn over with a wire-tined rake to remove dead grass bases and moss; choose mild spells if you are doing this in winter. Apply an appropriate lawn fertilizer in late winter and water in if need be. Dig out the worst broad-leaved weeds, if any, and apply a

Mark out the ground in 1 yd/m strips to ensure an even sowing of seed.

Sod should be laid in staggered rows working from one corner. If you need to cut a sod, use a half-moon edger and not a spade.

A square-point trowel can be used for firming the sod into place instead of a spade.

lawn weedkiller such as 2,4–D. If you take over the lawn in the spring to early autumn period, apply the fertilizers and weedkiller immediately after raking. If there are bare areas after weeding and using the weedkiller, loosen any compacted soil, rake it smooth and sow seed or insert a plug of sod. From now on, follow the lawn maintenance procedures as outlined for **Sowing**. A neglected lawn that receives treatment should be virtually back to normal again after one growing season.

Tools

There are certain basic tools needed to maintain a good lawn. Essentials are a lawn mower, digging fork, shovel, standard rake, wire-tined lawn rake, edging shears and a birch broom. A roller is not essential, especially if a cylinder mower with a roller attached is used. A fertilizer spreader and a leaf sweeper are very useful for a large lawn. If your lawn is on heavy soil which gets compacted and needs regular aerating, a hollow-tined spiker or a spiked roller is well worthwhile. A power-driven edger is definitely a luxury item but nevertheless nice to have.

The many lawn mowers available today can be classified into two groups according to the cutting design. Cylinder machines have a ring of blades curving round a central spindle which revolves when the machine is used, bringing each blade in turn across a fixed plate. A scissor-like action is created as each blade crosses the plate, and grass trapped between the two is cut cleanly. Whether motor-powered or hand-operated, cylinder machines give the neatest finish, providing the lawn surface is level and the grass dry.

Rotary mowers are always motor-operated. They have horizontally set propeller-like blades which cut the grass as much by their high speed as by their sharpness. They are best suited to the hard-wearing lawn or shallow rough banks where they will also deal effectively with grass which has been allowed to grow overly long. Rotary machines are either on wheels or operate on the hovercraft principle. If the lawn surface is uneven or the rough banks are steep, the hover type is the only mower that will do the job efficiently. It can also be used when the grass is wet.

Whichever machine you use it must be maintained in good order. Hand-operated machines must be regularly cleaned and oiled and the blades sharpened. Power mowers must be regularly serviced, ideally once a year. Do not expect to have a lawn worthy of admiration if your mower is not working efficiently.

ABOVE: *Again, mark out the ground in 1yd/m strips to ensure an even application of fertilizer or weedkiller.*

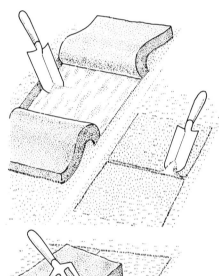

*To remedy bumps or hollows, make an H-shaped cut in the sod (**top left**), roll back the flaps and remove surplus soil or fill in with fresh compost.*
*Damaged patches of lawn can be re-seeded or lifted and replaced with new sod, (**bottom left**). Tamp down. Keep the area well watered for 2–3 weeks to help the edges knit together.*

Whether you decide to leave grass cuttings on the lawn after you have mown it or not is a matter of personal choice. If you do not have a machine that collects grass as you mow, you can rake it up afterwards. Or if you prefer you can leave cut grass on the lawn. Some experts say that the lawn will be greatly improved if the grass cuttings are left on it, while as many gardeners insist that you get better results if the lawn is raked clear. To date, no one has proved it either way!

Pests and diseases

Among the pests which affect a lawn are the grubs of beetles and chinch bugs, while worms leave unsightly casts. Grass which is in poor condition may suffer from various fungal diseases, notably dollar spot, snow mold and red thread. Fairy rings (rings of dark green grass caused by fungi growing on organic matter buried in the soil) do no lasting damage but they do spoil the overall appearance of a lawn.

GARDEN FLOWERS

I t would be an odd sort of garden that did not contain any of the annuals, perennials and bulbs that make up the bulk of cultivated flowering plants. Very varied in their height, mode of growth, flower size, shape and color, they can be used in every garden and all situations. Their primary limitation is lack of winter interest, but there are a surprising number of plants, mostly bulbs, which will flower over the winter months.

Annuals and biennials

These grow from seed, flower and die. Annuals do this within one growing season; biennials make leafy growth one year and flower the next. Few biennials are grown these days, the most popular being Canterbury bells and foxgloves. Some perennials are grown as biennials, for example English daisies (bellis) and wallflowers (cheiranthus).

A wide variety of annuals is available. They are indispensable for a quick display in a new garden and to fill in gaps among other plants, for example where spring bulbs have died down. There are two groups of annuals: hardy and half-hardy. The latter must be raised in warmth and the young plants set out when threat of frost has passed. Hardy annuals tolerate low temperatures and can be sown in spring or even the previous autumn in mild areas for an extra early flowering. Both sorts can also be used in their own right to fill beds and borders, creating a spectacular display in mid-summer. The only disadvantage of this sort of gardening is its fairly brief season – summer and early autumn. However, with the aid of biennials, notably forget-me-not (myosotis), wallflowers and English daisies, plus bulbs such as tulips, a spring display can be created. It gives you a colorful display, but this spring and summer bedding

approach to gardening requires planning and is fairly labor-intensive, what with the raising of young plants, first for the spring then the summer displays, the clearing out in between, the planting and weeding. Much depends on the size of your garden and the time you have to spare.

Perennials

These are more versatile and are basically long-lived plants which grow annually from a perennial root, bloom, and die back to ground level for the winter. The true herbaceous perennial dies away completely in autumn, but others retain their basal leaves and are essentially evergreen. Bergenia is a fine example of a perennial that maintains its handsome winter leaves except in the coldest zones. Beds and borders composed entirely of hardy perennials have long been popular, having something to offer the whole year, though there will be very little in winter. Perennial borders do require maintenance. Cutting down dead stems, staking tall species, feeding, weeding, and lifting and dividing every 3–5 years are essential for a lively and healthy display. Nowadays, mixed borders are gaining in popularity. Shrubs are used as the backbone of a bed or border and filled in with perennials, annuals and bulbs. A nicely chosen ensemble of plants can create a very satisfying display.

Bulbs

Our third category of garden flowers can be looked upon as full-grown plants in capsule form. Within each one are a flower spike and embryo leaves just waiting for sufficient warmth and moisture to pump them up to full size, hence the speed at which most bulbs perform when given the right conditions. Where would the spring garden be without its snowdrops, crocus, hyacinths, narcissi

and tulips? They are, in fact, perfect plants for providing winter and spring color in either the mixed, perennial or shrub borders, planted alone, or with a few biennials to provide the major display.

Cultivation

None of these garden flowers demands anything more than a reasonably well-drained ordinary garden soil. However, within reason, the better the soil the better the floral display. The lighter sandy or chalky soils in particular will benefit from organic matter. Rotted manure, garden compost, peat or composted bark at one 2 gal (9 liter) bucketful per sq yd (m) will condition the soil and greatly improve the plants' performance. Make sure that all perennial weeds are removed during soil preparation. Failure to do so could result in perennial plants being invaded by weed roots, spoiling their performance.

Planting

Hardy perennials can be purchased in containers or bare root direct from the nursery. The planting procedure is the same for both. Dig a hole with a trowel or spade about one and a half times as large as the root ball. Set the plant in the hole so that its crown (the point at which the annual stems arise) is about 1 inch (2.5 cm) below the surrounding soil surface. Fill in around the roots and firm with fists or feet, depending on the size of the plant.

Half-hardy annual plants raised under glass for setting out in late spring or early summer, though generally smaller, are dealt with in the same way as hardy perennials.

Bulbs, corms and tubers are bought in a dormant state and are more easily dealt with. Dig out a hole three times the length of the bulb. (For instance, place a 2 inch [5 cm] long narcissus bulb in a

hole 6 inches [15 cm] deep.) Fill in with soil and firm well. Some corms, notably crocus and gladiolus, are disc-shaped; plant these at a depth equal to three or four times their diameter.

The distance at which to space individual plants and bulbs is often found in books, on garden center information labels and on seed packets, but there is no immutable measurement laid down for each species. As a quick and easy guide, set plants at a distance apart equal to one half (for bulbs, one third) of their mature height.

Supporting

Although many sturdy wind-firm annuals and quite a number of perennials are available, there is still a host of desirable species liable to damage from a strong wind, especially if it is accompanied by rain. Annuals and perennials that exceed 2 ft (60 cm) in height are best given some means of support. This should be as inconspicuous as possible so as not to detract from the flowers. A time-honored method is to surround each plant with several short pea sticks. Push these in firmly so that the tops are about half the full-grown height of the plants (see illustration). Do this while the growth is still young and short. Ultimately the stems will grow up through and over the sticks and be perfectly supported. Really tall plants, like delphiniums, will need tying to stakes.

There are also custom-made supports available at garden centers based upon squares or circles of strong galvanized wire, usually with a grid of cross wires. These are placed over individual plants in the spring so that the stems can grow through and be supported. They are ideal for peonies and other heavy-headed perennials.

Bulbous species are mainly self-supporting, but large-bloomed gladioli and lilies can suffer in a summer gale and are best secured to slim stakes or stabilized with grids.

Maintenance

Weeding must be attended to early in the season or throughout the first year in a perennials border or bed. Once the plants are established and growing well, they knit together and suppress all summer weeds. Annuals also need weeding when young but should soon meet and prevent all but the odd extra-vigorous weed. Apply a mulch every other year unless the soil is very thin

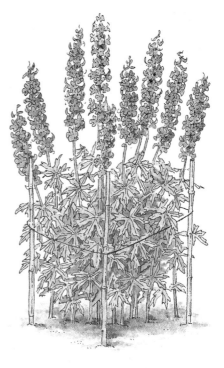

LEFT: *Dianthus, an easy rock garden plant.*
ABOVE: *Support a clump of tall plants by means of pea sticks and twine.*

LEFT: *Garden flowers can look as good in containers as in a formal flower bed.*
BELOW: *Outdoor cultivation – sow seeds in shallow furrows (**top**) and thin out to leave the strongest plants (**bottom**).*
BOTTOM: *Indoor cultivation – sow seed in an electric propagator or in a seed tray (**top**). Thin out to leave about 28 seedlings (**bottom left**). The plants can be hardened off in a cold frame (**bottom right**).*

and poor, in which case you should apply mulch yearly. In addition, on all but the richer soils, apply a dressing of general fertilizer annually in spring.

Propagation

The majority of perennials, annuals and bulbs are easily multiplied by one or several of the following techniques.
Seed: True annuals can only be propagated from seed and many perennials can also be easily raised by this means. Bulbs, too, are raised from seed by enthusiasts but, though easily done, one must expect to wait several years before the young plants reach flowering size.

Half-hardy annuals are sown in warmth from late winter to mid-spring. As comparatively small numbers of plants are needed for the average garden, fill 3–4 inch (7.5–10 cm) pots or 5 inch (13 cm) pans with a standard seed mix. Firm lightly and sow the seed thinly. Large seeds are best sown individually; for example, sweet peas can go in 1 inch (2.5 cm) apart. Cover the seed shallowly with the same soil at a depth no more than twice the diameter of the seeds. Water and place in a propagating case, enclosed in a plastic bag or covered with a sheet of glass, and keep out of direct sunlight. Most half-hardy annuals need a minimum temperature of 60°F (15°C) to germinate and respond even more positively to 65–70°F (18–21°C), though some appreciate even higher temperatures. When the seedlings appear, remove the glass or plastic and acclimatize them to bright light.

As soon as the seed leaves are fully expanded and one or two true leaves show, transplant the seedlings into separate containers. This involves carefully separating the tiny plants, handling them by their leaves only.

Hardy perennials can be set out in a cold frame, but seedling bulbs are best kept in pots in a cool or cold greenhouse. Most bulb seedlings, for example tulip, narcissus and hyacinth, make one leaf only in the first year and form a tiny

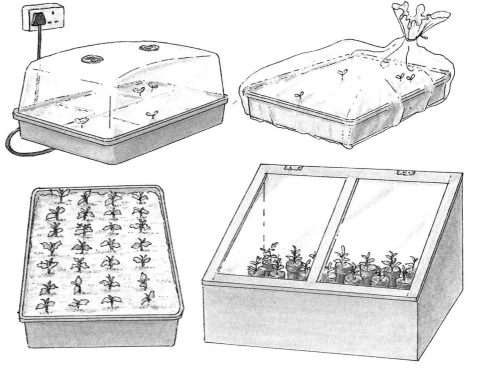

bulb, which is best grown on for a further year in containers before planting outside.

In late spring half-hardy annuals must be hardened off prior to planting out when the threat of frost has passed. Place the containers of young plants in a cold frame, or turn off the heat in the greenhouse. Ventilate on sunny days for the first 5 days, then take off the frame lid (light) each day and close at night; finally, leave the frames open all the time. Hardening off takes 10–14 days. Hardy perennials raised in warmth should also have a hardening-off period before planting out. They can also be sown in cold frames or outside in mid- to late spring, which is standard for biennials from late spring to early summer.

Division Among garden flowers this method is restricted to hardy perennials. Established clumps are lifted in late winter or early spring and divided. The easiest way is to thrust two forks back-to-back into the center of the clump then pull the handles apart. This can be repeated on the halves to make four nice plants. Some vigorous perennials, notably Michaelmas daisy (aster), are best reduced to small pieces with one to three shoots. Some woody-crowned perennials, for example peony, and thick fleshy ones such as anchusa, are best divided with the hands and judicious use of an old bread knife. Divisions are planted immediately where they are to bloom. Congested clumps of daffodil and snowdrop bulbs etc. can also be divided either when dormant or just after flowering.

Cuttings: These are of two kinds, stem cuttings and root cuttings. For both kinds some form of cold frame or propagating case is required; even one or two covered jars are suitable. Make sure the soil is sandy and well drained, or prepare a bed or box of 50–50 peat moss and coarse sand.

Stem cuttings: Choose basal shoots with 4–6 leaves (these are ready from mid-spring to early summer, depending on the species of plant). Cut off the shoots as near to ground level as possible, trim off the lowest leaf or two, dip in a rooting powder and insert the lower one-third in the rooting mixture. Space the cuttings about $1\frac{1}{2}$–2 inches (3–5 cm) apart each way. When they are well rooted and showing new growth, lift the young plants and grow them in nursery rows until autumn.

Root cuttings: Certain perennials, for example anchusa, Japanese anemones, dicentra and phlox, can produce shoots directly from their roots. In late winter, either lift a plant or carefully brush away the soil on one side to expose the roots. Fibrous-rooted plants such as Japanese anemones and phlox are easily dealt with in this latter way. Choose the thickest roots and cut them into 2–3 inch (5–7.5 cm) long pieces. Bury these horizontally about $\frac{1}{2}$ inch (1 cm) deep

Plan your planting carefully so that you can have color throughout the year. Also, take care to arrange plants so that taller varieties will not dwarf smaller ones.

in containers of sandy soil or insert directly into a prepared soil bed or a cold frame.

The deeply delving fleshy roots of anchusa are dealt with differently. Choose pieces of pencil thickness and cut into $1\frac{1}{2}$–2 inch (4–5 cm) lengths. Cut the tops (the end nearest the plant) straight and make a sloping cut at the bottom so that you know which way to plant. Insert these vertically with the tops just covered with soil. When the shoots are well developed, transfer them to a nursery bed and grow until autumn.

Layering: Another propagation method, especially suitable for carnations and pinks, is layering. A non-flowering shoot is covered with soil and pinned down by a stone or piece of tile (see illustration). The layered shoot is left attached to the parent plant until well rooted. It is then cut off and planted.

Pin down a shoot to be layered and cover it with soil and a stone.

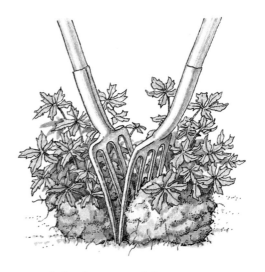

Divide hardy perennials by using two forks placed back to back in the plant.

A-Z
GARDEN FLOWERS

ACANTHUS ZONES 5–9
The best hardy member of acanthus or bear's breech is indispensable as a specimen plant in the flower garden. *A. mollis* forms bold clumps of arching, deeply dissected, dark glossy green leaves and erect 4 ft (1.2 m) tall spikes of foxglove-like mauve-purple bracts sheltering hooded white flowers in summer.
General care: A sunny sheltered site and a fertile soil give the best results.
Propagation: Divide in spring or take root cuttings in late winter.
Pests and diseases: Generally trouble-free.

ACHILLEA ZONES 2–8
All the yarrows have aromatic fern-like foliage and flattish clusters of small, closely packed flowers.

The following are good varieties for the herbaceous border: 'Coronation Gold' (hardy to zone 3), which flowers in mid-summer, bearing golden-yellow heads on slender stems clothed with silver-gray foliage, and grows 3 ft (90 cm) tall; 'Gold Plate', a taller variety that can grow up to 4 ft (1.2 m) tall and flowers from mid-summer through early autumn, bearing large golden-yellow flower-heads on stiff stems clothed in gray-green foliage; and 'Moonshine' (hardy to zone 3), a dwarf variety growing only 2 ft (60 cm) high, which is useful for

Achillea 'Gold Plate'

the front of the border. This is a new pale yellow hybrid with silver foliage and is a good variety. *A. ptarmica* 'The Pearl' (hardy to zone 2) is a neat 18 inch (45 cm) plant that produces double, pure white rosettes over a long blooming season.
General care: These hardy perennials do best in well-drained sunny situations and they should be divided and replanted in the spring. If they are left for several seasons the flowers deteriorate.
Propagation: Divide in autumn or early spring.
Pests and diseases: Generally trouble-free.

ACONITUM ZONES 2–8
Popularly known as monkshood, these are showy perennials that produce delphinium-like blooms from mid-summer through fall. Care should be taken with children and pets since all parts of the plant are poisonous. It does best in zones with cold winters and mild summer temperatures.

A. carmichaelii (hardy to zone 2) produces rich blue spikes on celery-like foliage in late summer through early autumn on stems 2–3 ft (60–90 cm) tall. 'Wilsonii' is a stately variety, growing 6–8 ft (1.8–2.4 m) tall with flower clusters measuring 10–18 inches (25–45 cm) long. 'Bressingham Spire' grows to

3 ft (90 cm) tall on sturdy stems with tapering spikes of deep violet-blue.

General care: Humus-rich, moist soil and light shade are all that is required. Mulch in winter in colder areas.

Propagation: Divide in autumn or spring every 2–3 years to promote vigorous blooming.

Pests and diseases: Generally trouble-free.

ACROCLINUM
See under Helipterum Roseum

ADONIS   ZONES 2–8
Commonly known as pheasant's eye, Adonis is often the earliest bloomer in the perennial garden. Buttercup-like blooms and finely divided foliage are at home in both the rock garden and the border. Adonis performs best in cool, coastal and mountainous regions where night temperatures drop below 65°F (18°C).

A. *amurensis* (hardy to zone 2) is particularly charming, growing 18 inches (45 cm) tall and bearing delicate yellow blooms. 'Fukuju Kai' is a popular double-flowered variety with red and yellow flowers that bloom in early

spring. A. *flammea*, native to Western Asia, is an annual variety, as is the popular A. *aestivalis*, which has bright red flowers and grows about 15 inches (38 cm) high.

General care: Ordinary soil is adequate. All do best in full sun with ample moisture.

Propagation: Sow seeds when fully ripe directly in the border in spring or autumn. Mature plants can be divided in fall.

Pests and diseases: Generally trouble-free.

AGAPANTHUS
ZONES 9 AND 10
Commonly known as lily-of-the-Nile, these plants are of South African heritage and can be grown in pots and tubs or outdoors in mild climates. They add a touch of the exotic to the summer garden and can be left outside in winter if the temperature stays above 25°F (–4°C). They form dense clumps of narrow strap-shaped leaves above which are carried globular heads of lily-like flowers in shades of blue, purple and white on stems to 3 ft (90 cm) tall.

General care: A sunny, reasonably sheltered site and ordinary but not dry soil is

all they require.

Propagation: Divide or seed indoors in spring.

Pests and diseases: Generally trouble-free.

AGERATUM
Soft cushion-like flower-heads are the feature of this edging or bedding annual.

The height of the different varieties varies from 6–18 inches (15–45 cm). The taller varieties provide a useful cut flower. The colors also vary from the clear blue of 'Blue Mink' to the bluish-mauve of 'Blue Blazer' and lavender blue of 'Blue Bouquet'.

General care: Given a moisture-retentive soil and a sunny position it will flower from summer until the first frost. In mild-winter areas, plant in mid-summer for fall bloom. Water it if there is any danger of the ground getting dry and dead-head when the flowers die.

Propagation: Sow indoors or in a cold frame in March or outdoors in May.

Pests and diseases: Whitefly can be a problem. Spray with malathion.

ALCEA   ZONES 2–10
The tall statuesque spires of hollyhocks are everyone's

favorites, and nowadays there are many kinds to choose from. Both the double and single varieties come true to color from seed. If you enjoy watching bees at work, grow Sutton's 'Single Brilliant-Mixture'; the bees simply love the wide-open flowers. For double flowers, Chater's 'Double Mixed' is an excellent selection. 'Summer Carnival' also produces a good mixture of fully double flowers that grow low down on the stems.

While hollyhocks can be grown as annuals or perennials, it is more usual nowadays to treat them as biennials. By doing so it is possible to minimize the risk of hollyhock rust, a disease that becomes a scourge on old plants, especially in the warmer and dryer parts of the country.

General care: All well-drained soils are suitable in a sunny site and with shelter from strong winds.

Propagation: Sow the seed outdoors in spring in a well-prepared seed bed. Space out the strongest seedlings to get robust plants for planting out in late summer.

Pests and diseases: Rust disease may spoil the foliage.

Adonis amurensis

ALCHEMILLA ZONES 3–8
This well-loved hardy perennial, *A. mollis*, popularly known as lady's mantle, produces its clouds of tiny lime-green flowers in summer. However, it is its pale green foliage that makes it so lovely.
General care: Any soil that is not waterlogged is suitable, in sun or deep shade.
Propagation: It is easily grown from seed, sown outside in spring, or by division from autumn to spring, and will seed itself freely.
Pests and diseases: Generally trouble-free.

ALLIUM ZONES 2–9
There are many different types of ornamental onion, some tall enough for the back of the border, others sufficiently small to make them suitable for the rock garden. Planted among low-growing shrubs, the taller alliums make effective and unusual displays.

A. *aflatunense* (hardy to zone 5) grows to 2½ ft (75 cm) tall and, with its large purple-lilac heads, is exceptionally ornamental. It blooms from late spring to mid-summer. A. *caeruleum* (hardy to zone 2) grows to 1½ ft (45 cm) high. It is a graceful plant with cornflower blue flower-heads carried on strong wiry stems in early summer. A. *moly* (hardy to zone 2) grows to only 1 ft (30 cm) high and is an old garden favorite. It has umbels of golden yellow flowers which appear in summer.
General care: All appreciate well-drained soil and as much sunshine as possible. Fall is the best time to plant all varieties. Once planted, leave them to multiply until the clumps become overcrowded, at which point the bulbs should be lifted and then replanted separately.
Propagation: Sow seed outside in a seed bed immediately after it has ripened or, if you buy it, try to make sure it is as fresh as possible. Leave for a season before transplanting the seedlings outside.

Ageratum 'Blue Mink'

Divide clumps in autumn or spring.
Pests and diseases: Generally trouble-free.

ALSTROEMERIA
ZONES 7–10
The Peruvian lily produces erect stems clad with narrow

upside-down leaves and broad clusters of beautifully colored funnel-shaped blooms in summer.

One of the hardiest species is A. *Aurantiaca* (hardy to zone 7) which grows to 3 ft (90 cm); its 1½ inch (4 cm) orange flowers are streaked red. The 'Ligtu' hybrids, which grow 2 ft (60 cm) tall, and are well known

for their pale pink, pale lilac or whitish trumpet-shaped flowers, are also a good choice. Both flower from late spring through summer and will provide excellent cut flower material.
General care and propagation: Peruvian lilies vary considerably in hardiness, so to be on the safe side, plant the fleshy roots at least 6 inches (15 cm) deep. It is a good plan to raise your own plants from seed which should be very fresh or foil-packed. Sow very thinly in flats or pots in spring, and put these in a cool greenhouse. Germination time will vary greatly in relation to the freshness of the seed; it can be from 1–6 months. When the seedlings are large enough to handle, put them individually into 3½ inch (8 cm) pots, trying to disturb the roots as little as possible. When they are well established, plant them outside about 12 inches (30 cm) apart in the warmest sheltered position possible, again with the minimum of root disturbance. They are happiest when the soil is deep, on the dry side with some sand in it, and drains well.

Alchemilla mollis

Alyssum saxatile and *Aubrieta deltoidea*

Pests and diseases: Young shoots are prone to attack by slugs and snails, so apply the appropriate bait as soon as growth begins.

ALTHAEA
See under Alcea

ALYSSUM ZONES 2–10
The commonly grown perennial rock plant, *A. montanum* (hardy to zone 2) has gray foliage and yellow clusters of flowers that appear in profusion in the spring. It grows to a height of about 12 inches (30 cm). *A. idaeum* (hardy to zone 6) performs best in rocky soils, growing to 5 inches (12.5 cm).
General care: All well-drained soils are acceptable, the poorer the better, plus full sun.
Propagation: Very easily propagated from cuttings of non-flowering shoots taken after the plant has flowered.
Pests and diseases: Generally trouble-free.

SWEET ALYSSUM
See under Lobularia

AMARANTHUS
The red version of *A. caudatus* is commonly known as love lies bleeding. It is tall enough to grow in the center of an annual bed or border. The flowers occur in long, graceful tassels from summer through early fall, and are ideal for cutting as they last well in water. The green variety 'Viridis', in particular, is prized by flower arrangers. *A. tricolor* (syn. *A. gangeticus*) is known as Joseph's coat and is grown entirely for its brightly colored leaves. Amaranthus grows to 2½–3 ft (75–90 cm) and is happiest in a sunny position.
General care: An ordinary soil is adequate, but more impressive growth will result from planting in a deep, rich soil.
Propagation: Sow indoors in

early spring or outdoors in early summer. Soil temperature should be at 60°F (15°C).
Pests and diseases: Generally trouble-free.

ANCHUSA ZONES 3–8
This genus is famed for its trusses of gentian-blue flowers. *A. azurea* is an erect, robust perennial which has given rise to several superior varieties. 'Loddon Royalist' is a splendid, relatively new variety. Although it grows 3 ft (90 cm) tall, it tends to be bushy and should not require staking to keep its large royal blue flowers off the ground. 'Morning Glory', which grows to 4 ft (1.2 m), has super gentian-blue flowers on tall stems, which will need support. 'Royal Blue' also has pure gentian-blue flowers which, like other varieties, appear in summer. It grows 3–4 ft (90–120 cm) high and needs staking, otherwise the plants will be untidy, and you will lose much of their beauty. Even taller, growing to 4 ft (1.2 m) is 'Dropmore', which has rich, deep blue flowers that appear just a little bit later on in the summer. *A. capensis* is a biennial from which a strain has been developed for

use as an annual. A good blue in the flower garden can be scarce at mid-summer, but from July through autumn, anchusa can fill the gap with its large forget-me-not flower-heads. A good variety is 'Blue Bird'.
General care: Ordinary but not dry soils are needed, ideally enriched with garden compost, well-rotted manure or peat and a general fertilizer. Choose a sunny, sheltered site.
Propagation: Sow seeds of *A. capensis* in March–May in open ground and transplant groups to the border. Growing to a height of 9 inches (23 cm), it is also ideal to grow in a container. Divide in spring or take root cuttings of *A. azurea*.
Pests and diseases: Generally trouble-free.

ANEMONE ZONES 3–10
The windflowers are a varied and highly decorative group of plants with many uses in the garden. Most widely grown are the so-called Japanese anemones (*A. x hybrida* syn. *A. japonica* [hardy to zone 5] of gardens). These form wide clumps or colonies in time, producing coarsely dissected foliage

and wiry erect stems 2 ft (60 cm) tall, bearing several bowl-shaped blooms in shades of pink and white. Go for the large 'White Queen', the soft pink 'September Charm' or the rosy-red, semi-double 'Bressingham Glow'.

Some of the most garden-worthy anemones are tuberous-rooted and can be used in the same way as bulbs. *A. coronaria* (hardy to zone 5) is the best of these, and is usually sold under the following names: 'De Caen', the single-flowered sort, is usually offered as a mixture of brilliant colors but named varieties are available in separate colors; 'St Brigid' has semi-double flowers and is not quite so free-flowering. Seed of both can be purchased for sowing any time, January–June, in a greenhouse or cold frame.

Among the small-flowered varieties for rockery and wild gardens is the easy-to-grow *A. blanda* (hardy to zone 6) which reaches a height of 4–6 inches (10–15 cm) and has blue flowers that bloom in the spring. It is delightful and is even successful when planted in semi-shade. *A. blanda atrocaerulea* is another small variety with lovely blue

Antirrhinum majus

flowers. It increases rapidly after planting. Separate colors are available, such as 'Charmer', pale pink, 'Radar', bright carmine and 'Splendor', white. You can also buy these as a mixture.
General care: Any moisture-retentive but well-drained soil is suitable. Japanese anemones thrive in sun or shade, the others are best in sun. Plant the tubers of *A. coronaria* at intervals from autumn to spring to get a long succession of flowers.
Propagation: Divide Japanese anemones in spring and divide or separate the tubers of the others when they are dormant. All may be raised from seed when ripe or in spring, but 2 or more years will elapse before seedlings bloom.
Pests and diseases: Generally trouble-free.

ANTHEMIS   ZONES 3–10
Very easy to grow, *A. tinctoria* (hardy to zone 3) is widely known as the golden marguerite. A native of Europe and Asia, this excellent mid-border plant, which grows 2–3 ft (60–90 cm) tall, has deeply cut, silver-gray aromatic foliage topped by profuse, yellow, daisy-like flowers that bloom from early summer until frost. Anthemis is tolerant of dry conditions.
    Varieties to try include 'Kelwayi', deep gold; 'Moonlight', soft yellow and 'E.C. Buxton', white with yellow centers. Deadhead after flowers fade to prolong bloom.
General care: Ordinary soil and moisture are all that is required. A sunny location ensures a long-flowering season.
Propagation: Sow seed in early spring or divide clumps in spring or fall.
Pests and diseases: Generally trouble-free.

ANTIRRHINUM
Favorites throughout the country, snapdragons are stars in sunny borders and as cut flowers. Native to the Mediterranean region, snapdragons are treated as annuals, but they will winter over in warm regions. They flower from winter to spring in warm-weather zones and from mid-summer to the first frost elsewhere.
    Modern varieties are available in all colors but true blue and in sizes ranging from the dwarfs, 6–9 inches (15–22.5 cm) tall; intermediates, 18–24 inches (45–60 cm) tall; and large, 3–4 ft (90–120 cm) tall. Large varieties include 'Sentinel', 3 ft (90 cm); the Rocket strain, 2½–3 ft (75–90 cm) and the Floradale giants, 3 ft (90 cm) tall. Intermediates include Bell-flowers, 2–2½ ft (60–75 cm) and 'Carioca', 12–18 inches (30–45 cm). Dwarfs ranging in size from 6–12 inches (15–30 cm) are Floral Carpet and Sweetheart hybrids.
General care: Snapdragons flourish in fertile, well-drained soil and full sun. Pinch back to increase bushiness and dead-head to prolong bloom.
Propagation: In warm climates sow seed in summer directly in the garden or sow in flats and transplant seedlings to the desired location. In cold climates, sow indoors three months before the planting season and set out while the weather is still cool, but after the danger of frost has passed.
Pests and diseases: Snapdragons are susceptible to rust. Choose rust-resistant varieties or treat infected plants with zineb.

AQUILEGIA   ZONES 2–10
There are many varieties of aquilegia, or columbine, to choose from. *A. vulgaris* (hardy to zone 2) has mainly blue or purple flowers with short spurs and is indeed inferior to some of the hybrids now available.

Aquilegia, short stemmed hybrid

The long-spurred hybrids are most attractive, with their many combinations of colors from crimson through to the delicate shades of pink, yellow and white. The 'McKana Giant Hybrids', which grow 2½–3 ft (75–90 cm) tall, are outstanding, and can be grown from seed sown outside or from plants purchased in the spring.

A. formosa (hardy to zone 2) has dainty brick-red flowers produced on slender stems. Growing to 3 ft (90 cm), it is so graceful and as a bonus it will come true from seed.

General care: Virtually any soil is suitable, even those which stay wettish for long periods. Partial shade is best but full sun is tolerated.

Propagation: Sow seed when ripe or in spring outside, thinning and transplanting as necessary.

Pests and diseases: Generally trouble-free, though aphids can be a nuisance. Spray with malathion.

ARABIS ALBIDA
ZONES 3–10
Rock cress forms low cushions or mats that grow no more than 6 inches (15 cm) high and are especially suitable for rockeries and walls.

Arabis albida

flowering shoots in summer.
Pests and diseases: Generally trouble-free.

ARCTOTIS
This gray-green-leaved annual, also known as African daisy, has large, daisy-like flowers which come in a wide range of both pale and bright colors from late June until the first frost. Some flowers have zones of contrasting color towards the center, making them particularly striking. They grow to a height of 1–2½ ft (30–75 cm), and the taller varieties may need some twigs for support. Arctotis makes an attractive, if short-lived, cut flower.

General care: Fertile, well-drained soil and a sunny, sheltered site are needed. After planting, pinch the growing tips at about 6 inches (15 cm) to encourage branching and cut or deadhead after the blooms have died to encourage further flowering.

Propagation: Sow inside in late winter at a temperature of 50–60°F (10–15°C). Plants survive as perennials in the mildest climates, but flower poorly after the first year.

Pests and diseases: Reasonably trouble-free.

ARGEMONE
Argemone or prickly poppy is usually grown as an an-

nual. Native to the dry desert areas of the West, it blooms throughout the summer. *A. grandiflora* is a showy variety, suitable for the back of the border. Its white flowers span 4 inches (10 cm), and the plant grows to about 3 ft (90 cm) tall. *A. mexicana* has smaller, yellow blossoms and grows 2–3 ft (60–90 cm) tall. The foliage has scalloped edges, rimmed with tiny spines.

General care: A sunny, hot location and sandy, well-drained soil are ideal for prickly poppies. They are very drought-resistant.

Propagation: Sow seeds indoors shortly before the last frost directly in peat pots as argemone are difficult to transplant, or sow outdoors directly in the garden bed.

ARMERIA   ZONES 3–10
Thrift or sea pink is a familiar plant of coastal areas and has produced several desirable garden varieties. *A. maritima* (hardy to zone 3), the wild species, is pink; 'Alba' is white, while 'Dusseldorf Pride' is richest pink and 'Ruby Glow' almost ruby-red.

General care: Any well-drained soil is suitable provided the site is a sunny one. Remove spent flowering stems promptly.

Propagation: Cuttings of single shoots or small branch-

Flowering commences early in spring and is a beautiful sight. This hardy perennial is easily grown, needing only plenty of sun and tidying up after flowering.

Seed in the separate colors (white, pink or rose-purple) is cataloged, as well as mixtures of the colors. All will give you mass displays of their tiny flowers.

General care: Any well-drained soil is suitable.

Propagation: Grow from seed sown either in a cold frame in early spring or outside in late spring. Alternatively, take cuttings of non-

Armeria maritima

Asclepias tuberosa

lets can be inserted outside in early spring or autumn. Sow seed in spring in pots in a cold frame.
Pests and diseases: Generally trouble-free.

ARTEMISIA ZONES 2–10

Most members of this genus, which is also known as wormwood, are grown for their silver or gray, often dissected, leaves which contrast so well with the more brightly colored flowering plants. They are clump-forming with unbranched stems which may or may not terminate in sprays of small grayish flowers. *A. absinthium* (hardy to zone 2) is woody-based, producing stems 3–4 ft (90–120 cm) in height clad in filigree foliage. *A. a.* 'Lambrook Silver' is bright gray, while 'Powys Castle' has a silver sheen. *A. lactiflora* (hardy to zone 3) is the odd man out, being grown for its astilbe-like, creamy-white floral plumes in late summer. *A. stellerana* (hardy to zone 2) 'Dusty Miller' is a popular variety for its dense, white-wooly foliage. This native of eastern North America is often used to accent more colorful flowers. It thrives near the seashore.
General care: Sun or light shade and ordinary soil are acceptable.
Propagation: Divide this perennial in early spring or take basal cuttings in late spring.
Pests and diseases: Generally trouble-free.

ASCLEPIAS ZONES 4–10

The milkweed family includes a few varieties suitable for the garden. *A. tuberosa* or butterfly weed grows 2–3 ft (60–90 cm) tall and has bright orange flowers throughout the summer. A native of the Eastern seaboard, it produces attractive seedpods after blooming.
General care: Asclepias needs a sunny location but will tolerate any soil that is well-drained.

Propagation: Sow seed in early spring or take cuttings in early spring.
Pests and diseases: Generally trouble-free.

ASTER ZONES 2–10

Michaelmas daisies, with their easy-going nature and wealth of colorful daisy flowers from early summer through autumn, are everybody's favorites. *A. novi-belgii* (hardy to zone 2) is the best-known species, but most of the many varieties are of hybrid origin.

There are many good named varieties with heights ranging from 2–4 ft (60–120 cm) in colors from crimson-red through to light pink and blue. A few well-known ones are: 'Ada Ballard', which has lavender-blue flowers and grows 3 ft (90 cm) tall; 'Crimson Brocade', which has semi-double, rose crimson flowers and grows 3 ft (90 cm) tall, and 'Pride of Colwall', which has double violet-blue flowers and grows 2½ ft (75 cm) tall. 'Jenny' (double red), 'Little Pink Beauty' (semi-double pink), 'Professor Kippenburg' (single blue) and 'Snow-sprite' (single white) are all under 12–16 inches (30–40 cm) in height and are more useful than the tall sorts.
General care: Any ordinary soil which does not dry out is suitable. A sunny site is best but partial shade is tolerated. In exposed areas staking will be needed for the tall growers.
Propagation: Divide in spring or fall, breaking each clump into small pieces with one to three shoots.
Pests and diseases: Mildew is the main nuisance. Spray with a fungicide.

ASTILBE ZONES 4–8

The ferny foliage and shapely, feathery plumes of astilbe place it among the most desirable of perennials where the ground is moist enough. Hybrids are the most popular, being available in colors from white through pinks and lilacs to deepest red. Good varieties include 'Bressingham Beauty', rich pink; 'Deutschland', intense white; and 'Fanal', deep red.
General care: Moisture-retentive to wet soil is essential for success unless one is prepared to water heavily in dry spells.
Propagation: Divide in spring just as the plants start into growth. Regular division every 3–4 years will keep them floriferous.
Pests and diseases: Generally trouble-free.

AUBRIETA DELTOIDEA
ZONES 4–9
This low-growing hardy perennial is well known for its mass displays early in the spring. Ideal for pockets in a dry wall, it will soon spread itself out into large mat-like plants. It is a particularly strong performer on the Northwest coast. If you plant named varieties or grow your plants from seed, you can have a considerable range of colors.

Of the named varieties, the following are recommended: 'Barker's Double', deep rosy purple; 'Bressingham Pink'; 'Dr Mules', violet-purple; and 'Riverslea', mauve-pink. Do not be afraid to cut aubrietas back immediately after flowering; they will benefit.

General care: Well-drained soil and full sun are essential to prolific blooming.

Propagation: Sow seeds in early spring in the greenhouse. When the seedlings are large enough to handle, transplant them into pots. They will be ready for planting in their final positions in the fall.

Pests and diseases: Generally trouble-free.

Aubrieta deltoidea, hybrid

AURINIA   ZONES 3–10
Once classified as an alyssum, *A. saxatilis* or basket-of-gold forms a cascade of golden yellow in the rock garden or the front of the border. Clusters of tiny gold flowers that bloom in spring and early summer top narrow gray-green leaves. This native of the Mediterranean grows 8–12 inches (20–30 cm) tall.

Varieties include 'Citrina' and 'Silver Queen', pale yellow; 'Plena', double yellow blossoms; and 'Compacta', a dense plant that grows 6–8 inches (15–20 cm) tall.

General care: Basket-of-gold prefers sandy, well-drained soil in full sun. Lightly shear after bloom to promote growth.

Propagation: Divide established plants every 3 years. Aurinia starts easily from seed. Sow indoors in late winter and set out in early spring.

Pests and diseases: Generally trouble-free.

BAPTISIA   ZONES 2–10
A member of the pea family, baptisia is a good candidate for the back of the border. Its spikes, which have sweet pea-shaped flowers, climb to 5 ft (1.5 m) high and spread rapidly. *B. tinctoria* (hardy to zone 5) is found from south New England to Minnesota and as far south as Florida. It bears yellow flowers in mid-summer and seed pods follow; both are interesting in floral arrangements. Tall varieties need to be staked. *B. australis* (hardy to zone 2) is prized for its blue flowers that blossom in early summer and its bluish-green foliage. Dead-head to prolong bloom.

General care: Ordinary soil is adequate. Baptisia sets down a deep tap root and can withstand heavy drought conditions. A sunny site is preferred although partial shade is acceptable.

Propagation: Sow seeds indoors in early spring and transplant outdoors after danger of frost has passed or divide established clumps in spring or fall.

Pests and diseases: Generally trouble-free.

BEGONIA   ZONES 8 AND 9
The 900 species plus many hybrids and varieties in this very garden-worthy genus are mainly tropical in origin and best known as pot plants for the greenhouse and home. Two different sorts are grown as summer bedding subjects outside. *B. x herbeohybrida* is tuberous-rooted. The best known sorts produce robust, erect stems, large ear-shaped leaves and massive double blooms rather like roses. More recent is the Pendula strain, having slimmer, lax stems and smaller, less stiff double flowers. Both have a wide color range. Long familiar as bedding plants are the fibrous-rooted *B. semperflorens*, low bushy plants with glistening rounded leaves and a profusion of small blooms composed of two large and two small petals. Try the delicate pink 'Pink Avalanche', the rose-pink 'Danica Rose' with bronze leaves and the brick-red 'Danica Red', also with bronze leaves. Alternatively, choose one of the mixtures which also includes white, for example 'Organdy' or 'Stara'; the latter has a cascading habit.

General care: Moisture-retentive, humus-rich soil gives the best results. Full sun and partial shade are acceptable. Plant out both sorts of begonia in late spring/early summer after the threat of frost has passed. Start tubers in warmth in boxes of compost two months before planting out, potting singly as growth starts. Lift in autumn, clean the tubers and store in dry peat at around 55°F (13°C).

Propagation: Cut tubers into two or more pieces, each with at least one shoot, just prior to potting, or take the shoots as cuttings. Sow seed in late winter. *Semperflorens*, though perennials, are raised annually from seed sown in warmth in late winter.

Pests and diseases: Generally trouble-free, but aphids can be a nuisance and sometimes virus appears. The latter shows as stunted, mottled shoots, and the plants must be destroyed.

BELLIS   ZONES 3–10
The common species, *B. perennis*, is the well-known, unloved lawn weed, also known as English daisy. There are various large-flowered and double miniature varieties well worth a space in the flower garden. For example *Bellis perennis* 'Monstrosa', with its double flowers that reach 2 inches (5 cm) or more across, has a color range from white through pink to scarlet red and makes an excellent bedding plant. It is at its best in early summer and is sometimes cataloged as 'Goliath Mixed'. Among the miniature varieties is 'Pompon-

ette', which has tightly quilled double daisies in shades of red, rose and white.

General care: Any soil is suitable, but humus-rich ones give the best results. Choose a sunny site.

Propagation: Seeds can be planted in late summer in a frame, protected over winter and set out in early spring.

Pests and diseases: Generally trouble-free except for aphids, which are easily controlled with diazinon or malathion.

BERGENIA   ZONES 2–10

Boldly handsome, paddle-shaped, evergreen ground-hugging leaves and clusters of pink to rose-purple flowers in early spring or earlier are the hallmarks of this desirable genus of perennials. They can be used as ground cover, specimen clumps or in the front of a shrub or perennials border. *B. cordifolia* and *crassifolia* (both hardy to zone 2) are the common ones often seen in old gardens. Modern var-

Brassica oleracea

ieties give better garden value. Try 'Admiral' with red flowers and glossy rich green leaves; 'Bressingham White' (pure white) and 'Sunningdale', a deep pink sort with leaves which take on dark bronze-red tints in winter.

General care: Almost any soil which is not waterlogged, though light, sandy and chalky soils should be enriched with garden compost or peat. Sunny or shady sites are equally acceptable.

Propagation: Divide in autumn or spring, separating single-rooted shoots. Plant 2 inches (5 cm) sections of leafless stems shallowly in a cold frame to produce plants.

Pests and diseases: Generally trouble-free, though leaf spot disease may disfigure the foliage. Remove the worst affected leaves and spray with captan or zineb, though neither is fully effective.

BRACHYCOME

B. iberidifolia, the Swan River daisy, produces fragrant cineraria-like flowers of blue, pink, purple and white shades from summer through autumn. Growing to

a height of 9 inches (23 cm), it is useful for group planting at the front of the border.

General care: Any well-drained soil is suitable provided it is in a sunny site.

Propagation: Sow seeds in early spring in the greenhouse or outside in late spring.

Pests and diseases: Generally trouble-free.

BRASSICA OLERACEA
ZONES 8–10

Decorative flowering cabbage is a bonus in fall and winter gardens where mild winters are the rule. Its curly, brightly colored leaves, which open out from the center, range from off-white to pink, rose, red and purple. Each head measures about 10 inches (25 cm) wide. It is prized as a striking addition to fall and winter flower arrangements.

General care: A sunny site and average soil are the only requirements.

Propagation: Sow seeds indoors in late winter and transplant after danger of frost has passed or sow directly in the garden in spring.

Pests and diseases: Generally trouble-free.

BROWALLIA

Spectacular in shady borders or hanging baskets, this summer-flowering annual is covered with star-shaped flowers in shades of violet, blue and white. Browallia performs equally well in the garden or as a house plant, displayed in a sunny window. *B. speciosa*, which grows 1–2 ft (30–60 cm) tall, acts as a perennial in the warmest zones and bears petunia-like flowers. Varieties include 'Blue Bells Improved', lavender-blue; 'Marine Bells', indigo blue; and 'Silver Bells', white. 'Sapphire', a 10 inch (25 cm) dwarf, is prized for its deep blue flowers contrasting with white throats.

General care: Moisture-retentive but well-drained soil and partial shade.

Propagation: Grown easily from seed sown directly in the garden after danger of frost has passed or indoors year-round.

Pests and diseases: Generally trouble-free.

BRUNNERA ZONES 3–9

Sometimes incorrectly classified as *Anchusa azurea*, *B. macrophylla* bears airy clusters of delicate, spring-blooming blue flowers that resemble forget-me-nots. A native of Siberia, brunnera grows 18 inches (45 cm) tall and features heart-shaped foliage that measures 6 inches (15 cm) across. It makes an attractive, informal ground cover.

'Langtrees' has leaves spotted with silver and 'Variegata' has white-spotted foliage.

General care: Plant in full or partial shade in deep, moist but well-drained soil that never dries completely.

Propagation: Seeds self-sow readily, but they are slow to germinate in the greenhouse. Try freezing them before sowing in late fall and transplant seedlings outside in spring. Divide established clumps in fall.

Pests and diseases: Generally trouble-free.

CALENDULA OFFICINALIS

Common or pot marigold re-

Brunnera macrophylla

wards the sower with a glorious summer show of orange and yellow shades for almost no effort. The large double daisy-type flowers look colorful and last well in water. Growing to 1–2 ft (30–60 cm) high, recommended varieties are 'Radio', deep orange; 'Lemon Queen', yellow; and 'Fiesta Gitana', a colorful mixture.

General care: Any soil that is not waterlogged is satisfactory. A sunny site is best, but partial shade is tolerated. Remove all faded blooms promptly or self-sown seedlings will create weeds.

Propagation: Sow seed outside in spring or early autumn for a much earlier display. Seedlings need to be protected in cold winters.

Pests and diseases: Trouble-free, except for occasional attacks of aphids and caterpillars; use diazinon or malathion.

CALLISTEPHUS

The big single and double daisy flowers of China aster have long been favorite half-hardy annuals. The original species *C. chinensis* is single and comes in a variety of colors. More popular are the varied double sorts, especially the elegant 'Ostrich Plume' with large flower-heads on plants to 1½ ft (45 cm). Other recommended varieties are 'Milady', dwarf selections in colors of rose, blue, white and mixed; 'Lilliput', miniature pompom; and 'Super sinensis', single. All are excellent for flower beds. There are several forms, ranging from the tall, feathery-headed ostrich plume type to the chrysanthemum-flowered ones, including those with incurving petals. There are also those with miniature pompom flowers.

General care: Moisture-retentive but well-drained, fertile soil and a sunny site are essential for success. Light, sandy and chalky soils must be liberally enriched with garden compost, decayed manure or peat and general fertilizer.

Propagation: Sow indoors in early spring and keep at 60–68°F (15–20°C) to germinate. Plant out in well-drained soil in a sunny position.

Pests and diseases: Aphids may curl and stunt young shoots. Spray with diazinon or malathion. Virus also stunts and mottles the leaves yellow. Destroy as soon as the trouble is recognized. Wilt disease causes wilting, yellowing, withering and death. Destroy plants and grow only wilt-resistant varieties.

CAMPANULA ZONES 2–9

The bellflowers form a large and varied genus of great garden value, ranging from dwarf alpines to large herbaceous plants. It is impossible to list more than a few, all of which make excellent subjects for the herbaceous border and which flower from spring to fall. They are *C. glomerata dahurica* (hardy to zone 2), which has violet-purple flowers and grows 18 inches (45 cm) tall; *C. lactiflora* 'Loddon Anna' (hardy to zone 5), which has lilac-pink flowers and grows 2½ ft (75 cm) tall; *C. l.* 'Pritchard's Variety' (hardy to zone 5), which has violet-blue flowers and grows 3 ft (90 cm) tall; and *C. latifolia* (hardy to zone 3), which has foxglove-like spikes of amethyst-violet flowers and grows 3½ ft (105 cm) tall. At the other end of the scale, there is *C. lactiflora* 'Pouffe', which at 9 inches (23 cm) is a

real dwarf. It has lavender-blue star-like flowers and is well worth considering. One of the most popular is the biennial *C. medium*, better known as the Canterbury bell. Best is the cup and saucer type *C. m. calycanthema*, which grows up to 2½–3 ft (75–90 cm) high and has softly colored flowers in white, rose and various shades of blue. Dwarf bedding mixture and 'Bells of Holland' seed is available for plants that only grow 18 inches (45 cm) high, but the flowers, although produced in a similar color range, have single blooms without 'saucers'.

General care: Ordinary soil, provided it is not waterlogged, is suitable, though sandy and chalky ones should be enriched with garden compost or peat and fertilizer.

Propagation: Perennials by division in early spring. Sow biennials in late spring in a cold frame. Thin and transplant seedlings as required, putting them into their flowering sites in autumn.

Pests and diseases: Slugs and snails are fond of young shoots; apply slug pellets when growth starts in spring.

CATANANCHE ZONES 4–10

Cupid's dart, *C. caerulea*, grows some 2 ft (60 cm) tall and has star-like purple-blue flowers in summer and early autumn that are not unlike cornflowers but with darker eyes. Anyone interested in flower arranging will find it useful for preserving.

General care: All well-drained soils in sunny sites are suitable. Dead-head regularly throughout the flowering season.

Propagation: Propagate from root cuttings taken in the autumn or from spring-sown seed kept in a cold greenhouse to germinate.

Pests and diseases: Generally trouble-free.

CATHARANTHUS ROSEUS ZONES 9–10

It is difficult to find a better choice than the periwinkle

for a spot of color in desert and city gardens. It withstands both urban pollution and strong summer heat. A perennial in warm climates, it is grown as a dependable annual in colder regions. Bushy varieties grow 1–2 ft (30–60 cm) tall and bear blankets of fragrant flowers in shades of white, pink, red, blue and lavender. Smaller varieties of 8–10 inches (20–25 cm) are often used as ground cover, in window-boxes or in the rock garden.

General care: Reasonably well-drained soil and full sun or partial shade is acceptable.

Propagation: Plants wintered over will self-sow readily, or sow seed indoors and keep in darkness until germination. Seeds are slow to germinate, and transplanting seedlings from the garden center may be more satisfactory.

Pests and diseases: Generally trouble-free.

CELOSIA

Celosia is useful and attractive as a pot plant and for bedding outside. *C. argentea pyramidalis* (syn. *plumosa*) is a half-hardy annual with an erect stem to 1½ ft (45 cm) tall. The upper third of this height is taken up by a plume of tiny, silky, yellow, red or pink flowers in summer. 'Fairy Fountains' grows to 1 ft (30 cm) only, while 'Geisha Mixed' is barely 8 inches (20 cm) tall. *C. a. cristata* is a mutant form known as cockscomb, having the flower cluster condensed and flattened with a crested top. 'Jewel Box Mixed' is the best variety, bearing its elaborate crests on 6–8 inch (15–20 cm) long stems.

General care: A sunny position and fertile soil that does not dry out are best.

Propagation: Sow seed in spring in warmth.

Pests and diseases: Generally trouble-free.

CENTAUREA

Cornflower, *C. cyanus*, is an easy hardy annual for any well-drained, sunny site. It

Centaurea cyanus

is a sturdy border and cut-flower plant, and may be either true corn-flower blue or red, pink, purple or white. The taller varieties grow up to 3 ft (90 cm) high. Another species is *C. moschata* or 'Sweet Sultan'. Its powder-puff flowers of yellow, pink, purple and white are sweetly scented and good for cutting. It grows to a height of 2 ft (60 cm) and so is suitable at the back of a border.

General care: Well-drained but not dry soils of all types are suitable; add organic matter to those that are sandy or chalky. Support tall varieties with stakes, especially in exposed sites where the flowers are likely to be blown over by strong winds.

Propagation: Sow seeds outside in spring or autumn in mild areas if extra-early flowers are desired.

Pests and diseases: Generally trouble-free.

CENTRANTHUS ZONES 4–9

One of the easiest to grow and longest lasting flowering perennials, Jupiter's beard produces fluffy clusters of white, pink and crimson flowers from early summer to the first frost. *C. ruber* is a bushy variety that grows to 3 ft (90 cm) high with bluish-gray leaves. It is a good cut flower and combines nicely with day lilies in the border. 'Roseus' has fragrant scarlet flowers in dense terminal clusters.

General care: Centranthus survives poor soils and little water, but it will bloom more profusely in enriched soil with moderate water in partial shade. Dead-head to prolong bloom.

Propagation: It self-sows readily from dandelion-like heads. Established clumps can be divided in spring.

Pests and diseases: Generally trouble-free.

CERASTIUM ZONES 2–10

An extremely adaptable perennial, *C. tomentosum* (hardy to zone 2), snow-in-winter, forms a dense mat of silver-gray leaves. It grows 3–6 inches (8–15 cm) tall, and each plant may spread to 2 ft (60 cm) wide. Widely used as a ground cover on steep slopes and sandy areas, it bears snow-white masses of star-shaped flowers in early summer. *C. alpinum* (hardy to zone 2) is very low-growing and spreads to 12 inches (30 cm) wide. 'Lanarth' is the most compact variety. Cerastium thrives from seacoast to desert and adapts to all zones.

General care: Plant in well-drained, ordinary soil in full sun or light shade in hot summer climates. Prune plants frequently to control prolific growth.

Propagation: Plants self-sow readily. Sow outside in late spring or take cuttings after flowering. Divide established clumps in the fall.

Pests and diseases: Generally trouble-free.

CERATOSTIGMA
ZONES 5–9

A very rewarding and colorful perennial, *C. plumbaginoides* (hardy to zone 5) forms a dense mat of phlox-like blue flowers. Plants grow 8–12 inches (20–30 cm) high and are excellent at the front of the perennial border, used as a ground cover or as an undercover to shrubs. The deep blue flowers bloom in mid-summer and last until frost. The foliage turns deep mahogany red in fall. *C. willmottianum* (hardy to zone 8) is a taller, less hardy, variety that grows 3–4 ft (1–1.2 m) high with profuse clusters of bright blue flowers. *C. griffithii* (hardy to zone 8) is similar to *willmottianum* but is more compact, growing 2½–3 ft (75–90 cm) tall.

General care: Ceratostigma is tolerant of many soil types and moisture levels and will thrive in partial shade or sun.

Propagation: Divide in spring or take cuttings from non-flowering stems.

Ceratostigma plumbaginoides

Pests and diseases: Generally trouble-free.

CHEIRANTHUS

Wallflowers, *Cheiranthus cheiri*, are particularly popular as late spring and early summer flowering bedding plants. Grown as a popular biennial in England, it performs well as an annual in the U.S. in certain areas of the East and in the moist Pacific Northwest.

There are numerous varieties to choose from; most of them make plants that grow 15–18 inches (35–45 cm) tall and which should be spaced about 12 inches (30 cm) apart. Recommended varieties are 'Fire King', a brilliant scarlet; 'Blood Red', with a color that is true to its name; 'Vulcan', a deep crimson; and 'Cloth of Gold', a yellow variety. For really startling displays in many colors plus plenty of fragrance, try either 'Persian Carpet' or 'Color Cascade'.

Seed of dwarf varieties that grow about 9 inches (22 cm) high in the usual range of colors is available and this, of course, can be planted a little closer together.

Siberian wallflowers, *C. x allionii*, which grow about 12 inches (30 cm) high and have brilliant orange spikes of flowers, can also be planted slightly closer together than the tall wallflowers.

General care: A well-drained soil is essential, and for the sturdiest growth it should be limy. A sunny site is also necessary for bushy plants and plenty of bloom.

Propagation: For best results sow the seed thinly in late spring in shallow furrows in a seed bed. When the seedlings are large enough to handle, transplant them into rows 6–8 inches (15–20 cm) apart. At the same time, in order to ensure bushy plants, pinch back the tips of the growing points. In October lift the plants and plant them where you want them to flower, bearing in mind they prefer a sunny position.

Pests and diseases: Generally trouble-free, but plants can be damaged or killed in severe winters.

CHIONODOXA ZONES 4–8

Commonly known as glory of the snow, these early spring flowering bulbs, with their dainty, small, star-shaped flowers artistically arranged on slender stems, are natives of the high mountains in Asia Minor. *C. luciliae*, with its vivid blue, white-centered flowers, is one of the best. *C. l.* 'Rosea' has pure pink flowers and can be recommended, as can *C. gigantea*, which has large pale blue blooms. All are ideal for naturalizing in short grass or among shrubs.

General care: Practically all soils are suitable provided they are not waterlogged. Plant as early in autumn as possible then leave undisturbed. Self-sown seedlings usually arrive to increase the colony.

Propagation: Divide clumps when dormant or sow seeds when ripe in a cold frame. Seedlings take 2–3 years to reach flowering size.

Pests and diseases: Generally trouble-free.

CHRYSANTHEMUM
ZONES 2–10

This large genus can be divided into four groups: 1, the florist's hybrids, *C. x morifolium* (hardy to zone 5) with mainly double flowers. The best known, these are now available in pots all the year round, but are still favorites as garden decoration, especially for cut flowers; 2, hardy border perennials as exemplified by the shasta daisy *C. maximum* (hardy to zone 4); 3, perennial rock plants and 4, the popular annuals *C. coronarium*, *C. tricolor* (syn. *carinatum*) and their hybrids.

For garden decoration,

spray varieties of florist's hybrids are best. These are allowed to grow naturally without disbudding. Recommended are: 'Pennine Bright Eyes', pink; 'Pennine Crimson', 'Pennine Orange', 'Pennine Yellow' and 'Pennine White', as well as some of the single spray varieties such as 'Pennine Dream', pink; 'Pennine Globe', gold; and 'Pennine Tango', a bronze. Most of these grow 3–4 ft (90–120 cm) tall. For the front of the border, 'Fairy' can be very colorful in late summer and early autumn. This is a dwarf pompom chrysanthemum which has numerous round rosy-pink flowers and grows to only 1 ft (30 cm).

Among shasta daisies, C. superbum, the 1½ ft (45 cm) tall 'Snowcap' takes some beating of those with single flowers, while 'Wirral Supreme' is probably the most reliable double daisy of all, although they do better along the Pacific Coast and in the East than in the dry and hot central U.S.

Among rock or front of the border species C. hosmariense grows to about 6 inches (15 cm) in height with silvery dissected leaves and white-petalled daisies off and on all the year in mild winters.

Annual chrysanthemums come in a wide range of colors, often two or more contrasting shades or colors in each bloom. Seed strains are listed as 'Special Mixture', 'Flame Shades', 'Double Mixed' and 'Court Jesters'.

General care: With the exception of the rock garden species which need a fairly poor, well-drained soil, chrysanthemums in general must have fertile, moisture-retentive but not wet rooting medium. Poorer soils must be enriched with rotted manure, garden compost or peat and general fertilizer. In windy sites the taller ones will need support. Young plants of florist's and annual sorts should have their growing points pinched back at 4–6 inches (10–15 cm) in height to promote branching.
Propagation: Sow seed of hardy annuals outdoors in

spring, the florist's varieties indoors in early spring. Divide hardy border perennials in spring and take cuttings of rock plants in spring or early autumn. Florist's varieties are usually propagated by cuttings taken from plants that have been dug up and overwintered in a cold frame. As soon as basal shoots are about 2 inches (5 cm) long, these are severed and placed in equal parts peat and sand in a propagating case; early spring is the best time.
Pests and diseases: Aphids and capsid bugs attack and cripple young shoots and leaves, earwigs and caterpillars eat leaves and flowers. For all these pests, spray with malathion. Leaf miner causes white lines in the leaves, weakening them and making them unsightly. Spray with disyston, or hand-pick if the attack is slight. Mildew fungus produces a powdery coating, then the leaves turn yellow and die prematurely. Spray with benomyl as soon as you see signs of powder.

Colchicum speciosum

CLARKIA
Native to the Pacific Coast, clarkia, also known as godetia, thrives in areas where nights are cool. Best known is *Godetia amoena var. whitneyi* (*G. grandiflora* of seed catalogs) in one of its modern selections . Try 'Tall Double Mixed', which grows to 2 ft (60 cm) or 'Double Azalea-flowered Mixed', which grows to 14 inches (35 cm). *Clarkia elegans* grows up to 2 ft (60 cm) high and produces long double flower spikes in shades of purple, red, pink and orange to white. *C. pulchella* grows to 18 inches (45 cm) high and has double and semi-double flowers of white, violet and rose.
General care: Any reasonably fertile soil which is not waterlogged and gets plenty of sun is suitable.
Propagation: Sow in spring outdoors.
Pests and diseases: Generally trouble-free.

COLCHICUM ZONES 4–10
This autumn-flowerer can be used to advantage in a shrub

border or even in rough grass. The flowers are held on naked stems, and they do make an attractive splash of color. While the flowers themselves take up only a small space, the large though handsome leaves can smother nearby plants in the spring. They also look untidy before they die back. It is important therefore to choose the planting site carefully.

C. autumnale (hardy to zone 4) is the most popular species. Native to Europe and northern Africa, its crocus-like flowers are a soft rosy lilac. The hybrid 'Waterlily' is darker and fully double. *C. speciosum* (hardy to zone 4), in its several forms – such as 'Album', a white, and 'Lilac Wonder', a pinkish lilac with a white throat – is probably best for garden planting.
General care: All garden soils that do not dry out when the plants are in full growth are suitable. A sunny site will ensure that the blooms open properly, but partial shade is acceptable. Plant the corms early, ideally in August.
Propagation: Separate offsets when dormant. Seedlings take up to 5 years to flower.
Pests and diseases: Generally trouble-free.

CONVALLARIA ZONES 3–9
Lily of the valley (*C. majalis*) is famed for its graceful 8 inch (20 cm) tall sprays of perfumed bell-shaped white flowers in spring.
General care: A moisture-retentive fertile soil and partial shade are required for success. To ensure the right growing conditions, prepare the ground by digging in a liberal quantity of well-rotted compost. The best time to plant is September/October in the colder zones; November in zones 8 and 9. When the bed becomes overcrowded – which it will after a number of years – lift and replant the rhizomes, having first replenished the ground with compost.
Propagation: Divide into

Convallaria majalis

single-budded crowns in autumn.
Pests and diseases: Generally trouble-free.

CONVOLVULUS
ZONES 7–10
C. tricolor or bush morning glory is a dwarf annual variety that grows to 12 inches (30 cm) tall. It has flowers that stay open all day, unlike *C. ipomoea*, common vining morning glory. Convolvulus forms solid mounds of blue, lilac, red, pink and white flowers that spread to 2 ft (60 cm) wide.

'Royal Ensign', bright blue, and 'Crimson Monarch', red, are widely available. *C. mauritanicus* (hardy to zone 7) is a fast-spreading blanket of color that is useful as a ground cover in dry, western regions. Its lavender-blue, funnel-shaped flowers bloom from early summer through late fall.
General care: Grow in full sun in well-drained soil. Avoid planting it in areas where it will receive frequent watering.
Propagation: Sow seed directly in the soil outside when night temperatures will not dip below 50°F (10°C) or sow indoors in

early spring and transplant to the garden in early summer. Nick the tough seed coats to hasten germination.
Pests and diseases: Generally trouble-free.

COREOPSIS
ZONES 3–10
Excellent for cutting, these daisy-like flowers are easy to grow. *C. grandiflora* (hardy to zone 7) is a robust native species that grows 18 inches (45 cm) high. Its leaves are

narrow and deeply toothed and its bright yellow flowers, measuring up to $2\frac{1}{2}$ inches (7 cm) across and carried on good stems, are first class for flower arrangements. Recommended varieties are 'Sunray', which grows 18 inches (45 cm) high and is very free flowering with double golden yellow flowers; 'Mayfield Giant', which grows 2 ft (60 cm) high and is a golden yellow; and 'Sunburst', also 2 ft (60 cm) high, a bright yellow, semi-double variety. 'Goldfink' is almost a miniature, rarely exceeding 10 inches (25 cm) in height. *C. verticillata* (hardy to zone 6) grows to 16 inches (40 cm), produces wiry stems, a froth of tiny grassy leaves and star-shaped bright yellow flowers.
General care: Ordinary fertile soil in sun is all that is needed for this hardy perennial.
Propagation: Division in spring or seed at the same time in a frame.
Pests and diseases: Generally trouble-free.

COSMOS
This is a tall-growing, elegant half-hardy annual with very broad-petalled daisy flowers and ferny foliage. It is

very useful for bringing color to the back of the flower border. *C. bipinnatus* is the best known species, with flowers in shades of rose, purple, pink and white on stems to 3 ft (90 cm) tall; 'Sensation Mixed' is a recommended variety. *C. sulphureus* is shorter than *C. bipinnatus*, and produces flowers in a range of shades from yellow to orange-red.
General care: Fertile but not over-rich soil and a sunny site are required. If the plant is grown in an exposed site, some support will be needed.
Propagation: Sow seeds inside in late winter or outside in early spring.
Pests and diseases: Generally trouble-free.

CROCOSMIA
ZONES 5–8
This genus includes the well-known montbretia *C. x crocosmiiflora* (hardy to zone 7). Sword-shaped leaves in clumps and sprays of small gladiolus-like flowers are the distinguishing features. 'Solfatare' has bronze-green foliage and apricot-yellow flowers. *C. masonorum* (hardy to zone 5) grows to $2\frac{1}{2}$ ft (75 cm) with flame-orange flowers

Convolvulus mauritanicus

on arching stems, making a superb display from mid-summer to autumn, and it is excellent for cutting, too. A newer hybrid is C. 'Lucifer', which has even finer and more colorful flowers of an intense brilliant flame red. These appear in June/July and the plant grows to a height of 3 ft (90 cm).

General care: Well-drained fertile soil in a sunny site is necessary. In cold areas choose a sheltered site. Plant the corms 4–5 inches (10–13 cm) deep in spring. Leave them until clumps form before lifting, separating and finally replanting.

Propagation: Divide congested clumps of corms in early spring.

Pests and diseases: Generally trouble-free.

CROCUS   ZONES 5–9

The chalice-shaped flowers of crocus are well known to all as heralds of spring. There are many sorts, however, some flowering in autumn and winter as well. While the large-flowered crocus may be the most spectacular, we should not forget the small-flowered species which flower in late winter. Try C. chrysanthus mixed, or C. tomasinianus (hardy to zone 5); they will quickly multiply and give an increasing display as the numbers build up. The same can be said for the large-flowered varieties, such as 'Queen of the Blues'; 'Pickwick', pearly gray with dark centers and striped dark lilac; 'Jeanne d'Arc', snow white; 'Remembrance', a large pale violet purple; and 'Large Yellow'. For autumn flowering try C. speciosus (hardy to zone 5) in shades of purple to lavender-blue. C. imperati (hardy to zone 7), violet from fawn buds, blooms during the winter.

General care: Any soil which is not waterlogged is suitable, plus a sunny site if the blooms are to open properly. Plant autumn flowerers in late summer or as soon as possible afterwards. The remainder can be planted in the fall.

Crocus hybrid and Chionodoxa luciliae (see p. 34)

Propagation: By separating clumps after flowering or when fully dormant. Seeds take 2–3 years to bloom.

Pests and diseases: Generally trouble-free.

CUPHEA   ZONES 9–10

Two tender members of this genus can be grown as perennials in zones 9–10 and as annuals in zone 1. They provide something colorful and different for the summer border or as fillers elsewhere.

C. ignea (syn. platycentra) is the cigar flower, a bushy slender-stemmed plant to 1 ft (30 cm) tall, bearing a profusion of narrowly tubular scarlet flowers with purplish-brown and white tips. C. miniata is more robust to 1½ ft (45 cm) or more tall, having vermilion blooms bearing rounded petals.

General care: A sheltered sunny site is necessary for the best results but ordinary soil will do.

Propagation: By seed in warmth in spring.

Pests and diseases: Watch for aphids.

CYCLAMEN   ZONES 5–10

The common hardy cyclamen (C. neapolitanum, syn. C. hederifolium) is half-sized version of the familiar greenhouse pot plant and just as, if not more, charming. It starts to flower in late summer or early autumn before the leaves unfold and finishes 6–8 weeks later, surrounded by silvery-patterned leaves that persist all winter. Pink and white flowers are available.

General care: All well-drained soils are acceptable, ideally in a partially shaded site. Plant the corms in summer, making sure they are covered by about 2 inches (5 cm) of soil, except for the florist's varieties, which should be planted with the upper half of the tubers above the ground. Roots appear only on the top side so this must be uppermost when planting.

Propagation: By seed, sown when ripe or in spring in a cold frame. Self-sown seedlings quite often appear.

Pests and diseases: Generally trouble-free.

DAHLIA   ZONES 9–10

Familiar even to non-gardeners, this is one of the top favorite summer flowers. There are hundreds of different varieties in a wide range

Cyclamen neapolitanum

of blossom shapes and colors. They are tender tuberous-rooted perennials.

General care: Dahlias require a sunny position in rich fertile soil that is moisture-retentive and well-prepared. As all parts of the plant are frost-sensitive, planting must be delayed until the risk of spring frost has ended. Dahlia tubers can be planted out, but it is advisable to use tubers that have been started in the greenhouse. However, best results of all are obtained with rooted cuttings, started in a warm greenhouse and hardened off before planting out. These methods are for the various decorative and exhibition types, which vary in height from 18 inches to 6 ft (45 cm to 1.8 m). All but the shortest varieties need staking and tying during the growing season. When frost blackens the foliage, cut back to just above ground level, lift the tubers, wash off the soil and store in dry peat in a frost-free place.

Propagation: Take cuttings in spring from tubers that have previously been started into growth at about 60°F (16°C). Divide tubers that have been started into growth so that each tuber or group of tubers has at least one good shoot. Sow seeds in early spring in warmth.

Pests and diseases: Aphids, stalk borer, caterpillars and earwigs can be troublesome. Spray with malathion.

DELPHINIUM ZONES 3–10
The genus *Delphinium* includes both the ever popular annual larkspur and the queen of the herbaceous border with its statuesque spires in shades of blue, pink, cream, yellow and white. The latter is classified under *D. elatum* (hardy to zone 2) but is really a group of hybrids among at least three species. The tallest exceed 7 ft (2.2 m) in height and though a splendid sight need to be staked very securely against the wind. Shorter varieties are now becoming more popular, the following being in the 4–5 ft (1.2–

Delphinium

1.5 m) category: 'Black Knight' (dark blue), 'Blue Jay' (mid-blue), 'Astolat' (pink) and 'Galahad' (white). These are all Pacific hybrids and are raised from seed, though some nurserymen sell them as plants. More graceful, with slimmer branched stems, are the Beladonna delphiniums. Try the 4–5 ft (1.2–1.5 m) tall deep blue 'Lamartine', and shorter, pinky-rose 'Pink Sensation'. Rocket larkspur *D. ajacis* syn. *D. ambiguum* and common larkspur *D. consolida* syn. *D. regale* are seldom listed by botanical name and are often confused in seed catalogs. Go for the double 'Stock-flowered Special Mixture', at 3 ft (90 cm) tall, and the long-spiked

'Rocket Mixed' at 2½ ft (75 cm). For a front of the border site there is 'Dwarf Rocket' at 1 ft (30 cm) tall.

General care: A sunny site and moisture-retentive fertile soil are essential for really fine spikes of bloom. Light soils should be heavily enriched with decayed manure or garden compost, plus a general fertilizer each spring. Lime should be added to very acid soils. When the first spikes have faded, remove them promptly and a second but poorer display often results. Larkspurs will thrive in less rich soils, but also need a sunny site.

Propagation: Divide or take cuttings of basal shoots in spring in a cold frame for the perennials. Sow seed in early spring under glass, or later outside. Sow larkspur seed outdoors in autumn or spring.

Pests and diseases: Slugs are the main problem on perennial varieties; larkspur is usually trouble-free.

DIANTHUS ZONES 2–10
There are no fewer than 300 species of dianthus plus numerous hybrids and varieties, although only about 30 species do well in the U.S. Among these are some of the best loved and most familiar of garden flowers: garden pinks, carnations, sweet Williams and Chinese pinks.

Garden pinks, derived from *D. plumarius*, are extremely popular. There are dozens of varieties in a range of colors. 'Pink Princess' is a good one to try, growing 10–18 inches (25–45 cm) tall with rose-colored blossoms. The best known carnations are grown as greenhouse plants, but for the garden there are border carnations. They are larger than pinks and are always double-flowered. They are best raised from seed strains, for example, 'Chabaud Mixed', 'Vanguard' (a mixture of bicolors) and 'Dwarf Fragrance Mixed', producing plants to 14 inches (35 cm).

Sweet William *D. barbatus* is a short-lived perennial. Its individual bi- or tri-colored flowers are small but gathered into broad, flattened clusters. *D. barbatus* grows to about 1½ ft (45 cm) in height and is obtainable in mixed or single colors. 'Double Mixed' has fully and semi-double blooms while 'Dwarf Mixed' and 'Wee Willie' only grow to 6 inches (15 cm) and can be treated as annuals.

The Chinese pink *D. chinensis heddewigii* is related to sweet William but has larger flowers in smaller clusters and lacks the clove scent. It is highly floriferous and is usually grown as an annual. Modern varieties grow 6–12 inches (15–30 cm) tall and contain shades of red, pink and white, single or double, making a glorious combination of colors in a border.

The popular sweet William, Dianthus barbatus

General care: All dianthus need a sunny site and well-drained limy soil. All will grow in the heavier soils, but are then inclined to be short-lived.

Propagation: Pinks and carnations can be raised from cuttings or layers in summer or early autumn. They can also be grown from seed sown indoors in early spring. Chinese pinks are sown at the same time. Sweet Williams are sown outside or in a cold frame in late spring unless the dwarf sorts are to be raised as annuals, when they must be sown early in warmth.

Pests and diseases: Generally trouble-free.

DICENTRA   ZONES 2–10

Growing some 2½ ft (75 cm) high, *D. spectabilis* (hardy to zone 2) is a tall, graceful plant. The rows of rose-pink and white heart-shaped flowers (from which this flower takes its popular name of bleeding heart) dangle from arched stems and are at their best in late spring and early summer. They are equally attractive in the flower bed or in a flower arrangement, and are plants for that shady sheltered corner, away from the wind and the spring frosts.

General care: Moisture-retentive but well-drained

soil is the ideal, liberally laced with organic matter, ideally leaf mold. Partial shade or full sun are acceptable.

Propagation: Taking root cuttings in late winter is the easiest way, or large plants can be divided at the same time.

Pests and diseases: Slugs, especially on the young shoots, are the primary pests.

DICTAMNUS   ZONES 2–8

A sturdy, enduring perennial that blooms faithfully for generations in cold climates, *D. albus*, or gas plant, gets its popular name from its pec-

uliar habit of emitting gas from glands on the flower spikes. Its leaves also give off a pleasant citrus odor when brushed against. *D. albus* deserves a prominent site in the garden to display its handsome, airy spikes of starry-white blossoms on stems that grow 3 ft (90 cm) tall. Flowers bloom from early to mid-summer. The flowers are attractive in bouquets and its seedpods make interesting additions to winter arrangements.

Robust varieties include 'Purpureus', purple, and 'Rubra', rosy-purple.

General care: Full sun or partial shade in ordinary soil are the only requirements. Dictamnus is best left undisturbed after it has established itself in an area.

Propagation: Sow seed indoors in the fall and grow in flats for one year before transplanting outdoors. Root cuttings may be taken from established plants any time during the spring.

Pests and diseases: Generally trouble-free.

DIERAMA   ZONES 6–9

Fairy wand is a spectacular focal point in the garden with arching stems that measure 4–7 ft (1.2–2.4 m) in

Dicentra spectabilis

length and stiff, sword-like foliage. A bulbous member of the lily family, *D. pulcherrimum* bears flowers that bloom in mid-summer, ranging from deep purple to near white. *D. pendulum*, an earlier blooming variety, has graceful flowers in shades of white, mauve and pink.

General care: Dierama does best in moisture-rententive soil in full sun.

Propagation: Divide corms in fall.

Pests and diseases: Generally trouble-free.

DIGITALIS   ZONES 3–10

An old-fashioned favorite that deserves a place in the garden. There are several fine selections stocked by seedsmen. Try 'Excelsior' at 5–6½ ft (1.5–2 m) with large spikes of white, cream or pink to purple flowers, all with delightfully spotted throats. The more recently introduced 'Foxy' strain is similar but not as tall.

General care: All but the wettest and driest soils are acceptable to foxgloves; the richer the soil the grander are the flowers. Partial shade is ideal, but full sun is tolerated.

Propagation: Late spring is the time to sow the very fine foxglove seed. Broadcast it over a well-prepared seed bed and lightly rake over the soil to cover the seed. When the seedlings are large enough to handle space them out, 6 inches (15 cm) apart. Plant them out in early autumn.

Pests and diseases: Generally trouble-free.

DIMORPHOTHECA
ZONES 9–10

D. sinuata, a bright daisy-like perennial from South Africa, is treated like an annual in cold areas.

General care: It loves a dry-ish border, but do not plant it in shade as its flowers open only in bright sunlight.

Propagation: Sow outdoors after danger of frost has passed.

Pests and diseases: Generally trouble-free.

DORONICUM   ZONES 4–9

This is the showy spring-flowering yellow daisy or

Epimedium pinnatum

leopard's bane, perfect for front or mid-border locations. Modern varieties are larger and finer, notably *D. caucasicum* 'Magnificum' at 2 ft (60 cm), and the somewhat shorter, double flowered 'Spring Beauty'. At 1½ ft (45 cm) or a little less is the very bright yellow, free-blooming single called 'Miss Mason', perhaps the most garden-worthy of them all.

General care: Sun or shade and ordinary soil are all that are required.

Propagation: Divide this perennial in autumn or late winter.

Pests and diseases: Generally trouble-free.

ECHINOPS   ZONES 3–9

The globe thistles, with their round, prickly, ball-shaped flower-heads and dramatic gray and green foliage are always majestic plants mid-summer to late fall. This is the time to cut and dry the flowers for winter use in

flower arrangements.

E. exaltus (hardy to zone 3) 'Taplow Blue' produces steel-blue flower-heads which turn silvery with age. It grows 5–6 ft (1.2–1.8 m) tall.

General care: Any moisture-rententive soil in sun or partial shade will grow the best known species and varieties.

Propagation: Divide in early spring or sow seeds a little later in a cold frame or in the flower bed. Seedlings usually take 2 years to bloom.

Pests and diseases: Generally trouble-free.

ECHIUM

The hardy annual *Echium plantagineum* has a long flowering season. If sown early it will start to flower in late May and go on continuously until the autumn. Its flowers come in shades of blue, white and pink. *E. p.* 'Bedding Mixed' and 'Dwarf Hybrid', both about 12 inches (30 cm) high, are

highly recommended.

General care: All soils are acceptable, even dry poor ones, though the best growth is made on those of medium fertility and moisture content. Choose a sunny site, although some shade is tolerated.

Propagation: Sow seeds outdoors in spring or, for early blooming plants, in autumn.

Pests and diseases: Generally trouble-free.

EPIMEDIUM   ZONES 3–9

A low-growing, rapidly spreading perennial, epimedium is an excellent choice for shade. The heart-shaped foliage is bronze-pink on the new plants, turns lush green and heralds autumn with shades of red-dish bronze. The plants do not perform well in the mild-winter regions of the South, Southwest and Southern California. Growing from 8–12 inches (20–30 cm) high, they are excellent small-

scale groundcover plants with their display of cup-and-saucer-shaped flowers.

E. pinnatum (hardy to zone 5) has yellow flowers that bloom in spring. E. grandiflorum (hardy to zone 3) has the largest flowers, 2 inches (5 cm) wide, in shades of white, red, purple and pink. E. rubrum grows 12 inches (30 cm) tall with appealing clusters of crimson, yellow and white flowers. Nurseries offer 'Pink Queen', rose-pink, and 'Snow Queen', white. E. perralderianum 'Frohnleiten' (hardy to zone 5), which grows to 12 inches (30 cm) high, is a recent German import with golden yellow flowers.

General care: Epimedium appreciates moist, acid soil, enriched with organic matter. It performs well in the shade but tolerates full sun if given ample moisture.

Propagation: Divide roots of established clumps with a sharp spade in spring or fall.

Pests and diseases: Generally trouble-free.

ERANTHIS ZONES 4–8

The winter aconite E. hyemalis (hardy to zone 4) is one of our earliest and brightest spring flowers. A wonderful bright golden yellow color, they are rather like large buttercups on short stems, set in rings of leafy bracts. Grown in masses, they are stunningly cheerful. They are ideal for naturalizing under trees.

General care: Moisture-retentive soil while the plants are actively growing in spring is essential to the long-term success of this plant. Plant the corm-like, dark brown tubers in autumn, the earlier the better.

Propagation: Established clumps can be divided after flowering or when dormant. Large tubers can be cut or broken into two or more pieces. Seed sown when ripe outside or in pots germinates freely but takes several years to reach flowering size.

Pests and diseases: Generally trouble-free.

Erigeron garden hybrid

ERIGERON ZONES 2–10

This ally of Michaelmas daisy bears flower-heads with many very slender petals which give them a distinctive elegance. There are now many fine hybrid varieties of E. speciosus in shades of violet, lavender and pink. All have a long flowering season, starting in early summer and continuing until the autumn. They last well when cut for indoor decoration.

The hardiest varieties include 'Darkest of All', which grows 18 inches (45 cm) high and has deep violet flowers with golden eyes; 'Dignity', which grows 2 ft (60 cm) tall and has flowers that are deep blue turning mauve; and 'Sincerity', which grows 2½ ft (75 cm) tall and has flowers that are lilac mauve with a clear yellow center. Those in the pink-rosy-carmine color range include 'Foersters Liebling', growing to 2 ft (60 cm) tall with semi-double, rosy-carmine flowers, and 'Gaiety', which grows to 2½ ft (75 cm) and has large pink flowers.

General care: A sunny site and any ordinary soil are the only necessities. Over-rich, moist soil will encourage soft, floppy growth.

Propagation: Division in spring is the usual method. Seed may be sown but does not come true to type.

Pests and diseases: Generally trouble-free.

ESCHSCHOLZIA

Grown as a hardy annual, E. californica (California poppy) produces masses of orange-yellow poppy flowers from summer to fall. 'Ballerina' Mixed is an interesting seed strain that has semi-double flowers with fluted petals in shades of orange, red, pink and yellow.

General care: California poppy does best in poorer sandy soils and is an ideal choice for a dry sunny border. Self-sown seedlings will flower well in succeeding seasons.

Propagation: Sow seed outdoors in spring.

Pests and diseases: Generally trouble-free.

EUPHORBIA ZONES 3–10

Although about 2,000 different species of spurge are known, for the flower garden we are only concerned with the hardy herbaceous or subshrubby members of the genus. The flowers of euphorbia are small and insignificant; it is the surrounding petal-like bracts that give the plant its beauty.

E. pulcherrima (hardy to zone 9) is the well-known poinsettia, an important greenhouse plant in the North, planted outside in subtropical zones. E. polychroma (hardy to zone 4)

(syn. E. epithymoides) is outstanding; growing to 18 inches (45 cm), it produces brilliant yellow bracts in early spring akin to a touch of sunlight. E. wulfenii grows to 2½ ft (75 cm) and has glaucous foliage and yellowish-green spikes appearing in spring. E. griffithii 'Fireglow' grows to 1½ ft (45 cm) and has orange-red bracts and pinky foliage. It remains splendid from spring to mid-summer.

General care: Ordinary soil will grow all these spurges well, though E. griffithii thrives best in the heavier or moisture-retentive ones. All will grow in sun or partial shade.

Propagation: Divide griffithii and polychroma in autumn or spring. Sow seeds of wulfenii when ripe or in spring in a cold frame.

Pests and diseases: Generally trouble-free.

FILIPENDULA ZONES 2–10

A member of the rose family, F. vulgaris (meadowsweet) is the most popular variety for garden cultivation, producing large sprays of double white flowers with a pink tinge. It grows 12–18 inches (30–45 cm) high and is a good choice for the middle of a shady border. The flowers bloom in late spring through mid-summer and bear some resemblance to astilbes. 'Flore-Plena' grows to 2 ft (60 cm) high and spreads to 18 inches (45 cm). F. rubra (hardy to zone 2) is a native of the eastern half of the country. 'Venustra' has strong stems that grow to 6 ft (1.8 m) tall and bear pink flowers from early to mid-summer. The bold foliage has large, jagged leaves.

General care: Filipendula prefers moist, enriched soil and partially shady conditions, but it will grow, less lushly, in sun and ordinary soil.

Propagation: Filipendula is easily propagated by seeds sown in early spring or by division of established plants in spring.

Pests and diseases: Generally trouble-free.

FRITILLARIA ZONES 3–9

There are two species within this group of hardy bulbs that are of particular interest to the gardener: *F. imperialis* (crown imperial, hardy to zone 3) and *F. meleagris* (snake's head, hardy to zone 5). *F. imperialis* is a robust plant to 3 ft (90 cm) or more tall bearing a terminal cluster of red or yellow bell flowers. *F. i.* 'Lutea Maxima' has deep yellow blooms and 'Rubra Maxima' has brick red flowers. The snake's heads, which are much lower growing at 10 inches (25 cm) high, have charming, solitary, drooping bell flowers in many shades of purple with a dark checkered pattern.

General care: Moisture-retentive but reasonably well drained soils are preferred, though *meleagris* tolerates some waterlogging. The bulbs are fleshy, easily damaged and must be planted as fresh as possible from August to October. Plant crown imperials 6–8 inches (15–20 cm) deep and snake's heads 4–6 inches (10–15 cm) deep.

Propagation: Remove offsets or separate clumps as the leaves die down.

Pests and diseases: Generally trouble-free.

FUCHSIA ZONES 5–10

This must rank among the most popular of all plants. Although it is seldom used as a hardy perennial, with some extra care several varieties can be left in the flower bed during winter. 'Mrs Popple' is one of the hardiest varieties, together with 'Riccartonii', but many others such as 'Celia Smedley', 'Madame Cornelissen' and 'Tom Thumb' do well.

General care: Any well-drained moderately fertile soil is suitable, preferably in a sheltered site. Put out young plants in late spring, planting them as deep as is practicable. This is the best protection you can give the plant against winter frost damage. Cut them back in November and put a layer of sand or peat on top to pro-tect the plants further. With nearly all varieties, new growth will come from the roots in spring and plants will start flowering from mid-summer. Regular feeding and watering during dry spells is essential for maintaining healthy and vigorous plants. They tolerate any soil as long as it is moisture-retentive.

Propagation: Take cuttings in late summer and grow the young plants in pots under cover until planting-out time.

Pests and diseases: Generally trouble-free, but watch for damage from aphids and spider mites.

GAILLARDIA ZONES 2–10

Inelegantly known as blanket flower, *Gaillardia* x *grandiflora* (hardy to zone 2) is a startlingly showy daisy with broad petals of bright red-purple and yellow. Sometimes listed under one or another of its parent species (*aristata* and *pulchella*), there are several variety and seed strains. Try 'Suttons Large-flowered Mixed' which grows to $2\frac{1}{2}$ ft (75 cm) or 'Goblin' (dwarf bedder), which is half the height at 15 inches (38 cm), 'Mandarin' (rich orange-red) and 'Croftway Yellow' (bright yellow).

General care: Blanket flowers do well in sun or light shade in almost any soil, although a well-drained one is best.

Propagation: Sow seeds under glass in early spring to make sure of flowers the first season. Alternatively, sow in late spring outside and transplant in early autumn.

Pests and diseases: Generally trouble-free.

GALANTHUS ZONES 3–8

The fair maids of February, better known as snowdrops, are one of the first outdoor bulbs to flower, and no garden is complete without them.

There are numerous varieties: *G. nivalis* (zone 3) is the common snowdrop and is usually chosen for natural-izing in the grass and in shade under shrubs. For open ground it is better to plant the large-flowered varieties, such as *G. elwesii* or *G. nivalis* 'Viridapicis' with its green-tipped petals. Reliable are 'Samuel (Sam) Arnot' which has large single flowers and *G. n. plenus*, with large double flowers.

General care: Snowdrops succeed in moist soils, particularly in heavy loams. Left undisturbed they multiply freely until, if grown in a border, they may need lifting and dividing to maintain maximum flower production. The time to lift and replant snowdrops is a couple of weeks after flowering while the foliage is still green. If dry bulbs are bought they should be very fresh; plant them immediately.

Propagation: Separate offsets or divide clumps when replanting.

Pests and diseases: Generally trouble-free, but narcissus-fly is sometimes a nuisance.

GALTONIA ZONES 5–10

Summer hyacinth is a summer-blooming member of the lily family from South Africa. The most common variety is *G. candicans*, which grows on sturdy stems that reach 3–4 ft (90–120 cm) tall with small, white and fragrant bell-shaped flowers. The summer hyacinth, which blooms for 3–4 weeks, is excellent for cut flowers and as a backdrop to shorter plants in the border.

General care: For best results plant in rich, moisture-retentive soil in sun or partial shade.

Propagation: Plant bulbs 6 inches (15 cm) deep in the fall and leave undisturbed. Mulch heavily in cold zones or lift and store in the fall.

Pests and diseases: Generally trouble-free.

GAZANIA ZONES 9–10

This is a half-hardy perennial from South Africa that loves sunshine; in fact, its brilliant daisy flowers open

Frost tender Fuchsia hybrid

Galanthus nivalis

only in direct sunlight. Seed mixtures are available which give flowers of yellow, pink and red shades as well as the more usual orange.

General care: Extremely well drained fertile soil and a sunny site are essential. In all but the mildest areas of zone 10, plants to be overwintered must be kept in a frame or greenhouse. Alternatively, take cuttings in late summer and overwinter these. They can also be grown as annuals.

Propagation: Sow seeds in warmth early to mid-spring. Set out the young plants only after the threat of frost has passed. Take cuttings of non-flowering shoots in late summer or spring.

Pests and diseases: Generally trouble-free.

GENTIANA ZONES 3–8

The blue trumpets of gentians are the highlight of the garden display. Most are difficult to grow unless soil conditions are perfect.

Recommended are the dwarf *G. acaulis* (hardy to zone 3), the blue trumpet gentian which flowers in late spring, *G. sino-ornata* (hardy to zone 4) with its brilliant blue flowers in early fall, and the 2 ft (60 cm) tall willow gentian, *G. asclepiadea*, which blooms in late summer and early autumn.

General care: *G. acaulis* needs a limy soil, *G. sino-ornata* an acid peaty one, while *G. asclepiadea* grows in any moisture-retentive rooting medium. Sun or partial shade is acceptable by all three.

Propagation: Plants can be propagated either from root cuttings taken in spring or by division of plants in March (*G. acaulis* should be divided in June). Sow seeds when ripe or in spring in a cold frame. Fresh seed sown in late summer and subjected to winter freezing in a cold frame generally germinates well.

Pests and diseases: Generally trouble-free.

GERANIUM ZONES 2–10

Geranium is the botanical name for cranesbill and must not be confused with the tender pot and bedding plants of that name which are technically members of the genus *Pelargonium*. Cranesbills are mainly hardy border and rock plants, some of which make splendid ground cover subjects.

G. psilostemon (hardy to zone 3), growing to $2\frac{1}{2}$ ft (75 cm) high, has numerous magenta red flowers with black centers and veins. In addition, it has beautifully colored leaves in autumn. *G. pratense* (hardy to zone 5), 'Meadow Geranium', grows 2 ft (60 cm) high and is available in several colors from white to violet blue; 'Flore Pleno' has double blue flowers. *G. macrorrhizum* (hardy to zone 2) 'Ingwersen's Variety' is often used as ground cover as it grows only to 1 ft (30 cm) high. It has soft pink flowers and masses of aromatic leaves that color beautifully in autumn. For the rock garden try the low-growing *G. cinereum* (hardy to zone 7) 'Ballerina' which reaches only 3–6 inches (7.5–15 cm) high and has pale rosy purple flowers deeply veined with crimson.

General care: A sunny site is best, though *G. macrorrhizum* and *G. pratense* are happy in partial shade. Any reasonably well drained soil is suitable.

Propagation: Division in spring is easiest, though all species can be raised from seed when ripe or in spring.

Pests and diseases: Generally trouble-free.

GERBERA ZONES 8–10

Native to South Africa, *G. jamesonii* or Transvaal daisy is the most elegant of the daisies. Slender-rayed petals of cream, yellow, orange, coral and red top 12–18 inch (30–45 cm) long stems. Gerbera is a beautiful, long-lasting cut flower as well as a good greenhouse plant in northern zones. After cutting, slit slightly before placing in water to increase its longevity. Although prime blooming season is in spring and fall, gerbera will bloom throughout the year in zones 9 and 10.

General care: Full sun or partial shade in hottest weather. Gerbera prefers deep watering and well-drained, humus-rich soil. Feed often.

Propagation: Sow seed indoors in winter at 70°F (21°C) or divide clumps in early spring.

Pests and diseases: Snails and slugs can be a problem.

Gentiana sino-ornata

Plant crowns of plants above the soil level to avoid root rot becoming troublesome.

GEUM ZONES 5–9

This genus of 40 evergreen and herbaceous perennials has long been a favorite for the flower border, with its basal pinnate leaves and flowers like small species roses. Among recommended varieties are: 'Mrs Bradshaw', growing to 2 ft (60 cm) with double flaming brickred flowers; 'Lady Stratheden' grows 2 ft (60 cm) high and has semi-double warm yellow flowers; and 'Fire Opal' grows $2\frac{1}{2}$ ft (75 cm) high and has semi-double flowers that are orange-scarlet with purple stems.

General care: Well-drained but moisture-retentive soil in sun or partial shade is the basic requirement.

Propagation: Plants can be raised from seed sown in late spring for planting out the following spring or by dividing the roots in spring.

Pests and diseases: Generally trouble-free.

GLADIOLUS ZONES 8–10

The gladiolus now takes its place in the top 10 of popular garden flowers. Thousands of varieties have been raised in every color of the rainbow except true blue. Best known are the large-flowered varieties with massive one-sided spikes $3\frac{1}{4}$–4 ft (1–1.2 m) tall. Better suited to general garden use and more graceful is the miniature *Primulinus*. 'Butterfly' is a good choice. Many varieties are available by mail order and from garden centers.

General care: Gladioli do best when planted in a sunny position where the soil has been well prepared. Some old compost or manure dug in also helps, as does good drainage. Most corms are frost-sensitive, so plant in late March/early April. There are extra hardy varieties now available that are hardy into Canada. The depth of planting is important – always plant at least 6 inches (15 cm) or even deeper, so unstaked

flower stems do not topple over, and if you are prepared to take a risk, the less hardy corms can be left in the ground through the winter in zones 6 and 7. If not planted as deep as this, the corms need lifting in the autumn. Dry them off quickly indoors and store in a frost-free airy place.

Propagation: Separate the smaller daughter corms and very tiny cormets known as 'spawn' when lifting in the autumn. Spawn should be sown in rows in spring and will produce flowering-sized corms for the following year.

Pests and diseases: Generally fairly trouble-free, but look out for thrips on the blooms and leaves, dry rot, corm rot and core rot on the corms.

GODETIA

See under Clarkia

GYPSOPHILA ZONES 2–8

Better known as baby's

breath or chalk plant, the lovely froth of tiny blooms of this plant makes it a wonderful accompaniment to sweet peas and other large flowers when gathered for a bouquet or vase arrangement. A free-standing plant in full bloom becomes a glorious hazy cloud of color.

'Bristol Fairy', which grows 4 ft (1.2 m) high, is a favorite and is probably the best double white for cutting; it is also a good, strong grower. The pale pink-flowered 'Rosy Veil' is a different type; growing only $1\frac{1}{2}$ ft (45 cm) high, it has a low, spreading habit. *G. elegans* is the popular annual with larger white or pink flowers.

General care: A sunny site and freely draining, limy, fertile soil are ideal, but most soils are suitable for this tolerant plant.

Propagation: By basal cuttings in late spring in a frame or greenhouse for the perennials. Sow seeds outdoors in spring for the annuals.

Godetia amoena (see p. 35)

Pests and diseases: Generally trouble-free.

HELENIUM ZONES 3–9

This member of the daisy family has the same growth habit and appeal as the Michaelmas daisy. By planting several varieties, the flowering season can extend from summer through October.

To start the season plant 'Moerheim Beauty', which flowers in mid-summer and reaches a height of 3 ft (90 cm). There is considerable warmth in its large, crimson-red, daisy-like flowers, which have a dark center. Another for mid-summer flowering is 'Coppelia', which grows 3 ft (90 cm) high and has coppery-orange flowers. For later flowering, 'Bruno' has really deep crimson-red flowers with a dark center. It grows to 3 ft (90 cm). After that try 'Butterpat', which also grows 3 ft (90 cm) tall and has bright yellow flowers that remain into mid-fall. The earlier flowering varieties, such as 'Moerheim Beauty', will sometimes produce a second flush of flowers during fall if they are cut down immediately after the first crop has finished.

General care: Ordinary garden soil that is reasonably moisture-retentive and a sunny site give the best results. Divide and replant every 3–4 years.

Propagation: Divide congested clumps in spring.

Pests and diseases: Generally trouble-free.

HELIANTHEMUM

ZONES 5–10

For brightening up the rock garden, front of a border or dry bank, sun roses have no peer. Pleasant in foliage all year, they really come into their own in early summer when the leafy mats are obscured by abundant rose-like blossom.

Some of the best named varieties are 'Ben Afflick', which has orange and buff flowers; 'Beech Park Scarlet' which, true to its name, is a crimson scarlet; 'Wisley Pink', a delightful pink; and 'Wisley Primrose', a soft yellow. Planting out time is fall or early spring when the soil is not frosted.

General care: Full sun and a sharply drained soil give the best results. After flowering, trim back to the leafy stem bases to maintain a compact habit. Severe winters may damage or even kill the plants.

Propagation: Take 3 inch (7.5 cm) cuttings of non-flowering growth with a heel, June–August. Over-winter newly-rooted plants in a cold frame and plant out in March or April when it is warmer.

Pests and diseases: Generally trouble-free.

HELIANTHUS ZONES 2–10

True perennial sunflowers are indispensable border plants, especially *H. multi-*

florus (hardy to zone 4) 'Loddon Gold' with fully double blooms on 5 ft (1.5 m) tall branching stems and the shorter, anemone-centered 'Morning Sun'. Among the annual sunflowers, *H. annuus* must be the most spectacular. Stems of 8–10 ft (3.2–4 m) topped by flowers measuring 12 inches (30 cm) across are by no means unusual. The 'Giant Yellow' variety is one of the largest. Smaller-flowered and in a range of yellow, bronze and maroon shades is 'Sunburst' at 4 ft (1.2 m) tall. Shorter varieties are available and they will flower impressively in the center of a bed or towards the back of the flower border, but remember the heads will always turn to face south. *H. gigantus* (hardy to zone 2) grows from 9–12 ft (2.7–3.3 m) and blooms from the summer through fall in the Northeast and Canada.

General care: A sunny site is required for all the varieties, and the flowers will happily survive a drought. The perennials thrive in all but the wettest and poorest soils, but the annuals must have a humus-rich, well-drained but moisture-retentive rooting medium. Even if you are growing the sunflowers against a wall or fence, most will need to be tied firmly to a long stake.

Helianthus 'Sunburst'

Gypsophila elegans

Propagation: Divide the perennials in early spring and sow seeds of the annuals outdoors mid to late spring.

Pests and diseases: Generally trouble-free.

HELICHRYSUM

The strawflower, *H. bracteatum*, is certainly attractive in the garden as a hardy annual bedding plant, but its great value is to the flower arranger for drying. The flowers are daisy-like in shape but the petal-like bracts are shiny and somewhat like straw. Flowers are produced from mid-summer to frost, and blooms for drying should be cut just as they are opening. If they are cut when fully open, seed development continues and the flower centers are spoiled. Try growing 'Hot Bikini', a bright red, and 'Bright Bikini', a colorful mixture, both of which grow to 12 inches (30 cm) high.

General care: A sunny site and ordinary soil are the only requirements.

Propagation: Usually best sown indoors in early spring, but can be sown outdoors in late spring.

Pests and diseases: Generally trouble-free.

HELIOTROPIUM X HYBRIDUM ZONE 10

Heliotrope or cherry pie is an evergreen shrub that responds to culture as an annual. It bears an abundance of somewhat forget-me-not-like flowers from spring to fall. The dark green to almost purple foliage of some varieties makes a useful contrast both to its own flowers and to other foliage. 'Marine', which grows 15 inches (38 cm) high, is outstanding.

General care: A sunny sheltered site and well-drained soil give the best results, but most ordinary soils are adequate. Plants can be lifted and potted and grown in a greenhouse or sunny window if desired.

Propagation: Sow in the greenhouse at a temperature of 60–68°F (15–20°C) in February/March and plant out when threat of frost has passed. Cuttings can be taken in late summer, and the young plants overwintered in warmth, or taken in spring from overwintered plants of the previous season.

Pests and diseases: Generally trouble-free.

The Christmas rose, Helleborus niger

HELIPTERUM ROSEUM

This is often listed by seedsmen as acroclinium. It has delicate daisy flowers like those of helichrysum but in shades of pink and white. 'Sandfordii' is an attractive yellow variety, growing 12 inches (30 cm) high. A delightful annual for the summer flower border and for drying for winter decoration.

General care: Sunshine and well-drained soil are essential. Avoid over-rich soil which will encourage soft, floppy growth.

Propagation: Sow seeds directly into their flowering position in late spring. Can also be sown earlier indoors.

Pests and diseases: Generally trouble-free.

HELLEBORUS ZONES 3–8

The hellebores are supreme among hardy perennials in producing their attractive bowl-shaped blooms in winter and early spring. It is such a thrill to have two or three Christmas roses (*Helleborus niger*, hardy to zone 3) as a centerpiece on the dinner table at Christmas time that it is worth all the trouble of dealing with the slugs to get them in bloom for that special occasion.

There are several forms of the Christmas rose, some with very much larger flowers than others. The best is 'Potter's Wheel', which has pure white, broad petals with no pink flush on the back of them. *Helleborus orientalis* (hardy to zone 6) and its hybrids, the Lenten rose, produce several large nodding flowers on each stem from late winter through spring. They vary in color from deep purple to creamy white with or without spots inside. *Helleborus corsicus* (hardy to zone 4) grows to 2 ft (60 cm) and makes quite a large shrubby plant. Its strong stems carry creamy-green flower trusses from winter through spring. Not only are the flower-heads sought after by flower arrangers but the seed pods that follow are just as interesting for the same purpose. *Helleborus foetidus* (hardy to zone 6) grows to 18 inches (45 cm). A native of England, it produces its flower-heads in shades of green and purple, followed again by attractive seed pods.

General care: Sun or partial shade are acceptable together with, ideally, a humus-rich soil that does not readily dry out.

Propagation: Sow seeds when ripe in a cold frame. (Dry seeds may take a year to germinate.) Divide clumps in spring as flowers fade.

Pests and diseases: Slugs can be a nuisance.

HEMEROCALLIS ZONES 2–10

Day lilies are easily grown plants of great appeal. They have a unique flower production system: a single flower on each stem opens in the morning and dies at night to be followed by a new fresh bloom on the same stem the next day. This flowering routine goes on without a break for 6–8 weeks and by growing several varieties of the best garden hybrids it is possible to have these beautiful lily flowers from June/July to September.

To start the flowering season plant 'Gold Dust', which grows to 18 inches (45 cm) tall and has yellow flowers with a dark reverse. Follow with 'Tejas', which grows to 2½ ft (75 cm). Its bright coppery-crimson flowers appear in mid-summer. If you like a bright clear yellow flower, grow 'Hyperion' instead: it grows to 3 ft (90 cm). For July/August you could choose from 'Kwanso', which grows to 2 ft (60 cm) high and has flowers with white-striped foliage, or 'Mrs John Tigert', grows 2½ ft (75 cm) tall and has coppery flowers with a dark center.

General care: Ordinary soils of moderate fertility and retentive of moisture are suitable; even wet soils are tolerated. A sunny site is best, but partial shade is acceptable.

Propagation: Propagation is by division of roots in late spring or early fall. Once planted take care not to disturb the roots. Seeds can be sown in spring, but varieties do not come true to type.

Pests and diseases: Slugs and snails attack young leaves.

HEUCHERA ZONES 3–9

H. sanguinea, coral bells, forms handsome mounds of shiny, ivy-shaped foliage.

Sprays of tiny bell-shaped flowers of pink, red and white top 1–2 ft (30–60 cm) slender, wiry stems. A native American perennial, coral bells is prized for its showy foliage and flowers that bloom from spring through mid-summer. The flowers attract hummingbirds.

'Green Ivory', which grows $2\frac{1}{2}$ ft (75 cm) tall, boasts numerous white flowers atop light green foliage. 'Matin Bells' is a good cut flower with its bright coral flowers that top 18 inch (45 cm) stems. 'June Bride' has large, vigorous pure-white flowers on 15 inch (38 cm) stems. 'Palace Purple' is beautiful year-round, with mahogany red foliage and sprays of small white flowers. It grows to 18 inches (45 cm).

General care: Plant in rich, moisture-retentive soil in sun or partial shade. Mulch well after the ground freezes in cold areas. Cut off spent flower stalks to encourage further blooming.

Propagation: Sow seeds indoors in early spring. Plant seedlings outdoors after danger of frost has passed, taking care to place the crowns just below the soil level.

Pests and diseases: Generally trouble-free.

HOSTA ZONES 3–9

The bold, spade-shaped leaves of the plantain lilies or funkias in many shades of gray, green and sometimes almost blue or golden yellow, with or without contrasting margins, make hostas great plants not only for the gardener but also for those interested in flower arranging. In addition they grace the garden with upright spikes of delicate lilac, lily-like flowers.

There are certainly too many varieties of hosta to list here, but two outstanding ones are: *H. fortunei* (hardy to zone 3) 'Albopicta', which has yellow leaves edged with pale green (in fact, there are several *fortunei* varieties in different combinations of green and yellow) and *H.*

Heuchera sanguinea

sieboldiana (hardy to zone 3) with lovely blue-gray crinkled and deeply veined leaves.

General care: Partial shade and humus-rich, moisture-retentive soils provide the best conditions.

Propagation: Divide the clumps in spring and replant immediately. Hostas can also be grown from seed sown in spring, but seldom come exactly true to type.

Pests and diseases: Slugs and snails are a primary nuisance on shoots, leaves and flowers.

HYACINTHUS ZONES 4–9

The sturdy, dense flower spikes of forced hyacinths at Christmas or bedded out in spring are a familiar and cheering sight. There are several cultivars, all derived from *Hyacinthus orientalis* and strongly fragrant. Recommended are: 'Anna Marie' (pale pink); 'Carnegie' (pure white); 'Delft Blue'

(light blue); 'Ostara' (deep blue); 'Jan Bos' (red).

General care: Ordinary soil, ideally enriched with organic matter, and a sunny site are all that is required. In the poorer, drier soils hyacinths tend to dwindle away.

Propagation: Separate long-established clumps or remove offsets when dormant.

Pests and diseases: Generally trouble-free.

IBERIS ZONES 2–10

Candytufts have long been gardening favorites, being of very easy culture and freely producing spiky, head-like white, pink or purple flowers. Among the low, shrubby perennials, *I. saxatilis* (hardy to zone 2) reaches 4–6 inches (10–15 cm) in height and is a spreading plant. It is well suited for a rock garden. The flat white flower-heads make a good show in early summer. *I. sempervirens* (hardy to zone 3), growing to 6–9

inches (15–23 cm), is taller and makes a larger spreading plant, reaching anything up to 2 ft (60 cm) across. It is more suitable for planting on top of a dry wall or for general open situations. Two good varieties are 'Little Gem' and 'Snow Flake', growing 6 inches (15 cm) and 9 inches (23 cm) tall respectively. Both have white flowers. Best known of the annuals is common candytuft, *I. umbellata*, bearing many clusters of pink, white or purple flowers. 'Giant Hyacinth', a white, and 'Red Flash', a vivid carmine red, are both successful varieties.

General care: A sunny site and well-drained soil are essentials. Poor soil is tolerated, but moderately fertile soil is recommended for the annuals.

Propagation: Take cuttings of the perennials, choosing non-flowering shoots in summer and placing them in a cold frame. Sow seed of the annuals outdoors in spring.

Pests and diseases: Generally trouble-free.

IRIS ZONES 3–10

There are 300 species of iris and many more hybrids and varieties. Some have rhizomes, others bulbs and among their ranks are some of the loveliest flowers for the garden. Among the many bulbous irises the best known is probably *I. reticulata* (hardy to zone 5) which grows 6–8 inches (15–20 cm) tall. It is often planted with good effect in rock gardens, and it produces its purple-blue flowers in late winter to early spring. The variety 'Cantab' is a lighter blue than 'J.S. Dijt', which is a near purple. *I. danfordiae* (hardy to zone 5) has vivid yellow flowers in February. The tall Dutch iris which grows $2\frac{1}{2}$ ft (75 cm) high is excellent for cutting in early summer. If left undisturbed it will flower for years, provided it has been planted about 5 inches (12.5 cm) deep. In fact, the same is true of the Spanish and English *I. xiphoides* (hardy to zone 7). Best known of the rhizome-bearing sorts is the huge assemblage of large-flowered bearded or flag irises, derived from *I. pallida* and allied species. These come in all colors of the rainbow and bloom in summer. There are so many varieties to choose from that it is best to consult a specialist's catalog or, better still, make a visit to a nearby nursery in June to see which are in flower. In addition to the taller varieties and hybrids there are many dwarf ones, some of which only grow to 4 inches (10 cm) high.

General care: A sunny site and well-drained fertile soil are essential for the success of the bulbous and rhizomatous irises mentioned here. Plant bulbous species in autumn, rhizomatous sorts after flowering in autumn or spring. Divide and replant rhizomatous irises every third year to maintain vigor.

Propagation: Divide rhizomatous irises after flowering or in spring. Separate clumps of bulbous irises or remove bulblets when dormant.

Pests and diseases: Slugs and snails damage flowers and leaves, leaf spot spoils the foliage, and bulbs and rhizomes are often prey to attack by soft rot.

KNIPHOFIA   ZONES 5–10
The brightly hued flower spikes and grassy foliage of red hot pokers have long assured their popularity in gardens as something different and desirable. Of the many varieties, 'Samuel's Sensation', which grows 5 ft (1.5 m) high, is outstanding with its bright scarlet blooms. 'Bressingham Torch', growing to 3 ft (90 cm), is also spectacular and has orange-yellow spikes.

General care: Although some shade is tolerated, a sunny, sheltered site and well-drained but moisture-retentive soil provide the best growing conditions. Plant in spring and subsequently protect the crowns with heavy mulch during the winter in cold areas.

Propagation: Divide estab-

lished clumps in spring or sow seeds at the same time under glass.

Pests and diseases: Generally trouble-free.

LANTANA   ZONES 8–10
Lantana produces lovely clusters of bright flowers on evergreen, shrubby plants. Grown as a perennial in the South, *L. montevidensis* (hardy to zone 8) provides summer color in any region. Trailing branches grow from 3–6 ft (90 cm–1.8 m) long and display a generous profusion of color throughout the year in warm regions. Lantana makes a lovely container plant, either in window boxes or hanging baskets. Selections include 'Carnival', pink, yellow, crimson and lavender; 'Confetti', yellow, pink and purple; 'Radiation', rich orange-red; 'Irene', magenta; and 'Kathleen', rose and gold.

General care: Plant in well-drained ordinary soil in full sun. Let soil dry out between waterings.

Propagation: Propagate from softwood cuttings or from seed planted indoors in late winter.

Pests and diseases: Mildew can be a problem if the plant is not placed in full sun.

LATHYRUS
The sweet pea, *L. odoratus*, is familiar to all and has long been a great favorite. From June to September the lovely flowers in shades of red, pink, salmon, blue, lavender and white are a delight in the garden and for indoor flower arrangements. The tall Spenser group of varieties all need sticks or some form of support, as does 'Jet Set' (mixed colors) which grows 3 ft (90 cm) tall. 'Snoopea' (mixed) is 12–15 inches (30–38 cm) tall and needs no support, making it excellent for a border.

General care: For the finest sweet peas, a rich, moisture-retentive soil and a place in the sun are required. Dress the poorer soils with rotted farmyard manure, garden compost or peat and fert-

The sweet pea, Lathyrus odoratus

ilizer, and if the soil is acid apply lime.

Propagation: Sow seed January–March under glass at a temperature of 60–68°F (15–20°C) or in April/May in open ground.

Pests and diseases: Generally trouble-free, but look out for thrips, slugs and snails and downy mildew disease, and treat accordingly.

LAVANDULA   ZONES 5–10
The English lavender *L. angustifolia* (*spica*), usually grown for its fragrant essential oil, is still popular in spite of the fact that its height – it grows to 3 ft (90 cm) – means it needs plenty of space. Its blue-purple flower spikes open from late summer through fall. The dwarf variety, 'Munstead', growing to 18 inches (45 cm), is ever a favorite with its blue spikes of flowers, and it is undoubtedly good for an average-sized garden. 'Hidcote' is another compact variety and has violet flowers. If you

want to dry the flower stems, cut them when the flowers are just showing color but are not fully open. The fragrance is then retained at its best.

General care: All but the wettest soils grow lavenders, but for long-lived, healthy specimens a well-drained, fertile, limy soil in a sunny site is best. Remove old flower spikes and at least 2–3 inches (5–7.5 cm) of stem each spring to keep the growth of the plant compact.

Propagation: Take 3 inch (7.5 cm) cuttings of ripe non-flowering shoots in late summer and, when rooted, overwinter them in a cold frame. Plant out in spring.

Pests and diseases: Generally trouble-free.

LAVATERA
The annual mallow, *L. trimestris*, is an erect plant which grows to around 2½ ft (75 cm) tall, branches naturally and is a good space filler. The wide petals of its pink or white flowers form a beautiful open trumpet up to 4 inches (10 cm) across

and appear from summer through fall. Recommended varieties are 'Silver Cup', which grows 2 ft (60 cm) tall, and 'Mont Blanc', which is white and a little shorter at 20 in (50 cm) tall.

General care: Ordinary, reasonably fertile, well-drained soil and a sunny site are all that is required.

Propagation: Sow seed outdoors in spring.

Pests and diseases: Generally trouble-free, but look out for aphids.

LEUCOJUM ZONES 4–10

The hardy snowflakes, with their snowdrop-like flowers, are welcome additions to the spring garden. *L. aestivum* grows 20 in (50 cm) tall and in spite of its common name – summer snowflake – actually flowers in springtime. It has pure white bells on each stem. *L. vernum*, smaller at 6 inches (15 cm) tall, is the spring snowflake, and it flowers soon after the snowdrop. This variety does not perform well in hot, dry regions.

General care: Although snowflakes will grow in ordinary soils, they thrive best where it is really moist, or even wet, during the growing period. Sun or partial shade is acceptable.

Liatris spicata

Propagation: Divide clumps or separate offsets, either just after flowering or when dormant. Seed may be sown when ripe (germinating the following spring), but takes several years to reach flowering size.

Pests and diseases: Generally trouble-free.

The annual mallow, Lavatera trimestris

LIATRIS ZONES 2–10

Liatris (gayfeather) has thick, tufted masses of spiked foliage and tall spires of rosy purple and white flowers. Gayfeather blooms through the summer and into fall, making a showy accent in the garden.

L. spicata 'Kobold' (hardy to zone 3) is the earliest to bloom. It grows 15–18 inches (38–45 cm) tall with 12 inch (30 cm) lavender spikes. *L. scariosa* 'White Spire' (hardy to zone 2) grows 3–4 ft (90–120 cm) tall and is a popular white variety. *L. elegans* (hardy to zone 7), a native of the South, has very narrow leaves with purple spires and grows 3–4 ft (90–120 cm) tall.

General care: Any well-drained location in full sun or partial shade is suitable for gayfeather. Water freely in hot, dry weather and dead-head to prolong bloom.

Propagation: Divide the established clumps every 3–4 years or sow seeds in frost-free climates in spring or fall.

Pests and diseases: Watch for slugs.

LILIUM ZONES 2–8

The majestic lily has never been more popular, mainly as the result of the arrival of many new vigorous hybrid varieties which are freely available commercially. There are two broad types of lily, those with trumpet-shaped flowers and those with reflexed petals, sometimes known as Turks-cap. Best known in the latter group is *L. martagon* (hardy to zone 3), an easy-going purple-flowered species to 4 ft (1.2 m) tall. A very familiar trumpet lily species is *L. regale* (hardy to zone 3), with fragrant red-purple budded white blooms. A long-lived and very easy Turks-cap with orange flowers in late summer is *L. henryi* (hardy to zone 4) which, when well grown, can attain 6½ ft (2 m) in height. The following trumpet hybrids can be recommended: 'Pink Pearl' (shades of pink); 'Royal Gold' (rich yellow); 'Green Dragon' (white from chartreuse-green buds); and 'Olympic Hybrids' (mixed colors). Among the Turks-caps, try the mixed colored 'Harlequin Hybrids', 'Citronella' (yellow) and 'Connecticut Yankee' (orange). There are many lily varieties which are halfway between the trumpet and Turks-cap, most with upward-facing blooms. Recommended in this group are: 'Enchantment' (brightest orange-red); 'Destiny' (lemon yellow); and 'Snow Princess' (ivory white).

General care: Ordinary, well-drained soil is suitable, ideally laced with leaf mold, garden compost or peat. Plant about 6 inches (15 cm) deep, ideally in late autumn, though any time until spring is satisfactory. Sun or partial shade is acceptable, but if in a sunny position place them in among dwarf shrubs or perennials to shade the soil and keep the bulbs cool. Staking may be needed in windy sites.

Propagation: Divide clumps or remove offsets when dormant. Some species and varieties, e.g. *L. tigrinum* (tiger lily) and 'Enchantment', produce aerial bulbils on the stem. Remove these in late summer and treat as seeds. Sow seeds when ripe or as soon as received and put them in a cold frame. Some species, e.g. *L. martagon*, germinate and form minute bulbs but no top growth until after they have been chilled by winter cold. This could mean 6–12 months before any obvious 'germination' occurs.

Pests and diseases: Slugs and snails damage young shoots, viruses may mottle and stunt growth and aphids deform shoot tips and flower buds.

LIMONIUM

Statice (*L. sinuatum*), a half-hardy annual, bears sprays of small yellow, pink, lavender, blue and white flowers during the summer. They thrive particularly well in coastal areas. They are excellent for drying if you cut them just as they begin to open. 'Rainbow' mixture is a recommended variety: it grows 18 inches (45 cm) tall.

General care: Any ordinary soil with a position in the sun is suitable for this plant.

Propagation: Sow at a temp-

Lilium regale

erature of 60–68°F (15–20°C) indoors for planting out in late spring. Alternatively, sow outdoors in late spring for late display of colorful flowers in early fall.

Pests and diseases: Generally trouble-free.

LINUM ZONES 3–10

Although flax blooms last for only one day, they appear profusely throughout the summer. The hardiest variety is *L. austriacum* (hardy to zone 3), which bears lavender-blue blossoms. *L. flavum* (hardy to zone 5) is compact and bushy, growing to 15 inches (38 cm) tall. The dwarf form *A. alpinum* (hardy to zone 4) is a candidate for the rock garden with small blue flowers borne on 4–6 inch (10–15 cm) stems. *L. perenne var. nanum* 'Saphyr' is a new version, outstanding for its compact, bushy plants and sky-blue flowers with white centers. Flax does not perform well in Florida or the Gulf Coast.

General care: Tolerant of dry soil conditions, flax prefers a sunny site.

Propagation: Any perennial seeds sown in spring will not bloom until the second year. Divide established clumps in spring or fall. Annual varieties reseed readily.

Pests and diseases: Generally trouble-free.

LOBELIA

The Oxford and Cambridge blue *L. erinus* has been a popular bedding and edging plant since Victorian times. Other colors are now available, e.g. 'Rosamond' (crimson and white) and 'String of Pearls' (mixed). *L. e. pendula* has prostrate stems and is useful for hanging baskets. Try 'Blue Cascade' (violet-blue) and 'Red Cascade' (purple-red).

General care: Ordinary, reasonably well-drained soil and sun or partial shade suit these half-hardy annuals. Plant out only when threat of frost has passed.

Propagation: Sow seeds indoors in late winter for planting out after the last threat of frost has passed.

Pests and diseases: Generally trouble-free.

LOBULARIA

A small, ever-popular edging plant, sweet alyssum (*Lobularia maritima* syn. *Alyssum maritimum*) is suitable for growing in the rock garden and in the crevices of paving or as an edging. A hardy annual, it flowers continuously throughout the summer. It grows to a height of 4–6 inches (10–15 cm) and popular varieties are 'Little Dorrit', white; 'Snowdrift', white; 'Rosie O'Day', pink; and 'Royal Carpet', purple.

General care: Grow in any ordinary well-drained soil in full sun.

Propagation: Sow indoors in late winter and keep at 50–60°F (10–15°C). Sow in open ground in spring.

Pests and diseases: Generally trouble-free.

LUNARIA

Honesty, *L. annua*, is a must for the flower arranger's garden, and the real interest will be in the stems of silvery seed pods produced at the end of the summer. These are always in great demand for dried winter floral arrangements. While the variety with purple flowers is generally the most popular, there are others which have white or pink flowers. The color of the flowers, incidentally, makes no significant difference to the quality of the seed pods. You will only need to sow honesty once if you allow the seed to shed and can resist cutting the stems for flower arranging. In fact, seedling production is so prolific that it can become a weed. The plant is a biennial, however, and is easily kept in check.

General care: Any ordinary soil and a site in sun or shade are suitable.

Propagation: To make a start sow the seed outside in early spring where you want it to flower. Thin out to 12 inches (30 cm) apart.

Pests and diseases: Generally trouble-free.

LUPINUS ZONES 3–9

The more than 200 species of lupine include both annuals and perennials, but it is the perennial strain of hybrids derived from *L. polyphyllus* (zones 3–10) that produces first-rate garden plants. The world-famous Russell strain has $3\frac{1}{4}$ ft (1 m) tall strong stems, plenty of vigor and a wide color range. Many varieties have bi-colored flowers. Recommended are: 'Chandelier' (yellow shades); 'My Castle' (red shades); 'Noble Maiden' (white and cream); 'The Governor' (blue and white); and 'Dwarf Lulu' (mixed colors on stems up to 2 ft [60 cm] in height). These can all be raised from seed or bought as plants. Russell lupines grow to about $3\frac{1}{2}$ ft (1.5 m) and flower in early summer. If the dead flower spikes are removed before seed formation, flowering will resume in a limited way. Worthy of special mention is the annual, 'Texas Bluebonnet'. The official flower of the Lone-Star state, it can thrive in gardens from Maine to California. It grows 8–12 inches (20–30 cm) tall and its blue flowers show themselves in early spring.

General care: Ordinary fertile soil which does not dry out and a sunny or slightly shaded site produce fine lupines; over-rich conditions promote extra tall soft stems liable to wind damage.

Propagation: Divide clumps in late winter, take cuttings of basal shoots in spring in a cold frame and sow seeds in a nursery row outside or in a cold frame in late spring.

Pests and diseases: Generally trouble-free, but powdery mildew can sometimes be a nuisance.

LYCHNIS ZONES 3–10

Lychnis includes both annual and perennial varieties which vary considerably in appearance but all offer bright color for the garden. *L. chalcedonica* produces dense clusters of mid-summer blooming scarlet flowers on airy stems that grow 2–3 ft (60–90 cm) high.

ABOVE: *Russell lupines*
LEFT: *Lunaria annua*

L. coronaria has silky white foliage with magenta flowers that bloom from late spring to mid-summer. *L. viscaria* 'Splendens', which grows to 12 inches (30 cm) tall, is compact with grass-like foliage and pink, long-lasting flowers – a good choice for the rock garden. *L. var. haageana* has large red and orange flowers that measure 2 inches (5 cm) wide. *L. arkwrightii* is a rare variety with a wide color assortment, including blue, pink, red, purple and maroon.

General care: Well-drained, rich soil in full sun is needed.

Propagation: Sow seed indoors in early spring or fall in warm zones and set out after frost or divide established clumps in spring.

Pests and diseases: Generally trouble-free.

LYTHRUM ZONES 3–9

L. salicaria is a very colorful perennial of regal bearing. The plants grow wild in marshy areas. The best selections from the wild form are the Morden Series. 'Morden's Pink' grows 3–4 ft (90–120 cm) tall and bears large quantities of deep pink spikes that rise from upright, leafy stems. They bloom from early spring to early fall and make excellent cut flowers. *L. salicaria* 'Firecandle' has intense rose-red flowers that bloom in mid-summer.

General care: Lythrum thrives in moisture-retentive, humus-rich soil in full sun, but it will tolerate some drought conditions if placed in partial shade.

Propagation: Self-sows readily. Divide clumps every 3–4 years or sow seeds indoors in late winter and transplant in early spring after danger of frost has passed.

Pests and diseases: Generally trouble-free.

MACHAERANTHERA

M. tanacetifolia or Tahoka daisy is a beautiful blue-flowered plant that has been domesticated from varieties that grow wild in the Southwest. The Tahoka daisy is a reliable performer and rivals the gerberas for cut-flower beauty and form. The lavender-blue, yellow-centered blossoms measure 2 inches (5 cm) across and grow on stems that grow to 2 ft (60 cm) tall.

General care: Water-retentive soil and a sunny site are necessary.

Propagation: Sow seed directly outside in late winter or in the early fall. Seeds germinate best at about 45°F (7°C).

Pests and diseases: Generally trouble-free.

MALCOMIA

The 8 inch (20 cm) high drifts of small rose, lilac and white sweet-scented flowers of *M. maritima* (Virginian stock) appear very quickly after sowing the seed of this hardy annual. It is a perfect stopgap plant, for example, for covering the sites of spring bulbs and for edging beds and borders.

General care: A sunny site and all well-drained soils are suitable.

Propagation: Sow seeds outdoors in spring, or 4–6 weeks before a display is required.

Pests and diseases: Generally trouble-free.

MATTHIOLA

The well-known night-scented stock *M. bicornis* is not much to look at during the day but at night it opens its pale lilac flowers and gives out a sweet, heavy scent. This hardy annual is especially fragrant on a still, warm evening. Mix it with the similar-sized Virginian stock to provide daytime color. Sow seed in early spring in place.

General care: Ordinary, reasonably fertile soils and a sunny or slightly shaded site are all that is required.

Propagation: Sow outdoors in spring and again in early summer to extend the display into autumn.

Pests and diseases: Generally trouble-free.

MECONOPSIS ZONES 5–8

Generally difficult to grow in the U.S. because of our hot summers, you will have your best chance with *M. betonicifolia* (syn. *M. baileyi*), the Himalayan blue poppy, which has delightful sky blue flowers with bright yellow anthers. It is a short-lived perennial (and often only biennial), reaching a height of 3 ft (90 cm). *M.*

grandis (hardy to zone 5) produces gentian-blue flowers and is a more reliable perennial. The yellow and orange-red *M. cambrica* (Welsh poppy) (hardy to zone 6) is attractive but can become a nuisance as it seeds very freely.

General care: The blue poppies require a humus-rich soil which is moist but not waterlogged. In limy soils they are mauve-blue unless treated with aluminum sulfate. Meconopsis can grow in the light of direct sun, but it cannot handle the heat – plant it in the coolest, partially shaded spot in the garden. It is recommended that the first flower spike on home-raised plants of *M. betonicifolia* be pinched back when young. This ensures a better floral display the following year and sometimes results in the plant persisting for several years.

Propagation: Sow seed as soon as ripe if possible, over-wintering the small plants in a frame. Alternatively, sow indoors in spring, transplant into boxes and plant out as soon as each young plant has 5–6 good-sized leaves.

Pests and diseases: Generally trouble-free.

MESEMBRYANTHEMUM ZONES 9–10

The Livingstone daisy *Dor-*

otheanthus bellidiformis syn. *Mesembryanthemum criniflorum* is a sun-loving, succulent-leaved native of South Africa which spreads brilliance over the driest of sunny sites. Masses of bight red, pink, and white daisy flowers appear continuously throughout the summer. Try growing 'Sparkles', which grows to 4 inches (10 cm). *D. oculatus* is similar in appearance but has yellow flowers. The variety *M. crystallinum*, called common iceplant, is often used as ground cover in the warm coastal areas of California.

General care: Sun and well-drained soil, preferably not too rich, are the basic requirements of this half-hardy annual.

Propagation: Sow seeds early to mid-spring indoors and set out young plants when the threat of frost has passed.

Pests and diseases: Usually trouble-free, but in a wet season slugs and snails can eat leaves and flowers, so put out slug pellets as soon as you see tell-tale signs.

MIMULUS

The strikingly colored monkey flowers, with their somewhat antirrhinum-shaped blooms, can be used as bedding annuals and in a bed of perennials. Species names are rarely mentioned in seed catalogs, but the various seed strains are hybrids known as *M.* x *variegatus*. 'Giant Mixed' has large yellow to red, darker blotched flowers. 'Royal Velvet' has entirely mahogany-red blooms with yellow throats. The new 'Malibu Orange' is a clear vivid orange on compact plants.

General care: Humus-rich soil which does not dry out and a sunny or slightly shady site are required for the best results. Pondside or other wet sites are ideal as monkey flowers are always associated with water in the wild.

Propagation: Divide established plants in spring. To

Meconopsis cambrica

grow as an annual, sow seed in early spring indoors.
Pests and diseases: Generally trouble-free.

MIRABILIS   ZONES 9–10

Mirabilis jalapa is grown as a perennial in its native Peru and as an annual in colder climates. It gets its strange nickname 'four o'clock' from its curious habit of staying closed until mid-afternoon unless the day is cloudy. Plants grow to 2 ft (75 cm) tall and produce long, trumpet-shaped flowers of white, pink, lavender, red and yellow. Flowering is from mid-summer to frost. The new 'Jingles' strain is smaller and has tri-colored flowers. Four o'clock is very tolerant of urban smog and dirt and offers color in late summer and fall when other flowers in the garden may be past their prime.
General care: It needs well-drained soil and a sunny location.
Propagation: Sow seed indoors a month before the last frost or outdoors in spring. Mirabilis forms tuberous, dahlia-like roots, which may be dug up in the fall and stored over in the winter.
Pests and diseases: Generally trouble-free.

MOLUCELLA

The tall flower spikes of bells of Ireland *M. laevis* reach up to 3 ft (90 cm) and consist of tiny white flowers, each surrounded by a light green large shell-like calyx. These half-hardy annuals are highly valued by flower arrangers for drying and cut flower use.
General care: Ordinary fertile soil that is reasonably well-drained and a sunny position are all that is required. For drying, cut the stems just as the flowers appear and hang up in bunches in an airy place out of direct sunlight.
Propagation: Sow seeds indoors in early spring and plant out in early summer or sow outdoors in late spring.
Pests and diseases: Generally trouble-free.

Monarda didyma or bee balm

MONARDA   ZONES 4–9

Irresistible to hummingbirds, *M. didyma* is a native of New England with unusually formed, fragrant bracts. Known popularly as bee balm, it thrives in cool temperatures. The scarlet flowers provide color throughout the summer on stems that grow to 3 ft (90 cm) tall. Quick-growing and perfect for cutting, bee balm is a good choice for the middle or the rear of the border. 'Cambridge Scarlet' is a long-time favorite. Other hybrids include 'Adam', rich cerise-red; 'Mahogany', deep red; 'Snow White'; 'Craftway Pink'; and 'Lavender Queen'.

General care: Moisture-retentive, enriched soil and full sun or partial shade in the hottest weather ensure good results. Make sure that the soil is never allowed to dry out completely.
Propagation: Divide established clumps in spring or fall.
Pests and diseases: Generally trouble-free.

MUSCARI ZONES 2–10
With their little inverted grape-like clusters of rounded bells, the grape hyacinths are so different and cheerful they demand a place in every spring garden. Try the 4–6 inch (10–15 cm) tall *Muscari betryoides*, with deep blue flowers, and its pure white form, 'Alba'. Vigorous and very free-flowering is *M. armeniacum* (hardy to zone 4), which grows to 8 inches (20 cm). The best forms are 'Cantab' (sky blue), 'Early Giant' (deep blue) and 'Blue Spike', the latter having crowded double flowers of flax blue.
General care: Ordinary soil that is reasonably well-drained is perfectly adequate and, ideally, a sunny site, though some shade is tolerated. Plant in autumn. Lift and replant when clumps get congested as soon as the leaves yellow and die down.
Propagation: Divide clumps or separate offsets or bulblets when replanting.
Pests and diseases: Generally trouble-free.

MYOSOTIS ZONES 2–10
Forget-me-nots are everyone's favorites and make a splendid accompaniment to tulips and other spring bulbs. Even when grown without the company of other plants, the dainty flowers carried on thin stems are a delight in April and May. Species names are only rarely given in seed catalogs, but the taller, 10–12 inch (25–30 cm) varieties are preferable to the annual variety *M. sylvatica*, the wood forget-me-not, and the dwarf sorts to *M. alpestris*, (hardy to zone 2), alpine forget-me-not, or are otherwise hybrids. 'Royal Blue', which has rich dark blue flowers and grows 12 inches (30 cm) tall, is an excellent choice. 'Dwarf Royal Blue' grows only 7 inches (18 cm) tall and has a more bushy habit. 'Miniature Blue' reaches only to 5 inches (12.5 cm) in height. Varieties in colors other than blue are 'Carmine Red' and 'Victoria White'.

Nemesia 'Carnival Mixed'

General care: Ordinary well-drained soil is satisfactory in sun or shade. To avoid hordes of self-sown seedlings, which can be as bad as weeds, pull up the plant as the last flowers fade, or before if possible.
Propagation: Sow seed outside around mid-summer and plant into permanent sites in autumn.
Pests and diseases: Generally trouble-free, though mildew is sometimes a nuisance.

NARCISSUS ZONES 4–10
These are the hardy flowering bulbs which are such a delight in spring and easily recognized by even the non-gardener. To many people the terms 'daffodil' and 'narcissus' mean two different plants, but botanically they are both members of the genus *Narcissus*. True daffodils have a trumpet equal in length to the petals. Outstanding large golden-yellow trumpet daffodils include 'Golden Harvest' and 'Rembrandt', but there are long lists to choose from in the bulb catalogs. Among the pure white-flowered sorts, old 'Mount Hood' is one of the best. Among large-cupped narcissus cultivars,

try 'Carbineer' (yellow and orange-red); 'Ice Follies' (white and cream); 'Stadium' (yellow and white). Small-cupped sorts are 'Blarney' (white and salmon-orange) and 'Verger' (white and scarlet). For the rock garden or front of beds and borders do not neglect the small wild species such as: *N. bulbocodium* (hardy to zone 6), hoop petticoat daffodil; *N. asturiensis* (syn. *minimus*) (hardy to zone 4), a perfect miniature trumpet daffodil; and *N. triandrus albus* (hardy to zone 4), the creamy white angels' tears.
General care: Practically all soils will grow narcissus, but they must be moist during the growing season. Sun or shade is equally acceptable.
Propagation: Divide clumps or separate offsets when dormant or when in full leaf after flowering.
Pests and diseases: Generally trouble-free, but narcissus fly attacks the bulbs, and viruses cripple the whole plant.

NEMESIA
This early flowering annual, which resembles a small, broad-flowered antirrhinum in a wide color range, puts on a show from late spring through the summer, but wilts under heavy heat. It is

recommended for mountain or coastal regions where nighttime temperatures dip below 70°F (21°C). Growing to a height of 8–12 inches (20–30 cm), it is a good subject for beds and borders. 'Carnival Mixed' produces compact plants of glorious colors. Keep the soil moist if the plants are to flower well for a long time.
General care: Sunshine and a fertile soil which is well-drained but not dry provide ideal conditions.
Propagation: Sow seeds in warmth in spring and plant out as soon as the threat of frost has passed.
Pests and diseases: Generally trouble-free, but watch for aphids.

NEMOPHILA
The hardy annual *N. insignis* (syn. *N. menziesii*) has a useful spreading habit, and in summer it forms a carpet of bright blue, white-centered saucer-shaped flowers. It makes a lovely edging to a bed or can be sown to cover gaps where spring bulbs have died down. It also looks choice enough to be grown in the rock garden.
General care: Ordinary well-drained soil and a site in the sun are all that is required.
Propagation: Sow seeds out-

doors in spring.

Pests and diseases: Generally trouble-free.

NEPETA ZONES 3–10

This attractive aromatic plant, with its blue-gray foliage and misty mauve flower spikes, is often used as an edging plant. It does well in light soils in full sun but tends to die out fairly quickly on heavy, cold, poorly drained soils.

N. faassenii (syn. N. mussinii) (hardy to zone 3), which grows to 18 inches (45 cm) high, is the commonly grown catmint, but the variety 'Six Hills Giant', which grows to 2 ft (60 cm) and has violet-blue flowers, makes a better and more positive display.

General care: A sunny site and well-drained soil are the basic requirements; even poor soils are suitable.

Propagation: Divide in spring or take cuttings of basal shoots at the same time or in late summer in a cold frame.

Pests and diseases: Generally trouble-free.

NICOTIANA ZONES 9–10

The beautiful, trumpet-shaped scented white flowers of the tobacco plant are borne through the summer. Older varieties open in the evening only, while newer varieties open during the daytime as well. N. alata grandiflora (syn. N. affinis) is a tender perennial to 3 ft (90 cm) tall grown as an annual in the northern areas. Seed strains with pink and red flowers are hybrids known as N. x sanderae. Choose from 'Evening Fragrance', mixed colors growing 3 ft (90 cm) tall; 'Crimson Rock', growing 18 inches (45 cm) tall; and 'Lime Green', growing to 2½ ft (75 cm) tall.

General care: For the best results, choose a sunny site and provide a humus-rich soil that is drained but does not dry out.

Propagation: Sow seeds under glass in March at 60–65°F (15–18°C) for planting out in May.

Pests and diseases: Generally trouble-free, but look out for the crippling yellow mottle caused by virus.

NIEREMBERGIA
ZONES 7–10

An import from Argentina, this member of the nightshade family grows as a summer-blooming annual in the North. Slender stems support narrow leaves and dainty flowers of white, blue and lavender. An excellent edging plant, N. hippomanica violacea (hardy to zone 7) forms a 6 inch (15 cm) sprawling clump of tiny, cup-shaped violet blue flowers. N. scoparia (hardy to zone 7) grows to 3 ft (90 cm) tall with white flowers tinted with blue. The most popular variety is N. repens, which grows to 6 inches (15 cm) tall with white flowers.

General care: Nierembergia prefers full sun where summers are cool or partial shade in hot-summer zones. Enriched, moisture-retentive soil and regular watering will ensure blooms all summer.

Propagation: In the North, sow the seed indoors in late winter and plant out in late spring. In the South, where grown as a perennial, divide established plants, take cuttings or sow seed 3 months before desired flowering date.

Pests and diseases: Generally trouble-free.

NIGELLA

A native of North Africa, this annual, known as 'Love-in-a-mist', resembles cornflowers in shape and color. The 18 inch (45 cm) stems have lacy foliage, and the flowers, which bloom from late spring to early summer, come in shades of blue, white, pink, rose and purple. In fall the seed pods are an interesting addition to dried arrangements.

'Miss Jekyll', white, and 'Persian Jewels', mixed colors, are superior strains.

General care: Nigella tolerates ordinary soil but will thrive in humus-rich soil. Full sun is best.

Propagation: Sow seeds outside as early after the first frost as possible as nigella does not transplant easily. Two or three sowings a month apart will ensure continuous bloom.

Pests and diseases: Generally trouble-free.

Nigella damascena

OENOTHERA ZONES 4–10

An American native, evening primrose produces a continuous flush of cup-shaped flowers that open in the afternoon and stay open through the next day. It blooms throughout the summer. *O. deltoides* (hardy to zone 5) grows to 18 inches (45 cm) high with lance-like foliage and flowers that turn from white to pink as they fade. *O. fruticosa* (hardy to zone 4) 'Youngi' has lemon-yellow flowers and is particularly effective when planted in a clump of 6–8 plants. 'Rosea' is an ideal candidate for the front of the border, growing 6–12 inches (15–30 cm) tall with light pink flowers. *O. missourensis* is one of the most beautiful varieties with velvety 5 inch (12.5 cm) leaves and yellow flowers that measure 3–5 inches (7.5–12.5 cm) across.

General care: Light, well-drained soil in sun or light shade is sufficient.

Propagation: Sow seeds indoors in late winter and set out after danger of frost has passed. Plants self-sow readily. Divide established plants every few years to promote vigorous growth.

Pests and diseases: Generally trouble-free.

OXALIS ZONES 4–10

This group includes more than 300 species of annual and perennial plants that feature clover-like foliage and small yellow, white and red flowers. Hardy *O. montana* (hardy to zone 4) grows 6 inches (15 cm) tall and features delicate white flowers that bloom from spring through late summer. *O. purpurea* (hardy to zone 9) blossoms from late fall to early spring and is grown mainly as a house plant in the North for its flowers, which grow 2 inches (5 cm) wide. 'Grand Duchess' comes in rose pink, white and lavender. *O. lasiandra* (hardy to zone 9) features crimson flowers and is usually grown as a greenhouse or house plant.

General care: Plant in sun or partial shade in well-drained soil. Oxalis is very drought-tolerant.

Propagation: Oxalis can be propagated by bulbs planted 3 inches (7.5 cm) deep in the fall or by seed sown indoors in late winter. Divide established plants in fall for planting in early spring.

Pests and diseases: Generally trouble-free.

PAEONIA ZONES 3–8

There are several different types of peony, including the old-fashioned, cottage-garden types with their green foliage and fully double flowers. The double Chinese peonies, *P. lactiflora*, are now very popular; they have a greater range of delightful colors and the added virtue of being scented. Among the old cottage peonies (*P. officinalis*), which grow to 3 ft (90 cm) tall, there are 'Alba-plena', a double white; 'Rosea-plena', a double pink; and 'Rubra-plena', a double crimson. All flower in late May. Among the many excellent double Chinese peonies, all of which flower in May, are: 'Adolph Rousseau', a crimson; 'Alex Fleming', bright rose-pink; 'Kelway's Glorious', pure white; and 'President Wilson', pale cream pink. Single bloom varieties include 'Globe of Light', a pink with a large cream-yellow center; 'Jan van Leeuwen', pure white with a golden center and 'Soshi', rose with a yellow center.

General care: A moisture-retentive but not wet soil, well laced with organic matter, is necessary for the best results. Sun and partial shade are equally acceptable.

In windy sites the taller varieties will need support.

Propagation: Divide the roots in October or early spring. Once planted, on no account disturb them.

Pests and diseases: Generally fairly trouble-free, but grey mold (botrytis) can be a nuisance on flower buds if the season is damp and cool.

PAPAVER ZONES 2–10

The boldly colorful bowl-shaped flowers of poppies have a perennial charm and have long graced our gardens. Best known is the oriental poppy *P. orientale* (hardy to zone 2) and its hybrid varieties with their massive flowers on 3 ft (90 cm) stems and hairy, coarse ferny leaves. Try 'Glowing Embers' (orange-red, ruffled petals); 'Beauty Queen' (buff apricot-orange); 'Midnight' (salmon-pink); and 'Perry's White'.

The common annual field poppy *P. rhoeas* has given rise to 'The Shirley', a strain of mixed shades of red, pink and white, often with picotee edges. It can attain 3–4 ft (90–120 cm) in height.

General care: A sunny site and ordinary soil are required. Over-rich soil promotes tall, soft stems liable to wind blow.

Propagation: Divide perennials in early spring or take root cuttings at the same time in a frame or cool greenhouse. Sow annuals outdoors in spring.

Pests and diseases: Generally trouble-free.

PELARGONIUM
ZONES 9–10

This genus contains several kinds of popular plants, generally called geraniums, that are grown as annuals in colder climates. They are bright and showy, and thrive equally well as windowsill pot plants or in beds outside in summer. Best known is the so-called zonal geranium, *P.* x *hortorum*, a hybrid race containing hundreds of varieties with rounded

Double white peonies

clusters of five-petalled or double blooms in shades of red, white and pink for most of the year. The rounded leaves may or may not have a ring-like bronze zone, and several varieties are strikingly variegated, e.g., 'Mr Henry Cox'. Most *hortorum* geraniums grow $1\frac{1}{2}$ – 2 ft (45–60 cm) tall, but there is a dwarf race about 8 inches (20 cm) or under, e.g., 'Red Black Vesuvius'. Best grown as a pot plant is the regal or show geranium *P. x domesticum*. It has larger, often bi-colored flowers mainly from spring to fall. Useful for hanging baskets is the trailing *P. peltatum* or ivy-leaved geranium. The different varieties have almost fleshy, lobed leaves and single or double blooms in reds, pinks, mauves and white. Generally less showy, but Grown for their aromatic leaves, are the so-called scented geraniums. Several different species are involved, among them rose-scented *P. capitatum*, lemon-scented *P. crispum* and peppermint-scented *P. tomentosum*.

General care: Any standard compost or ordinary well-drained soil is suitable and as much sun as possible.

Propagation: Take tip cuttings in warmth in late summer, early autumn or spring.

Pests and diseases: Watch for aphids, caterpillars and rust disease.

PENSTEMON   ZONES 2–10

This native American comes in a number of varieties, which have widely different growth characteristics and climate needs. Check with your nursery for the best ones in your own area. The different varieties reach heights from 1–4 ft (30–120 cm), but these very different cousins do share a common family trait: attractive, brightly colored flowers that bloom through the summer. The species with the best chance in most areas is *P. gloxinoides* (hardy to zone 6). It also presents some of the most colorful flowers in a summer display. Within this

species, 'Garnet' is just about the hardiest. It makes a neat bushy plant and produces spikes of deep red flowers. 'Firebird' has the same growth habit, but its flowers are bright scarlet. Various seed mixtures are available, such as 'Grandiflorum Excelsior' which grows to $2\frac{1}{2}$ ft (75 cm) or 'Skyline', which has a more bushy growth habit. Both have a lovely mixture of colors.

General care: A sheltered sunny site and well-drained but not dry humus-rich soil give the best results.

Propagation: Take cuttings of non-flowering shoots in late summer and overwinter the young plants in a frame. Sow seeds in warmth in early spring and grow on (i.e., don't starve or allow to become dry) for flowers the same year. Sow seed outside in a seed bed in summer and transplant to flowering positions in fall. The plants will flower the following season.

Pests and diseases: Generally trouble-free, but watch for aphids and caterpillars. Severe winters can damage the plants.

PETUNIA

The wide range of dazzling colors, a long and prolific flowering season and ease of cultivation have put petunias among the favorite annual flowers. Some are self-colored, others bi-colored in radiating stripes. A few seed strains are double-flowered. Some of the newer varieties are earlier, freer flowering and more weather-resistant than their predecessors. Try 'Resisto Rose' and 'Red Joy', plus other colors in the same series. Also recommended are the purple and white 'Telstar', red and white 'Star Jay', yellow 'California Girl' and the mixed doubles 'Super Fanfare Mixed'.

General care: Ordinary fertile soil and a sunny site are necessary.

Propagation: Sow seeds thinly in early spring in warmth. Transplant the tiny seedlings with care. Plant out when the threat of frost has passed.

Physalis alkekengi

Pests and diseases: May be subject to attack by aphids, but generally trouble-free.

PHACELIA

The California bluebell *P. campanularia* is a bushy annual growing 1 ft (30 cm) high and flowering through summer. The freely borne flowers are a wonderful gentian-blue and bell-shaped, and the foliage gives off a fragrance when bruised.

General care: This plant does best in a light, well-drained soil and is well suited for small informal sowings towards the front of the border.

Propagation: Sow seeds outdoors in spring.

Pests and diseases: Generally trouble-free.

PHLOX   ZONES 4–10

The bright clean colors and sturdy, reliable growth of

border phlox *P. paniculata* (hardy to zone 4) make them indispensable for a late summer display. Their erect, almost woody stems never need staking and bear terminal trusses of flowers which, individually, resemble primroses in shape. Recommended are: 'Cinderella', which has lilac-pink flowers with rose eyes and grows to 3 ft (90 cm) tall; 'Firefly', which grows to $2\frac{1}{2}$ ft (75 cm) tall and has pink flowers with crimson eyes; 'Rembrandt', which is pure white and grows 3 ft (90 cm) tall; and 'San Antonio', which is claret red and grows $2\frac{1}{2}$ ft (75 cm) tall. The only variegated type, with pale mauve flowers, is 'Norah Leigh', which grows 2 ft (60 cm) tall. A bright addition to the border, it is less vigorous than the others.

Similar in flower shape, but with bushy annual growth up to 1 ft (30 cm) in height, is *P. drummondii*, which is first-rate as a bedding plant and for patio containers. Try the 6 inch (15 cm) tall 'Beauty Mixed', the starry flowered 'Twinkles' at 7 inches (18 cm) and the full-sized 'Large Flowered Mixed'.

General care: Although phlox will perform reasonably well in ordinary soil, they respond well to a humus-rich rooting medium which does not dry out. Sun or shade are acceptable.

Propagation: Divide established clumps in spring or take root cuttings in late winter in a frame or greenhouse. Sow seeds of annuals in warmth in spring, planting out when fear of frost has passed. They can also be sown outdoors in late spring.

Pests and diseases: Generally trouble-free, but look out for stem eelworm and powdery mildew.

PHYSALIS   ZONES 2–10
Chinese lantern *P. alkekengi* (syn. *P. franchetii*) (hardy to zone 2) is grown for the ornamental calyx, which looks like an orange lantern. If cut while the color is still good the stems of lanterns can be dried for winter indoor decoration, but remove the foliage first.

General care: All but the wettest soils and a site in sun or shade are acceptable. Physalis is likely to become invasive, especially in the richer soils, and it is usually best to keep its roots confined with vertically sunk slates or tiles.

Propagation: Divide any time from late autumn to spring.

Pests and diseases: Generally trouble-free.

PHYSOSTEGIA ZONES 3–10
A good addition to the perennial border, late summer-blooming physostegia, false dragonhead, bears a resemblance to foxglove. White, lavender and pink spires of flowers grace slender, upright stems that grow 3–4 ft (90–120 cm) tall. A wildflower in the Midwest, it can be found along riverbanks

Physostegia virginiana

and in wooded areas.

P. virginiana 'Summer Snow' is a handsome garden plant that is not as inclined to spread as most varieties. 'Grandiflora' grows to 5 ft (1.5 m) tall, bearing pink flowers. 'Vivid', which grows to 2 ft (60 cm) tall, features rose-pink flowers.

General care: Physostegia grows easily in ordinary soil in a sunny site with regular watering in hot weather, so

there is no danger of the earth becoming completely dry.

Propagation: Sow seeds inside in late winter or in the garden in early spring. Divide established plants in spring or autumn every 2–3 years.

Pests and diseases: Generally trouble-free.

PLATYCODON ZONES 3–9
Fine, free-blooming perennials with glossy foliage and star-shaped flowers, the bal-

loon flower's buds resemble waxen balloons, hence its name. These plants, which bear violet, white and pink flowers, are in the campanula family and are among the best for the perennial garden. *P. grandiflora* grows to 2½ ft (75 cm) tall and bears flowers of lavender-blue, white and pink from early summer to early fall. 'Komachi', which grows to 10 inches (25 cm) tall, is a new variety that maintains its unique balloon shape

when the flowers open. *P. var. mariesii* and 'Apoyama' are dwarf varieties that grow to 18 inches (45 cm) tall.
General care: Plant in well-drained, sandy or loamy soil in full sun, except for 'Pink Shell', which prefers light shade. Dead-head plants often to prolong flowering.
Propagation: Sow seeds in early spring after danger of frost has passed.
Pests and diseases: Generally trouble-free.

POLEMONIUM ZONES 2–8
P. caeruleum (hardy to zone 2) or Jacob's ladder is a graceful specimen for partially shaded spots in the garden. Lush rosettes of small, cup-shaped blue flowers, edged with delicate, fernlike foliage, bloom from late spring to mid-summer. They grow to 1½–2 ft (45–60 cm) high and combine nicely with bleeding hearts and ferns in the cool, shady perennial border. *P. reptans* 'Blue Pearl' (hardy to zone 2) is a dwarf variety that grows to 9 inches (23 cm). It produces a profuse display of blue flowers in late spring and is a charming addition to the rock garden.
General care: Normal, moisture-retentive soil and partial shade are needed. Water frequently.
Propagation: Sow seeds in early spring after the danger of frost has passed. Take cuttings in mid-summer or divide established clumps in early fall.
Pests and diseases: Generally trouble-free.

POLYGONATUM
ZONES 2–10
Solomon's seal, *P. x hybridum* (syn. *P. multiflorum* of gardens) forms elegant colonies of erect, unbranched stems with arching tops 2–3 ft (60–90 cm) in height. In early summer, the white, waisted flowers hang gracefully down in clusters of two or three almost along the full stem. They are set off by a background of equi-spaced oblong mid-green leaves, which turn a lovely shade of yellow in the autumn.
General care: Partial shade and ordinary soil which does not dry out readily provide the ideal conditions.
Propagation: Propagation is by division of rhizomes in early spring or from small rhizome eyes potted on and kept in a cold frame or greenhouse until large enough to be planted out.
Pests and diseases: Generally trouble-free, but in some areas Solomon's seal sawfly can strip the leaves.

PORTULACA
This somewhat neglected half-hardy annual deserves wider use. It is a neat plant with succulent foliage that enables it to withstand a degree of drought. It can really only be said to grow 6 inches (15 cm) tall as the stems tend to lie along the ground. Semi-double flowers with prettily ruffled petals in shades of most colors (except blue) appear successively throughout the summer. The flowers wait for sunlight before opening fully and then form a complete carpet of color and decorative foliage. Recommended varieties are *P. grandiflora* 'Double Mixed' and 'Calypso'.
General care: A sunny site and well-drained, even poor, soil are essential for a good floral display.
Propagation: Sow seeds in warmth, early to mid-spring. Handle the fleshy seedlings with care and allow the compost to almost dry out between waterings.
Pests and diseases: Generally trouble-free.

PRIMULA ZONES 3–10
There are no fewer than 400 species of primrose. Primrose (*Primula vulgaris*) (hardy to zone 5) is much grown in gardens, especially in its mixed color seed strains, e.g. 'Juliet'. The large-bloomed and variably colored hybrid between primrose and cowslip *P. veris* (hardy to zone 3), known as polyanthus, has long been a popular garden plant and there are many first-rate seed strains, e.g. 'Triumph', available mixed or in separate color shades of white, yellow, pink, red and purple-blue. The extra-large flower 'Pacific' strain is also good, especially the low-growing 'Pacific Dwarf Jewel'. The claret-crimson *P. x* 'Wanda' has long been a favorite. It is derived from the dwarf *P. juliae* and *P. vulgaris* and is like a smaller, rounder-leaved primrose in habit. Very popular is the drumstick primrose, *P. denticulata* (hardy to zone 4), a Himalayan species with small lilac-to-purple flowers aggregated into dense, spherical heads.

Some of the finest border primulas belong to the Candelabra group. These have erect stems to 2 ft (60 cm) tall with several whorls of flowers. *P. japonica* is red-purple, *P. bulleyana* light orange, *P. pulverulenta* red, and *P. helodoxa* (hardy to zone 7), yellow. Even taller is the so-called giant cowslip *P. florindae*, with its large, loose, terminal cluster of bright yellow, sometimes red-flushed, fragrant flowers.

Many primulas are small or very small and are among standard plants for the rock garden. Best known is the easy going *P. auricula* (hardy to zone 2) and its many hybrid varieties in almost every shade of the rainbow. Also recommended and well worth trying are *P. marginata* (blue-lilac), *P. frondosa* (rosy-lilac), *P. x pubescens* 'Falconside' (crimson) and *P. rosea* (bright pink).
General care: With the exception of *P. auricula, marginata* and *x pubescens*, which require moist but well-drained soil, all other species need constantly moist soil to really thrive, though they will grow in ordinary soil that is watered during dry spells. The Candelabra group and *P. florindae* grow best in waterside or bog conditions. Divide clumps at least every third year to keep them vigorous and floriferous.
Propagation: Divide after flowering, late summer or spring. Sow seeds when ripe or in spring in a cold frame.
Pests and diseases: Vine weevil grubs may attack the roots, bryobia mites brown or bronze the leaves and birds shred the flowers.

PULMONARIA ZONES 2–8
A native of Europe, the lungwort is a good choice for a shady, damp spot. *P. augustifolia* grows to 12 inches (30 cm) tall, bearing blue, funnel-shaped flowers that bloom in spring. *P. saccharata* is distinguished by its white-spotted foliage. It grows to 8 inches (45 cm) tall with pink, blue and white

Alpine Primula

flowers. 'Mrs Moon' has large pink buds that open into showy gentian-blue flowers. 'Sissinghurst White' has rougher-textured, dark green spotted leaves that grow up to 12 inches (30 cm) long and white spring-blooming flowers.

General care: Lungwort prefers partial shade and cool, porous, moisture-retentive soil.

Propagation: Sow seed or divide plants in late summer. Water heavily after transplanting.

Pests and diseases: Generally trouble-free.

PYRETHRUM ZONES 2–10

With leaves more finely cut than most ferns and large, brightly hued, golden-centered daisy flowers in early summer, the pyrethrum has long been a favorite perennial. *P. roseum* is the basic species (now classified by botanists as *Chrysanthemum coccineum*). Only varieties are commercially available. Recommended are: 'E. M. Robinson', a pale pink; 'James Kelway', a crimson red; and 'Marjorie Robinson', a deep pink. Try also the double pink 'Princess Mary' and the carmine 'Red Dwarf' at only 1 ft (30 cm) tall.

General care: A sunny site and fertile, moisture-retentive but well-drained soil provide ideal conditions. The support of stakes is advisable as stems bearing flowers in full bloom are likely to collapse in strong wind and heavy rain.

Propagation: Propagation is by division of the roots in the spring, which is also the time for planting new stock. Autumn planting can result in considerable losses. Large-flowered hybrids can be raised from seed sown in summer outside or in a cold frame.

Pests and diseases: Generally trouble-free, but watch for aphids.

RESEDA

Mignonette is renowned for its breathtaking fragrance. Once grown by the perfume trade for its precious oils, reseda should be planted in doorways, under windows and along paths to be fully enjoyed. Its sweet fragrance atones for its somewhat plain appearance. Most varieties grow from 12–18 inches (30–45 cm) tall and feature cone-shaped clusters of greenish-yellow to brownish-red spikes that bloom from early to mid-summer. Cut flowers will stay fresh for as long as a week. 'Common Sweet Scented' and 'Machet' are the sweetest varieties.

General care: Mignonette needs rich, water-retentive soil in a sunny location in cool areas and partial shade in hottest weather.

Propagation: Sow seeds 10 inches (25 cm) apart outside where you want them to grow after danger of frost has passed. This plant does not transplant easily. In zones 9 and 10 plant in late fall for early spring bloom.

Pests and diseases: Generally trouble-free.

RUDBECKIA ZONES 3–10

Popularly known as cone flowers because of the thimble-shaped centers to their daisy-like flowers, rudbeckias are indispensable perennials for late summer and autumn color. Try 'Goldquelle' which, with its bushy habit, grows 3–4 ft (90–120 cm) high and has large double yellow flowers that open from mid-summer through fall; 'Goldsturm', which grows to 2 ft (60 cm) and blooms from mid- to late summer, bearing flowers with long, deep golden yellow petals surrounding a black center; and *R. newmanii* (syn. *R. fulgida speciosa*), the original black-eyed Susan, which has yellow flowers with black centers opening on branching stems from mid-summer to fall.

General care: Ordinary soil is adequate, provided it does not dry out unduly. A sunny site is best but partial shade is tolerated.

Propagation: Divide in spring or autumn immediately flowering ceases. Some sorts are easily raised from seed sown in a frame in spring.

Pests and diseases: Generally trouble-free.

SALPIGLOSSIS

Sometimes known as painted tongue, *S. sinuata* is so beautiful and exotic to look at that it gives the impression it is harder to grow then it really is! Trumpet-shaped flowers, some attractively veined, are carried on slender stems and open in succession from mid-summer to early fall. At a height of 2–2½ ft (60–75 cm), it is a striking mid-border plant; try growing 'Splash', 'Suttons Triumph' or the 1 ft (30 cm) tall 'Ingrid', all in shades of red, purple, blue and yellow.

General care: A sunny site and ordinary fertile soil are all that is required. Support the tall sorts with stakes.

Propagation: Sow seed indoors in late winter to plant out in spring.

Pests and diseases: Generally trouble-free.

SALVIA ZONES 4–10

With their freely produced dense spikes of tubular, hooded flowers, the annual and perennial sages are undoubtedly worthy of a place in the flower border. The most familiar annual is the brilliant scarlet *S. splendens*. Recommended varieties are 'Carabiniere', scarlet-red, growing 15 inches (38 cm) tall and 'Volcano', an intense bright red, which grows to the same height. *Salvia* x *superba* (hardy to zone 5) grows to a height of 3 ft (90 cm) and is fully perennial. It makes a bushy plant with violet-purple flowers that appear in mid- to late summer. *Salvia superba* 'Lubec', at 18 inches (45 cm) tall, is a shorter, more compact plant. *S. uliginosa* reaches 5 ft (1.5 m) in height, producing long spikes of sky-blue flowers in autumn.

General care: Reasonably fertile soil that is drained but moisture-retentive, plus a sunny site, provide the best conditions.

Propagation: Divide fully perennial species in spring. Sow seed of *S. splendens* in warmth in early spring.

Pests and diseases: Generally trouble-free but watch for aphids and capsid bug.

SCABIOSA ZONES 2–10

The large, pincushion-shaped, pastel-toned flowers of *S. caucasica* (hardy to zone 2) are a must for garden decoration and for cutting. They bloom from mid-summer to autumn. The ever-popular 'Clive Greaves', which grows 3 ft (90 cm) high, produces a constant supply of large lavender-blue flowers on long stems which do not require staking. 'Miss Willmott', with its white flowers, has a similar growth habit. Very different is the mauve-flowered *S. graminifolio* (hardy to zone 6) which blooms at the same time on 18 inch (45 cm) tall stems above wide mounds of silvery, grassy foliage.

General care: Ordinary, fertile, preferably limy soil and a site in the sun are basic requirements.

Propagation: Propagation is by dividing roots in the spring or by cuttings taken after flowering. Planting out should always be done in the spring.

Pests and diseases: Generally trouble-free.

SCHIZANTHUS

Native to Chile, butterfly plant or poor man's orchid produces large quantities of orchid-like blooms in variegated colors of red, pink, rose, lilac and white, all with yellow throats. The common variety, *S. pinnatus*, is best suited to coastal climates where nights are cool and days are sunny but not too hot. It grows to about 18 inches (30–45 cm) tall and has ferny foliage. It performs well both as a container plant and in the garden with its brilliant display of flowers.

General care: Fertile, moisture-retentive soil in sun or partial shade is best.

Propagation: In warm zones sow seed outside in the fall

Schizanthus pinnatus

for bloom in early spring. In colder climates, start seed indoors and transplant outdoors after danger of frost has passed. Seed germinates best if you leave it to grow in a fairly dark place.

Pests and diseases: Generally trouble-free.

SCILLA   ZONES 2–10

This genus of mainly spring-blooming bulbous plants includes the squills and the familiar bluebell. The dwarf squills are well worth a place in any rock garden. There is a choice of several varieties: *S. sibirica* (hardy to zone 2) 'Spring Beauty', which grows 6 inches (15 cm) tall and is a bright blue, and *S. bifolia* (hardy to zone 4) bear-

ing bright mauve-blue flowers on 4–6 inch (10–15 cm) stems. *S. nutans* (hardy to zone 5) (syn. *Endymion nonscriptus*) is the English bluebell with its elegantly nodding flower spikes of narrow blue bells; pink and white forms are available. *S. campanulata* (hardy to zone 4) (syn. *Endymion hispanicus*) is the Spanish bluebell, a similar plant but with wide bells and a straight flowering stem. Bulbs under this name in catalogs are usually hybrids between English and Spanish and blend the characteristics of both.

General care: Ordinary soil which is moist during the growing season is all that is required. Sun or partial shade is tolerated.

Propagation: Divide clumps or separate offsets when

dormant. Sow seeds when ripe indoors; several years elapse to flowering.

Pests and diseases: Generally trouble-free.

SEDUM   ZONES 2–10

At least 500 species of stonecrop are known. Most of them are smallish and the hardy ones are best for the rock garden, e.g. *Sedum album* (hardy to zone 3) (white), *S. cauticolum* (hardy to zone 3) (rose-purple), *S. floriferum* (hardy to zone 3) (yellow), *S. spathulifolium* (hardy to zone 5) 'Purpureum' (yellow with gray-purple leaves) and *S. spurium* (hardy to zone 3) (pink or red).

Among taller sorts for the perennial border are the gray-leaved *S. spectabile*

(hardy to zone 3) with wide heads of pink flowers on 16 inch (40 cm) stems. Its variety, 'Autumn Joy', is salmon-pink and grows to a height of 2 ft (60 cm). The dwarf variety, 'September Ruby', growing only to 1 ft (30 cm) has deep rose-pink flower-heads. *S. maximum* 'Atropurpureum' is undoubtedly the most striking stonecrop with stems to $2\frac{1}{2}$ ft (75 cm) tall, bearing dark red-purple leaves and reddish flowers.

General care: A sunny site and almost any well-drained soil are suitable.

Propagation: Divide the deciduous clump-formers in spring and take cuttings of non-flowering shoots of the rest, any time from spring to early autumn.

Pests and diseases: Generally trouble-free.

SIDALCEA ZONES 5–9

A native perennial of the Rocky Mountains region, the flowers of S. candida (hardy to zone 5) resemble miniature hollyhocks. They provide a striking vertical accent in the garden, growing to 3 ft (90 cm) tall with blooms from mid- to late summer. Showy varieties include 'William Smith', salmon pink, and 'Elsie Heugh', light pink. S. malviflora (hardy to zone 8) is a native Californian perennial that grows to 2 ft (60 cm) tall. 'Rosy Gem', 'Pink Beauty' and 'Rose Queen' are excellent choices for warm climates.

General care: Sidalcea prefers well-drained, ordinary soil in sun or light shade. Water frequently and deadhead to prolong the blooming season.

Propagation: They grow readily from seed sown indoors in late winter and planted out in spring or by division taken in spring.

Pests and diseases: Generally trouble-free.

SILENE ZONES 3–10

This genus of the pink family includes many species, some perennial, some annual, that are good choices for beds, borders and rock gardens. Many varieties of S. armeria have a sticky substance on the leaves, which is the source of the common name sweet William catchfly. S. armeria is native to Europe but has become naturalized in many of the eastern states. It grows 12–18 inches (30–45 cm) tall and bears clusters of deep pink flowers that bloom from mid-summer through fall.

S. acaulis (hardy to zone 5) is a good choice for the rock garden. It is a mosslike plant, growing to 2 inches (5 cm) tall, with reddish-purple flowers. S. californica is native to the Northwest. It has flame red flowers on branching stems growing 6–16 inches (15–40 cm) tall. S. pendula grows 6–10 inches (15–25 cm) tall and bears drooping sprays of profuse pink, salmon, scarlet and white flowers. 'Compacta' is a particularly dense variety, and 'Rosea' features deep pink flowers.

General care: Silene does best in full sun in well-drained soil.

Propagation: Sow seeds outdoors in the fall for an early summer show or in early spring for a mid-summer display.

Pests and diseases: Generally trouble-free.

SOLIDAGO ZONES 3–10

For a patch of frothy bright yellow in late summer and autumn, goldenrods have no peer. The old varieties were inclined to be weedy, but the newer ones are all desirable and recommended: 'Cloth of Gold', which grows to 18 inches (45 cm) and makes a robust plant with deep yellow flowerheads; 'Crown of Rays', which grows to the same height and has attractive horizontal golden spikes; 'Golden Thumb', which grows to 1 ft (30 cm) and is a neat plant with yellow fluffy flower-heads; and the tall 'Mimosa', which grows 5 ft (1.5 m) high and is a trouble-free plant with yellow flower-heads.

General care: For the best goldenrods choose a sunny site with moisture-retentive fertile soil.

Propagation: Divide roots in early spring. Plants can also be grown from seed sown indoors in late winter.

Pests and diseases: Generally trouble-free, but mildew can sometimes be a nuisance.

STACHYS ZONES 2–10

The popular name of S. byzanthina (hardy to zone 4) is lamb's ears, which comes from the soft, elliptical leaves that are covered with white wooly hairs. Growing 12–18 inches (30–45 cm) tall, stachys spreads rapidly and is an excellent ground cover, pretty as an edging for a walkway, under tall trees or at the front of the border. It is grown more for its striking foliage than for its flowers. The small purple blooms open in summer. 'Sheila McQueen' has larger leaves and flowers, and 'Olympica' has pink flowers. S. grandiflora (hardy to zone 2) is a hardy native of Asia Minor and has deep purple flowers.

General care: Any ordinary, well-drained soil is adequate. Plant in sun or partial shade. Stachys is relatively drought-resistant.

Propagation: Start new plants from root divisions in spring.

Pests and diseases: Generally trouble-free.

STOKESIA ZONES 5–9

A wonderful, low-maintenance, easy-to-grow plant, S. laevis rewards the gardener with long-lastïng blooms that resemble asters and measure 3–4 inches (7.5–10 cm) across. Stokesia will bloom all year in Southern California if spent flowers are faithfully pruned. It blooms all summer in the Northeast and will often produce a second show in the fall in the Southeast. Ranging in height from 1–2 ft (30–60 cm), the fluffy-flowered plants are valued for cutting and as potted plants.

'Blue Danube' has light blue flowers that measure 5 inches (12.5 cm) across. 'Silver Moon' is white with lavender centers and 'Cyanea' is lavender-blue with silvery green foliage.

General care: Plant in full sun in the North and semi-shade in the South in warm, well-drained, sandy loam.

Propagation: Divide established plants every 4–5 years or grow from seed sown indoors in early spring.

Pests and diseases: Generally trouble-free.

TAGETES

Best known as African and French marigolds, tagetes are top-ranking half-hardy annuals of great popularity. T. erecta, the African marigold, is the tallest and largest-flowered. It usually begins its flowering a little later than the smaller types. It provides large lemon-yellow to bright orange blooms from early summer until the first frosts and is always splendid. Try 'Crackerjack Mixed', which grows 2 ft (60 cm) tall. T. patula, French marigolds, are compact, bushy and very free-flowering. They blossom from late spring until the first frosts and can completely clothe the planting area with masses of individual, long-lasting blooms. There are singles, doubles and variants in plenty; try 'Queen Sophia', which is an outstanding double. Among the new Afro-French hybrid marigolds 'Suzie Wong', 'Moll Flanders' and 'Nell Gwyn' are all excellent, and grow to a height of 12 inches (30 cm). T. tenuifolia var. pumila (syn. signata) is the plant commonly known as tagetes. Small, bushy plants with finely cut foliage are covered with small, single, gold, lemon or mahogany daisy-like flowers through the summer. It is a particularly good edging plant; try 'Golden Gem' at 7 inches (18 cm) tall.

General care: A sunny site and ordinary well-drained soil are suitable.

Propagation: Sow all types in the greenhouse in early spring at a temperature of 60°F (15°C) for planting out in late spring.

Pests and diseases: Generally trouble-free.

TIGRIDIA ZONES 6–10

The Mexican shell flower has 12–18 inch (30–45 cm) swordlike leaves and brilliantly colored, chalice-shaped flowers in shades of orange, yellow and purple. They bloom from mid- to late summer. Each bloom lasts only one day, but spaced plantings will ensure a continuous display of color. A tender cormous plant from Mexico, tigridia is cultivated like the gladiolus.

General care: Tigridia likes rich, porous soil and full sun. Water frequently and feed with liquid fertilizer.

Propagation: In cold areas, lift the corms in fall and store in dry peat. Divide and plant after the ground thaws. In

Stokesia laevis

zones 9 and 10, corms may be left in the ground. Divide every 3–4 years.
Pests and diseases: Watch for red spider mites.

TORENIA

A native of Vietnam, the wishbone flower gets its name from the pair of stamens which form a wishbone shape. The tubular flowers, which look like miniature gloxinias, bloom from late summer to first frost. *T. fournieri* is one of the few summer annuals that thrive in the shade. Growing to 12 inches (30 cm) high, the plant bears hosts of light blue flowers rimmed with deep purple. Some varieties are white with yellow throats, or yellow with purple throats. Torenia thrives as a potted plant and will bloom from fall through the winter inside. 'Nana Compact Blue' is an 8 inch (20 cm) tall bushy plant that is ideal for containers or as an edging plant.
General care: Torenia need warm, humus-enriched, moist soil in partial shade or full sun in cool climates.
Propagation: Sow seed indoors in late winter. Germination takes three weeks. Transplant seedlings outside in late spring or sow seed outdoors in late spring.

Pests and diseases: Generally trouble-free.

TRACHELIUM ZONES 8–10

Although it is commonly known by the unappealing name of throatwort, *T. caeruleum* is strikingly beautiful as a border plant or as a cut flower. Bearing cloudlike clusters of tiny delicate blue and lavender flowers, it sends up wiry stems that grow 2–3 ft (60–90 cm) tall. Throatwort is grown as an annual or greenhouse plant in the North and as a perennial in warm zones. A Mediterranean native, it blooms from early summer to early fall. 'Album' is a new white variety.

General care: Throatwort requires little maintenance and grows in ordinary soil in full sun or partial shade.

Propagation: Sow seeds indoors in late winter and

Trachelium caeruleum

transplant outdoors after danger of frost has passed. New plants will bloom approximately five months after they are sown in normal weather conditions.

Pests and diseases: Generally trouble-free.

TRACHYMENE

Trachymene, a native of Australia, resembles Queen Anne's lace with its umbrella-shaped plume of sky-blue flowers measuring 3 inches (7.5 cm) across. *T. coerulea* grows to 2 ft (60 cm) tall and blooms throughout the summer where temperatures stay cool. It is an outstanding, long-lasting cut flower. 'Lace Veil' bears fragrant white flowers.

General care: Trachymene prefers light but moisture-retentive soil in sun, but it does not perform well in hot weather.

Propagation: Sow seeds outdoors in spring or inside two

months before the last frost is expected.

Pests and diseases: Generally trouble-free.

TRICYRTIS ZONES 4–9

A member of the lily family, tricyrtis (toad lily) is an outstanding performer in cool, shady locations. The 3 ft (90 cm) stems bear clusters of orchid-like flowers in fall when little else is in bloom. *T. hirta* (hardy to zone 5) has white flowers, spotted with purple and black. *T. formosana* (hardy to zone 6) is a new, long-blooming variety with blue flowers marked with white throats.

General care: Ordinary, well-drained soil in partial or full shade.

Propagation: Easily propagated by division, the roots should be lifted and stored in dry peat in the autumn in cold climates.

Pests and diseases: Generally trouble-free.

TROLLIUS ZONES 3–9

The globeflower contributes brilliant colors and deeply lobed, fernlike foliage to the damp, lightly shaded areas of the garden. Growing from 1–2 ft (30–60 cm) tall, *T. europaeus* has buttercup-like, globular flowers in lemon yellow that bloom from late spring through the end of summer. 'Superbus' is a strain from Holland with soft yellow flowers. Other varieties include 'Alabaster', very pale yellow; 'Canary Bird', lemon-yellow; 'Commander in Chief', deep orange; and 'Fireglobe', deep orange-yellow. *T. ledebouri* grows to 2 ft (60 cm) tall; the variety 'Golden Queen' has deep orange flowers. *T. var.* 'Orange Princess' is one of the best selections for cut flowers.

General care: The globeflower thrives in damp, boggy, humus-enriched soil in partial shade or filtered

Tulipa kaufmanniana hybrid

sun. Dead-head to prolong bloom.

Propagation: Plants sown from seed will not mature for 3–4 months. It is more practical to buy from nursery stock or divide established clumps in the spring.

Pests and diseases: Aphids can be a problem.

TROPAEOLUM

To provide a quick temporary screen of attractive leaves and flowers, the common nasturtium, *Tropaeolum majus*, cannot be surpassed. For a few weeks in early summer this hardy annual will cover banks, fences or any 'eyesore' with great efficiency. It blooms through the summer with minimum demands on soil or gardening skill. Try 'Mixed Tall Single', a climbing variety which grows up to 6 ft (1.8 m). The dwarf varieties will grow happily in any sunny spot in need of color. Best are the 'Gleam' hybrids, which have double flowers and grow 15 inches (38 cm) tall.

General care: Ordinary soil and sun are quite adequate, but for fastest growth a humus-rich, well-drained but moisture-retentive rooting medium is best.

Propagation: Sow seeds outdoors mid- to late spring. For an earlier display, sow singly in 3½ inch (9 cm) pots indoors in early spring.

Pests and diseases: Generally trouble-free, but in some seasons the caterpillars of

large and small white butterflies can strip leaves.

TULIPA   ZONES 4–10

The tulip ranks high in the top 10 favorite bulbs. It has graced gardens for centuries, and its beauty and simplicity ensure its continued popularity. There are well over 50 wild species, and thousands of varieties have been raised in a wide range of colors; only true blue is missing. They range from about 6 inches (15 cm) to 2½ ft (75 cm) tall. Because of this variation, it is important to find out about the growth habit of the different types. While most hybrid tulips, such as the tall Darwins and May-flowering varieties, deteriorate if left in the ground from season to season, some of the species persist well, and in fact will multiply freely. For long-term planting, try *T. fosteriana* 'Madame Lefeber', which grows 18 inches (45 cm) tall and is a striking vivid scarlet, *T. greigii* 'Red Riding Hood', which grows 1 ft (30 cm) tall or *T. kaufmanniana* (water-lily tulip), 1 ft (30 cm) tall. 'The First' is a very early variety with pure white blooms tinted carmine-red on the reverse of the petals. It grows to 8 inches (20 cm). To make your choice, look through a bulb specialist's catalog, which always has dozens of different varieties and several species.

General care: A sunny site and well-drained fertile soil are required. Bulbs used for

bedding can be lifted after flowering while in full leaf, and if replanted in a spare corner can still be expected to bloom the following year, though not so splendidly.

Propagation: Separate offsets when dormant.

Pests and diseases: Generally fairly trouble-free but beware of tulip fire (botrytis) and gray bulb rot.

VENIDIUM

V. fastuosum, monarch-of-the-veldt, is an annual native to South Africa. It grows 2 ft (60 cm) tall with daisy-like flowers that measure 4–5 inches (10–13 cm) across and bloom from mid-summer to the first frost. Colors range from brilliant orange to cream with dark brown and purple centers. It is an excellent cut flower although the blossoms close in low light.

General care: Monarch-of-the-veldt needs sandy, well-drained soil and full sun.

Propagation: Sow seeds indoors two months before the first frost is expected and transplant outside when night temperatures stay above 60°F (16°C)

Pests and diseases: Generally trouble-free.

VERBASCUM   ZONES 3–10

Although somewhat short-lived, the mulleins always capture attention, especially when they flower majestically as individual plants in a garden. They are so stately, often towering above their surrounding neighbors to show off their long, thick and sometimes wooly spires of flowers which appear in mid- to late summer, and are a must for any flower garden. Of perennial duration is *V. phoeniceum*: 'Cotswold Queen' grows 4½ ft (1.3 m) high and has branching stems and buff-orange flowers. 'Gainsborough' grows 4 ft (1.2 m) high and is the most beautiful of them all with its graceful spikes of clear yellow flowers. 'Pink Domino' is the same height and is rose-pink, a rare color in the mulleins.

General care: Sun and ordi-

nary soil are the basic requirements. Over-rich conditions will encourage taller, softer stems prone to wind-blow.

Propagation: Take 3 inch (7.5 cm) long cuttings of named varieties in late winter for rooting indoors, or from root cuttings taken in mid-winter. To grow from seed, sow 'Choice Mixed' indoors in spring for flowering the following year.

Pests and diseases: Generally trouble-free.

VERBENA X HYBRIDA

The heads of these half-hardy annual, primrose-like flowers come in shades of red, pink, blue and white, and are often faintly scented. They are borne in profusion by sturdy little plants from June until the first frosts. Outstanding varieties are: 'Derby Salmon Rose' and 'Derby Scarlet'; 'Springtime' is a reliable mixture.

General care: For most satisfactory growth, a humus-rich, well-drained but not dry soil and a sunny place are required.

Propagation: Sow seed indoors in February at temperatures of 60–68°F (15–20°C) for planting out in late spring.

Pests and diseases: Generally trouble-free.

VERONICA   ZONES 2–10

Among the 300 species of speedwell are several first-rate border plants that mostly occur in shades of blue, purple and mauve. *V. gentianoides* (hardy to zone 4) grows 2 ft (60 cm) high and is sometimes planted for ground cover. It produces slender spikes of palest blue flowers in spring. *V. incana* (hardy to zone 3) 'Saraband' grows 18 inches (45 cm) high and has beautiful gray foliage followed by violet-blue flowers that appear through the summer. *V. spicata* 'Barcarolle' usually grows to 18 inches (45 cm) and makes a neat carpet of dark foliage punctuated by narrow spikes of deep rose-pink flowers in summer. *V. s.* 'Red Fox'

*Veronica gentianoides,
or speedwell*

grows to 15 inches (37 cm) and has red flowers all summer. *V. teucrium* 'Shirley Blue' grows to 1 ft (30 cm) tall and bears a profusion of bright blue flowers from late spring through mid-summer. *V. t.* 'Trehane' has golden green leaves.

General care: Ordinary fertile reasonably well-drained soil and a sunny position produce excellent results. It will also grow in light shade.

Propagation: Divide established clumps in spring or early autumn. Sow seeds in late spring indoors.

Pests and diseases: Generally trouble-free.

VIOLA   ZONES 3–10

This large genus of 500 species includes both the viola and the garden pansy (*V. x wittrockiana*), which is still the most popular.

The superb strain of Swiss giant pansies called 'Roggli Giant Mixed' is well known, and a packet of seed will have many colors. 'Tiara Mixed', which has large flowers, is a good variety, as is 'Engelmann's Giants'.

The lighter colored faces of 'Love Duet Mixed' are simply charming. Among the faceless pansies, 'Azure Blue', which is a clear blue with a yellow eye, is excellent and 'Golden Champion' and 'Clear Crystal Mixed' also deserve a mention. There are many more.

Bedding violas or tufted pansies, *V. x williamsii*, make compact plants with somewhat smaller flowers freely produced throughout the spring and summer in a wide range of mainly self colors. They are fully perennial. Try 'Irish Molly' (copper-yellow), 'Maggie Mott' (silvery blue), 'Nora Leigh' (light violet-blue).

True violets are well worth a place in every garden. Sweet violet, *V. odorata* (hardy to zone 6), is best known, but also good are the horned violet, *V. cornuta*, the heavily blue-purple-freckled white *V. cucculata* 'Freckles' and the purple-leaved *V. labradorica* 'Purpurea'.

General care: Ordinary fertile soil that does not dry out is essential for all the violas mentioned here. Sun is best for pansies and bedding violas, partial shade, how-

ever, is needed for the violets.

Propagation: Divide violets and bedding violas in spring or early autumn. Take cuttings of bedding violas in late summer indoors and over-winter there. Favorite pansies can be propagated in the same way but they are usually raised from seed sown in spring indoors or outside in early summer. There are also seed strains of bedding violas, which are dealt with in the same way. True violets are also raised from seed, ideally sown when ripe or as soon after as possible and placed in a cold frame.

Pests and diseases: Generally trouble-free, but watch for aphids.

XANTISMA

X. texanum, star-of-Texas, is a native annual of that state and bears yellow, daisy-like flowerheads on 1½–2 ft (45–60 cm) long stems. The flowers bloom mid-summer through to the first frost and are excellent for cutting.

General care: Star-of-Texas will thrive in poor, dry soil in full sun. Staking may be necessary in windy areas.

Propagation: Seeds may be sown indoors in early spring and seedlings transplanted in late spring. In warm zones,

Viola x wittrockiana hybrid

seeds may be sown in early fall for early spring bloom.

Pests and diseases: Generally trouble-free.

XERANTHEMUM

The immortelle *X. annuum* is one of the best plants to grow for the production of everlasting flowers. Growing to a height of 2 ft (60 cm), the strawy-petalled white, pink, lilac or purple daisy-like flowers keep their true colors for years if cutting and drying are carried out properly (see under *Helichrysum bracteatum*, page 00).

General care: Sun and ordinary soil are all that is required.

Propagation: Sow seed inside in spring.

Pests and diseases: Generally trouble-free.

ZANTEDESCHIA
ZONES 9–10

Native to South Africa, calla lilies are excellent in the summer garden with their arrow-shaped foliage and sculptural flower spathes that bloom throughout the season. The most common is *Z. aethiopia*, which grows 3 ft (90 cm) tall and bears cream 8 inch (20 cm) bracts. *Z. albomacula* grows to 2 ft (60 cm) tall with cream-colored flowers accented with purple throats and deep

Zantedeschia aethopia

green leaves mottled with white. *Z. rehmannii* features delicate pink to rose bracts on 1–1½ ft (30–45 cm) stems. A long-lasting cut flower, *Z. elliottiana* bears rich golden yellow bracts that tend to grow as high as 2 ft (60 cm).

General care: Will tolerate ordinary soil but thrives in wet, bog-like conditions and a sunny site.

Propagation: Plant rhizomes indoors in early spring and transplant outside when danger of frost has passed. Lift in fall and store in peat in colder zones.

Pests and diseases: Aphids can be a problem. Root rot will cause yellowing of the leaves. Dry old rhizomes carefully before storing.

ZEA

The half-hardy annual ornamental maize, *Zea mays* 'Japonica', produces an ornamental corn cob which can be cut when fully ripe for drying and winter decoration. *Z. m.* 'Japonica Variegata' has white-striped leaves. Try 'Strawberry Corn' which grows to 3 ft (90 cm) and produces small, broad, strawberry-shaped cobs.

General care: A sunny sheltered site and humus-rich moist but not wet soil are required for the best results. Set out the plants in groups of not less than three together to ensure cross-pollination.

Propagation: Sow indoors in late winter at a temperature of 60–68°F (15–20°C). Plant out in late spring.

Pests and diseases: Generally trouble-free.

ZINNIA

The half-hardy annual zinnias are highly distinctive members of the daisy family with very broad ray petals. Modern seed strains are mostly semi- or fully double in a wide range of bright clear colors and open from mid- to late summer. The large-flowered popular varieties are derived from *Z. elegans*. Some are quite tall, growing up to 3 ft (90 cm), but the strong stems and firm flower-heads are excellent for cut-ting. Try 'Ruffles Mixture' or select separate colors; they grow 2 ft (60 cm) high. 'Thumbelina' to 6 inches (15 cm) and 'Persian Carpet' to 10 inches (25 cm) tall form bushy plants with many small flowers. They are derived from *Z. haageana*.

General care: Humus-rich, moisture-retentive but well-drained soil and a sunny site give the best results. Tall varieties may need support, especially in windy places.

Propagation: Sow in the greenhouse in late winter at a temperature of 60–68°F (15–18°C) for planting out in late spring.

Pests and diseases: Generally trouble-free, but watch for gray mold during cool, wet summers.

SHRUBS AND CLIMBING PLANTS

Both in actuality and in many classic paintings, the idealized country cottage invariably has a rose, clematis or similar climber on its walls. The blank brick walls of starker, modern suburbia cry out for the same treatment, and yet all too many home-owners are either dubious or actually against the idea. There are stories that roots get into and damage foundations and brickwork and that a covering of vegetation on the walls encourages 'creepy-crawlies'. There is no real evidence to support these assertions. The roots of most climbers are either deeply delving or widespreading and remain small in diameter. Even the trunk-like stems of 100-year-old wisterias have not been reported as doing any damage. In fact, climbers mold to their supports. To undermine and weaken them would be self-defeating. The aerial stem roots of

ivy are surface stickers and are more likely to hold up a wall than break it down. Many a picturesque ruin owes its unchanging existence to a mantle of ivy, which very effectively protects the walls from rain, heat and cold. Foliage on a wall will, of course, provide a home for wildlife, and a few extra little creatures may find their way into the home. None should cause alarm. Indeed spiders, for example, as eaters of flies, should be positively encouraged.

House and garden should be harmoniously merged whenever possible by planting climbers and shrubs where they meet. This is known as foundation planting, an apt and descriptive term. Shrubs and climbers go hand-in-hand. All the less hardy shrubs benefit for being grown against or trained to walls, and some of the hardy ones have just the right shape for this treatment, e.g. garrya and *Cotoneaster horizontalis*. Free-

standing shrubs in groups or as solitary specimens are essential in the garden to create that furnished, mature look which is the essence of good gardening. Like the climbers, if chosen with care they can be colorful and attractive in their own right while also providing a background for the smaller annuals and perennials.

Before choosing what you need, look around and see what is being grown in your area and then browse around the nurseries and garden centers nearby. The latter usually have a wide selection of suitable plants. The tables on page 78 are arranged in useful categories to cover most parts of the garden. When choosing climbers and shrubs, make sure that some are evergreen so that the garden does not have that dreary, bare look in winter. There are also shrubs and a few climbers which flower during mild winter spells; look in the A–Z section for *Jasminum nudiflorum*, chimonanthus, *Cornus mas*, garrya and chaenomeles.

Soil
All the plants described in the A–Z will grow in the ordinary soil of your district. Ideally it should not be dry or waterlogged. The latter situation is practically non-existent where modern houses are built, and even the older properties are adequately drained in the vicinity of the building. If it is a bit wet on the surface, work in coarse sand or grit or raise the surface about 6 inches (10–15 cm) by digging out paths and placing the soil on the adjacent beds. Dry soils must be laced with decayed manure, garden compost or peat using at least one 2-gal (9-liter) bucket full per sq yd (m). Fork

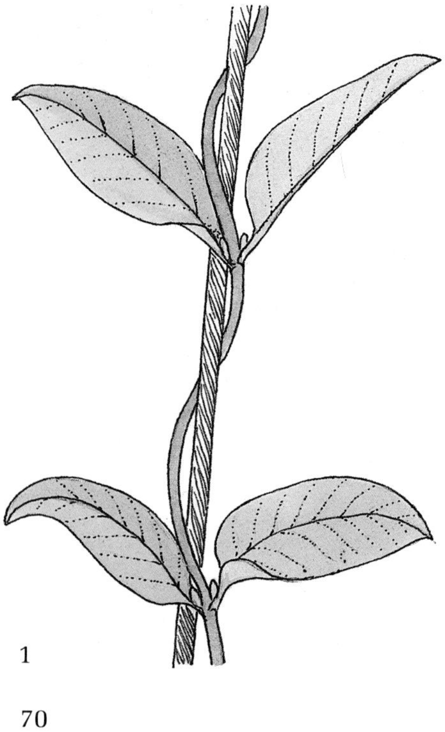

LEFT: *Climbers have a built-in means of clinging to a support. Some twine themselves around a frame or wires by their growing tips (1) or tendrils (2).*

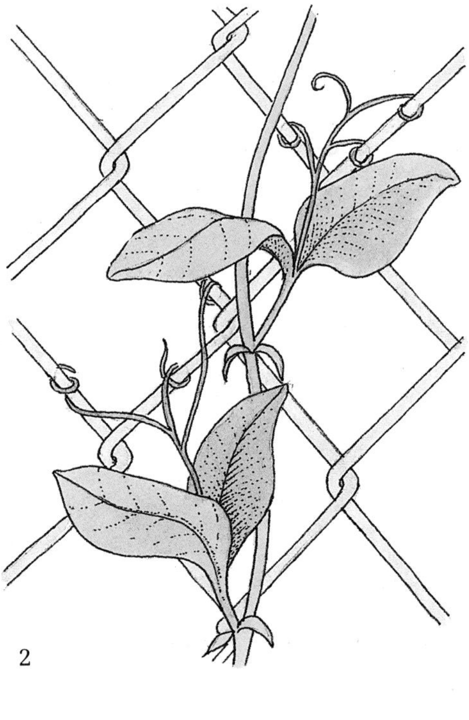

1

2

over the surface to remove perennial weeds or treat with a weedkiller well before planting time.

Supporting

Climbers and taller wall shrubs will need life-long support, which must be put in place before planting. Secure horizontal galvanized wires at 1½ ft (45 cm) intervals to walls and fences, using eyed bolts (vine eyes) embedded in rawl plugs. If you prefer a wooden trellis or a wood arbor or pergola, make sure it is treated thoroughly with a preservative. Ideally, poles or posts should not be less than 4 inches (10 cm) in diameter and should be deeply set in a concrete base.

Planting

Containerized shrubs and climbers pur-chased from a garden center can be planted at any time of the year provided the soil is not too wet or frozen. In areas where spring or early summer droughts are likely, try to plant ever-greens in autumn, the earlier the better, so that they can get established. Many nurseries still sell plants 'bare root', that is, dug directly from the nursery soil. Such plants are available from late autumn to early spring, which is the traditional time for planting hardy trees and shrubs. Some of the finest wall shrubs are not reliably hardy, espe-cially in hard winters and when young. These are always sold in containers and should not be set out until spring, after the worst of the frosts is over. If you buy plants from a garden center, choose the healthiest and best-looking speci-

*Not all climbers need support and some use aerial roots to climb by themselves (**top left**). The Virginia creeper (**bottom left** and **above**) uses adhesive pads that will attach themselves to any rough surface.*

men available. Look for vigorous, leafy growth with unblemished foliage of a good green (not yellowish) color. Buy-ing a good plant will make all the difference in the way it performs, at least initially.

Whether the plants are in containers or bare root, dig out a hole somewhat larger than the root system in both width and depth. For containers make the depth a few inches (3–5 cm) more than the root ball. For bare-root specimens look for the soil mark on the stem and make the hole deep enough just to cover

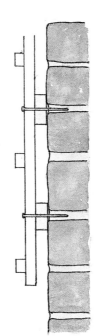

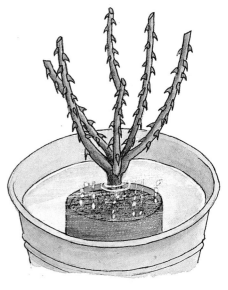

ABOVE: *Plunge a container-grown plant in a bucket of water before planting.*
BELOW: *Cut away some of the burlap from the sides of the root-ball before filling in.*

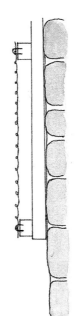

*To support climbers, fix wooden trellis away from the wall (**top**) and away from direct contact with the soil. Stretch mesh over panels made with battens (**above**), fixing the mesh with staples. Fix the panels to the wall or fence. Wire laced through vine eyes (**below left**) provides strong support for permanent planting.*

it when filled in with soil. Once the plant is in place, spade or trowel the soil around the roots. Bare-root plants should be gently bumped up and down a few times to work the soil among the roots. When the hole is loose-filled, firm with fists or feet, then top up and firm again. Finish off so that there is a shallow saucer-shaped depression around the stem base to facilitate watering.

There is no set distance apart at which to set climbers and shrubs. So much depends upon what sort of effect is desired, whether each species is to be treated individually or several are to be grown harmoniously intermingling. In the latter case, climbers and wall shrubs can be set 3–6 ft (1–2 m) apart, and shrubs at about half their ultimate height. For specimen status, space shrubs at a distance apart equal to their ultimate (catalog or book) height. Climbers should be spaced at about two-thirds this distance.

Maintenance

For the one or two years following planting, watering, weeding and training must be regularly attended to. Dur-

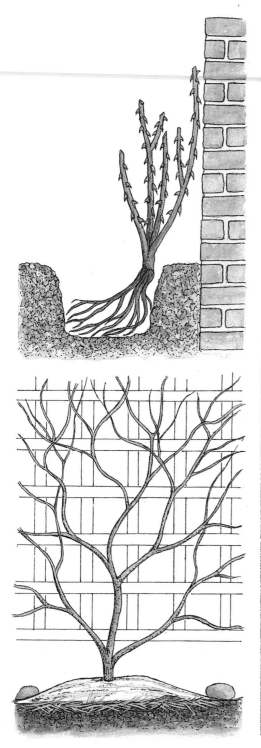

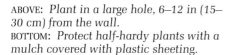

ABOVE: *Plant in a large hole, 6–12 in (15–30 cm) from the wall.*
BOTTOM: *Protect half-hardy plants with a mulch covered with plastic sheeting.*

ing all dry spells, water thoroughly once or twice a week. In the spring following planting, apply a mulch of peat, strawy manure, composted bark, etc., and repeat this a year later. If growth seems slow, apply a light dressing of a general fertilizer. Climbers and tall-growing shrubs will need an initial tie to the first supporting wire. If the climber is a twiner, vertical strings secured to the wires will aid its ascent.

Pruning

Both climbers and shrubs will be more effective if they branch fairly close to ground level. The spring following planting, reduce the height of the young plants by two-thirds to a half. This will stimulate growth low down and create bushy shrubs and well-branched climbers. The growth which results after this pruning will become the main framework of the mature plant. Thereafter, climbing plants should be pruned annually after flowering, when spent blooms are removed and crowded stems lightly thinned, and in winter when further thinning is well worthwhile.

Wall shrubs need little pruning other than to remove stems which grow too far forward from the wall. Most free-standing shrubs can also be allowed to grow naturally, though it pays to thin out congested growth. Vigorous summer bloomers such as philadelphus (mock orange) and weigela greatly respond to an annual thinning after the first two or three years. Remove whole flowered branches back to near the base to encourage young replacement stems. Spring flowerers such as forsythia, kerria and ribes should be pruned only immediately after blooming; winter pruning destroys potential flowers.

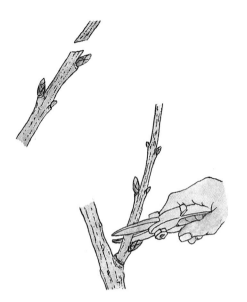

Special pruning requirements for individual plants are given in the A–Z section.

To prune climbing and wall plants, make a clean, slanting cut across the stem, just above a bud if you are trimming back a branch (**above**) or where a side branch joins the main stem (**far left**).

Propagation
There are various ways of propagating shrubs and climbers, the easiest being suckers, layering and hardwood cuttings. Semi-hard and softwood cuttings and seeds require more skill and patience.

Suckers: A few shrubs and climbers, e.g. berberis, hydrangea, kerria, mahonia, ribes and viburnum, often produce shoots from below ground level at or near the base of the plant. These are suckers. When one or two years old they usually have some roots of their own and can be removed and planted independently. Dig away the soil down to where the sucker is attached and carefully pull or cut it free. Do this between autumn and early spring and replant immediately. Cut back the top by half.

Layers: Practically all woody-stemmed plants can be layered. First, in late summer or spring, a low branch is pulled down to soil level and pinned or tied in position. Next, one-year-old stems from this branch are bent into a U-shape so that the bottom of the U can be buried shallowly with the free tip erect. Loosen the soil with a fork and then make a shallow hole. Work some coarse sand into the bottom of the hole if the soil is not free-draining. Nick the stem at the bottom of the U, dust with hormone rooting powder and bury it about 2 inches (5 cm) deep. Secure the free end to a short cane. Make sure that the shoot is kept moist in dry weather and one year later sever it from the main branch, dig up the rooted layer and replant immediately.

Forsythia planted with clematis.

ABOVE RIGHT: *To increase a plant by layering, nick the underside of the chosen shoot (1) and peg the shoot into the soil (2) with the nick still on the underside.*
RIGHT: *For air-layering, dip the stem in rooting compound, wrap it in moist sphagnum moss and cover it tightly with clear plastic, ensuring that the nick in the stem remains open. Once the roots push through the moss, remove the covering and sever the new plant below the level of wrapping.*

LEFT: *Semi-hardwood cuttings are taken from shoots removed with a heel attached (1). Remove the lower leaves (2) and place cuttings to root around the rim of a pot (3). Cover with a plastic tent (4) to increase humidity.*

Hardwood cuttings: All deciduous shrubs and climbers and some of the evergreens (e.g. euonymus and ligustrum) root easily from hardwood cuttings. These are mature stems of the previous season severed in autumn or early winter. Each stem must be cleanly cut above and below a bud and should be 8–12 inches (20–30 cm) long. Any leaves are removed from the lower part, the end is dipped in rooting powder and the cutting inserted two-thirds deep in sandy or sharply drained ground in a sheltered, partially shaded site. One year later the rooted cuttings can be lifted and replanted in permanent sites.
Semi-hardwood and softwood cuttings: For these techniques some kind of propagating case is necessary. This can be improvised from a seed tray covered with plastic sheeting supported by U-shaped lengths of galvanized wire. Single pots can be put inside plastic bags. Best of all are the custom-made propagators with a clear rigid top and a heating element in the bottom. Semi-

hardwood cuttings can also be placed in a shaded cold frame.

Softwood cuttings are sappy, recently formed stems with active growing tips. They are taken in spring and summer, severed with 2–3 inches (5–7.5 cm) of stem and cut beneath a node (bud or leaf). The lower leaves are cut or nipped off, and the base is dipped in rooting powder and inserted one-third deep in pots of equal parts sand and peat, or perlite. A case or a plastic bag is needed, and bottom heat around 60–70°F (18–21°C) hastens rooting.

Semi-hardwood cuttings are the current season's stems starting to become woody at the base. They are taken in late summer and early autumn, severed at the base and trimmed to 3–4 inches (7.5–10 cm) by reducing the top. With some shrubs (e.g. ceanothus, cistus, elaeagnus, ilex, pyracantha) this kind of cutting roots more successfully if it has a heel of parent stem. The cuttings are carefully pulled or sliced off to leave a shield-shaped base of older wood. The tail of tissue from this shield is pared off, and the cutting is then treated as described above. A propagating case is needed and bottom heat is an advantage.

Seeds: Many shrubs and climbers can be raised from seed, but if they are hybrids or selected forms they will not come true to type. Most of them germinate and grow well, but the seedlings usually take several to many years to reach flowering size. Easy genera to try are: berberis, buddleia, chaenomeles, cotoneaster, potentilla, pyracantha, rose, syringa, viburnum and weigela. The seed is best sown when ripe or as soon afterwards as possible. Dried, packeted seed may take more than a year to germinate. As usually only a few new plants are needed, use 3–4 inch (7.5–10 cm) pots. Fill these with a standard seed compost then sow the seed thinly. If it is large enough to handle with the fingers or tweezers then space the seeds ½ inch (1 cm) apart each way. Seed embedded in berries (berberis, cotoneaster and

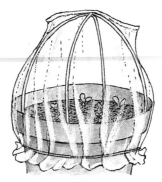

When sowing seeds in a pot, cover with a plastic bag until the seeds have germinated.

pyracantha) should be squeezed or tweezed out of the surrounding pulp and sown immediately. Press the seeds into the surface of the compost, cover with ½ inch (1 cm) of grit, then water and put outside in a sheltered place or a cold frame. Many shrub and climber seeds, especially those from berries, need a period of low temperature (winter) before they can respond to spring warmth. Pots left outside all winter are best put in a frame or greenhouse in early spring and the seeds should soon germinate.

CLIMBERS AND SHRUBS FOR SPECIAL PURPOSES

CLIMBERS	SHRUBS FOR WALLS	SHRUBS FOR THE OPEN GARDEN
Sheltered north walls: Celastrus Parthenocissus Clematis (some) Polygonum Hedera (E) Rosa (some) Hydrangea (partially E) Jasminum Tropaeolum Lonicera speciosum	**Sheltered north walls:** Camellia (E) Garrya Cotoneaster Kerria Daphne (some E) Mahonia Euonymus (E) Ribes Forsythia Skimmia (E)	**Shady sites:** Berberis (some E) Prunus (some E) Cornus Ribes Cotoneaster Salix Elaeagnus (some Skimmia (E) E) Spiraea Forsythia Symphoricarpus Ilex (E) Viburnum Kerria (some E) Mahonia (E)
South walls: Campsis Rosa (some) Clematis (some) (partially E) Ipomoea Tropaeolum Lathyrus tuberosum Passiflora Wisteria	**South walls:** Abutilon Escallonia (E) Buddleia (some) Garrya (E) Ceanothus Magnolia (E) Chimonanthus Pyracantha (E) Choisya (E) Santolina (E) Cistus (E) Senecio (E)	**Sunny sites:** Buddleia (some E) Potentilla Chaenomeles Prunus (some E) Cistus (E) Santolina (E) Conifers (E) Senecio (E) Cytisus (E) Spiraea Erica (E) Syringa Philadelphus Weigela
East and west walls: All those for north walls, plus: Campsis Wisteria Lathyrus *E = Evergreen	**East and west walls:** All those for north walls, plus: Buddleia (some E) Magnolia (E) Chimonanthus Rhododendron (E) Choisya (E) Viburnum Elaeagnus (E) (some E) Escallonia (E) Weigela	**Exposed sites:** Berberis (some E) Potentilla Buddleia davidii Ribes Conifers (E) Santolina (E) Cotoneaster (some E) Senecio (E) Cytisus (E) Spiraea Elaeagnus (E) Viburnum Erica (E) (some E) Ilex (E) Weigela

A-Z

SHRUBS AND CLIMBING PLANTS

ABELIA ZONES 5–10
A. grandiflora (hardy to zone 6) is the most popular, free-flowering and hardy of these deciduous and evergreen shrubs, prized for their graceful arching branches and glossy foliage. The summer-blooming flowers, tubular in shape, grow in clusters of one to four and in shades of pink, purple

Abutilon vitifolium

and white. The foliage turns bronze in the autumn. *A. grandiflora* grows from 6–8 ft (1.8–2.4 m) and is useful as an informal flowering hedge. *A.* x 'Edward Goucher' is a smaller variety that grows to 3–5 ft (90 cm–1.5 m) high and produces small purplish-pink flowers with orange throats. 'Sherwood' grows to 3 ft (90 cm) tall. *A. grandiflora* dies back in colder climates, but will re-main evergreen in the South.

A. floribunda (hardy to zone 8) grows to 6 ft (1.8 m) with large red flowers.
General care: Abelias should be pruned in spring as they develop on new growth. In coldest climates, prune the plant to 3–5 inches (8–13 cm) and mulch heavily. Abelias prefer partial shade, although *A. floribunda* will take full sun. Plant in well-drained soil.
Propagation: Abelias are easily propagated from soft-wood or hardwood cuttings or sow ripe seeds in the spring.
Pests and diseases: Generally trouble-free.

ABUTILON ZONE 10
Abutilon is mostly tropical in origin and is usually grown as a greenhouse, conservatory or pot plant in this country, but two of the species can be grown outdoors in favored sites in the South and are well worth attempting for the sake of their beautiful, exotic-looking flowers. *A. vitifolium* is the hardier, and if grown as a wall shrub in a sheltered position could even succeed in areas further north. It grows to 6 ft (1.8 m) – more in a good site – and produces masses of large mauve flowers all summer, or later in good years. 'Album' is a white variety. *A. megapotamicum* is less hardy but is worth attempting for its unusual flowers,

produced from late April right through the summer; red and yellow and pendant, they look like fuchsia flowers. It can grow to 8 ft (2.4 m) in good conditions. *A. m.* 'Variegatum' has yellow and green leaves.
General care: Abutilon prefers a sunny site, as sheltered as possible, preferably against a wall. Any garden soil will do. Depending on the site, it will probably need protection with straw in anything but the mildest winter, and in any case the young plants should be given routine winter protection until they are fully grown. Little pruning is needed, apart from removal of dead or diseased shoots in the spring.
Propagation: All the species can be raised from seed, which is freely produced. Sow in pots in spring at 65°F (18°C). Named varieties will only come true if raised from semi-hardwood cuttings. Take shoots any time in the summer and strike in pots of a 50–50 mixture of peat and sand.
Pests and diseases: Generally disease-free, but mealy bugs cause sticky brown patches on the leaves. Spray with malathion.

AKEBIA ZONES 4–9
Native to China, Korea and Japan, *A. quinata* is one of the best of the foliage vines. Its large, semi-evergreen leaf stalks bear five leaflets,

Antigonon leptopus

which measure 3–5 inches (7.5–13 cm) long. Rapidly growing to a height of 30–40 ft (9–12 m), the vines feature fragrant clusters of small purple flowers that appear in spring, followed by purple, sausage-shaped fruit in fall. Its underground runners spread rapidly. Leaves fall late in the year in zones where winter temperatures drop below freezing. *A. trifoliata* is similar to *A. quinata*, but it is distinguished by having three rather than five leaves on a stalk.

General care: Akebia is tolerant of both sun and shade. The plant grows most thickly in moist, rich soil, but it will grow satisfactorily in ordinary, well-drained soil.

Akebia needs support to climb on, and it benefits from annual pruning.

Propagation: Sow seed as soon as it is ripe or take softwood and hardwood cuttings.

Pests and diseases: Generally trouble-free.

ANTIGONON ZONES 9–10
This deciduous vine is a native of Mexico and thrives in the low deserts of the Southwest. In Mexico it is called 'chain of love' because its rose-pink flowers resemble a chain of little hearts. *A. leptopus* climbs by tendrils to a height of 30–40 ft (9–12 m). Its dark green, heart-shaped leaves have a rough texture. The flowers bloom mid-summer to fall on

long trailing sprays, creating a lovely canopy of shade for a terrace or cover for a fence or trellis. 'Albus' is a white variety.

General care: Antigonon thrives in hot summer heat, but it will tolerate ordinary soil. Mulch heavily when temperatures dip below 25°F (−4°C).

Propagation: Propagate by seed or cuttings in spring.

Pests and diseases: Generally trouble-free.

BEAUMONTIA ZONE 10
An import from India, *B. grandiflora* is an evergreen, tropical vine, dubbed the Easter lily vine, that climbs to 30 ft (9 m) high. One of the tropics' showiest specimens, the plant bears fragrant,

trumpet-shaped flowers that bloom from mid-spring through summer, measuring 5 inches (13 cm) across. The vine is a vigorous climber and features dense, 8 inch (20 cm), dark green leaves. *B. jerdoniana* is a woody vine, used in wedding bouquets in Hawaii. It bears bell-shaped, fragrant flowers in large clusters in winter and early spring.

General care: Beaumontia prefers deep, rich, well-drained soil and a sunny site. It requires a sturdy support in a warm, sheltered location. Prune after flowering but leave a good base of 2- and 3-year-old wood.

Propagation: Beaumontia is easily grown from stem cuttings taken after flowering.

Pests and diseases: Generally trouble-free.

BERBERIS ZONES 4–9
Berberis is a trouble-free, easy shrub grown for its striking flowers and berries. It will succeed almost anywhere and does not need the protection of a wall, but is often placed near one because it looks so good there. A word of caution: many varieties of the barberries are restricted by the U.S. Department of Agriculture because they act as alternate hosts for the devastating black stem rust of wheat. Those varieties and hybrids are prohibited in wheat-producing areas. The ones listed here are among the many that have U.S.D.A. approval. *B. darwinii* (hardy to zone 7) is one of the most splendid species, growing to 10 ft (3 m), evergreen, with tiny holly-like leaves and masses of dark yellow or orange flowers in spring followed by blue-purple berries. It makes a fine screen or hedge plant. Another good spring-flowering screen shrub is *B. gagnepainii* (hardy to zone 5), evergreen, up to 6 ft (1.8 m) in height, with an upright growth habit. *B. thunbergii* (hardy to zone 4) is deciduous, with brilliant red autumn colors. The variety 'Atropurpurea' has purple leaves.

General care: Berberis is easy

to look after, and is tolerant of poor soil conditions. Plant in March and, if using for screen or hedging, set about 2 ft (60 cm) apart. No pruning is needed, except for trimming of hedges.

Propagation: Berberis grows readily from seeds sown in spring in a cold frame or from berries collected in autumn.

Pests and diseases: Generally trouble-free.

BRUNFELSIA   ZONES 9–10

An evergreen shrub in the warmest zones, *B. pauciflora calycina* 'Floribunda' is an excellent container plant or specimen plant for a shady spot. Its common name of 'yesterday, today and tomorrow' can be attributed to the flowers, which open a deep purple (yesterday), fade to light lavender (today) and turn white (tomorrow). *B. pauciflora calycina*, a native of Brazil, is an upright or spreading shrub that grows to 6 ft (1.8 m).

The 2 inch (5 cm) flowers are profusely produced from spring through the summer. 'Eximia' is a compact dwarf that produces somewhat smaller flowers in heavy quantities over a shorter period in spring. 'Macranthra' has larger leaves and flowers, measuring 4 inches (10 cm) across, that do not change color as dramatically as 'Floribunda'. *B. latifolia* (hardy to zone 10) is a native of South America with blue flowers turning to lavender which bloom during spring and fall. The shrub's variable coloring includes white flowers that fade to yellow.

General care: Brunfelsia requires rich, well-drained, slightly acid soil and ample supplies of water and fertilizer. For maximum bloom and foliage, plant in light shade. Prune lightly in spring to maintain a neat shape. Mulch heavily in winter months.

Propagation: Propagate from cuttings taken in spring.

Pests and diseases: Treat plants that show evidence of chlorosis with iron chelate.

BUDDLEIA   ZONES 5–9

Buddleia davidii (hardy to zone 5), the so-called butterfly bush, is too often seen to need a description and too easy to grow to waste a wall on, but many of the buddleias are half-hardy, or only just hardy, and are worth growing with the protection of a wall. *B. alternifolia* (hardy to zone 5) is the hardiest of the woody buddleias. Known as the 'Fountain', it produces a springtime spray of small, purple flowers. It grows to 12 ft (3.6 m) and provides early seasonal color in a cascading pattern. In a warmer climate,

LEFT: *Berberis thunbergii* 'Atropurpurea'
BELOW: *Buddleia davidii hybrid*

you might try *B. asiatica* (hardy to zone 8). This dwarf grows only 2–6 ft (60 cm–2 m), but its fragrant white flowers burst in early spring over leaves that are green on top and ruddy underneath.

B. globosa (hardy to zone 7), 6½–10 ft (2–3 m), is evergreen in most winters, and is hardy in a sheltered site. Its clusters of orange ball-shaped flowers are a charming sight in late spring and early summer.

General care: Plant buddleia in early spring, half-hardy ones against a west- or south-facing wall. They are happy in most soils, including limy ones, but like a sunny position.

Propagation: Take semi-hardwood cuttings in late summer and pot in a 50–50 mixture of peat and sand.

Pests and diseases: Generally trouble-free.

CALLISTEMON ZONES 9–10
The bottlebrush is prized in the warm regions of the Southwest and Florida for its bright color, long blooming period and the lasting quality of the blossoms in floral arrangements. A native of Australia, callistemon produces spectacular, bristle-like, bright red stamens. Varieties vary widely in height; most are useful as accent specimens, wall covers and windbreaks. *C. citrinus*, lemon bottlebrush, grows to 15 ft (4.6 m), blooming in mid-winter and intermittently throughout the year. Leaves appear coppery-colored on the new growth and turn vivid green with maturity. The 6 inch (15 cm) bright red bristles are irresistible to hummingbirds. 'Improved' and 'Splendens' are good selections with good-sized flowers. 'Compacta' grows to 4 ft (1.2 m) with smaller spikes; 'Jeffersii' grows to 6 ft (1.8 m) and bears reddish-purple flowers fading to lavender. 'Rosea' is similar in habit but bears rose-pink blooms.

C. *viminalis*, weeping bottlebrush, will grow to 20–30 ft (6–9 m) with low-sweeping, pendulous branches. It breaks into bloom during periods of hot weather, bearing dense red spikes. It may need staking. 'Captain Cook' is a dwarf useful as a low hedge, and 'McCaskillii' is a vigorous producer. *C. salignus*, white bottlebrush, features coppercolored new foliage and white to pale yellow flowers. *C. phoeniceus*, fiery bottlebrush, grows 6–8 ft (1.8–2.4 m) high and has denser foliage with rich red flowers. 'Prostratus' has floppy stems that grow to the contours of the terrain.

General care: *C. citrinus* is the most tolerant of poor soil, dry conditions and extremes of cold and hot weather, but callistemon thrives in full sun and moist, well-drained soil. *C. viminalis* needs to be thinned of surplus branches to avoid top-heaviness, and the young plants require

Callistemon citrinus

ample watering.
Propagation: Propagate by leaf cuttings as seed germina-tion seldom produces good results.

Pests and diseases: All varieties are susceptible to chlorosis. Treat with iron chelate.

CALLUNA (HEATHER)
See under Erica

CAMELLIA ZONES 7–10
This is one of those exotic-looking plants that is easier to grow than it might appear. Camellias have been pleasing American gardeners since the early 1800s, when they were first imported from the Far East. In 150 years they have spread coast to coast and to thousands of varieties, a testimony to both their beauty and their easy care. All camellias are evergreens, and hate lime soil.

C. *japonica* (hardy to zone 7), the common camellia, can grow to 20 ft (6 m), although 6–10 ft (2–3 m) is more usual. It is generally hardy, although it benefits from the protection of a wall, especially in the North. The site should be chosen carefully, since the plant needs some shelter from cold north and east winds and, because it can bear its flowers from fall through winter, depending on local conditions, it should be away from the early morning sun or the flowers will be frost-damaged.

A vast number of varieties is available which, like that

Camellia japonica

of roses, is constantly being added to. They can be red, pink, white or bi-colored, and single, double, or semi-double. The safest way of buying is to see the camellias in flower, rather than choosing from a catalog or description. Among the japonicas, 'Professor C. S. Sargent' is one of the hardiest. Its double red flowers show themselves under less than ideal conditions, and with less than doting care. Among the whites, 'Alba Plena' is worth a try. It is one of our oldest varieties, with double flowers that measure up to 4 inches (10 cm) wide. *C. sasguansa* (hardy to zone 7) is a 20 ft (6 m) evergreen which produces flowers in fall. Its individual blossoms are thinner than japonica, but it blooms in such profusion that it sprays ample color across the gray autumn landscape. *C. reticulata* (hardy to zone 8) and its varieties are considered the least hardy of the camellias.

General care: Camellias hate dry, limy soils. Before planting, the site should be dug over and plenty of compost or peat added, with extra nourishment given in the form of mulches after planting. They like cool roots, so a south wall with no protection should be avoided. The best aspect is west, or north if the wall is sheltered from winter winds. Plant in spring and give support until the plant is established on the wall. Young plants should be given plenty of water during the summer, and good frost protection in the winter. Keep the soil round the plant well mulched. Camellias do not need any routine pruning.

Propagation: Take semi-hardwood cuttings in the summer and plant in pots of a 50–50 sand and peat mixture.

Pests and diseases: Frost damages the buds. Leaf discoloration is probably caused by too much lime in the soil. Treat with chelated iron.

CAMPSIS   ZONES 4–10
Campsis, or trumpet vine, is a deciduous climber producing orange and red trumpet flowers in late summer. It grows up to 40 ft (12 m) under ideal conditions and will climb a wall by means of its tiny aerial roots. *C. radicans* (hardy to zone 4), is the most common species, and the hardiest, but *C. x tagliabuana* 'Mme Galen' (hardy to zone 4) has finer flowers.

General care: To give of its best, campsis needs a sunny, warm, sheltered site and a humus-rich, well-drained soil. Plant out in the winter or early spring. The plant will have to be tied to the wall until it produces its own aerial shoots. Once it is established on the wall, campsis has to be pruned every winter to encourage the flowers: cut back the previous season's growth to within a few buds of the old wood. The flowers appear at the end of the current season's shoots.

Propagation: Campsis can be propagated readily by layering long shoots in the autumn and separating them from the parent a year later and also from semi-hardwood cuttings taken in late summer and grown in a cold frame.

Pests and diseases: Aphids attack tender young shoots, causing flower loss. Spray with dimethoate or malathion. Flower bud drop is caused by low temperatures and dry roots. Guard against the latter by mulching.

CEANOTHUS   ZONES 4–10
This native American includes several varieties, each with its own geographical preference. Many of them flourish on the West Coast, particularly in California, but whatever your locale, your nursery can probably recommend some varieties that will succeed. *C. americanus* (hardy to zone 4) grows to 3 ft (1 m) and presents clusters of white flowers in early summer. Commonly known as New Jersey tea, the name dates to the Revolutionary War when Washington's troops used its leaves as a substitute for tea. *C. thyrsiflorus* (hardy to zone 8) is about the hardiest of the evergreen species, and will grow almost anywhere, given the protection of a wall. It produces masses of light blue flowers in late spring and early summer, is very floriferous, and grows to 20 ft (6 m) on a good site. *C.*

impressus (hardy to zone 8), 9 ft (2.7 m) tall, bears masses of dark blue flowers in May and June. 'Autumnal Blue' is a hybrid of uncertain parentage. It is a vigorous grower, is evergreen and hardy and, as its name suggests, produces its dark blue flowers from late summer through to the autumn.

General care: Ceanothus likes a sunny site, preferably a west- or south-facing wall. It does best in a light, well-drained soil. The spring-flowering species need only light pruning when flowering is over, but 'Autumnal Blue' should have the previous year's growth cut back in spring.

Propagation: From heeled cuttings taken in late summer and planted in pots of a 50–50 peat and sand mixture with bottom heat.

Pests and diseases: Generally trouble-free.

CELASTRUS   ZONES 2–10
This is a deciduous shrub which climbs by twisting its stems. Its flowers are inconspicuous, and it is grown for the beauty of its fruits, which split open in the autumn to reveal scarlet seeds behind which the inner yellow surface of the

Ceanothus hybrid

Celastrus orbiculatus

seed capsule appears like the petals of a flower. Luckily the fruits do not seem attractive to birds, so they last for months, sometimes well into the new year.

Celastrus is a vigorous grower, and the most popular species, *C. orbiculatus* (hardy to zone 4) can reach 40 ft (12 m). It usually has male and female flowers on separate plants, in which case you have to grow one of each to get berries. There is, however, a hermaphrodite form, with male and female flowers on the same shrub, and you should be sure to choose this form if you are growing only one.

General care: Celastrus grow well in most garden soils, but they do not like lime or excesses of wet or dry. Being vigorous growers, they need a lot of feeding, and like regular mulches. Dig in plenty of compost before planting, which can be carried out any time in the winter. Celastrus do not need regular pruning, merely a tidying up of the old wood in the winter.

Propagation: Best by layering one-year-old shoots in the autumn, choosing a hermaphrodite parent plant, or you can root semi-hardwood cuttings in the summer or hardwood cuttings in the winter, using a 50–50 peat and sand mixture.

Pests and diseases: Generally trouble-free.

CHAENOMELES
ZONES 4–10

This is the flowering quince and is a hardy, deciduous wall shrub. It is related to the common quince

and its fruits can be eaten. *C. speciosa* is the most commonly planted and is the one which often starts flowering before Christmas, although its main flowering comes in spring. It is a spreading, rather untidy shrub, up to about 6 ft (2 m) tall on a wall. The flowers of the species are red, but it has been cultivated for centuries, and there are at least a dozen varieties still available with different colored flowers: 'Cardinalis' (dark red), 'Moerloosii' (pink and white), 'Nivalis' (white), 'Phillis Moore' (semi-double pink), 'Umbilicata' (salmon-pink). There is a confusion here as to nomenclature. *C. speciosa* is often referred to as *C. japonica*, but *speciosa* is *not* Japanese quince; it is Maule's quince, and to add to the confusion the true Japanese quince is sometimes sold under the Latin name *Cydonia japonica*. Maule's quince is low and spreading compared with the true Japanese quince – it seldom grows higher than 3 ft (90 cm) – and has orange-red flowers. *C.* x *superba* is a cross between these species, and has a number of named varieties in shades of red, pink and orange.

General care: Chaenomeles is happy in any garden soil, prefers sun but will tolerate shade, and likes a wall or fence against which to grow. Prune after flowering, tidying up the shoots as far as possible and reducing the previous year's growth to a couple of buds.

Propagation: Most successful from heeled cuttings, taken in the summer and potted in a 50–50 peat and sand mixture.

Pests and diseases: Generally trouble-free.

CHIMONANTHUS
ZONES 7–10

Winter sweet is a shrub which is not planted as often as it deserves to be. It has many merits. It bears its exotic-looking, fragrant flowers right through the

Chaenomeles japonica

winter, from November onward, and will provide cut flowers for the house. Its only fault is that it takes some years to come into full flowering. *C. praecox* is deciduous and hardy, although it does best on a wall, where it can reach 10 ft (3 m). The species flowers are yellow, with purple inner petals. *C. praecox* 'Grandiflora' has larger flowers, but with less scent, and *C. praecox* 'Luteus' is pure yellow.

General care: Chimonanthus likes a south or west wall, but will tolerate any soil conditions provided they are well-drained. Plant in the spring. Once it is established and flowering, prune it every spring by removing most of the shoots that have just flowered, leaving only a few buds on each.

Propagation: Can be raised from seed, but you may have to wait 10 years from sowing before you get flowers. Layering in fall is the easiest way of propagating, but wait two years before severing the shoot from the parent plant.

Pests and diseases: Generally trouble-free.

CHOISYA ZONES 7–10
The Mexican orange blossom bears its white, orange-blossom-like scented flowers on and off right through the summer, and even into the winter if it is a mild one; its main flowering is in spring. It is evergreen and hardy, but should be grown as a wall shrub in cooler regions and even in the South it does better on a wall, reaching a height of 6–10 ft (2–3 m). Not only the flowers are fragrant: the leaves, too, give off scent when crushed.

General care: Choisya is tolerant of most soils, but not heavy clay. In the North it should be given a south-facing wall. In the South it is not so fussy and will tolerate some shade, but shelter is important. Plant in spring. Regular pruning is not needed, but any tidying up should be done in early summer. Any frost-damaged shoots should be cut right out in the spring.

Propagation: From semi-hardwood cuttings taken in summer and planted in a 50–50 sand and peat mixture.

Pests and diseases: Generally trouble-free.

CISTUS ZONES 7–10
The sun rose is among the most colorful and attractive of evergreen shrubs and bears a profusion of single rose-like flowers in summer. It grows in poor, dry, sandy and chalky soils to perfection, but must have plenty of sun and freedom from severe frost. One of the best is *C. x purpureus* which bears large, rose-purple, chocolate-blotched flowers on gray-green rounded bushes to 3 ft (90 cm) in height. Somewhat hardier is *C. ladanifer*, the so-called gum cistus, bearing white, crimson-purple-blotched flowers on dark green erect bushes to 6 ft (1.8 m) or more tall. Hardiest of all is the similar *C. laurifolius*, which produces slightly smaller, white, yellow-blotched blooms. Also fairly hardy are the pink-flowered 'Anne Palmer' and the white *C. salvifolius*, both of which are about 2 ft (60 cm) in height.

General care: It does not require pruning and is best without it, except for removing untidy or dead shoots. The sun rose must have a sheltered site and must be protected from freezing winds.

Propagation: From heeled cuttings taken in late summer and inserted in pots of 2 parts sand and 1 of peat in a case with bottom heat.

Pests and diseases: Generally trouble-free.

CLEMATIS ZONES 2–9
There are a great many species and hybrids of clematis. All climb readily by twisting their leaf stalks round the nearest available support. The hybrids, which produce large, exotic-looking blooms, are easier to grow than they look. Each

variety keeps to a timetable for blooming, so by planning you can have a succession of clematis flowers right through the summer. All of the following are deciduous.

C. montana (hardy to zone 6) is vigorous, hardy, and easy to grow. It climbs as high as 20 ft (6 m), producing small white flowers, slightly scented, in late spring. The main problem is to keep it under control. *C. jouiniana* (hardy to zone 4) grows to 10 ft (3 m), but needs tying to supports to help it climb. It produces lilac flowers from late summer through fall.

C. x jackmanii (hardy to zone 5) is easy to grow and vigorous. Growing to 20 ft (6 m), it produces masses of large purple flowers, with a darker stripe, from mid-summer onward. Similar in appearance, but not in the same grouping, are the large-flowered hybrids such as 'Nellie Moser' (pink and mauve flowers in spring and fall), 'The President' (purple flowers, summer and fall), and 'Ville de Lyon' (carmine red flowers, summer and fall). All grow to about 10 ft (3 m) tall. Clematis gives a mass of growth starting from a small base, so a lot of plants can be put into quite a small plot.

General care: Clematis is tolerant of a lot of different growing conditions but prefers its roots in the shade in moisture-retaining soil with some lime. Its top growth likes the sun but some flowers, such as 'Nellie Moser', bleach in sunlight and should be planted on a north wall. Heavy clay soil should be lightened with peat or leaf mold. Clematis does not like its roots disturbed, so always use container-grown plants, putting them in at any time during the winter.

Correct pruning is essential if clematis is to give of its best in flowers. *C. montana* blooms on the previous year's growth so pruning, if done at all, should be carried out just after flowering. *C.*

Choisya ternata, Mexican orange blossom

Clematis 'Nellie Moser'

jouiniana may need some top growth cut back after a few years to encourage basal shoots. *C.* x *jackmanii* flowers on the current year's growth, and should be cut right back in February to encourage young shoots. 'Ville de Lyon' needs the same treatment, but 'Nellie Moser' and 'The President' need only light pruning to tidy the plant.

Propagation: Clematis can be raised from seed, but the offspring are often not as good as the parents. Cuttings can be taken in summer and rooted in a 50–50 mixture of peat and sand, but the most reliable way of propagating on a small scale is to layer shoots in the spring and separate them from the parent a year later.

Pests and diseases: Clematis wilt causes shoots – often a whole young plant – to wilt and die rapidly, but fresh shoots may appear from the base later. There is no reliable cure.

CLERODENDRUM
ZONES 6–10
C. thomsoniae (hardy to zone 9) is an attractive evergreen shrubby vine in warm climates and can be grown as a climbing wall plant indoors. A native of West Africa, this twining vine, which can grow to 6 ft (1.8 m) if left untrimmed, is prized for its red-centered white flowers. They are borne in clusters in late summer through the early autumn. *C. trichotomum* (hardy to

zone 6) is an unusual shrub from China and Japan which grows to 15 ft (4.6 m) tall with many branching stems. White, star-shaped, fragrant blossoms appear in late summer, followed by highly decorative bright blue berries surrounded by red calyces in the autumn. *C. fragrans pleniflorum* (hardy to zone 9) grows 10 ft (3 m) tall and bears small pink double flowers in tight clusters. It grows by root suckers, which can be trimmed to control growth.

General care: Plant in partial shade in ordinary well-drained soil. Prune after flowering.

Propagation: Stratify seed as soon as ripe at 40°F (5°C) for 3 months or store in an airtight container in a cool place and then stratify.

Easily propagated from softwood cuttings and root cuttings.

Pests and diseases: Generally trouble-free.

CLETHRA
ZONES 3–9
The genus includes both deciduous shrubs and some tender evergreen trees. *C. ainifolia*, summersweet or sweet pepper bush (hardy to zone 3), is a native of the eastern part of the country. It grows 9 ft (2.7 m) tall and features 4–6 inch (10–15 cm) spires of deliciously fragrant small white flowers that bloom from mid to late summer. The foliage is a handsome green and turns yellow and orange in the autumn. 'Rosea' has pink flowers and 'Pinkspire' is an improved selection distinguished by the intensity and depth of color of its deep pink flower spikes. *C. ainifolia* thrives in coastal settings and is ideal as a decorative hedge.

General care: Prefers a moist, acid soil similar to that in which both azaleas and rhododendrons thrive. Condition surrounding soil with peat moss or ground bark to prevent salt build-up. It will tolerate full sun in cool weather but prefers light shade in warm weather.

Propagation: Propagate by seeds, cuttings made in late summer and layering.

Pests and diseases: Spray to control red spider mite.

CLYTOSTOMA
ZONES 9–10
C. callistegioides, violet trumpet vine, is a vigorous growing, highly adaptable decorative climber. Although it is slow to start growth, it will eventually spread to 15–20 ft (4.6–6 m) wide and almost twice as tall. It climbs by tendrils and needs the support of a trellis to cover walls. The trumpet-shaped flowers are violet, lavender or pale purple and measure 3 inches (7.5 cm) long. Cascading masses of bloom are in evidence from early spring through the summer. In cold climates, treat as a perennial and mulch heavily in late fall.

Cobaea scandens

General care: Clytostoma is amazingly tolerant of soil and sun conditions, thriving in anything from sand to clay, from full sun to shade, which makes it an extremely useful plant. Prune in late winter to control growth.

Propagation: Propagate by cuttings in early spring.

Pests and diseases: Generally trouble-free.

COBAEA ZONES 9–10
A native of Mexico, *C. scandens* can be grown as an annual in any zone. Known as the cup-and-saucer vine,

it is a fine ornamental that rapidly climbs to 25 ft (7.5 m) by means of tenacious tendrils that will scale a wall without support. In zones 9 and 10 the plant will grow to 40 ft (12 m) and blooms for six months, beginning in early spring. The plants will reach a height of 25 ft (7.5 m) in one season when grown in a greenhouse. The flowers, which are bell-shaped with a green, saucer-like collar, come in shades of violet, rose-purple and white, and bloom throughout the summer to early fall.

General care: Plant in full sun in ordinary soil. Supply ample water in dry periods

and keep sheltered from strong winds.

Propagation: Start seeds indoors, nicking them with a knife to speed germination and pressing them into moist potting soil. Transplant outdoors when danger of frost has passed. The plant will bloom during its first year of growth.

Pests and diseases: Check new growth for aphids.

CONIFERS ZONES 2–10
Pines, firs, spruces, redwoods, hemlocks, cedars, larches, cypresses, junipers and yews are all described as conifers. In the main they are

forest trees and too large for the average garden. However, many of them have produced smaller or really dwarf mutations which collectively are known as dwarf conifers. Those, by reason of their neat architectural shapes and wide range of foliage colors and textures, have become popular garden plants in recent years. The most useful of all are the many junipers, most of which are normally bushy or prostrate shrubs. They make splendid ground cover which, when established, requires virtually no maintenance. For this purpose, *Juniperus sabina* (hardy to zone 4) 'Blue Danube', *J. squamata* (hardy to zone 4) 'Blue Carpet', with gray-blue-green foliage, and the rich green *J. communis* (hardy to zone 2) 'Green Carpet' are to be recommended. Among taller junipers, look out for the 6 ft (2 m) tall deep green *J. chinensis* (hardy to zone 5) 'Kaizuka', the spreading gray-green *J. virginiana* (hardy to zone 2) 'Gray Owl' and the golden 'Old Gold', both about 4 ft (1.2 m) in height.

Among small pines, try the 6½ ft (2 m) tall *Pinus parviflora* (hardy to zone 5) 'Glauca', with blue-green leaves, or the 3 ft (90 cm) tall *P. mugo* (hardy to zone 2) 'Ophir', with bright gold leaves in winter. Long known and still one of the best dwarf spruces is *Picea glauca* (hardy to zone 2) 'Albertiana Conica', which forms a dense wide cone eventually to 6½ ft (2 m) or more. Among the firs, *Abies balsamea* (hardy to zone 3) 'Hudsonia' ('Nana') has long graced our gardens. It develops into a compact, rounded green bush to 1 ft (30 cm) or so in height.

A most satisfying dwarf spreading and weeping conifer is the Canadian hemlock (*Tsuga canadensis*) (hardy to zone 4), known as 'Jeddeloh'. Eventually it can exceed 1 ft (30 cm) in height and double this in width. It combines well with the dwarf Lawson cypress (*Chamaecyparis lawsoniana*) (hardy to zone 5) called 'Ellwood's Pillar'. Blue-gray in leaf, it eventually forms dense columns to about 2 ft (60 cm) tall. Best known of all conifers nowadays is Leyland cypress (x *Cupressocyparis leylandii*) (hardy to zone 5). It has a potential height in excess of 100 ft (30 m) but stands clipping well and makes a good windbreak or hedge. There are green, grayish and yellowish foliaged sorts to choose from.

General care: With the exception of the firs (*Abies*) which are best in an acid soil, all the conifers mentioned here will grow in most soils provided they are not waterlogged. For wet ground, try the deciduous dawn redwood (*Metasequoia glyptostroboides*) (hardy to zone 5). Except for hedging, conifers do not need pruning and are best without it.

Propagation: Dwarf conifers and those of hybrid origin (e.g. Leyland cypress) must be propagated by heel cuttings in early autumn in a cold frame. True species of pine, spruce, fir, cypress, etc., come easily from seed sown in autumn or spring in a frame. Some of the really small varieties of pine and spruce are difficult and very slow to root, and nurserymen graft them on to seedlings of true species.

Pests and diseases: Generally trouble-free.

CORNUS ZONES 2–9
Although collectively known as dogwoods, the genus *Cornus* is a varied one, including trees and shrubs grown either for summer flowers, autumn fruits and foliage or colored winter stems. All the hardy species are deciduous. Their flowers are small, borne in compact rounded heads and are not showy. In the so-called flowering dogwoods, however, each flowerhead is surrounded by four or more large, colored, petal-like leaves known as bracts. The best known and most reliable of this sort is *C. kousa* (hardy to zone 5), a large shrub to 10 ft (3 m) or more with profusely borne white bracts followed by pendant strawberry-like fruits and good autumn color. *C. florida* (hardy to zone 4) is even better, with bracts of white, pink or red, but it is not so easy to grow. Colored twigged dogwoods are *C. alba* 'Sibirica' (hardy to zone 2) (red) and *C. stolonifera*

'Flaviramea' (olive-yellow). *C. mas* (hardy to zone 4) is the cornelian cherry and provides a profusion of yellow (bractless) flowers on naked twigs in spring followed by edible fruits in late summer.

General care: Colored twigged dogwoods will grow in any soil, even wet ones. Cornelian cherry is also adaptable but the soil must be well drained. Flowering dogwoods need moisture-retentive acid land, though *C. kousa* will stand some lime. Colored twigged species are best pruned back to 1 ft (30 cm) above ground each spring. All the others are best left to grow naturally, except for removing untidy stems in late winter or after flowering.

Propagation: Cuttings with a heel in late summer for all species, also hardwood cuttings in the open ground in October for the colored twigged sorts. *C. mas, C. florida* and *C. kousa* can also be layered in autumn or raised from seed sown as soon as ripe in a cold frame; germination sometimes takes 15 months or more.

Pests and diseases: Generally trouble-free.

COTONEASTER ZONES 4–9
Cotoneaster is an easy-to-grow, red-berried shrub that includes species suitable for screening and hedges, as well as for training on walls. The two varieties most suitable for screening are both semi-evergreen: *C. x watereri* and *C. x* 'Cornubia', both of which can reach 10 ft (3 m) or more, and spread almost as wide. When used as a screen, *C. watereri* should be planted 5 ft (1.5 m) apart, at least. These planting distances will give a very thick screen, and if they are exceeded you will still have satisfactory screening eventually. Another semi-evergreen is *C. simonsii* (hardy to zone 5), seldom growing above 7 ft (2.1 m), but because of its upright habit of growth, suitable for a screen or hedge. Plantings

Cotoneaster horizontalis

for the latter use should be 1 ft (30 cm) apart. *C. horizontalis* (hardy to zone 4) is a deciduous species whose shoots and laterals form a regular herringbone pattern which looks very effective when trained on a wall or wooden fence and, as it is deciduous, you get the bonus of the autumnal tints before leaf-fall. It will reach a height of 6–8 ft (1.8–2.4 m) when trained in this way. The prostrate evergreen *C. dammeri* (hardy to zone 5), and 'Skogholm' provide good ground cover on banks and between shrubs.

General care: Cotoneaster is not fussy about site or soil, and in fact seems to prefer poor soil. Plant any time in the winter and, if growing for hedging, shorten the shoots to encourage a bushy growth habit. Routine pruning is not needed, but hedges should be trimmed.

Propagation: It can be grown easily from seed harvested in the autumn, but is unlikely to grow true to type. It is better to use heeled cuttings, taken in late summer and planted in a 50–50 peat and sand mixture, or to layer some shoots, which can then be separated from the parent a year later.

Pests and diseases: Birds often eat the berries. Aphids can be sprayed with malathion. Fireblight, which is on the increase, can affect cotoneaster. Its symptom is dark brown, shriveled leaves, caused by a bacterium. There is no chemical cure. Infected branches should be cut back well below the infected area and burned. Pruners should be disinfected afterwards.

CYTISUS   ZONES 5–9
Cytisus is the well-known and popular garden broom (*C. scoparius*). There are many varieties, in shades of yellow, pink, red and white. Well worth growing as a wall shrub is the very different *C. battandieri*, the Moroccan or pineapple broom, so called from the scent of its bright yellow flowers which are borne in summer. It is a spec-

Cytisus battandieri, pineapple broom

tacular shrub that will grow up to 15 ft (4.6 m) on a wall, its light green leaves covered in silky hairs looking particularly good when they are seen in contrast with deep red brick. It is evergreen, but may lose most of its foliage in a severe winter.

General care: A sunny site and rather poor soil are preferred. Some lime is tolerated. Use container-grown plants, putting them in in September or March. Prune in the summer, removing the shoots which have just finished flowering, and you will get young shoots to provide next year's flowers.

Propagation: Best grown from seed. Leave some pods on the plant to ripen, and harvest when they turn brown. Keep in a cool place throughout the winter, and sow seeds in 4 inch (10 cm) pots of soil-less compost in spring.

Pests and diseases: Generally trouble-free.

DAPHNE   ZONES 3–10
Renowned for its scented blossom, daphne contains no fewer than 70 species, few of which are in general cultivation. They are small shrubs, some evergreen, others deciduous, usually freely bearing their clusters of small tubular flowers. Best known is the erect, 3–4 ft (90–120 cm) tall, deciduous mezereon (*D. mezereum*) (hardy to zone 4), with rose-purple flowers on naked twigs in winter and spring. *D. m.* 'Alba' is white-bloomed. About the same height but more widespreading is *D. odora* (hardy to zone 7), a splendid evergreen with red-purple buds opening to almost white in late winter or spring. The most common form has narrowly yellow-margined leaves ('Aureo-

Daphne odora 'Aureomarginata'

marginata'). Mat-forming and magnificent when well grown is *D. cneorum* (hardy to zone 4), aptly known as the garland flower. It is not a very distinguished evergreen until early summer, when every shoot tip bursts into a little posy of rich pink, highly fragrant blossom.

General care: Almost any well-drained soil is acceptable provided it is neither too dry nor too wet. *D. cneorum* must have a sunny site; the other two will stand partial shade. *D. odora* is not totally hardy and needs a position sheltered from cold winds.

Propagation: By taking cuttings with a heel in late summer for the evergreen species or by layering in autumn or spring and leaving for at least

a full year. *D. mezereum* is easiest by seed, which must be sown when ripe in a cold frame if germination is to occur in the next spring. Seedlings may flower the second spring and certainly the third.

Pests and diseases: *D. mezereum* in particular is prone to virus infection which causes a yellow mottling and crippling of the leaves, then die-back and death. It is best to destroy any plant as soon as the virus symptoms are recognizable. All daphnes are liable to die suddenly, though this is not as common an occurrence as statements in the popular gardening press would suggest. Virus infection may be a contributing or major cause of death.

DEUTZIA ZONES 4–9

This genus of carefree shrubs is prolific with its trusses of five-petalled white or pink flowers. *D. x rosea* (hardy to zone 5) forms rounded bushes to 4 ft (1.2 m) in height with pink flowers. *D. x 'Montrose'* (hardy to zone 5) is almost twice as tall and bears purplish-rose blooms. *D. scabra* (hardy to zone 5) is erect and can exceed 8 ft (4.2 m). The pink-tinted buds open pure white. *D.s. 'Flore Pleno'* is double white tinted rose-purple.

General care: Ordinary soil and sun or partial shade are all that is needed.

Propagation: Take hardwood cuttings in autumn or semi-hardwood cuttings in late summer.

Pests and diseases: Generally trouble-free.

DISTICTIS ZONES 9–10

An import to Southern California from Mexico, distictis is a quick-growing evergreen which climbs by tendrils and features trumpet-shaped flowers that bloom from early summer to early fall. *D. buccinatoria*, red trumpet vine, has shiny foliage and bears clusters of 4 inch (10 cm) vivid orange-red flowers that turn to rose-red as they mature. It grows to 20 ft (6 m)

Elaeagnus pungens

tall in one season. *D. laxiflora* has flowers that open violet and fade to white, emitting a sweet vanilla-like scent. It needs less pruning than other varieties. *D. riversii* is the most vigorous and floriferous variety. The purple flowers, marked with orange throats, will bloom throughout the year during periods of warm temperatures.

General care: Distictis will thrive in well-drained soil in full sun. Vigorous varieties need regular pruning to maintain shape and a strong support such as a fence or sturdy trellis. Removal of blooms as they die will encourage more flowers to blossom on the plant.

Propagation: Distictis roots rapidly from cuttings.

Pests and diseases: Generally trouble-free.

ELAEAGNUS ZONES 2–8

Grown for its decorative foliage, elaeagnus is particularly useful for screening or hedging, especially near the sea, owing to its ability to stand up to salt-laden winds. Some elaeagnus are deciduous, but

the two sorts described and recommended here are evergreens. *E. x ebbingei* (hardy to zone 5), introduced from Holland in the 1930s, is particularly useful because of its speed of growth. It will reach a height of 9–10 ft (2.7–3 m) a few years after planting. Its leaves are deep glossy green above, silvery beneath and there is a named variety, 'Gilt Edge', which has yellow leaf margins. *E. pungens* (hardy to zone 7), which can grow to the same height but is slower to do so, has a number of named cultivars that do not grow so tall or so fast as the species: 'Dicksonii' (broad yellow leaf margins) and 'Frederickii' (yellow leaves with green margins) grow only to 6 ft (1.8 m); 'Maculata' (variegated yellow and green) to 8 ft (2.4 m).

General care: Elaeagnus is very accommodating as to site and soil, being happy in poor, thin conditions and tolerant of lime. Plant container-grown specimens 18 inches (45 cm) apart in spring if grown for hedging, 3 ft (90 cm) apart if for screens. Shorten the shoots to encourage bushy growths. No routine pruning is needed, but hedges should be trim-

med in mid-summer. Remove any all-green shoots as soon as they appear on variegated varieties.

Propagation: From semi-hardwood cuttings taken in summer.

Pests and diseases: Generally trouble-free, though *E. x ebbingei* is heir to a die-back of branches, occasionally the whole plant, caused by coral spot fungus. Remove and burn dead stems promptly.

ERICA and CALLUNA ZONES 4–10

The heaths (erica) and heathers (calluna) are inseparable in their garden value and so close botanically as to have once been classified together. Those mentioned here are hardy, wiry-stemmed shrubs with tiny leaves and a profusion of little bell-flowers throughout the year. They provide ground cover which is highly decorative in its own right. Beds or whole gardens devoted to them have become popular as a labor-saving device during the past 20–30 years.

There are hundreds of varieties of calluna, some with colored foliage and producing flowers in a wide range of red, pink, purple and white shades. Only a few can be mentioned here, many more being found in garden centers and nurseries. All grow about 1 ft (30 cm) in height and bloom in late summer and early autumn. 'Anne Marie' has fully double pale pink and cerise flowers. 'Anthony Davis' has gray foliage and white flowers. 'Beoley Gold' bears white flowers above bright gold foliage. 'Darkness' is dark green with crimson blooms. 'Golden Feather' is yellow in summer, reddish-orange in winter and produces unremarkable mauve flowers. 'Robert Chapman' has purple flowers and foliage which changes from gold to bronze to red.

Following true heather is the so-called winter heath *Erica herbacea* (hardy to zone 5), which flowers mainly in

Erica herbacea hybrids

winter and spring and rarely exceeds 10 inches (25 cm) in height. 'Anne Sparkes' has bronze and orange-red tinted foliage and red-purple flowers. 'January Sun' is half the normal size with pink flowers and gold-green leaves. 'King George' is an old variety but still one of the best pinks. 'Ruby Glow' has a compact habit and ruby-red blooms. 'Springwood White' is mat-forming and vigorous, producing its white flowers freely.

The best summer ericas are *E. cinerea* and *E. vagans* (both hardy to zone 5). The latter grows to 1½ ft (45 cm) or more in height with a greater spread. 'Lyonesse' is white, 'Mrs D. F. Maxwell' rose-crimson and 'St Keverne' salmon pink. The bell heather (*E. cinerea*) forms spreading bushlets to 8 inches (20 cm) tall. 'Foxhollow Mahogany' has dwarf foliage and mahogany red flowers. 'Hookstone' is a strong-growing white. 'Pink Ice' is a glowing pink. 'Stephen Davis' has blooms of a startlingly bright magenta. The white 'Rock Pool' is largely grown for its gold foliage, which takes on attractive coppery-bronze

hues in the winter months.
General care: Well-drained soil and sun are essential for the heaths and heathers and, except for *E. herbacea*, lime-free soil is needed. Pruning is controversial but cutting off the spent flower spikes does promote compact, floriferous plants of lawn-like neatness.
Propagation: Cuttings in late summer in a cold frame in 50–50 peat and sand is the easiest method, but for just a few extra plants layering in spring is recommended, severing one year later.
Pests and diseases: Generally untouched by pests but die-back can be a nuisance in some areas. Foliage yellows and looks small and thin, dying first in patches, then whole plants. Destroy infected plants promptly. In future make sure the site is well-drained and keep watering, feeding and mulching to a minimum.

ERYTHINA ZONES 8–10
The coral tree includes more than 100 species of shrubs, most of which are acclimated to relatively cool and dry tropical climates. 'Erythina' is Greek for red, but its flowers range from pink, coral, and red to orange-yellow. *E. herbacea* (hardy

to zone 8) is the heartiest of the species. A native of the Gulf Coast, it bears bright showy flowers surrounded by prickly petioles. *E. coralloides* is one of the most colorful varieties. The bright red blossoms form in clusters at the ends of the sculptural branches. It grows to about 30 ft (9 m) and needs regular pruning. *E. crista-acanthocarpa* is more suitable to the small garden. It grows to 4 ft (1.2 m) and is hardy to zone 8. *E. bidwillii* grows to 8 ft (2.4 m) with deep scarlet flowers which bloom from spring until winter.
General care: Plant in well-drained soil in full sun. Water well during dry seasons. Prune bushes after flowering to avoid cutting away next year's buds, with the exception of *E. bidwillii*, which forms new flowering branches each spring.
Propagation: Erythina grows readily from cuttings.
Pests and diseases: Generally trouble-free.

ESCALLONIA ZONES 7–10
This South American shrub is much favored for its pretty red or pink flowers which are sometimes borne right through the summer and autumn. It is hardy only in warmer regions; elsewhere it needs the protection of a wall. The most popular of

Euonymus 'Emerald 'n' Gold'

the evergreen species is *E. rubra* (hardy to zone 8) and, near the sea, its variety *macrantha*, a favorite for hedging and screening and in seaside towns for its ability to stand up to salt-laden winds. More useful is its variety 'C.F. Ball' which is hardier and bears red flowers. Hybrid varieties suitable for hedges or screening include 'Donard Seedling', 6 ft (1.8 m), pink, fragrant flowers in summer; 'Crimson Spire', 6 ft (1.8 m), quick-growing red flowers; and 'Slieve Donard', 7 ft (2.1 m), pink flowers in June, probably the hardiest of all.
General care: Escallonia is happy in any well-drained soil, including chalk. It likes a sunny site. Plant in spring 18 inches (45 cm) apart if it is being used for hedging, and 30 inches (75 cm) apart for screens. Routine pruning is not needed, and hedges should be lightly sheared once after flowering only, or you will get few flowers the following year.
Propagation: From heeled cuttings, taken at the end of summer, and planted in 50–50 peat and sand mixture.
Pests and diseases: Generally trouble-free.

EUONYMUS ZONES 3–9
The form of euonymus grown on walls is the evergreen *E. fortunei* (hardy to zone 5), also known as winter creeper. Like ivy, it climbs by the roots which

appear along its stems. Flowers and fruits are insignificant and the plants are grown for their foliage. The species plant, which has dark green leaves, grows to a height of 15 ft (5 m), but the named varieties are usually lower-growing. 'Colorata', which reaches the same height as the species, has unusual foliage that turns purple in winter and changes back to green in spring. 'Emerald 'n' Gold' and 'Emerald Gaiety' are native varieties, both with green leaves edged with yellow, and are low climbers. 'Variegatus', also known as 'Gracilis' and 'Argenteomarginata', has white bordered leaves and can attain 10 ft (3 m).

General care: Plant in spring in any ordinary soil. Will tolerate lime and any aspect. A poor soil often produces better leaf variations and colorings. No pruning is needed, apart from what is necessary to keep the plants going in the right direction. Like ivy, they sometimes need encouragement to start them climbing.

Propagation: Either soft or semi-hardwood cuttings pulled from the plant in late summer and pushed into a 50–50 peat/sand mixture.

Pests and diseases: Aphids can be troublesome and should be sprayed with malathion or a systemic insecticide of some sort.

FORSYTHIA　ZONES 4–9
Forsythia is an easy-to-grow, popular shrub whose brilliant yellow flowers appear in spring before the foliage. Some forsythia are especially suitable as wall shrubs, or for hedging or screening. *F. suspensa* (hardy to zone 5), the weeping forsythia, is suitable for a north or east wall, where it can reach 10 ft (3 m). It has a number of varieties: *F. s. fortunei* is the tallest; *F. s. sieboldii* has thin, very pendulous shoots; *F. s. atrocaulis* has pale, lemon-yellow flowers and stems that are purple when young. *F.* x *intermedia*, a hybrid of *F. suspensa*, is

most suitable for hedging or screening. It grows to 8 ft (2.4 m) or more, and carries masses of flowers. It is most commonly grown as 'Spectabilis' but 'Lynwood' has richer-hued flowers.

General care: Forsythia is very easy to grow and is happy with any soil and aspect. It is especially successful in town gardens where its bright yellow flowers brighten a dull corner. Plant any time in the winter. If using *F.* x *intermedia* as hedging, space the young plants 18 inches (45 cm) apart; if for screening, 30 inches (75 cm) apart. Prune *F. suspensa* and its varieties as soon as they have flowered, cutting back the laterals to leave a couple of buds on each. *F.* x *intermedia* grown as a hedge or screen should be clipped lightly only after flowering. Too-vigorous pruning of forsythia will reduce next year's flowers.

Propagation: Cuttings 12 inches (30 cm) long of the

current year's growth, taken in the autumn and pushed into the soil, will be ready for transplanting a year later.

Pests and diseases: Birds eat the flower buds, especially in country gardens. Spray with a bird repellent if you can find an effective one; if not, use a net. Otherwise trouble-free.

FUCHSIA　ZONES 5–10
For grace, beauty and eye-catching color the fuchsia is hard to beat. Excellent as pot plants, many are also surprisingly hardy and can be used as hardy perennials or shrubs. Hardiest of all is the Chilean species *T. magallanica gracilis* (hardy to zone 5), with slender red and purple blooms. Its variegated form 'Versicolor' has grayish leaves splashed pink and white. Best known are the many large-flowered varieties, some double, in shades of white, pink, purple, almost blue and red. Recommended for garden use are

'Alice Hoffman' (pink and white single), 'Brilliant' (red and purple double), 'Mme Cornelissen' (red and white single), 'Mrs Popple' (red and purple with cerise veins, single).

General care: Ordinary soil, ideally enriched with humus, and sun or partial shade give good results.

Propagation: Take cuttings in spring, summer or autumn, either soft tips or more mature growth.

Pests and diseases: Watch for capsid bugs and aphids.

GARRYA　ZONES 6–10
The evergreen garrya is grown for its long, pendulous catkins, which it bears from winter until spring. It is hardy in the South, but needs the protection of a wall in colder regions. *G. elliptica* (hardy to zone 8) is a native of the Pacific Coast. The green-gray male catkins, about 8 inches (20 cm) long, are the most spectacular, and male plants are the ones usually available at nurseries and garden centers. If a female plant is bought and planted nearby, it will produce brown-purple berries. 'James Roof' is an American variety with especially long catkins, about 12 inches (30 cm) in length. Garrya does not like damp sites. It will tolerate any aspect, but a south-facing wall produces the best catkins.

General care: Garrya hates being transplanted, so make sure the site is right before you plant, and use container-grown specimens. Garrya grows in any soil, but it must be well-drained. Give some protection to the young plant in the first winter or two, especially if they are hard, by means of straw or bracken, or some glass leaning up against the wall. Tidying up is the only pruning needed. Garrya does not like to be cut back too vigorously.

Propagation: Take semi-hardwood cuttings at the end of summer and root them in 3½ inch (9 cm) pots of 50–50 peat and sand mixture.

Forsythia x intermedia

Pests and diseases: Generally trouble-free, but any frost-damaged shoots should be pruned away in the spring.

GAULTHERIA ZONES 3–8

Gaultheria (wintergreen) is a handsome small evergreen in the heather family bearing urn-shaped flowers and berry-like fruit. *G. ovatifolia* (hardy to zone 5) is native to the Pacific Northwest. It makes a handsome ground cover for a shady location and grows to 8 inches (20 cm), featuring trailing branches covered with leathery, dark green leaves and small white flowers followed by red berries that attract birds. *G. procumbens* (hardy to zone 3) bears waxy, white, bell-shaped flowers in spring followed by scarlet berries. It grows to 6 inches (15 cm). Both the glossy leaves and berries have a wintergreen flavor. *G. shallon* (hardy to zone 5) grows to 18 inches (45 cm) with small pink and white flowers, followed by decorative purplish-black fruit. *G. miqueliana* is a Japanese native which grows to 8–10 inches (20–25 cm) with striking white fruit.

General care: Plant in humus-enriched, acid, well-drained soil in shade. The leaves can be damaged by overhead watering.

Propagation: Propagate by seed, layers and softwood cuttings.

Pests and diseases: Generally trouble-free.

GELSEMIUM ZONES 6–10

A handsome evergreen vine, *G. sempervirens*, or Carolina jassamine, is a moderate grower, reaching to about 20 ft (6 m) tall. The fragrant, tubular-shaped yellow flowers bloom from late winter to early spring although established plants may bloom as early as late November and continue through late spring. Gelsemium is prized for its glossy green foliage, which forms a delicate green spread of color for use as a screen, or to grow up the trunks of small trees. Gelsemium is the state flower of South Carolina. All parts of the plant are poisonous. 'Plena' displays a profuse show of double flowers from late winter to late spring.

General care: Plant in full sun in ordinary soil. Prune severely if the vine gets top-heavy. Gelsemium is moderately drought-resistant, but it is more attractive and long-lived with regular watering.

Propagation: Easily propagated from seed or cuttings.

Pests and diseases: Generally trouble-free.

HAMAMELIS ZONES 4–8

Witch hazels are very fragrant, hardy, ornamental bushes that bloom at the first sign of warmth – as early as February in the South. The well-known medicinal lotion is derived from an extract of the plant dissolved in alcohol. *H. x intermedia* (hardy to zone 5) is a hybrid of *H. mollis* and a Japanese witch hazel that has some lovely flowering varieties. 'Arnold Promise' has large golden yellow flowers that bloom in the early spring, and downy gray-green foliage which turns bright orange in the fall. It reaches a height of 20 ft (6 m) with a spreading habit. 'Diana' is a rare variety, prized for its unusual copper-red flowers and yellow and red fall color. Other selections include 'Jelena', large yellow flowers with red, orange and scarlet fall color; 'Magic Fire', coppery-orange flowers; and 'Ruby Glow', coppery-red flowers.

H. vernalis (hardy to zone 4) is among the earliest of all woody plants to add floral interest to the landscape. It grows 6–8 ft (1.8–2.4 m) tall and bears soft yellow flowers with red toward the base. 'Christmas Cheer' has excellent red fall foliage.

General care: The witch hazels grow well in sun or partial shade and prefer peaty, sandy soil and regular watering in dry weather.

Propagation: Take cuttings from soft wood or stratify seeds for 5 months at 40°F (5°C). If they fail to germinate, keep the seeds cool for an additional 3 months.

Pests and diseases: Generally trouble-free.

HARDENBERGIA
ZONES 9–10

Perfect as an airy vine for covering fences or retaining walls, hardenbergia climbs by means of twining stems. *H. comptoniana* has small lavender flowers that bloom from late winter through mid-spring. A native of Aus-

Garrya elliptica

tralia, it grows to 10 ft (3 m) tall. *H. violacea* is a denser, faster growing variety that bears flowers ranging from violet to pink and white. It needs less shelter from the wind and full sun than its more delicate cousin.

General care: Hardenbergia prefers sandy, well-drained soil in sun or light shade. Cut back after bloom to prevent tangling.

Propagation: Propagate from seed of green wood cuttings.

Pests and diseases: Hose off in dry weather to prevent thrips. Watch carefully for spider mites and nematodes.

HEBE ZONES 5–10

Although this native New Zealander is prized more for its form and foliage, some varieties add lovely flower displays. Hebe is very tolerant of salt air and sea winds and thrives in cool coastal areas. The evergreen shrubs are close to the veronica genus and feature neat leaves and spikes of lavender, mauve and white flowers. Heights vary from 6 inches (15 cm) to 5 ft (1.5 m).

H. buxifolia (hardy to zone 7) forms an attractive 3 ft (90 cm) hedge with white, 1 inch (1.5 cm) spikes. *H. x andersonii* (hardy to zone 7) is a compact hybrid that grows to 6 ft (1.8 m) tall. It features handsome clusters of white flowers edged with purple which bloom from late summer to early fall. 'Variegata' has creamy white flowers. *H. decumbens* (hardy to zone 5) is a rare, hardy succulent that grows 12–14 inches (30–35 cm) tall with leaves edged red and white and small white flowers.

H. speciosa (hardy to zone 10) is a showy plant that grows 3–5 ft (90 cm–1.5 m) tall with purple-crimson flowers in mid-summer. 'Imperialis' has red foliage with magenta flowers. 'Coed' is a compact, 3 ft (90 cm) shrub with small pinkish-purple clusters of flowers which bloom from late spring through summer. 'Desilor' has deep lavender blue flowers which bloom from spring until frost.

Hamamelis or witch hazel (see p. 95)

General care: Hebe will tolerate full sun in a coastal setting, but it needs shade in hot, inland areas. It requires well-drained, sandy soil.

Propagation: Propagated from seed or softwood cuttings taken in the autumn.

Pests and diseases: Generally trouble-free.

HEDERA ZONES 5–10

Hedera (ivy) is a vigorous, evergreen climber which clings to walls by means of aerial roots. Old ivy plants which have reached the top of their supports cease to produce the aerial roots, but change to an adult form of the plant with flowers and fruits. *H. helix* (hardy to zone 5) is the common English ivy, with plain dark green leaves. *H. colchica* (Persian ivy) (hardy to zone 5) and *H. canariensis* (Canary Island ivy) (hardy to zone 7) have larger, more handsome leaves, the former being the best and hardiest. Varieties of all these species are available, with variegated leaves, including mixtures of yellow, cream, silver and white. They are known by various different names, some confusing to the non-expert, and the safest and easiest way of getting the variations you want, since the plants are evergreen, is by looking before you buy.

General care: Ivies are very tolerant of soil and site conditions, but a sunny wall encourages them to produce the best color variations in their leaves. Plant out in the spring, pegging the stems flat to the soil with the growing tips pointing to the wall.

Propagation: From cuttings, taken in summer and put into pots with a 50–50 peat and sharp sand mixture, or by layering at any time. If you want climbing plants, take your material from juvenile shoots with aerial roots. If you propagate from adult growth, the plants will become ivy bushes.

Pests and diseases: Generally trouble-free.

HIBBERTIA ZONES 9–10

Native to Australia, the hibbertia genus includes both evergreen shrubs and vines. *H. cuneiformis* is a shrub that grows to 4 ft (1.2 m) tall with attractive, glossy, serrated foliage. The yellow flowers, which bloom from early spring to mid-summer, are wild rose-like in appearance and grow on new wood. Prune after blooming to control the shape. *H. scandens* is a fast-growing, shrubby vine with glossy dark green leaves. It grows from 8–10 ft (2.4–3 m) tall and is an attractive vine for a stone wall or fence. It can also be trained as a ground cover. From late spring to mid-fall, it bears yellow, rose-like flowers. Known as guinea gold, *H. scandens* is perfect for a moist, shady location protected from drying winds and hot sun.

General care: The shrub variety will take full sun or light shade in well-drained soil. Guinea gold prefers light shade and thrives when given ample moisture, so try to water it regularly during hot, dry weather.

Propagation: Propagate from softwood cuttings.

Pests and diseases: Spray *H. scandens* with water frequently in dry weather to ward off thrips.

HIBISCUS ZONES 5–10

Although mainly a tropical genus, there are two hardy hibiscuses, *H. sinosyriacus* and *H. syriacus* (hardy to zone 5). Both are similar deciduous shrubs of rounded habit to 6½ ft (2 m) in height. In late summer and autumn they bear single or semi-double blooms in a range of colors. *H. sinosyriacus* 'Ruby Glow' is white and cerise. *H. syriacus* 'Bluebird' is violet-blue, 'Pink Giant' has large rose-pink blooms, and 'William R. Smith' is pure white. *H. rosa-sinensis* (hardy to zone 9), the Chinese hibiscus, is popular in parts of Florida, California and Texas.

General care: Ordinary, even poorish soil is acceptable but the site must be sunny.

Propagation: Take cuttings with a heel in late summer.

Pests and diseases: Generally trouble-free.

HOYA ZONE 10

H. carnosa is grown outdoors in warm climates or in conservatories, but other wax plants are grown primarily as climbing plants indoors. *H. carnosa* is a climbing vine which grows to 15 ft (4.6 m) tall. Lustrous, leathery foliage and dense clusters of fragrant, creamy white, star-shaped flowers are the prime attraction. The flowers have pink centers and bloom throughout the summer. 'Variegata', although less vigorous, has interesting foliage, edged with white and pink. 'Exotica' has yellow and pink-marked leaves. *H. bella* is a shrubby plant, usually grown in hanging baskets. It grows to 3 ft (90 cm) tall and has white, purple-centered flowers.

General care: Plant in loose, rich, well-drained soil in partial shade. *H. carnosa* grows best with infrequent but deep waterings. Avoid pruning flowering wood as new buds form on old wood.

Propagation: Propagate from softwood cuttings.

Pests and diseases: Generally trouble-free.

HYDRANGEA ZONES 4–10

Hydrangea petiolaris (hardy to zone 4) is the climbing version of the common hydrangea. It is deciduous, hardy and vigorous, and can reach as high as 50 ft (15 m). It climbs like ivy, by aerial roots on its stems. In summer it produces masses of flat, white lacy heads of flowers. It likes a shady site – a north wall is ideal, if you have one in your garden.

General care: Plant in the spring in well-drained soil which has had plenty of

Hydrangea petiolaris

compost added to it. Secure the stems to the wall to give the growing tips a chance to cling firmly, and water during dry spells. Once they are established, they need very little attention beyond light pruning in the winter or spring to keep them tidy. A well-established plant is self-supporting.

Propagation: Cuttings of non-flowering shoots, about 3–4 inches (7.5–10 cm) long, taken in summer and put in a 50–50 mixture of peat and sand will root by autumn.

Layering in spring is even more certain.

Pests and diseases: Generally trouble-free.

HYPERICUM ZONES 2–9

The flowers of St John's wort have something of the appeal of a rose but are always in a shade of cheerful yellow. *H. calycinum* (hardy to zone 6) is widely used for ground cover and can be invasive. *H.* 'Hidcote' is a true, almost evergreen shrub eventually 3 ft (90 cm) or more tall and blooms over a long period. *H. prolificum* (hardy to zone 4) forms a slightly smaller, rounded bush with flowers having long, dense stamen brushes of great charm. *H. kalmianum* (hardy to zone 2) is a hardy native from Quebec to Maine.

General care: Ordinary fertile soil and sun or partial shade are basic requirements.

Propagation: Divide *H. calycinum* in autumn and spring. Take cuttings of the other varieties some time during late summer.

Pests and diseases: Generally trouble-free.

ILEX ZONES 3–10

Ilex is the botanical name for holly. The evergreen forms

Hoya carnosa

are very useful for hedging and screening, especially as they are tolerant of quite hard pruning and trimming. *I. x altaclarensis* (hardy to zone 6) is hardy and evergreen, and will in time attain a height of 30 ft (9 m). It is particularly useful in seaside areas, owing to its ability to stand up to salt-laden gales. *I. aquifolium* (hardy to zone 6) is the renowned English holly. It does not grow quite so tall – 25 ft (7.6 m) – but has the advantage of yielding the familiar red berries for Christmas decorations. Male and female flowers are borne on separate plants and the berries appear only on the female plants, but some male plants must be grown nearby to fertilize the females. There are also one or two hermaphrodite varieties of *I. aquifolium* that can produce berries without males. There are a large number of named varieties of both these species of holly, with variegated leaves and different colors of berries.

General care: Holly will tolerate any aspect and soil, although it prefers some moisture at its roots. Plant in spring about 2 ft (60 cm) apart for hedging and at least 4 ft (1.2 m) for screening. Make sure you plant some males to fertilize the females if you want berries. If you are planting on an exposed site, erect small screens of polythene sheeting or burlap to protect against the prevailing wind until the young plants are established. Trimming and pruning should be done in spring.

Propagation: Take small heeled cuttings in autumn from that year's growth and plant in a 50–50 mixture of peat and sand. Alternatively, layer some shoots in October or November. In either case, wait two years before putting the young plants into their permanent positions.

Pests and diseases: Birds take the berries, and are difficult to stop. Brown blotches on the leaves are caused by holly leaf miner. Spray with malathion. Later use a systemic insecticide, e.g. dimethoate.

Ilex aquifolium 'Aureomarginata'

IPOMOEA　ZONES 5–10
Ipomoea is the Latin name for morning glory, so called because its flowers open in the morning sunshine but fade by the end of the afternoon. It comes from South America, and is not hardy in many areas. 'Heavenly Blue' is the most popular variety – a cultivar of *I. tricolor* (hardy to zone 5), which produces purple and blue flowers throughout the summer. It grows to about 10 ft (3 m). The annual *I. purpurea* is similar but has smaller flowers and is slightly hardier. The species' flowers are purple, but there are other varieties, including 'Alba' with white flowers and 'Rosea' with pink.

General care: Ipomoea likes a warm, sunny, sheltered site, although *I. purpurea* will tolerate some shade. It can be grown up a south-facing wall or fence, or up sticks or poles in a sheltered corner. It likes a compost-rich soil, and needs plenty of water during the growing season. Plant out 12 inches (30 cm) apart in late spring, when all danger of frost has passed, but in a cold spring delay planting until the weather warms up.

Propagation: Germinate the seeds at a temperature of 65°F (18°C) in a soil-less compost after soaking for 24 hours. Transplant into 4 inch (10 cm) pots, and harden off carefully.

Pests and diseases: The young shoots may be attacked by aphids, leaf hoppers or thrips. Spray with malathion at once. Generally disease-free.

Ipomoea, morning glory

JASMINUM　ZONES 5–10
There are 200–300 species of jasmine but most are suitable only for a conservatory or greenhouse, or occasionally for warm and sheltered positions in the West and South. The two jasmines most widely grown in this country are *J. nudiflorum* (hardy to zone 5), producing yellow flowers at intervals throughout the winter, and *J. officinale* (hardy to zone 7), the common jasmine, producing fragrant white flowers from mid-summer to early autumn. They are both tolerant of shady sites, and need only ordinary, well-drained garden soil. *J. officinale* climbs by twisting its stems, is a vigorous grower, and will go up to 30 ft (9 m) if it can find the support. It is deciduous, but will retain its leaves in a mild winter or position. *J. nudiflorum*, which can reach a height of 15 ft (4.6 m), is not a climber

Kalmia latifolia

and must have its leading shoots fixed to the wall or fence. The laterals will curve downwards by themselves.
General care: *J. officinale* should not be pruned unless it is necessary to keep it in shape, and pruning too hard will cause it to miss a year's flowering. *J. nudiflorum*, however, needs a lot of pruning to encourage plenty of flowers in the winter. As soon as it has finished flowering, prune the laterals back to within a few inches of the leading shoots to encourage the new growth, which will bear the coming winter's flowers. Cut old wood back to the ground from time to time to encourage young basal shoots.
Propagation: Take semi-hardwood cuttings at the end of summer and root in a 50–50 peat and sand mixture, or layer one-year-old stems in spring.
Pests and diseases: Generally trouble-free.

JUNIPERUS
See under Conifers

KADSURA   Zones 7–10
An evergreen twining vine native to Japan and Korea, *K. japonica* has alternating, glossy, dark green leaves which measure 4 inches (10 cm) long and turn reddish during cold weather. It grows to 15–20 ft (4.6–6 m) and needs sturdy support. It bears small white flowers in mid-summer, but it is prized more for its bright scarlet, berry-like fruit which appears in fall and winter. It is an attractive cover for a pillar or fence. Kadsura will only bear fruit when both male and female plants are grown together. Without pollination, it is a handsome foliage vine.
General care: Kadsura will take full sun along the cool, coastal regions, but it prefers partial shade in hot inland areas. Ordinary, well-drained soil is adequate.
Propagation: Propagate by softwood cuttings.
Pests and diseases: Generally trouble-free.

KALMIA   Zones 4–9
Mountain laurel is a familiar, favorite evergreen shrub that provides beauty throughout the year. *K. latifolia* is native to the eastern part of the country and is the state flower of both Connecticut and Pennsylvania. A well-formed, hardy shrub, it grows to 6–8 ft (1.8–2.4 m) tall and spreads as far. It produces masses of pinkish-white flowers and deep green, leathery foliage. The flowers, which are borne in showy clusters, bloom from late spring to early summer. Many varieties have been cultivated, including 'Clementine Churchill' and 'Ostbo Red', red flowers; 'Bullseye', white flowers edged with purple; 'Olympic Fire', dark red buds that open to pink blooms; and 'Elf', a floriferous miniature that grows to 2½ ft (75 cm). Kalmia combines well in woodland settings with rhododendrons and azaleas.
General care: Kalmia prefers cool, moist, well-drained, acid soil in partial shade. Mulch in summer to conserve moisture.
Propagation: Propagate by semi-ripe cuttings or layering. Seed germination is difficult but benefits from 3 months of stratification at 40°F (5°C).
Pests and diseases: Kalmia is subject to infestation by rhododendron lacebug and borer. Weevil grubs may attack the roots. Spray plants affected with leaf spot with a fungicide.

KERRIA   Zones 4–9
Kerria is a 4 ft (1.2 m) tall, deciduous shrub with green stems, bearing bright yellow flowers in spring. It is most commonly seen in its double-flowered variety, 'Pleniflora', or bachelor's buttons, which grows much taller than the single-flowered species, reaching 6½ ft (2 m) or more. It is quite hardy, but in cold northern sites it is happier grown against a wall.
General care: Kerria is happy with any ordinary soil, and a sunny or half-shady site. Plant any time during the winter. Cut back the flowered shoots of 'Pleniflora' to promote the new growth on which the plant will flower next year. At the same time remove a few of the old shoots at ground level to promote new basal growth. The original species is best left to develop its normal spreading and shapely habit.
Propagation: The easiest way is to divide the clump of shoots any time during the winter. Alternatively, take cuttings from the lateral growths at the end of the summer and plant them in 50–50 sand and peat.
Pests and diseases: Generally trouble-free.

KOLKWITZIA   Zones 4–9
This very hardy deciduous shrub can attain 10 ft (3 m) tall on good soil. In early summer, every twig is wreathed in a cloud of exquisite pink foxglove-shaped flowers and it then fully merits its vernacular name, beauty bush.
General care: Ordinary soil that does not dry out is suitable and a site in partial shade or sun, the latter assuring a heavy crop of bloom.
Propagation: Take cuttings with a heel in late summer or sow seed in spring.
Pests and diseases: Generally trouble-free.

LAGERSTROEMIA
Zones 7–10
Crape myrtles include a large group of deciduous shrubs and trees. They flower freely in areas with hot summer weather. *L. indica* (hardy to zone 7) ranges in height from 6–30 ft (1.8–9 m). Shrub forms are slow-growing and spread as wide as they are tall. The privet-like foliage is

Ligustrum ovalifolium
'Aureum', *golden privet*

light green, tinged bronze in spring and turns yellow in the autumn. Its conical clusters of crinkled flowers come in shades of white, pink, red and lavender and appear on the current season's growth throughout the summer. There are many shrub varieties, including 'Gendora White', 'Shell Pink', 'Gray's Red', 'Majestic Orchid' and 'Watermelon Red'. Smaller choices are 'Petite Red Imp', 'Petite Orchid' and 'Petite Pinkie'. A new strain called 'Crape Myrtlettes' grows from seed to a maximum of 3–4 ft (90–120 cm). They range in color from dark red through rose, pink and lavender to white.
General care: Grow in full sun with good air circulation, in moist, well-drained, organically enriched soil. Prune heavily in spring.
Propagation: Propagate by seed or softwood cuttings.
Pests and diseases: Crape myrtle is susceptible to mildew. Space plants so that there is free air circulation and spray with fungicide. The new 'Indian Tribes' selections are mildew-resistant.

LATHYRUS ZONES 3–10
This is the group which includes sweet peas and everlasting peas. All are hardy. *L. odoratus* is the familiar garden sweet pea, an annual producing fragrant flowers all summer. There are many named varieties in a vast range of colors, but not all are fragrant. They climb by tendrils to a height of up to 9 ft (2.7 m), depending on variety and growing conditions. Among the perennial species are *L. latifolius* (hardy to zone 3), height to 8 ft (2.4 m), purplish flowers from June to September; and *L. rotundifolius* (hardy to zone 5), the Persian everlasting pea, height to 6½ ft (2 m), pink flowers from June to August. Lathyrus like full sun, and a rich, well-drained soil with some lime.
General care: Plant annuals 10 inches (25 cm) apart, and perennials 2 ft (60 cm). Grow up pea sticks, mesh, trellis, etc. Sweet peas need plenty of nourishment: dig a lot of compost into the site before planting, and give a weekly feed of a liquid fertilizer while they are in flower. Annuals and perennials should have the seed pods removed as they appear, to encourage repeat flowering.
Propagation: Nick the seed coats to encourage germination. Annuals sown in fall for the following year give the earliest flowers. Sow in seed boxes of compost, or directly into the site. Otherwise, sow in spring in boxes or into the soil. Perennials should be sown in boxes in a cold frame in spring, potted on, and planted out in fall.
Pests and diseases: Aphids and thrips should be controlled with malathion. Lathyrus are subject to a number of fungal diseases. Some cause the leaves to brown and develop white patches and the plant to wilt.

LIGUSTRUM ZONES 3–10
This is the familiar privet, common and uninspiring, but still useful for situations where nothing else will grow, such as in poor soil, or in atmospheric pollution. *L. ovalifolium* (hardy to zone 5), the California privet, is the most common, with glossy oval green leaves and

Lonicera periclymenum
'Belgica' *(see p. 102)*

short panicles of creamy flowers produced in mid-summer. It will grow to 15 ft (4.6 m), but is usually kept lower by clipping. Varieties include 'Aureum', the golden privet, and 'Variegatum', which has cream leaf margins. They do not grow so tall. *L. vulgare* (hardy to zone 4), the common privet, has narrower leaves than the California privet and will survive in colder climates. 'Densiflorum' is a good choice.

General care: Privet is very easy to grow, and will put up with poor soil and other adverse conditions. Plant 18 inches (45 cm) apart in spring and cut back all shoots by half. Each autumn reduce new shoots by half to encourage the shoots at the base and to prevent the plant becoming leggy. Privet will take any amount of clipping.

Propagation: By hardwood cuttings taken in the autumn and planted in the open ground.

Pests and diseases: Generally trouble-free.

LONICERA ZONES 2–10
The honeysuckle can be grown in every state in the union. All species climb by twining, but not all are fragrant. *L. sempervirens* (hardy to zone 3), the trumpet honeysuckle, is a twining vine that does well in a hostile climate. Native to the eastern states, it is the hardiest of the genus. It can achieve heights of 50 ft (15 m), and produces orange, scarlet or yellow flowers. *L. x brownii* (hardy to zone 5), scarlet trumpet honeysuckle, grows to about 12 ft (3.6 m) and flowers from summer well into the fall. It is evergreen in mild winter conditions, and is available in a number of striking named varieties, but it has no scent. *L. caprifolium* (hardy to zone 5), goat-leaved honeysuckle, grows to 20 ft (6 m). *L. japonica* (hardy to zone 4), Japanese honeysuckle, is the most vigorous species of all, climbing sometimes to 30 ft (9 m). It is evergreen, and produces very sweetly

fragrant flowers in summer and autumn but they are not as large as those of most of the other honeysuckles.

General care: Plant deciduous climbers in the winter, evergreens in spring. Honeysuckles need a good soil, with plenty of humus. They will grow in sun and shade. Prune lightly to remove old wood and tidy the plant up. Too-heavy pruning will reduce flowering.

Propagation: Raise from cuttings taken in the autumn or by layering shoots bent down in October, which can be severed and planted out a year later.

Pests and diseases: Aphids can stop the plant from flowering. Spray with malathion or a systemic insecticide. Dust powdery mildew with sulphur.

MAGNOLIA ZONES 4–10
If you have a south-facing house wall, there is no finer thing you can plant against it than a *M. grandiflora* (hardy to zone 7), a magificent wall shrub native to the southern states. Given time, it will grow to 25 ft (7.5 m) or more. An evergreen, it flowers from July to September, with – as its name suggests – the biggest blooms of any

Magnolia grandiflora

magnolia, creamy white, heavily fragrant, and up to 9 inches (22.5 cm) across the bowl. Unlike some magnolias it is not a lime-hater. Among the varieties available are two which, unlike many of the magnolias, produce flowers on young plants. They are 'Exmouth' and 'Goliath' which, as its name suggests, has bigger flowers than those of the species.

General care: Plant in spring and provide shelter from cold winds, especially when the plant is young. Put in stakes for its support until it is established on the wall, and give a spring mulch of compost or leaf mold. Only its main shoots need to be tied to the wall. In spring cut out basal shoots that are facing away from the wall.

Propagation: Layering is the most successful method. Peg the shoots down in the spring, but allow at least two years before separating from the parent.

Pests and diseases: Generally trouble-free, but frost-damaged shoots may become diseased. Guard against this by cutting back the damaged shoots in spring.

MAHONIA ZONES 5–10
Glossy, large, evergreen leaves which are handsome

in their own right and showy yellow flowers from autumn to spring are the hallmark of this genus. Best known is the Oregon grape (*M. aquifolium*) (hardy to zone 5), a suckering species to 4 ft (1.2 m) or more tall with leaves that often take on red or bronze tones in winter. Its rich yellow flowers borne in early spring are followed by blue-black edible berries. Finest of the hardy larger sorts is the hybrid 'Charity', an erect shrub to 6½ ft (2m) or more with leaves 1½–2 ft (45–60 cm) in length, and long trusses of yellow flowers in autumn and early winter. Less statuesque but still very good garden value is *M. japonica* (hardy to zone 7), one of 'Charity's' parents. Slower growing but eventually to the same height, it has somewhat shorter leaves and paler flowers which open successively from autumn to the following spring.

General care: Mahonias will grow in any well-drained, but not dry, fertile soil. Enrich sandy and chalky soils with plenty of organic matter, e.g. peat, garden compost or leaf mold. Pruning should be restricted to the removal of dead or untidy stems.

Propagation: True species are easy from seed sown when ripe in a cold frame but

seedling growth is fairly slow. *M. aquifolium* is best divided in spring or early autumn; suckers can be removed from 'Charity' and *japonica* at the same time.
Pests and diseases: Generally trouble-free.

MANDEVILLA ZONE 10

Although it can only be grown outside in the warmest regions of zone 10, mandevilla is dramatically beautiful as a greenhouse vine that can shuttle outside during the summer. It climbs 20–30 ft (6–9 m) outside, much less as a container plant. It has glossy, deeply veined, dark green foliage and produces clusters of clear pink, funnel-shaped flowers from spring through early fall. It should be supported by a trellis or stake and pinched back to encourage bushiness. 'Alice du Pont' is a popular selection.
General care: Plant in rich soil and water freely during growth spurts. Mandevilla can tolerate full sun near the coast but prefers light shade inland.
Propagation: Propagate by softwood cuttings.
Pests and diseases: Watch for spider mites.

MINA ZONE 10

Spanish flag is a perennial vine only in the warmest areas of the country, but it is frequently grown as a summer annual. A native of Mexico, it is a relative of the morning glory and will grow to 20 ft (6 m) in one season. It features interesting, three-lobed leaves and garlands of flowers which open a fiery scarlet and change to yellow and white. Mina is a good choice to shade a patio.
General care: Ordinary, well-drained soil in full sun is adequate.
Propagation: Propagate from seeds soaked in warm water in spring.
Pests and diseases: Generally trouble-free.

NANDINA ZONES 7–9

The popular heavenly bam-

Mahonia 'Charity'

boo, *N. domestica* is not a true bamboo, but its airy foliage and cane-like stems are suggestive of that plant. Native to central China and Japan, nandina grows to 6–8 ft (1.8–2.4 m) tall but it can be pruned to maintain a more compact shape. The delicate foliage is composed of many 1–2 inch (2.5–5 cm) leaflets and changes from pinkish-bronze to delicate green to red and purple in autumn. It produces 12 inch (30 cm) long clusters of tiny white to pink flowers in mid-summer and small red berries in the fall. Useful as a screen, accent plant or hedge where

planting space is narrow, nandina is graceful and colorful throughout the year.

Varieties include 'Alba', white fruit; 'Nana Purpurea', 2 ft (60 cm) high with purple-green foliage; 'Moyers Red', brilliant red fall color; 'Pygmaea', 8–10 inches (20–25 cm) tall and dense, and 'Umpqua Chief', vigorous with brilliant red fall color.
General care: Nandina performs best in rich soil with an ample supply of water. It will grow in light shade or sun, but it colors more brilliantly in full sun.
Propagation: Sow ripe seed in warm, humid conditions. Germination takes several months.
Pests and diseases: Generally trouble-free.

NERIUM ZONES 9–10

N. oleander is a popular flowering shrub in the warm climates of the southern half of the United States. It thrives in the desert and hot inland regions as well as in coastal areas and zones with near-tropical humidity. Heights vary from 8–20 ft (2.4–6 m). It features leathery, dark green, glossy leaves that grow to 12 inches (30 cm) long. It usually has many

Mandevilla

branches growing from ground level but they can be cut back to create a single-trunked shrub. The flowers, which bloom from late spring through early fall, come in shades of red, coral, pink and white. Some varieties have fragrant blooms, and some are double. All parts of the plant are poisonous.

The most vigorous selection is 'Sister Agnes', which grows to 20 ft (6 m) and bears single white flowers. 'Petite Pink' grows 3–4 ft (90–120 cm) tall, and 'Mrs Roeding' has double pink flowers and grows 6 ft (1.8 m) tall.
General care: Oleander will thrive in any type of soil and is very drought-resistant. Flowering is more profuse in full sun and high temperatures.
Propagation: Propagate from softwood cuttings.
Pests and diseases: Spray with malathion to control scale insects.

PANDOREA ZONES 9–10
A vigorous evergreen vine P. jasminoides is a native of Australia and grows from 20–30 ft (6–9 m) tall. Its glossy, dark green foliage is graced with tubular, pink flowers from mid-summer through early fall. 'Alba' has pure white flowers. P. pandorana is more vigorous and its glossy green foliage looks attractive throughout the year. Heavy clusters of yellow and pinkish-white flowers, marked with purple and brown throats, bloom from early spring through summer.
General care: P. jasminoides will tolerate full sun along the coast, but it needs some shade inland. Water frequently during dry weather. Ordinary, well-drained soil is adequate for both varieties. P. pandorana will grow in sun or shade and is drought-resistant once established. Prune heavily after spring bloom.
Propagation: Propagate by seed or, alternatively, by softwood cuttings.
Pests and diseases: Generally trouble-free.

PARTHENOCISSUS
ZONES 3–10
This group of vigorous climbers includes the Virginia creeper, and that name is often applied to the whole group. They are deciduous, climb by tendrils, which often have sticky pads on the ends, and are grown for their ornamental leaves, which change color spectacularly in the autumn. P. quinquefolia (hardy to zone 3) is the true Virginia creeper, which has been cultivated for centuries. Since it can climb to 70 ft (21 m) it can be difficult to control, and is best left to clamber up tall trees. P. tricuspidata (hardy to zone 4) is often incorrectly called 'Virginia creeper' – in fact, it comes from Japan. It is the Boston ivy, commonly planted on walls, where it can go to 50 ft (15 m) or more, and gives a marvelous display of crimson foliage in the autumn. P. henryana (hardy to zone 8), Chinese Virginia creeper, grows to 25 ft (7.6 m) and has distinctive rich green, silvery-veined leaves in summer which also turn red in autumn. It needs a sheltered site.
General care: Dig a large planting hole, about 18 inches (45 cm) square, and fill with a humus-rich soil. Use container-grown plants, as parthenocissus does not like any root disturbance. Support it with sticks until it climbs by itself. Once established, it needs little attention.
Propagation: Take hardwood cuttings in late autumn and push them into the ground to root, or layer long shoots. Semi-hardwood cuttings can be taken in late summer and rooted in pots.
Pests and diseases: Generally trouble-free.

PASSIFLORA ZONES 7–10
There are hundreds of species of passion flowers, but only two are hardy enough to be grown outdoors in many parts of this country and even they must have sheltered sites. Frost may cut the tops to the ground, but the plant usually grows back in the spring. P. caerulea (hardy to zone 7), the blue or common passion flower, is the one most often planted in this country. It climbs to about 25 ft (7.6 m). The species' flowers are blue, purple and white, but there is a variety, 'Constance Elliott', which is entirely white; both open from mid- to late summer into autumn. Egg-shaped, pale orange-yellow fruits may follow.
General care: Find a sheltered site, preferably with full sun. Plant in ordinary garden soil when danger of frost has passed, and while the plant is young give it winter protection with bracken, straw, glass or plastic sheeting. Help the young plant to climb by tying it to a trellis or mesh until it has started to pull itself up. Confine pruning to tidying up and removing any weak growth that has sprouted.
Propagation: Take semi-ripe cuttings in summer and root them in pots of 50–50 peat and sand mixture, or grow from seed, germinating at a temperature of 70°F (21°C) and planting out in spring after hardening off.
Pests and diseases: Generally trouble-free.

PHILADELPHUS ZONES 3–9
Mock orange has long been a garden favorite with its profusion of white, sweetly scented flowers in summer. There are a few species and several good hybrids readily available from garden centers and nurserymen. All are vigorous, deciduous shrubs, the smaller varieties being best value in the garden. Recommended are: 'Belle Etoile' varieties of compact habit to 6½ ft (2 m) tall, bearing white flowers with a purple eye. P. coronarius 'Aureus' (hardy to zone 5), is a spectacular yellow-leaved rounded shrub to 8½ ft (2.5 m) in height with heavily scented creamy-white flowers. It makes a particularly fine accent plant in the garden. A special hybrid devel-

Passiflora caerulea or common passion flower

Philadelphus hybrid

oped for northern climates, 'Minnesota Snowflake' (hardy to zone 3) grows to 6 ft (1.8 m) and is able to withstand severe winters.

General care: Mock orange grows well in all but really wet soils, though light sandy or chalky ones should be enriched with organic matter. To build up shapely, free-blooming shrubs, cut back flowered stems by two-thirds once the last blossom has faded.

Propagation: Take semi-hardwood cuttings in late summer in a propagating case. Take hardwood cuttings in late autumn when they can be inserted in the open ground.

Pests and diseases: Generally trouble-free.

PHOTINIA   ZONES 4–10
The evergreen members of this genus of shrubs and small trees make splendid specimen plants and hedges with a difference. One of the best is *P. x fraseri* 'Red Robin' (hardy to zone 7), which grows 6–8 ft (1.8–2.4 m) in height. The glossy leaves start bright red and are produced in flushes in spring

and summer. There is also a bonus of clustered small white flowers in summer.

General care: Most soils which do not dry out are suitable, including those containing lime.

Propagation: Take cuttings in late summer, ideally with bottom heat.

Pests and diseases: Generally trouble-free.

PLUMBAGO   ZONES 9–10
P. auriculata or Cape plumbago, a South African native, is a large, sprawling evergreen shrub, which can grow 10 ft (3 m) tall and wide if not kept pruned. It is useful as a background shrub or as a camouflage for a wall or fence. When supported, it will climb to 12 ft (3.6 m) tall. The foliage is light to medium green, and the phlox-like clusters of flowers bloom over a long season, from spring to early winter (and most of the year in frost-free zones). Colors range from white to light blue.

General care: Plumbago is tolerant of most soil conditions provided the drainage is adequate. Plant in sun or light shade. Frost will blacken the foliage, but it recovers well.

Propagation: Propagate from softwood cuttings in spring so that the plants are well established before winter.

Pests and diseases: Generally trouble-free.

Plumbago auriculata

with grayish leaves and pure white flowers; 'Goldfinger' has glowing, deep yellow blooms; while 'Katherine Dykes' is primrose yellow. Pink fading to almost white typifies the new 'Princess'. 'Red Ace' is red but fades badly in hot sun. 'Tangerine' has a low spreading habit and reddish-copper flowers which contrast nicely with the cream ones of 'Tilford Cream', an equally low-growing but more compact sort.

General care: Shrubby cinquefoils grow in practically all soils, even those that are seasonally wet. Pruning is not required except to keep them shapely. Untidy specimens can be cut down to a few inches above soil level and will soon regenerate.

Propagation: Easy by seed sown in spring, but plants so raised from varieties will not come true to type. Semi-hardwood cuttings taken in late summer or autumn and placed in a cold frame will root readily.

Pests and diseases: Generally trouble-free.

Potentilla fruticosa
'Tangerine'

Polygonium baldschuanicum,
or Russian vine

POLYGONUM Zones 3–10
P. baldschuanicum, or Russian vine (hardy to zone 4), is about the fastest-growing climber that is cultivated. It can put on 16 ft (4.9 m) per season and cover a small house in a couple of summers. The problem is keeping it in check. It is a deciduous, twining climber, producing masses of long panicles of pale pink or white flowers all summer. *P. aubertii* (hardy to zone 4), which has similar, white flowers, is very like *P. baldschuanicum,* and is often sold under that name – in fact, most of the Russian vines growing here are *P. aubertii.* It will tolerate any soil, even lime, and any site.

General care: Plant in early spring. Some care of the young plant is needed, including stakes to start it climbing, and pinching out the leading shoots to encourage side growth, but once it is established all the Russian vine needs is controlling.

Propagation: Take semi-hard wood cuttings in late summer and root them in a 50–50 mixture of sand and peat.

Pests and diseases: Generally trouble-free.

POTENTILLA Zones 2–9
The shrubby cinquefoil, *P. fruticosa* (hardy to zone 2) is a twiggy, bushy plant of variable habit but seldom much above 3–4 ft (90–120 cm) in height. It has small, neat, fingered leaves and a long succession of five-petalled flowers like small dog roses but in shades of yellow, pink, red and white. Totally hardy and requiring virtually no maintenance, it is a perfect shrub for the casual or uncommitted gardener. Among the best are: 'Abbotswood',

Pyracantha coccinea

PRUNUS   ZONES 2–9

Prunus is a genus of plants that includes apricots, peaches and cherries. *P. triloba* (hardy to zone 5) does best on a wall, preferably fan-trained, as it is doubtfully hardy in some regions, and in any case produces far more flowers on a sunny wall. The species carries single flowers and is seldom seen. The Chinese variety 'Multiplex' is the variety commonly available. It grows 12 ft (3.6 m) or more on a sunny wall and carries masses of large double pink flowers from early spring. *P. cerasifera*, the cherry plum (hardy to zone 3) is an excellent screen tree, growing to 20 ft (6 m) or more. It carries white flowers in late winter and early spring and eventually small cherry-plums. The varieties, which can be mixed in with the species in the screen, have different colors: 'Atropurpurea' has purple adult leaves, and 'Nigra' purple leaves and pink flowers. The cherry plum is deciduous, but another prunus, *P. laurocerasus*, the cherry laurel (hardy to zone 6) is evergreen, and therefore more commonly planted for screening. It is fast-growing to 10 ft (3 m) or more and produces candles of white flowers in spring and fruit similar to cherries which are red at first and turn black as they ripen. Among a number of named varieties is *P. l.* 'Otto Luyken', a low-growing plant which makes excellent ground cover.

General care: Prunus are happy in any ordinary, well-drained garden soil, and most prefer a trace of lime in it. The evergreen species should be planted in spring, the remainder in autumn and winter. For hedging, plant 2 ft (60 cm) apart, and for screening 5 ft (1.5 m) apart, cutting back the tips of the shoots if planting for hedging. Prune back hard as soon as the flowers are finished on *P. triloba* as well as the screening prunus to encourage young flowering shoots for next year, and use pruning shears rather than hedge trimmers to trim the screening prunus if they need it.

Propagation: All are easiest from cuttings taken in August and rooted in a 50–50 sand and peat mixture.

Pests and diseases: Birds eat the flower buds. Try net, or cotton. Blackfly should be sprayed with malathion. Peach leaf curl may be controlled by spraying with Bordeaux mixture in the winter.

PYRACANTHA ZONES 5–10

Pyracantha, or firethorn, is a popular wall shrub grown chiefly for its fire-colored berries, although its flowers are not unattractive. It is evergreen and hardy so does not need the protection of a wall, but it does seem to go naturally there, being erect growing and easy to train, with dense vegetation which can be used to cloak an unsightly support. *P. coccinea* (hardy to zone 6) is the most popular species. It grows to a height and spread of 12 ft (3.6 m), and provides a profusion of white flowers in summer, followed by bright red berries in the autumn. 'Lalandei' (hardy to zone 5) is the most popular variety, and with its erect habit of growth it is more suitable for a wall or fence. It can reach 20 ft (6 m), has larger leaves than those of the species, and its berries are more orange. *P. crenulata* 'Rogersiana' (hardy to zone 6), generally known as *P. rogersiana*, grows to 12 ft (3 m). Its larger white flower clusters are borne in summer and are followed by orange berries. Among its varieties is 'Flava', which has yellow berries. *P.* 'Mohave' (hardy to zone 5) is an American hybrid with orange-red berries from late summer onwards. Another very popular hybrid is the Dutch *P.* 'Orange Glow' (hardy to zone 6), which makes an excellent specimen plant, very vigorous and free-fruiting. Both of these are said to have some resistance to scab.

General care: Pyracantha are happy with almost any soil, including lime, but not those which are waterlogged. Both sunny and partially shaded sites are acceptable. Plant container-grown specimens in spring, watering in well and making sure that they do not dry out. Tie to wires or trellis as they grow up the wall. Trim back the current year's growth in June.

Propagation: Pyracantha will grow readily from seeds harvested in the autumn, but if the seed is from hybrids, the resulting plants are unlikely to grow true. It is safer to take semi-ripe cuttings of the current year's growth in the summer and plant in a 50–50 sand and peat mixture.

Pests and diseases: Birds take the berries, especially of *P. coccinea.* Try cotton strung between the shoots. Scale insects should be sprayed with diazinon when seen. Pyracantha scab causes a brown coating on leaves and fruit. Spray every two weeks with captan. Fireblight, a bacterial disease which causes leaves to turn dark brown and wither, is on the increase. Cut away the shoots well beyond the infection and burn, and disinfect the pruning shears.

PYROSTEGIA   Zone 10

Pyrostegia or flame vine is a natural climbing shrub with self-clinging tendrils and loose clusters of brilliant orange, trumpet-shaped flowers which bloom during fall and early winter. Suitable for only the warmest climates, *P. venusta* can curtain walls that face the sun. In the low desert and other warm locations it grows quickly to 20 ft (6 m).

General care: Any ordinary soil will do, but flame vine needs heat and full sun to thrive.

Propagation: Propagate from cuttings or layering.

Pests and diseases: Generally trouble-free.

RAPHIOLEPIS   Zones 7–10

R. indica, Indian hawthorn (hardy to zone 8), is an excellent, adaptable choice for mass plantings and hedges. The evergreen foliage is glossy and forms a sturdy, dense, compact shrub which grows 5–6 ft (1.5–1.8 m) high. It blooms from late fall or mid-winter to early spring with loose clusters of flowers ranging from white, pink, and rose to red. The flowers are followed by blue-black, berry-like fruit. The plant size and flower color differ according to variety. Selections include 'Ballerina', rosy pink, 2 ft (60 cm) tall; 'Clara', white flowers, 4–5 ft (1.2–1.5 m) tall; and 'Coates Crimson', coral-pink, 4–6 ft (1.2–1.8 m) tall.

R. umbellata (hardy to zone 7) are more vigorous and grow to 10 ft (3 m) tall. They have round, dark, leathery leaves and produce white flowers.

General care: Ordinary soil is adequate. The flowers are more numerous in full sun, but Indian hawthorn will grow happily in light shade. It is somewhat drought-resistant, but does not object to frequent waterings.

Propagation: Propagate from softwood cuttings.

Pests and diseases: Watch for aphids and spray with fungicide to avoid fungus spotting on the foliage.

RHODODENDRON
Zones 2–8

Queen of the evergreen flowering shrubs, the rhododendron has much to offer those who are lucky enough to garden on acid soil. Apart from prodigious displays of blossom in practically all colors of the rainbow, some sorts also have foliage which is attractive at all times. In stature they range from mats and buns under 1 ft (30 cm) in height to large shrubs up to 10 ft (3 m) plus, some trees eventually to three times this. About 800 true species are known, and literally thousands of hybrid varieties

Pyrostegia venusta

Rhododendron, hardy hybrid

have been raised, so it is impossible to do justice to them here. All the species and varieties stocked by nurserymen at garden centers are good and worth trying in the garden.

Depending on the height required, look out for the following. Under 1 ft (30 cm): *campylogynum* 'Crushed Strawberry' (hardy to zone 5) (pink), *hanceanum* 'Nanum' (hardy to zone 4) (yellow), *keleticum* (hardy to zone 6) (purple-crimson), *pemakoense* (hardy to zone 6) (lilac pink).

1–4 ft (30–120 cm): 'Blue Tit' (hardy to zone 5) (lavender blue), 'Cilipinense' (hardy to zone 4) (white flushed pink), 'Elizabeth' (hardy to zone 3) (scarlet), 'Bow Bells' (hardy to zone 4) (shell-pink, darker buds), 'Chikor' (hardy to zone 5) (yellow).

Under 6½ ft (2 m): 'Don-caster' (scarlet), 'Pink Pearl' (hardy to zone 3) (pink), 'Blue Peter' (hardy to zone 2) (lavender blue), 'Cunningham's White' (hardy to zone 2) (white), 'Yellow Hammer' (yellow; can eventually exceed 6 ft [1.8 m]).

General care: Plant in spring, in lime-free soil which has got some humus or compost in it, adding peat or manure if necessary. Rhododendrons are surface-rooting, and must have some moisture-retaining material in the topsoil. Set the plants 3 ft (90 cm) apart if for a hedge and 5 ft (1.5 m) apart or more for a screen, depending on the thickness of the screen required. Water on planting, and keep watering if the first spring is dry. They need no pruning, apart from any trimming necessary to keep them in shape, which should be done in the winter. Dead-head flowers to stop the seeds forming, unless they are needed for propagation.

Propagation: Seeds sown in spring in pots or pans of soil-less compost. Alternatively, to obtain a flowering-sized plant quickly, layer some long shoots in the summer.

Pests and diseases: Rhododendron bud blast turns the flower buds brown or black in the autumn. Control is by killing the carrier, the rhododendron leaf hopper, by spraying with fenitrothion in late summer. Leaf-yellowing caused by chlorosis means that your soil is too alkaline to grow rhododendrons. You can try making it more acid by adding quantities of peat and watering with ammonium sulfate.

RIBES ZONES 2–10

Flowering currants have lost some of their popularity over the years mainly because most of them are forbidden in areas where the white pine grows – the currants act as hosts for white pine blister rust. However, the following are worth mentioning for their spring color. Best known is *R. sanguineum* (hardy to zone 5), an erect shrub to 8½ ft (2.5 m), with maple-like leaves which are barely showing when the pendant spikes of deep pink flowers appear in spring. The varieties 'King Edward VII' and 'Pulborough Scarlet' have more intensely hued blossom; 'Tydermann's White' is pure white, while 'Brocklebankii' has golden foliage. *R. aureum* and *odoratum* (hardy to zone 4) are much alike and are confused in gardens. Known as yellow or buffalo currant, they are erect in habit to about 7 ft (2.2 m) tall with loose spikes of fragrant, tubular yellow flowers with the young leaves in spring.

General care: Ribes grow in all but the wettest soils in sun or partial shade. Light sandy or chalky soils should be enriched with garden compost or peat, etc. Pruning is a matter of expediency. If the shrubs are to be kept under 6½ ft (2 m) cut back flowered stems by two-thirds annually as soon as the last blossoms fade. Alternatively, remove only untidy stems or branches.

Propagation: By semi-hardwood cuttings in late summer in a frame, or hardwood cuttings in late autumn in the open ground.

Pests and diseases: Generally trouble-free.

Ribes sanguineum

ROSES

It is impossible to imagine a flower garden, however small or large, without at least a few roses. There are literally hundreds of roses to choose from, but as their growth and flowering habits vary greatly the first thing to do is to decide on the type you want to grow. Choose varieties that are suitable for your climate – local nurseries are the best source for plants that will thrive in your region's conditions. Most roses will survive cold winters if they are given proper protection.

The majority of roses sold in nurseries are hybrid teas, which produce large individual blooms on single stems; grandifloras, which have hybrid tea-type flowers borne singly or in long-stemmed clusters; floribun-das, whose characteristic of many blooms produced in clusters has made them very popular for mass color displays; and climbing roses. Specialty garden centers and mail-order nurseries offer old roses and modern shrub roses. Hybrid teas range from 2–6 ft (60 cm–1.8 m); grandifloras are more vigorous, reaching 8–10 ft (2.4–3 m) tall; and floribundas range from 2–4 ft (20–120 cm).

For covering arborways, walls or fences, roses with vigorous growth habits are needed. These are classified as climbing or rambling roses, the older varieties of which will mostly flower only once during the summer. Some of the more recent additions, however, provide repeat displays of blooms throughout or later on in the season. Some of the modern shrub roses, too, have the same repeat-flowering qualities and merit consideration, not only as individual plants

Whisky Mac

*To prune roses, use sharp secateurs to make a clean cut on a slant (**below**). Climbers and ramblers should be pruned to a framework of healthy wood (**right**) and bush roses cut right down in late autumn (**bottom**).*

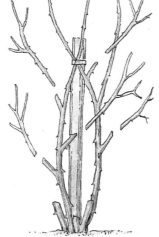

in a bed or border but also for planting as flowering hedges throughout the garden.

The first golden rule for success with roses will always be the preparation of the soil before planting. A heavy clay soil, which is the best type for growing roses, often lacks good drainage; digging in home-made, well-rotted compost or a mixture of peat and sand will improve it. With lighter soils, it is advisable to step up the water-holding capacity by digging in well-rotted compost or manure. If neither of these is available, use peat on its own.

General care: Feed them with a rose fertilizer, first in early spring, followed by a repeat application in early summer. Try to get manure to use as a top dressing early in spring.

Pruning: The pruning of roses is a controversial subject. Early spring is the recommended time, but it can be carried out from late autumn onwards during mild spells. Generally, the best pruning time for most roses is at the end of the dormant season when the buds begin to swell. Remove all very thin growth from bush roses and cut back all the previous season's growth to one-third on hybrid teas and grandifloras. Cut floribundas back only to two-thirds or one-half to maintain a bushier plant. Make sure that your pruning shears are really sharp so that you achieve a clean sloping cut without crushing the wood. Bush roses should also be pruned just after their first flowering to encourage a second flush of blooms.

Climbers and ramblers should be pruned back to a framework of healthy wood; with shrub roses it is wise to cut out all the thin, straggly growth and cut back the strong wood by one-third.

Propagation: Nurserymen propagate the bush roses by bud grafting (budding) on to wild species (usually dog rose) in summer. Roses can also be raised from cuttings. Take these in early fall, selecting strong shoots of the current season's growth and cutting a 7–8 inch (18–20 cm) length of stem cleanly below a node at the base and just above a node at the top. Carefully remove all the leaves without damaging the buds, then dip the bottom end of the cutting in a rooting powder or solution. These cuttings are now ready for planting in a prepared position outside. When doing so, make sure that only one-third of the cutting is above ground, otherwise too much drying out will occur. Rooted cuttings will be ready for transplanting to their permanent positions in late fall the following year.

Pests and diseases: Black spot, rust and powdery mildew are the chief dangers. Aphids are always a problem on shoot tips and buds.

HYBRID TEA ROSES

'Brandy' has burnt-orange buds that open to rich apricot blooms that emit a classic tea fragrance.

'Christian Dior' has magnificent, non-fading flowers of bright crimson on erect stems.

'Double Delight' is a showy bicolor that opens creamy white splashed with red and has a spicy fragrance.

'Eclipse' features long, slender buds with rich, golden flowers growing on upright, bushy plants.

'Friendship' has huge 6 inch (15 cm) flowers that range from deep coral to light pink and are abundantly produced.

'Mr Lincoln' has deep maroon buds that open to

Charisma

LEFT: *The free-flowering Iceberg*

rich red, double flowers on long stems.

'Oregold' has double 5 inch (12.5 cm) lemon-yellow flowers borne on long, erect stems that are perfect for cutting and arranging.

'Pascali' has compact blossoms of clear white with a beautifully sculpted form, borne on glossy, dark-green foliage.

'Peace' has large creamy-yellow edged and shaded pink blooms which are never produced very freely, but it makes a spectacular show.

'Red Queen' has large, double, fragrant flowers of rich red that grow on vigorous upright plants.

'Sterling Silver' has unusually colored silvery-lavender flowers, that are produced abundantly on firm, upright stems.

'Tiffany' has beautifully formed, soft pink flowers with graceful, light-green foliage.

'Tropicana' is a vigorous, disease-resistant plant that features orange-red flowers and a delightful scent.

'Whisky Mac' has ruffle-edged blooms of bright apricot-peach, which are exceptionally long-lasting, against deep-green foliage.

FLORIBUNDAS

'Allgold' is a free-flowering, rich-colored yellow rose bush that is amazingly disease-resistant.

'Betty Prior' has elegant pink flowers that grace the bush from mid-spring through the autumn.

'Charisma' produces masses of vermilion and yellow flowers that mature to bright red. The plant is vigorous and mound-shaped, suitable for planting in a border or grown as a specimen.

Sundowner

'China Doll' is a lavish producer of bright pink double blooms that work particularly well in the garden as a low hedge.

'Europeana' is the brightest of the bright reds. It is heat-resistant, long-lasting and vigorous.

'Fashion' has beautiful luminous coral flowers edged with gold that open from clear red buds.

'French Lace' has classically formed creamy white blooms with ruffly edges.

'Frensham' has abundant, satiny, bright red flowers borne on rich green foliage.

'Iceberg' is probably the finest white floribunda of all time and has been popular for almost 30 years.

GRANDIFLORAS

'Ambassador' yields glowing orange-red, classically shaped flowers on strong, upright stems.

'Gold Medal' has deep gold flowers with splashes of orange-red. These plants are very hardy and don't fade in the summer heat.

'Queen Elizabeth' has great vigor and height and plenty of soft clear-pink flowers.

'Sonia' is a very popular florist's rose. Its classic buds open to delicate pink with coral and yellow undertones.

'Sundowner' is a vigorous, tall plant that boasts flowers that open orange, edged with red and purple, and change to clear salmon.

'White Lightnin'' has clear white, ruffly flowers with a characteristic lemony fragrance. The flowers often take on a faint pink blush.

SHRUB ROSES

These are a real asset to any garden but generally need more space than either hybrid teas, floribundas or grandifloras. In a smaller garden a single specimen is acceptable, but if the garden is on the large side these shrub roses look well planted in groups of three.

'Bonica' is a ruggedly hardy, perpetual blooming plant with glossy green foliage and rich pink double, 3 inch (7.5 cm) flowers. It will grow to 4 ft (1.2 m).

'Carefree Beauty' is wonderfully disease-resistant and boasts double pink, hybrid-tea quality flowers and bright orange fruit for winter color.

'Nymphenburg' features attractive bronze-tinted foliage. Its apricot buds mature to rich salmon pink. It will grow to 7 ft (2.1 m) tall with an equal spread.

'Sir Thomas Lipton' grows 4–5 ft (1.2–1.5 m) tall and produces large, double white blooms on vigorous, trouble-free shrubs.

'The Fairy' bears graceful clusters of pink flowers from early spring to the first frost. It is a good perpetual bloomer for use as a low hedge.

'Therese Bugnet' is an exceptionally hardy and fragrant plant which produces large clusters of red buds that open to a delicate lilac-pink. It blooms on old wood and should be pruned only to limit growth.

CLIMBING ROSES

Any long-stemmed rose can be grown as a climber. Some species climb naturally and go higher than any cultivated roses. Being disease-resistant, they do better than modern roses in the close conditions near to walls and fences. The modern climbers offer repeat flowering; they need little pruning and are more-or-less disease-resistant.

'Blaze' has brilliant scarlet clusters of flowers in great quantities.

Bonica

A discreet, yet well-constructed arch support shows the natural attributes of climbing roses to good advantage.

'Climbing Peace' stars the world-famous huge blossoms of 'Peace', colored yellow tinged with pink.

MINIATURE ROSES

While some of the miniature roses are recommended for open ground planting, practically all exceed their catalog heights even during their first year outdoors. However, there is undoubtedly a place for them in containers or pots where root restriction has a considerable effect on the size of the plant.

'Alfie' is a vigorous variety that grows from 15–18 inches (38–45 cm) tall. The flowers are double, rich rose-pink tinged with lavender.

'Holy Toledo' has beautifully formed, bright orange flowers with a hint of yellow. It grows from 2–2½ ft (60–75 cm) tall.

'Hombre' has mid-sized, delicate pink flowers on compact, bushy plants.

'Red Cascade Starina' features free-flowering bright scarlet fragrant flowers edged in yellow. The plant grows from 8–12 inches (20–30 cm) tall.

'Rhonda' has large double flowers of clear pink with shadings of coral and deep green foliage.

'Rise 'n' Shine' is a beautiful miniature yellow rose that grows on vigorous 15 inch (38 cm) plants.

'Spectra' has unusual flowers that change from rich gold buds edged with red to open flowers of gold and crimson. Their color intensifies as the sun gets hotter.

ROSMARINUS ZONES 6–10

Fragrant leaved, lavender-blue flowered rosemary has a variety of roles in the garden; as a hedge, a scented evergreen flowering shrub and as a herb. There are several different sorts. Best for hedges is 'Miss Jessop's Upright', an erect-growing variety to 6 ft (1.8 m). 'Severn Sea' is dwarf and arching with bright blue flowers. 'McConnells Blue' makes a low hummock.

General care: Well-drained, even poor, sandy or chalky soil is ideal, plus a sunny, reasonably sheltered site.

Propagation: Take tip cuttings in late summer in a cold frame, or use longer, more woody stems planted outdoors in autumn.

Pests and diseases: Generally trouble-free.

SALIX ZONES 1–10

There are no fewer than 300 species of willow plus many more hybrids and varieties. All are deciduous and produce minute flowers in catkins, the best known being those of the pussy or goat willow *Salix caprea* (hardy to zone 4). Salix contains tiny matformers, shrubs of various sizes and quite tall trees. It is the shrubs that are of most value in the garden. *S. caprea* is too large a shrub for the smaller garden and anyway can be enjoyed in the countryside. Its now popular weeping form known as Kilmarnock willow (*S. c.* 'Pendula'), however, makes a nice little weeping tree for a small lawn. Far better to plant this than the common weeping willow. (*S. x chrysocoma* [hardy to zone 7], syn. *S. alba* 'Tristis' and *S. a.* 'Vitellina Pendula'), which rapidly outgrows its space in the smaller garden and becomes a lovely nuisance. A willow of quality is *S. fargesii*, a comparatively slow grower for the genus, eventually to 6½ ft (2 m). It has robust, polished winter twigs set with sealing-wax red buds. The leaves too are large and handsome. The dwarf alpine pussy willow, *S. hastata*

'Wehrhahnii' is rarely above 4 ft (120 cm) tall. Erect and compact-growing with age it bears a profusion of silvery, then yellow catkins before the leaves in spring. Huge pussy willow catkins are produced by the wooly willow *S. lanata* but they are borne with the large, gray, wooly young leaves in late spring or early summer. In time it forms a spreading bush 3–4 ft (90–120 cm) tall. The black pussy willow *S. melanostachys* (syn. *S. gracilistyla* var. *melanostachys*) (hardy to zone 5) eventually reaches 8½ ft (2.4 m) in height. It has bright green leaves and, before they expand in early spring, almost black catkins set with red anthers which finally turn yellow with pollen. For the rock garden, *S. x boydii* is a must, a gnarled shrublet of slow growth rarely above 1 ft (30 cm) in height, bearing small corrugated gray leaves.

General care: Almost any soil is acceptable, although *S. x boydii* does not like wet conditions. Pruning is not necessary except for removing untidy stems or branchlets.

Propagation: By semi-hardwood cuttings in a cold frame in late summer or hardwood cuttings in the open ground in late autumn to late winter.

Pests and diseases: Generally trouble-free.

SANTOLINA ZONES 6–10

The gray frothy foliage of cotton lavender or lavender cotton (*S. chamaecyparissus*) (hardy to zone 6) has been a garden standby for at least 200 years. It is an evergreen shrub to 2 ft (60 cm) tall or more, but is best cut back close to ground level annually and then rarely exceeds 1–1½ ft (30–45 cm) in height. In late summer the stem tips produce flowerheads like lemon-yellow buttons. Some people remove them because they spoil the smooth gray outline of the foliage, but they are not without charm. *S. c. insularis* (syn. *S. neapolitana*) (hardy to zone 6) has looser, taller, more feathery foliage, which in the variety 'Sulphurea' is topped by primrose-yellow buttons.

General care: Any well-drained soil is suitable, growth being more compact in the poorer sandy or chalky

ones. Full sun is essential. Cut back annually in spring.

Propagation: Take semi-hardwood cuttings in late summer or hardwood in autumn, both in a cold frame.

Pests and diseases: Generally trouble-free.

SENECIO ZONES 4–10

Gray-leaved plants have a wide appeal and when they are garnished with bright yellow daisy flowers they become desirable garden decoration. *S. x* 'Sunshine' (syn. *S. greyi* and *laxifolius* of gardens) (hardy to zone 5) is just such a plant, forming a low, compact evergreen shrub to 3 ft (90 cm) tall. An excellent plant for windswept sites by the sea but suffers damage in severe winters, *S. monroi* has smaller, beautifully crimped-edged leaves which are dark green above and white-felted beneath. Yellow daisy flowers similar to those of *S. x* 'Sunshine' appear in summer.

General care: Any well-drained site, preferably in sun, is suitable. In cold areas the foot of a south wall is best.

Propagation: Take semi-hardwood cuttings with a heel in late summer and root them in a propagating case.

Pests and diseases: Generally trouble-free.

SKIMMIA ZONES 7–9

This genus of smallish shrubs is valuable for its fragrant, spring-borne flower clusters, crimson berries and evergreen leaves. The hardiest and best known species, *S. japonica* (hardy to zone 7), unfortunately has male and female flowers on separate plants. To get the bonus of berries, therefore, at least two specimens must be planted. Should you have room for only one, then choose *S. j.* 'Rubella', a rounded male plant 3–4 ft (90–120 cm) in height, with dark foliage and red-budded white flowers. If red berries are desired, plant

Senecio x 'Sunshine'

S. j. 'Foremannii', a large-fruited female, beside it. Less hardy and needing acid soil, S. reevesiana (hardy to zone 7) is the only species generally available which has hermaphrodite flowers and so can produce fruit without a companion plant.
General care: S. japonica will grow in any soil which is not too dry, but chalky and sandy soils should be enriched with peat, leaf mold or garden compost. S. reevesiana must have a lime-free rooting medium. Both will grow in sun or partial shade. Pruning is not required.
Propagation: Take cuttings of semi-hardwood in late summer, or hardwood in autumn, placing them in a cold frame.
Pests and diseases: Generally trouble-free.

SPIRAEA   ZONES 2–9

No garden should be without at least one member of this large genus of deciduous trees and shrubs. All those offered at garden centers are hardy and easily grown, producing their frothy clusters of small white, pink or red flowers in abundance. Best known is S. japonica (hardy to zone 5), a twiggy shrub to 5 ft (1.5 m), but only half this if annually pruned. In late summer it produces large flattened clusters of pink to red flowers. S. j. 'Anthony Waterer' has a scattering of cream and pink variegated shoots and crimson flowers. S. j. 'Bumalda' (syn. S. x bumalda) is more compact, bearing carmine flowers above rich green leaves. S. j. 'Little Princess' (dark pink) and 'Snowmound' (white) form dense low mounds wider than high and are best not pruned. S. x vanhouttei (hardy to zone 4) achieves 6½ ft (2 m) or more in time, and pure white floral pompoms smother its arching stems in early summer. Quite different are S. douglasii, S. salicifolia and their hybrid x billiardii (hardy to zone 4). All are upright in growth to 7 ft (2.2 m) tall, and they bear erect

Skimmia japonica 'Foremannii'

terminal plumes of pink to rose flowers in late summer. The best of the bunch is S. x billiardii 'Triumphans' (syn. S. menziesii 'Triumphans'), which bears large clusters of rose-purple blossoms. S. latifolia (hardy to zone 2) grows wild throughout the country between Newfoundland and North Carolina.
General care: Almost any soil is suitable, even a wettish one, though a moist but well-drained site is best. S. x vanhouttei will grow in quite dry places. Sun or partial shade is acceptable. Cut all stems of S. japonica back to 2 inches (5 cm) every spring if desired.
Propagation: Take semi-hardwood cuttings in late summer or hardwood ones in autumn and insert in a cold frame. S. x billiardii and its allies produce suckers, which can be severed from late autumn to early spring.
Pests and diseases: Generally trouble-free.

SYMPHORICARPOS
ZONES 2–10

Symphoricarpos, or snowberry, is a useful hedging or screening plant that will grow practically anywhere, producing large, white, marble-like berries in the autumn which then last through most of the winter. S. albusis (hardy to zone 3) is an evergreen growing up to 7 ft (2.1 m) or taller under good

soil conditions. Of the varieties, 'Laevigatus' has even bigger berries and 'White Hedge' (syn. 'White Hedger') is a compact, erect grower which is considered best for the purpose.
General care: Snowberry will grow anywhere – sun or shade, or under trees – and in any soil, no matter how poor. Plant any time in the winter, 18 inches (45 cm) apart for hedging, and 30 inches (75 cm) or more apart for screening, depending on how thick a screen you want. The young plants should then be cut down to within 10 inches (25 cm) or so of the soil, and the growing tip pinched out from time to time to encourage branching. No routine pruning is needed, and hedges and screens can be trimmed as and when required.
Propagation: Take cuttings in the autumn and plant in a 50–50 sand and peat mixture or remove suckers any time from late autumn to early spring.
Pests and diseases: Generally trouble-free.

SYRINGA   ZONES 2–8

Although syringa is sometimes, quite wrongly, used as a common name for philadelphus, it is strictly the botanical name for lilac. Syringa vulgaris (hardy to zone 3) is common lilac, that deservedly popular deciduous shrub so prodigious of its trusses of fragrant flowers in

late spring and early summer. Bluish-purple is the basic color but there are many varieties in shades of purple, red, pink and yellow, both single and double. Recommended are: 'Firmament' (almost blue), 'Charles Joly' (rich purple-red, double), 'Esther Staley' (pink), 'Maud Notcutt' (white), 'Primrose' (pale yellow), 'Sensation' (red-purple edged white, very striking). S. x prestoniae (hardy to zone 2) is a hybrid of S. reflexa and makes large vigorous bushes with more plumy flower trusses than those of S. vulgaris. Among the best of the named varieties are 'Bellicent' (clear pink) and 'Elinor' (lilac to violet-pink). If space is at a premium and a really small lilac is desired, go for S. microphylla 'Superba' (hardy to zone 5). This small-leaved sort grows to 5 ft (1.5 m) or more in height and bears fragrant, rosy-pink blossom in early summer. Unlike other lilacs it gives an encore in autumn, though the display is on a lesser scale.
General care: All soils that are not too dry or wet are suitable, though light sandy and chalky ones should be enriched with garden compost, leaf mold or peat. Pruning is not necessary except to maintain a shapely outline.
Propagation: Take semi-hardwood cuttings in late summer and root in a propagating case or cold frame.
Pests and diseases: Generally trouble-free.

TAMARIX   ZONES 2–10

The tamarisks are graceful deciduous shrubs with slender arching branches, tiny, juniper-like foliage and feathery plumes of pink flowers. They are particularly suited to the desert areas of California and Arizona, where they have proved to be tolerant of drought and high winds, and to coastal areas where they withstand both saline soils and salt spray. T. parviflora (hardy to zone 4), which is often sold mistakenly under

Thunbergia alata

the name of *T. africana*, grows to 15 ft (4.6 m). It produces clusters of pink flowers in spring on the previous year's growth and should be pruned after flowering to maintain its shape and to encourage more flowering.

T. chinensis (hardy to zone 3) varies in color and blooming season, according to selection, from early spring to fall in shades of white to pink to purple. All selections have lovely blue-gray foliage. 'Rosea' has rose-pink flower plumes that are excellent for cutting. It grows to 8 ft (2.4 m), but can be pruned to 4–6 ft (1.2–1.8 m).
General care: Tamarisk prefers sandy, well-drained soil, but is very tolerant of poor soil. Plant in sun or light shade.
Propagation: From softwood or hardwood cuttings or from seed.
Pests and diseases: Generally trouble-free.

TECOMARIA   ZONES 8–10
T. capensis, Cape honeysuckle, is a wonderfully adaptable plant for growing in warm zones. It performs as a vine, growing 15–25 ft (4.6–7.5 m) tall when given support, as a shrub growing to 6–8 ft (1.8–2.4 m) when pruned regularly and as a ground cover in a variety of climate and soil conditions. The prime attraction of Cape honeysuckle is its brilliant orange, 2 inch (5 cm), trumpet-shaped flowers which bloom in compact clusters from mid-summer through the autumn. A native of South Africa, Cape honeysuckle is well-adapted to both coastal and desert regions. 'Aurea' is a yellow-flowered form which is less vigorous and produces smaller flowers.
General care: Any soil conditions are adequate if drainage is good. Plant in a sunny location.
Propagation: By cuttings, from seeds and by layering.
Pests and diseases: Generally trouble-free.

THUNBERGIA ZONES 8–10

Thunbergia is a tropical, twining, perennial vine which can be grown as an annual in cold climates. It is grown for its striking curtain of brilliant, funnel-shaped flowers. *T. alata* (hardy to zone 9), the black-eyed Susan vine, is the most popular variety. Selections include 'Alba', white with black centers and 'Aurantiaca', orange-yellow flowers. All varieties will bloom during the first summer after planting.

T. grandiflora (hardy to zone 8) is an evergreen from India with spectacular 3 inch (7.5 cm), sky blue, tubular flowers which grow in long, pendulous clusters. It climbs to 20 ft (6 m) with lush, light green, heart-shaped leaves. A white version of the vine is also available.

T. gregorii (hardy to zone 10) produces bright orange flowers throughout the year in warm climates and all summer when grown as an annual in colder climates. It has rich, evergreen foliage and climbs to 6 ft (1.8 m) tall. It is a showy vine for a trellis or hanging basket.

General care: Thunbergia requires rich, porous soil in full sun, protected from wind and frost. Prune in summer when the spring flowering is over.

Propagation: Sow seed indoors in early spring or propagate from softwood cuttings taken in summer.

Pests and diseases: Generally trouble-free.

TRACHELOSPERMUM ZONES 7–10

T. jasminoides (hardy to zone 9) is the ever-popular star jasmine, one of the most common and versatile evergreen twining vines grown in warm climates. Its delightful jasmine fragrance is a welcome addition to a sunny patio. The tiny, white, star-shaped flowers bloom from early spring through the summer and contrast beautifully with the lustrous oval dark green foliage. Star jasmine reaches 10–15 ft (3–4.6 m) tall. Without support, it will grow into a shrubby ground cover if its upright shoots are pruned back. 'Variegatum' is a rare selection that features cream-variegated leaves. 'Madison' is an extra-hardy version of star jasmine with cream-colored flowers.

T. asiaticum (hardy to zone 7) is similar to the star jasmine, but it bears yellow flowers in the shape of a pinwheel which bloom from early spring to mid-summer and has smaller, less lustrous foliage.

General care: Plant in a sunny location or light shade in very hot regions in well-drained, enriched soil. Prune back older plants by about one-third each year to prevent sparse, woody inner growth.

Propagation: Propagate by cuttings after blooming.

Pests and diseases: Spray for scale, mealy bug and red spider mites with a solution of insecticide such as diazinon or malathion.

TROPAEOLUM ZONES 7–10

This group includes the familiar garden nasturtium and Canary creeper, which climb like clematis, twisting their leaf stalks round any available support. *T. majus* is the common nasturtium, an annual growing to 7 ft (2.1 m) or more and flowering through the summer. Dwarf and trailing strains are available. *T. peregrinum*, Canary creeper, is also an annual. It is a rapid climber, up to 10 ft (3 m) in a season, and produces its bright yellow flowers all summer. *T. speciosum*, or flame nasturtium

Trachelospermum jasminoides, or star jasmine

(hardy to zone 9), grows to about 12 ft (3.6 m) with flame-red flowers from mid- to late summer. It is the only one of the group that does not like full sun, and although it comes from Chile, it seems to prefer cool, damp conditions – a north-facing wall is ideal. *T. tuberosum* (hardy to zone 8) is a vigorous climber, up to 10 ft (3 m), with red and orange flowers. Some strains do not flower until the end of summer and are then cut down by frost. Look for the early-flowering variety 'Ken Aslet', which blooms in early summer.

General care: Canary creeper needs average garden soil but the other annuals should be given poor soil or they will produce a lot of vegetation at the expense of the flowers. Most of the perennials will thrive in any good fertile soil, but *T. speciosum* must have an acid soil. Add peat if necessary to achieve this. *T. tuberosum* grows from tubers which will survive the winter only in the mildest areas. If in doubt, lift and store in a frost-free shed, planting out again when all danger of frost has passed.

Propagation: The annuals can be grown from seed sown in April into the flowering site, or sown in pots of

Tropaeolum speciosum

Viburnum tinus

soil-less compost in March for planting out later after hardening off. The tubers of *T. tuberosum* can be separated when they are lifted for over-winter storage. The other perennials can be propagated by dividing the roots in March.

Pests and diseases: Tropaeolum are attacked by aphids, cabbage caterpillars and thrips; malathion will deal with all these.

VIBURNUM ZONES 2–9
The viburnum genus includes a very wide variety of evergreen and deciduous shrubs, flowering in winter, spring and summer. Some are grown for their flowers, some for their berries, some for their colorful autumn leaves, and some for all three. Certain species are best grown as bushes, but many make excellent wall shrubs. Although most viburnums are hardy, they flower earlier and better on a wall or fence. *V. x burkwoodii* (hardy to zone 5) is a spreading semi-evergreen which grows to about 7 ft (2.1 m) and bears clusters of fragrant white flowers in spring. *V. farreri* (hardy to zone 6), formerly known as *V. fragrans*, is a deciduous winter-flowering species. It grows to 10 ft (3 m) or more against a wall, and bears its fragrant white and pink flowers through the winter intermittently in spells of fine weather. The leaves follow the flowers in spring. *V. x bodnantense* (hardy to zone 5) is a useful hybrid of *V. farreri* and *V. grandiflorum*, since it is more vigorous, growing to 12 ft (3.6 m) and hardier than either. It is deciduous, and carries white-pink fragrant flowers on the bare wood, sometimes from fall through winter. 'Dawn' is the variety usually available, but 'Deben' has a longer winter-flowering period than any, from October to April if the weather is mild. *V. rhytidophyllum* (hardy to zone 5) is an upright evergreen species, 12 ft (3.6 m) tall, with whitish flowers in late spring, followed by red berries that turn black when ripe. It is, however, mainly grown for its large oblong leaves, which have a finely wrinkled glossy surface.

General care: Viburnums grow in most soils, ideally with compost dug in, and a mulch of leaf mold from time to time. Plant deciduous varieties any time in the winter, and evergreens in spring. A west-facing wall is ideal. Viburnums do not need regular pruning: any tidying up needed should be done when they have finished flowering.

Propagation: Take cuttings at the end of the summer and root them in a 50–50 sand and peat mixture, or layer shoots at this time and separate a year later.

Pests and diseases: Generally trouble-free.

WEIGELA ZONES 4–8
This is undoubtedly one of the 10 most popular garden shrubs. *W. florida* (syn. *Diervilla floribunda*) (hardy to zone 5) is a hardy, easy to please, deciduous species growing to 7 ft (2.2 m) tall which, without fail, produces numerous small trusses of foxglove-shaped flowers in summer. Several good varieties are available, the best being 'Bristol Ruby' (ruby-red), 'Abel Carrière' (rosy carmine), 'Avalanche' (white), 'Folliis Purpureis' (rose-pink with purple foliage) and 'Variegata' (pale pink with yellow-margined leaves). If you would like to try something different, look out for the smaller-growing sulphur-yellow, *W. middendorffiana* (hardy to zone 4).

General care: All but the wettest soils are suitable but light sandy and chalky ones should be enriched with garden compost or peat, etc. To maintain a compact bush, cut back flowered stems by two-thirds to three-quarters as soon as the last blossoms have faded. Weigelas flourish when they are pruned vigorously so do not be too gentle.

Propagation: Take semi-hardwood cuttings in late summer in a propagating case, or hardwood cuttings either in a cold frame or in the open ground.

Pests and diseases: Generally trouble-free.

WISTERIA ZONES 4–10

Wisteria sinensis (Chinese wisteria) (hardy to zone 5) is the most popular species – not surprisingly, for it is fragrant and spectacular, the long racemes of mauve flowers appearing in spring before the leaves, with a smaller second flowering in warm summers in August. There are several varieties, including 'Plena' (double flowers) and 'Alba' (white flowers). *W. floribunda* (Japanese wisteria) (hardy to zone 4) is similar, but not so vigorous, growing up to 30 ft (9 m). Many varieties have been produced, some with extra-long racemes of flowers, notably 'Macro-botrys', whose purple racemes are 3 ft (90 cm) long. These look best when they are trained over an arch or pergola so that the racemes of flowers hang down clear of the plant.

General care: All wisterias prefer a sunny site, such as a south-facing wall, except for *W. floribunda*, which will tolerate some shade. They like a rich moist soil with plenty of compost dug into it. The young plants can be put in at any time during the winter, and need support until they can start twining and climbing. Eventually wisteria will grow into a self-supporting tree with a head of new young growth. Prune unwanted climbing shoots back to five basal leaves in summer to promote more flowering spurs and generally to keep the plant looking tidy and under control.

Propagation: Take cuttings 4 inches (10 cm) long of the current year's growth in late summer and plant them in a 50–50 mixture of peat and sand, or layer in spring and remove one year later.

Pests and diseases: Generally trouble-free.

BELOW: *The spectacular purple flowers of Wisteria sinensis provide excellent cover for a south-facing wall.*

ABOVE: *The dazzling white mass of flowers of the cultivar Wisteria sinensis 'Alba' flourish in a sunny position.*

HOUSE PLANTS

Not only do plants embellish the décor of one's home, but they provide an important link with the natural world. A whole new industry has arisen to meet the tremendous demand for house plants from dwellers in crowded cities and suburbia. New plants are continually being tested for their suitability and, indeed, never before has there been such a wide variety of plants for the home.

Where do house plants come from? Most are native to warm countries, some from the shady floors of tropical forests, others, the epiphytes or air plants – e.g. orchids and bromeliads – from the branches high above. The succulent plants with fleshy stems and/or leaves come from the semi-deserts. A surprising number come from temperate climates, e.g. ivy from the forests of Europe and Asia, aspidistra from similar shady places in China and cyclamen from mountain woods in the eastern Mediterranean. As this indicates, house plants come from habitats with extremes of shade or exposure – not surprising when you consider the climate of an average house. In most homes the atmosphere is very dry, the light, except near windows, is poor and, unless there is central heating, the temperature fluctuates widely between day and night, especially in winter. Despite this there are species suitable for most sites in the house. The best localities are window-sills, tables and shelves nearby and room corners. Plants can be used as dividers in larger rooms, to embellish the harshness of a fireplace in summer or simply to brighten a dull corner.

Light is essential to all plants, though some need a lot more than others. The desert dwellers obviously need lots of direct sunlight, while forest or jungle plants tolerate shade.

The more shade-tolerant species will also thrive under artificial light, and nowadays there is a variety of custom-made units to take either one plant or a whole shelf or trayful. By such means plants can be grown in the darkest of rooms and even in basements and windowless cellars. Not only is it important to purchase the right plant for the right situation, but the plant itself should be the best available. Shop around before you buy what you want. Look for sturdy specimens with leaves of a good green color. Do not purchase plants with a lot of bare stem or with yellowish or brown-marked leaves. Check for such pests as aphids, whitefly, mealy bug and red spider (see pests chart on page 228). Get the plant home as soon as possible in cold weather because chilling can trigger premature leaf or flower drop.

Watering
The correct watering of a containerized plant is essential if it is to flourish. Without doubt, most plants perish as a result of too much or not enough water. Frequency of watering depends upon the stage of the plant's development, temperature and time of year. A newly potted plant, for example, with unexploited soil around its roots, will need less water than one which is pot bound (the pot container tightly filled with roots). Plants actively growing and producing new leaves and perhaps flower buds also will need more water than those which are dormant. With most plants the aim is to keep the potting mix moist but not wet. There are a few exceptions. *Cyperus alternifolius* is a waterside plant and is best kept wet. All succulents, including cacti, do better if they are allowed to dry out between waterings and then kept dry or very nearly dry throughout the winter.

The most reliable means of deciding when a plant needs water is to scratch into the soil surface with the tip of the finger. If it feels dry on the surface and dryish for about ½ inch (1 cm) down, watering is necessary. Do the job thoroughly, filling up the space between the soil surface and rim of the container. Rain water is ideal, but tap water is perfectly adequate.

Humidity
Plants whose native homeland is forest or jungle thrive more happily if some sort of humidity can be provided. The easiest way is to stand the pots on gravel-filled trays with water just below the surface. Alternatively, deeper trays or troughs can be filled with moist peat and the pots sunk in this up to their rims. A little water from time to time keeps the peat moist. Another method is to dampen the foliage daily with a small spray adjusted to produce fine droplets.

Feeding
Sooner or later the plants will exhaust the potting mix of its essential nutrients. If feeding, top-dressing or repotting is not carried out, the growth of the plant will slow down or cease, leaves will be small and yellowish and flower buds will fall or fail to develop. Liquid fertilizer is the best way of feeding containerized plants. All the well known proprietary sorts are suitable, but must be used according to the maker's instructions. It is usual to carry out feeding from spring to autumn, but plants which continue to grow in winter should still be fed, though preferably at half strength.

Potting soil
The quality of the rooting medium – potting soil – is crucial to the health and vigor of a containerized plant. As

Select plants with healthy-looking leaves, sturdy stems and, if choosing a flowerer, plenty of buds.

the root system is packed into a small space, the soil must be richer than that in the garden. For this reason it is best to purchase a properly formulated mixture rather than try to mix garden soil, peat and fertilizers. There are packs of plant food especially formulated to mix with a set amount of peat and perlite, thus creating a fairly cheap potting mix. If garden soil is used, mix it with equal parts of peat and apply a liquid feed regularly.

Potting on

If a bigger, finer plant is needed, then a larger container and more soil is the answer. Choose a new container that is large enough to allow about 1 inch (2.5 cm) or more space all around the root ball. Make sure the new pot is clean, put a single crock over the drainage hole followed by a handful of compost. Take the plant to be potted and turn it upside down on to your hand with the stem between the fingers. Holding the pot itself with the other hand, rap the rim against a hard surface, preferably a wooden one. The pot will then lift off. Place the root ball in the new container, adjusting so that when filled around it will be covered with about ½ inch (1 cm) of new soil and, most important, there will be a space for watering. If in doubt, leave a gap between soil surface and rim equivalent to about one-seventh or one-eighth of the container depth. After filling with potting soil, water and return the plant to its original site.

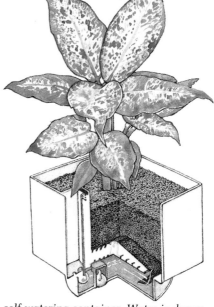

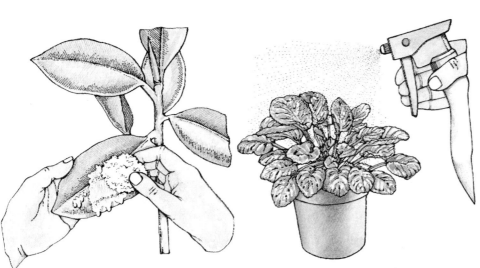

To remove dust or dirt from tough-leaved specimens (e.g. Ficus elastica) wipe leaves gently with a damp pad of cotton wool.

Plants with leaves that are delicate or awkward to clean (e.g. Saintpaulia) should be sprayed with tepid water.

A self-watering container. Water is drawn up from a reservoir by a wick, which distributes moisture through the soil.

Repotting

This is a means of giving a long-term pot plant some fresh soil while preventing it from getting much bigger. Turn the plant out of its pot as before, then with a hand-fork and, if necessary, a knife reduce the root ball by one-third. Return it to the same pot, or preferably a clean one of the same size, and fill in with fresh soil. This repotting operation should be done in late winter or spring or while the plant is semi-dormant. The top growth should be trimmed at the same time to balance the shoot/root ratio. Repotting can be carried out annually on a vigorous plant such as bougainvillea or x fatshedera or at intervals of several years as with palms (howeia and phoenix).

Top dressing

This is an alternative to repotting and is usually done annually or biennially in early spring. Strip away the top layer of soil, removing up to a quarter of the total depth of the root ball. Any fibrous roots in the way can go but avoid damaging the thicker main ones. Replace the old soil with a fresh mix, firm lightly and water, using a rose-nozzled can to settle it in.

Supporting

House plants with a climbing mode of growth, e.g. ivy, stephanotis and bougainvillea, must be given a support system. Custom-made structures of plastic or wire are obtainable, or a U-shaped support of galvanized wire can easily be made. Alternatively, several slim green canes or spills can be inserted in a fan-shape to one side of the pot. Sometimes plants splay or collapse, perhaps due to an over-warm or under-lit site. Such plants can be made tidy with a few small stakes around the base or a green spill carefully secured to each stem with a tie. Try to keep the support inconspicuous.

Propagation

Raising new plants for presents or for a charity sale can be an absorbing and satisfying pastime. Many house plants root easily from cuttings or can be increased from seed without much skill or knowledge. Some kind of propagating case is necessary to ensure success. This can be improvised from a seed tray covered with plastic sheeting and supported by U-shaped lengths of galvanized wire. Single pots can be placed in plastic bags with or without a support. Best of all are the custom-made structures with a clear rigid top, ideally with a heating element in the bottom. A number of the less easy plants to propagate root as cuttings when provided with bottom heat.

ABOVE: *A simple method of repotting using a pot the same size as the outgrown one as a guide. This enables the new pot to be filled to the correct height with soil, leaving a hollow the right size for the root ball.*

BELOW: *Propagate from stem tip cuttings by taking a stem with several leaves attached from the top of a mature plant and pot up in a peat and sand mixture.*

Softwood cuttings: These are stem tips in a state of leafy growth provided in abundance by such plants as beloperone (shrimp plant), coleus (flame nettle), hedera (ivy), impatiens (busy lizzie) and tradescantia (wandering Jew). Any time from early spring to early autumn, sever stem tips 2–3 inches (5–7.5 cm) long. Cut beneath a node (leaf or bud), remove the lowest leaf or two and insert the basal one-third into pots of equal parts of peat/moss and coarse sand. Water with a rosed can and place in the propagator. For a more sure rooting, the cuttings can first be dipped into one of the hormone rooting powders. The actual pot size to use is a matter of choice. Single cuttings can be put into 2–2½ inch (5–6 cm) pots, or several set around the edge of larger containers at 1–1½ inch (2.5–4 cm) apart. At a minimum temperature of 65°F (18°C) rooting takes anywhere from 10–30 days, depending on the type of plant. Once growth recommences, pot singly into 3–3½ inch (7.5–9 cm) containers of potting soil, water and keep lightly shaded for a few days.

Semi-hardwood cuttings: These are the current season's stems which are just starting to get woody at the base. Shrubs and woody climbers such as cissus, codiaeum (croton) and ficus (ornamental fig) often root more successfully when starting to become more woody. Sever whole side shoots, then trim off the soft tip so as to make a cutting 3–4 inches (7.5–10 cm) long. Remove the lower leaves and treat as for softwood cuttings.

Hardwood cuttings: These are fully woody stems that have stopped growing. Very few house plants are propagated in this way, the only one mentioned here being bougainvillea. Cut 4–6 inch (10–15 cm) lengths of dormant leafless stems (prunings are often used), treat with a rooting powder and place in a heated propagating case; late winter to early spring is the best time.

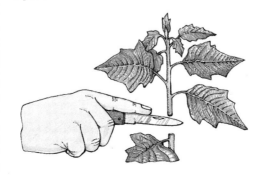

Leaf cuttings: Certain plants can regenerate from a single leaf or even a piece of one; begonia, peperomia, saintpaulia, sansevieria and streptocarpus come into this category. Small leaves, e.g. peperomia and saintpaulia, are usually used whole. Take a mature (fully sized) but not old leaf, remove all but about 1 inch (2.5 cm) of leaf stalk and insert ¾ inch (2 cm) of this into a 50–50 peat and sand mix in the same way as for softwood cuttings. Streptocarpus and sansevieria leaves are cut transversely into 2–3 inch (5–7.5 cm) long sections, which are then inserted obliquely so that the lower one-third is buried.

Large begonia leaves can be used whole or cut into 1 inch (2.5 cm) squares. If used whole, only a stub of stalk is left and this is pressed into the surface of the same sandy compost so that the blade lies flat. Take a sharp, pointed knife or razor blade and pierce all the main veins at ¾–1 inch (2–2.5 cm) intervals. The tiny plants that will develop from some of these wounds can be separated from the leaf and potted singly when well rooted. Place the leaf squares on the surface of a container of soil so they are close but not touching. One or more plantlets will arise from most of the squares. Both the squares and whole leaves must be kept warm and humid in a propagating case. If they don't sit flat on the soil, anchor with U-shaped pieces of thin wire or small pebbles.

Leaf-bud cuttings: These are single leaves attached to short sections of stem. Ficus elastica is entirely propagated in this way by nurserymen. Cut a mature stem into pieces about ¾–1 inch (2–2.5 cm) long so that each piece has one leaf. Loosely roll each leaf cigar-fashion and secure with an elastic band. Apply rooting powder to the stem and insert up to the base of the leaf blade. A short spill of cane through the rolled leaf will hold it erect. A temperature of not less than 75°F (24°C) is necessary for success. When the lower parts of dieffenbachia and dracaena stems become leafless and unsightly, take the top as a soft or semi-hardwood cutting then cut up the bare stem into 2 inch (5 cm) lengths. Lay them on their sides and barely cover with soil. In time, each will produce one or more shoots and grow into a young plant. These are in effect leafless leaf-bud cuttings.

Air-layering: For information on basic layering see under Shrubs and Climbing Plants, p. 75. Basic layering is not always easy to carry out in the home, especially if a plant has stiff, erect stems, as have ficus elastica and dracaena. These two plants frequently become bare and unsightly, and air-layering is a sure way of rooting the top, allowing new shoots to form below. Nick or make a shallow slice in the stem about 6–8 inches (15–20 cm) below the growing tip and dust with rooting powder. If the slicing method is used, wedge it open with a tiny pebble. Cut a piece of 'lay-flat' plastic tubing that opens to a tube diameter of not less than 3 inches (7.5 cm). Bunch the leaves and slip the tubing down to the nicked area of the stem, positioning it so that its middle point is opposite the wound. Secure the base of the tube to the stem with insulating tape. Now, firmly pack the tube with a mixture of equal parts of moist potting or seed sowing soil and moss, ideally sphagnum moss. Secure the top of the tube in the same way as the base. Rooting may take several months. When a good network of roots is visible, sever below the layer, remove the tube and pot up. Keep partially shaded and humid for 1–2 weeks to aid establishment.

Division: Several house plants, most notably asparagus fern, true ferns, cyperus, fittonia, maranta, saintpaulia, etc., can be divided as described under Garden Flowers (p. 20). For the smaller plants, however, two handforks placed back to back will give the essential leverage; a knife may also be useful. Pot each division as soon as it is made and water carefully until established.

Seeds: Comparatively few plants for the home are regularly raised from seed though many can be when seed is available. For the procedure, see the seed-sowing entry under Garden Flowers, p. 19. Most house plant seed germinates bst at between 65–75°F (18–24°C).

LEFT: *Propagation by leaf cuttings (**top**) and by leaf-bud cuttings (**below**). For leaf cuttings, take a mature healthy leaf with a stalk attached and insert it in a pot of seed compost, ensuring that the base of the leaf is clear of the compost. For leaf-bud cuttings, take a 4 in (10 cm) cutting with a leaf attached and pot it in a mixture of sand and peat. Support the cutting by means of an elastic band secured to a stake.*

A-Z
HOUSE PLANTS

ACACIA

A lovely winter-flowering shrub, A. *armata*, kangaroo thorn, bears a close resemblance to mimosa. It thrives in cool temperatures and bears fuzzy yellow flowers, surrounded by dense, waxy, green foliage on thorny branches. It will grow to 5 ft (1.5 m) indoors, and established plants may need staking.

General care: Situate in a well-lit position in a cool location where temperatures in winter will stay below 50°F (10°C). It needs well-draining soil and prefers standard potting soil with some sand added. Pinch back new growth to encourage bushiness. Fertilize every other week in spring and summer. Water moderately and syringe occasionally with tepid water.

Propagation: Propagation is best achieved from cuttings as the seed does not germinate easily.

Pests and diseases: Watch for mealy bugs, scale and whiteflies – all may occur.

ACALYPHA

These plants are native to Australia and are prized both for striking, dark green, leathery foliage and interesting flowers which bloom most heavily in fall and early winter. A. *hispida*, known as red-hot cat's tail and the chenille plant, has characteristic, bright red, pendulous flowers which can grow as long as 20 inches (50 cm) and look somewhat like cats' tails and drapery fringe. 'Alba' has pinkish-white flowers.

A. *wilkesiana* has less showy flowers but its foliage qualifies it as a prime plant for display in the house. Mature plants have handsome copper-red leaves with hints of pink which grow 8 inches (20 cm) long. 'Obovata' has olive-green leaves, edged with orange. 'Musaica' features brownish-orange foliage laced with pink.

General care: These plants need high humidity and ruthless pruning to do well and maintain good form.

Asplenium, (see p. 132) Howeia (see p. 145) and Adiantum

Place in a well-lit space, but out of direct sunlight on the hottest days. They need a constant temperature of approximately 60°F (15°C). Straggly plants can be revived by pruning them down to 4–8 inches (10–20 cm) in spring. Plant in standard potting mix with a bit of peat moss added and feed with mild liquid fertilizer from early spring through fall. Mist regularly. Remove spent blooms.

Propagation: Take cuttings in spring, dip them in rooting hormone and set in sandy potting mix. Bottom heat speeds root formation.

Pests and diseases: Watch for mealy bugs, red spiders and scale insects.

ACHIMENES
Relatives of African violets and gloxinias, achimenes offer many colorful species and varieties to choose from. They provide a lengthy blooming season from early summer through autumn with satiny, tubular flowers in a wide range of colors, including pink, blue, violet, lavender, deep purple and pure yellow with silvery foliage. They normally grow between 8–12 inches (20–30 cm) tall and have roundish, hairy foliage. They are particularly striking planted in hanging baskets.

General care: Water the plants abundantly and feed every other week while they are in flower. Plant in acid, porous soil; standard potting soil mixed with peat and sand works well. They like high humidity and good light but no direct sunlight. Pinch back young plants to increase bushiness. Night temperatures of 65–70°F (18–21°C) and day temperatures of 75°F (24°C) are preferred. After flowering, the plants will die back. Cease watering, remove the withered leaves and store the dormant rhizomes in dry peat moss during the winter.

Propagation: New plants are most easily started by dividing the rhizomes of a mature plant during dormancy. To speed growth, dip the rhiz-

omes in hot water, then plant them 1 inch (2.5 cm) deep in moist peat moss in early spring and water sparingly until growth appears. Alternatively, sow seeds in a heated propagator or take stem cuttings in spring.

Pests and diseases: Generally trouble-free.

ADIANTUM
The best known species grown as a pot plant is *A. raddianum*, commonly known as maidenhair, which is one of the most popular ferns. Its delicate fronds, rosy pink when young, mature to a fresh bright green when the plant has become established.

General care: The maidenhair fern requires a humid environment. It will tolerate temperatures as low as 50°F (10°C), but its optimum temperature is 70°F (21°C). It needs a situation well away from direct sunlight. Make sure the soil never dries out. If this happens, and the plant looks as if dehydration has killed it, don't give up. Provided it has not been allowed to stay dry for too long, it is possible to rejuvenate the plant. Cut off the dead fronds about ¼ inch (0.5 cm) above soil level and carefully water

Aeschynanthus lobbianus

the plant over the next few weeks. Usually the plant will eventually produce fresh growth and regain its former glory.

Propagation: Adiantum can be propagated from spores in the same way as other ferns (see Asplenium). However, division in spring is a much easier and quicker method.

Pests and diseases: Generally trouble-free.

AECHMEA FASCIATA
The aechmea or urn plant is a member of the bromeliad or pineapple family. Its large, greenish-gray, strap-like leaves radiate upwards and outwards. At their center, where water collects, the large pink bracted flower spike emerges. The spike produces flowers of violet-blue that are relatively short-lived. They are, however, produced in succession and the flower spike can live for as long as 6 months. They normally appear in autumn.

General care: Aechmeas are relatively easy to look after. A semi-shaded position away from direct sunlight is best, with a temperature of about 50–65°F (10–15°C); they will tolerate lower temperatures, however. During the growing period, give the plants rainwater (if possible) in the central funnel

and in the soil. Though the soil may be allowed to dry out, do not let the funnel run dry. Remove the flower spike when it has faded by gently pulling; if it does not come away easily do not tug too hard, but wait a little longer. Clean the leaves by rinsing them with tepid water. Never wipe them with a cloth, for this removes the decorative banding.

Propagation: Once the plant has finished flowering it will usually produce one or more offsets. When these have grown to approximately one-third the size of the parent, cut them off and pot singly into 4 inch (10 cm) pots of a sandy lime-free soil. Keep extra humid until rooted, then place in 6 inch (15 cm) pots of an all-peat mix.

Pests and diseases: Aechmeas are sometimes attacked by root mealy bugs and aphids on the flower spike, but generally they are trouble-free.

AESCHYNANTHUS
The lipstick plant is so named because of its striking red tubular flowers that bloom in spring. They are epiphytic plants, originating in damp forest regions where they grow in the branches of trees. They are best displayed in hanging baskets

because of their trailing stems which measure 2–3 ft (60–90 cm) long. *A. lobbianus* has yellow-throated, scarlet flowers with purple outer petals and dark green elliptical leaves; *A. pulcher* has drooping stems with green outer petals. The flowers of *A. speciosus* are waxy, bright yellow and orange. 'Black Pagoda' has dark green leaves, mottled with blackish purple, and deep orange flowers which bloom intermittently throughout the year.

General care: The lipstick plant performs best in a greenhouse because of its love for warm, humid places, but a steamy bathroom or kitchen location would be suitable. Plant in loose, fibrous, peaty potting soil which should be kept moist but not soggy. Lipstick plants enjoy temperatures that do not drop below 70°F (21°C), and should be placed away from drafts and high light conditions with protection from full sun in the summer. If the foliage turns faded green, it is an indication that the plant is receiving too much direct sunlight. After flowering, prune the plants to 6 inches (15 cm). Feed monthly with mild, acid fertilizer.

Propagation: Propagate from cuttings taken in spring. Place the cuttings under glass or plastic and add bottom heat.

Pests and diseases: Generally trouble-free.

AGAVE

The agaves are succulent plants which grow wild in Mexico and the warmer parts of the United States. All members of the genus carry their well-defined succulent sword-shaped leaves in the form of a rosette. One of the most attractive varieties is *A. americana* 'Marginata', with its variegated green and cream leaves. *A. victoriae-reginae* has dark green fleshy leaves with white margins.

General care: Agaves must be given full light and kept on the dry side. Excessively wet conditions spell the

Agave americana 'Marginata'

rapid demise of the plant. Agaves may eventually flower from the center of the rosette if grown in tubs or similar large containers. After flowering most agaves will produce offsets around their bases and then die. *A. victoriae-reginae* does not produce offsets.

Propagation: Carefully remove offsets produced around the base of the plant and pot them singly in 5 inch (13 cm) pots of standard potting mix in a 50–50 mixture with sand. Spring is the best time to do this. Propagate from seed by germinating in a mixture of 4 parts potting mix to 1 part fine sand at about 65°F (18°C), transplant the young plants when they are large enough to be handled; pot individually in a similar mixture.

Pests and diseases: Mealy bugs and sometimes root mealy bugs attack agaves, but they are troubled by very little else. Take immediate action if bugs occur.

AGLAONEMA

The Chinese evergreen is very tolerant of most household conditions and is a pleasant change from the equally problem-free, omnipresent philodendron. Chosen for its variegated foliage, aglaonema is a native of Southeast Asia. *A. costatum* has ivory-ribbed dark green leaves and grows to 12–18 inches (30–45 cm) with a spreading habit. *A. modestum* is larger, growing up to 3 ft (90 cm). *A. trewbii* 'Silver Queen' has lance-shaped, silver-gray leaves 5–6 inches (12–15 cm) long.

General care: Grow at temperatures between 60° and 70°F (15° and 21°C). Aglaonema tolerates both deep shade and diffused sunlight. Water deeply and then let the plant almost completely dry out before watering again. Plant in standard potting soil and feed twice a month with diluted liquid fertilizer. Aglaonemas can also be grown in water, laced with a bit of charcoal. Mist

frequently with a fine spray.

Propagation: Propagate by division, separating young shoots with leaves and roots in spring. Keep at a temperature of at least 70°F (21°C) until they have rooted. They can also be propagated from cuttings from leafy stem tips in a propagator or under glass or plastic.

Pests and diseases: They are prone to mealy bug infestation.

ALOCASIA

Elephant's ear is a magnificent, lush, foliage plant with large, arrow-shaped leaves. *A. sanderiana* has the smallest leaves, measuring 18 inches (45 cm) long and 6 inches (15 cm) wide. The leaves of *A. macrorhiza* grow to 2 ft (60 cm) on 5 ft (1.5 m) stalks. It produces tiny, calla-like, greenish-yellow spathes and reddish fruit.

General care: The elephant's ear likes a good deal of moisture and light shade in a location protected from

Anthurium scherzerianum and Aphelandra

drafts. Temperatures should not fall below 65°F (18°C). Plant in an organically enriched potting soil and feed with liquid fish emulsion from spring to fall.
Propagation: Propagate from shoots or by dividing plants.
Pests and diseases: Generally trouble-free.

AMARYLLIS
See under Hippeastrum

ANANAS
Although the pineapple plant rarely produces fruit in moderate climates, *A. comosus* and *A. nanus* are prized for their stiff ornamental leaves. *A. comosus* grows to 2 ft (60 cm) and has gray-green leaves with cream-colored margins. 'Variegatus' is much larger, growing to 3 ft (90 cm), with barbed foliage edged with cream; older plants have hints of pink. When grown under the right conditions, violet flowers bloom from the large spike. *A. nanus* produces a 15 inch (38 cm) spike of red buds resembling a pincushion which open into purple flowers.
General care: Plant the pineapple plant in a potting mixture that consists of half coarse sand and half peat moss. Place in full sun and provide ample moisture both to the vase-shaped trunk and the potting mixture. Feed monthly with diluted fish emulsion. The pineapple plant prefers warm temperatures above 65°F (18°C).
Propagation: Propagate from the suckers that form at the base of the plant after flowering. Plants can also be started from commercially grown pineapples. Cut off the top foliage of a pineapple, including about 1 inch (2.5 cm) of the pineapple crown. Let it dry for 2–3 days and place the crown in sandy potting soil. Keep warm to hasten root development.
Pests and diseases: Generally trouble-free.

ANTHURIUM
The anthurium, or flamingo flower, is an unusual plant which produces colorful spathes that look like exotic flowers. The two most commonly grown are *A. andreanum*, which has a shield-shaped flowering spathe of white, pink or brilliant red from which a finger-like flower spike protrudes, and *A. scherzerianum*, which has an orange-red spathe and a piglet's tail-like flower spike.
General care: The flamingo flower needs a fair amount of care and attention. It prefers a temperature of 65–70°F (18–21°C) and humid conditions. While it does not like too much direct sunlight, it will not thrive in excessive shade. A well-lit position where the temperature is reasonably constant will provide a good growing situation. Do not let the plant dry out, especially during the growing season. Mist regularly with tepid water. Feed once a month from April to September with a tomato fertilizer applied at half strength.

The flowers, which appear throughout the year, can be used in cut flower arrangements where they may live 3–4 weeks or more. If they are left on the plant, however, they may last for up to 8 weeks.
Propagation: Sometimes the plant will produce an offset at its side. This can be separated when it is about 6 inches (15 cm) tall and potted individually in a mixture of equal parts potting compost and moss peat. Alternatively, anthuriums can be raised from seed produced from the true flowers. This should be sown in half pots of seed compost and lightly covered. To germinate, keep the pots at 70°F (21°C), enclosed in a polythene bag to conserve water and heat. When large enough to handle they can be transplanted and potted singly.
Pests and diseases: Mealy bugs can sometimes be a nuisance and aphids occasionally attack young leaves and flowers.

APHELANDRA
Zebra plant or *A. squarrosa* bears cones of bright golden-yellow flowers on a flower spike rising from luxurious leathery green leaves with white veins. The flowers last several weeks before they eventually fade and fall off. Flowering takes place annually in autumn and winter, sometimes later.
General care: The aphelandra likes lots of light. Avoid drafts and aim for a temperature of about 65°F (18°C). It likes water and will suffer if left to dry out. Once the plant has flowered, it tends to produce rather straggly growth. This can be controlled a little by careful pruning and by feeding with half-strength tomato fertilizer. Spring pruning, cutting back after flowering to above the last pair of leaves, will encourage a good shape and improve the chances of it flowering again.
Propagation: When you prune the plant back in spring, use the prunings as cutting material. Cut up the stem, leaving about 2 inches (5 cm) below each pair of leaves. Dip each cutting in hormone rooting powder and insert singly in 3½ inch (9 cm) pots of loam-based potting mixture. Cover with polythene bags and keep them at a temperature of 70°F (21°C) until rooted. Grow on and eventually pot up into 5 inch (13 cm) pots to grow to maturity.
Pests and diseases: Scale insects on the undersides of the leaves and on the stems are the worst nuisance. Aphids attack the young leaves and flowers in spring and summer.

ARAUCARIA EXCELSA
Better known as Norfolk Island pine, *A. excelsa* (syn.

A. *heterophylla*) is a very close relative of the monkey puzzle tree – the tall, pine-like tree that is often seen in gardens. The Norfolk Island pine is an elegant plant resembling a Christmas tree that normally grows to between 4 and 6½ ft (1.5 and 2 m) in the house. It is not a hardy plant and must be grown indoors.

General care: The adaptable araucaria tolerates a wide range of conditions. As an optimum, it prefers a temperature of 60–65°F (15–18°C) and a reasonably well-lit position, even in full sun. The plant can, however, be grown at lower temperatures down to 50°F (10°C) with more shade. Leggy plants can be cut back hard and will grow again. The one thing araucaria does not like is too much water. Allow the soil to almost dry out between waterings. The soft spine-like foliage collects dust which is best removed by regularly spraying the plant with tepid water.

Propagation: The easiest way to propagate araucaria is from seed, which should be sown in a pot half-filled with a seeding mixture. Lightly cover the seed with the mixture and keep at 68°F (20°C) until germinated. When the seedlings are large enough to handle – approximately 2 inches (5 cm) tall – gently transplant them individually into 3½ inch (9 cm) pots filled with potting soil. Shoots from cut-back plants can be taken as cuttings in late summer, inserting them in a 50–50 peat and sand mix in a propagator.

Pests and diseases: Generally trouble-free, but may be attacked by mealy bugs and root mealy bugs.

ARDISIA

The coral berry's principal attraction is its crop of brilliant scarlet berries which may linger on for as long as a year. *A. crenata* is a shrubby plant. It grows slowly, but with adequate warmth and humidity it will eventually reach 4 ft (1.2 m) high and nearly as wide. Its shiny, elliptical

green foliage and spire-like clusters of pinkish and white flowers which bloom in spring make it worth the time it takes to reach maturity. *A. japonica* grows to 2 ft (60 cm) tall. After the plants reach 18 inches (45 cm), they shed their lower leaves and appear treelike.

General care: The coral berry prefers bright light but no direct sunlight. Water and spray freely in fall and feed every other week with diluted liquid fertilizer. Ordinary potting soil is adequate. Temperatures should not fall below 50°F (10°C) at night or 70°F (21°C) during the day. Prune the plant down to 2 inches (5 cm) in spring and keep dry until new shoots appear.

Propagation: Sow seed from ripe berries in peat moss in early spring or take cuttings from lateral shoots.

Pests and diseases: Generally trouble-free.

ASPARAGUS FERN

Not all types of asparagus are grown to be eaten! Of the ornamental varieties suited to pot culture, two make excellent house plants: *A. plumosus* (syn. *A. setaceus*) and Asparagus 'Sprengeri'. They produce beautiful, bright green feathery foliage which is, incidentally, invaluable in flower arrangements. They are displayed to good advantage in a hanging basket or on a high shelf.

General care: Although asparagus ferns prefer not to be allowed to dry out completely, they can tolerate this condition even in summer. Nevertheless, the soil is best kept relatively moist through the growing season, and drier in winter. A lightly shaded situation is best, although they will tolerate direct light or deeper shade. During the growing season, provide a temperature of around 55–65°F (13–18°C). A minimum temperature of about 50°F (10°C) is required in winter.

Propagation: Propagate by division in spring. Water the plant well first to ease separation. Gently tease the roots apart using a sharp knife to cut cleanly through any parts that do not separate easily. Pot up each piece into a suitably sized pot containing a loam-based seeding mixture, and grow on. They are also easy to grow from seed sown in spring at 65°F (18°C).

Pests and diseases: Generally trouble-free, but look out for scale insects.

ASPIDISTRA

Although not a spectacular plant, aspidistra is extremely reliable. The dark green leaves are held erect by the plant, which needs a striking container to set it off.

General care: Aspidistra does not demand a great deal of attention. A temperature of around 60°F (15°C) is ideal and a position away from direct sun is most satisfactory. A dry environment may cause the leaf tips and edges to turn brown; if this occurs, try misting the leaves with tepid water. Clean the leaves, which tend to trap dust, by lightly wiping with a cotton wool pad moistened with water.

Allow the plant almost to dry out in between waterings. Do not overwater, particularly in winter.

Propagation: This is carried out by division of the roots in spring or summer.

Pests and diseases: Watch for spider mites and mealy bugs.

Ardisia crenata

ASPLENIUM

Asplenium nidus, or bird's-nest fern, has broad, strap-like fronds radiating from a central rosette.

General care: One of the easiest ferns to grow, it is quite happy at relatively low temperatures, down to 50°F (10°C), although it prefers to be kept at around 65°F (18°C). It is also rather more tolerant than other ferns of a dry atmosphere, although it shares with them a preference for semi-shade, away from direct sunlight. It is less susceptible than many other ferns to over- or underwatering.

Propagation: This fern is propagated from minute dust-like spores produced from dark brown gill-like objects on the underside of mature fronds. Collect these spores carefully and sprinkle them on to the surface of a half pot filled with a peat-based mixture. Place the pot in a plastic bag and keep it moist at about 70°F (21°C) until the spores germinate. Leave until large enough to handle, then transplant.

Pests and diseases: Scale insects are the most likely pests.

AUCUBA

A. japonica, gold dust plant, is a hardy shrub that grows 15 ft (4.5 m) tall. It can be grown outside in frost-free places, but it has established itself as a good house plant for cool, dark corners. The plant is densely covered with glossy dark green leaves that vary from 3–8 inches (7.5–20 cm) long. It produces tiny dark red flowers in early spring, followed by clusters of red berries if male and female plants are grown close to each other. Its popular name comes from the gold-spotted leaves of 'Variegata' and 'Crotonfolia'.

Other selections include 'Fructu Albo', green leaves edged in white and pinkish-beige berries; 'Picturata', yellow leaves rimmed with dark green spotted with gold; and 'Sulphur', green leaves edged in yellow.

General care: Aucubas will tolerate very low light and low temperatures. Mist and water in summer and occasionally in spring. Pot in humus-enriched potting soil that is about one-quarter sand. Prune in late winter to maintain form and wash the foliage regularly to protect against pests.

Propagation: Sow ripe seeds or take cuttings in spring.

Pests and diseases: Watch for mealy bugs and mites.

AZALEA

Rhododendron indicum hybrids, the so-called Indian azaleas, are most colorful flowering plants that are seasonal from autumn to spring. Azaleas are available in a wide range of colors from white, rose-pink and salmon to cerise-red. If looked after reasonably well, they will last in flower for up to 8 weeks.

General care: Keep azaleas reasonably moist but not over-wet. Azaleas that are allowed to get dry seldom recover and rapidly decline. Temperature and light are equally important. A light and airy situation – a bedroom windowsill, for example – at not above 60°F (15°C) is ideal. Central heating can often be fatal and will certainly reduce the flowering period to as little as 2 weeks.

When the plant has finished flowering it can be placed outdoors in the summer. Plunge the pot in a peat bed and keep it moist throughout the summer. Feeding with a tomato fertilizer at about half strength once a month will assist growth. One or two applications of iron chelate will prevent yellowing of the leaves. When they have been brought back indoors in September, most azaleas will flower reasonably well. They can be made to flower in greater profusion, however, by a simple technique. In the evening, spray the plant with tepid water and iron chelate. Repeat this for a few weeks and you will find that the relatively high temperature and humidity have helped to produce flowers. Do remember to place the plant in full light during daylight hours.

Propagation: Azaleas can be raised from cuttings in summer or seed in spring but the results are usually so disappointing that it is not worth trying.

Pests and diseases: Azaleas suffer from few pests, although aphids can sometimes be a problem on the flower buds.

BEGONIA REX

Begonia rex or fan plant is available in a wide range of leaf colors and patterns. The leaves are roughly heart-shaped with prominent fleshy veins on the underside. The small, insignificant flowers may be pale pink or white.

General care: *Begonia rex* must be kept away from direct sun. It is therefore best to place the plant on a shaded windowsill or even up to 5 ft (1.5 m) away from the window. The plant is fairly tolerant of a warm dry environment and is usually happy at a temperature of about 65°F (18°C). Water regularly but in moderation; reduce the watering to a minimum in winter or the plant may rot.

Propagation: The method of propagation is by leaf cut-

Azalea indicum hybrids come in a wide range of colors

tings. Select a well-formed mature (not old) leaf, lay it face down and cut into postage-stamp squares using a sharp knife. Gently lay right-side up on the surface of a seed tray filled with moistened seeding mixture. Cover with a plastic bag and keep at about 70°F (21°C). Remove any cuttings that wither or rot; about half should 'take'. Remove the cover when the little plantlets start to grow from the cut edge of the pieces. When they are large enough to handle, pot singly in potting soil.

Pests and diseases: Generally trouble-free.

BELOPERONE GUTTATA

Beloperone guttata (syn. *Justicia brandegeana*) is known as the shrimp plant because of the oddly shaped shrimp-like flower spikes it produces. They are small and white, enclosed in reddish-brown bracts, and last several weeks before dropping off.

General care: Since the beloperone likes plenty of light, put the pot in a well-lit window. During the winter months, the plants may become straggly. Prune in early spring to encourage more compact growth. Feed once a month with half-strength tomato fertilizer rather than a house plant fertilizer in order to induce sturdy growth and plenty of flowers rather than leaves. In the flowering period, give water freely. In the winter, give just enough to prevent the compost drying out.

Propagation: When you prune the plant in spring, make the trimmings into cuttings 2–3 inches (5–7 cm) in length. Dip into hormone rooting powder and insert in individual pots of equal parts of peat and sand. Cover the pots with plastic bags to conserve moisture and keep at about 68°F (20°C). Pot on into a loam-based seeding mixture when they have rooted well.

Pests and diseases: May be affected by red spider mites or whitefly.

BILLBERGIA

Of the bromeliad family, billbergia is one of the easier members of the group to cultivate. It grows quickly with dramatic, summer-blooming flower shafts that spiral 2 ft (60 cm) high surrounded by strap-like leaves which form a cup. The most common variety is *B. nutans*, known as angel's tears or queen's tears because of its arching tubular pink bracts with blue-edged green flowers. Its foliage is gray-green and grass-like.

B. windii has green leaves which grow to 15 inches (38 cm) long and pale green flowers, tinged with blue and

Beloperone guttata (front) and Bougainvillea

with bright yellow stamens. 'Fantasia' has leaves marked with pale green or cream-colored spots. When given lots of sun, the foliage turns bronze. The flower bracts are deep coral with indigo blue flowers. *B. horrida tigrina* has rust-colored leaves edged with silver and lavender-tipped green flowers. Billbergia's blooms do not last as long as many in the bromeliad family, but several rosettes flower simultaneously in mature plants.

General care: Billbergia does well in regular potting soil with no lime and a good percentage of sand and peat moss. Add a layer of gravel to the bottom of the pot to ensure good drainage. It needs full sun to flower well, but it will tolerate some shade. Keep in a relatively constant temperature of 65°F (18°C) or warmer in the summer. Make sure that the center of the plant is kept filled with water and keep the soil moist during the summer. Mist the foliage frequently on hot summer days. Reduce the watering in the winter and move to a cooler location. Feed with diluted fish emulsion every other week.

Propagation: Propagate from shoots that appear on the base after flowering.

Pests and diseases: Generally trouble-free.

BOUGAINVILLEA

The bougainvillea or paper flower provides a glorious display of color. It needs the support of stakes or a frame. As with poinsettias, the flowers are insignificant – it is the papery bracts surrounding them that provide color – pink, red, magenta or orange. The flowering period usually lasts from midsummer well into the autumn.

General care: Bougainvillea needs as much light as possible during the active growing season. A temperature of about 65–68°F (18–20°C) is ideal and a fairly humid environment is essential. Mist regularly with tepid water during spring and summer and take care to prevent the soil drying out between waterings. Good drainage is essential, however, and the pot must not sit in a saucer of water for long periods. Weekly feeding with a diluted tomato fertilizer will promote flowering.

Billbergia nutans

Over winter, keep the plant on the dry side at a temperature of around 50–55°F (10–13°C). In spring, prune lightly, reducing the plant by a quarter of its height to encourage bushy, well-shaped growth.

Propagation: To succeed with bougainvillea cuttings you will need a propagator that can provide a constant bottom heat of 70–75°F (21–24°C). Take 3–4 inch (7.5–10 cm) cuttings in summer and insert in 2 inch (5 cm) pots of

4 parts seeding mixture to 1 part sand. Keep in the case until rooted – about 3 weeks – and allow the young plants to adjust gradually to room conditions.

Pests and diseases: Aphids, mealy bugs or red spider mites may attack.

CALADIUM

Fancy-leaved caladiums are among the most beautiful of the foliage plants. There are many different-colored varieties but they all share large, 12–18 inch (30–45 cm)

long, heart-shaped leaves, some of which are nearly translucent. The masses of foliage range from red to bright pink, creamy whites and pale greens to various combinations. Caladiums grow 2–3 ft (60–90 cm) tall and spread to 4 ft (1.2 m) wide. Some striking selections include 'Clarice', pinkish-white centers with red veins bordered in rich green; 'White Queen', white leaves turning to light green on the edges with red veins; 'Postman Joyner', dark red leaves with deeper red veins edged in dark green; and 'Ivory', ivory white shaded with pale, cool green.

General care: Caladiums thrive in partial shade and filtered sunlight – direct sun will sear the leaves. They prefer warm temperatures that do not fall below 65°F (18°C). Plant in acid soil, mixing standard potting soil with sand, a bit of charcoal and some bonemeal. Water and mist frequently and feed every other week.

Propagation: Caladiums are tuberous. Plant tubers, one to a pot, in early spring. Supply high humidity and temperatures at about 75°F (24°C). Feed with dilute fertilizer when growth first appears. In fall decrease the water supply as the leaves begin to shrivel. Remove all the dead leaves and keep dry for 2 months.

Pests and diseases: Watch for aphids, mealy bugs and red spider mites.

CALCEOLARIA

The unusual flowers of calceolaria look like half-inflated balloons of bright yellow, orange or red. The flowers are often spotted or streaked and are borne on short stems above a rosette-like cluster of broad leaves. It lasts fairly well indoors and usually flowers in spring and summer for 2–3 months. It is best disposed of after flowering.

General care: Calceolaria will not give of its best in warm, dry conditions, and prefers a fairly cool, light position such as a north-facing windowsill. A temperature of 50–60°F (10–15°C) is best. Temperatures may well rise during summer, but this will not seriously affect the plant – it is only troubled by constant high temperature. Always keep the soil just moist but not wet. Occasional feeding with diluted tomato fertilizer will encourage the plant to remain fairly stocky and to carry a good show of flowers.

Propagation: Calceolaria seed should be germinated from late spring through mid-summer in seed trays filled with seeding mixture. Keep the temperature around 65°F (18°C) until the seed has germinated and grow on until large enough to handle. At this stage, transplant the seedlings and pot individually in 3½–5 inch (9–13 cm) pots of soil. For sturdy plants, grow in a cold frame or greenhouse and only bring indoors when the weather cools in autumn.

Pests and diseases: Often attacked by aphids and whitefly.

CAPSICUM

The ornamental pepper plant, *C. annum*, is an annual from tropical America which grows to 12 inches (30 cm) and is prized for its pungent, bright red fruit. The peppers, which are very hot but edible, appear in summer and change from green to white, then from yellow to red. It is difficult to grow without a greenhouse, and most plants are purchased when the fruit is already in evidence. 'Christmas Greeting' has green, purple, yellow or red fruit; the fruit of 'Fiesta' ripens from yellow to orange to red; and 'Rising Sun' has red, tomato-like fruit.

General care: Capsicum likes bright light, but shies away from the hot sun of mid-day. Plant in standard potting mix and feed monthly until the fruit sets. Keep moderately moist and water freely when the temperature rises.

Propagation: Propagate from seeds in early spring in a propagator in darkness.

When the seeds germinate, give them some light and thin out seedlings. Transplant into separate pots when the plants have reached about 3 inches (7.5 cm) high.

Pests and diseases: Watch out for whitefly.

CATTLEYA

Cattleya is the most familiar of the orchid family, the most widely cultivated and the easiest to grow. The flowers are exquisite, fragrant and commonly used as corsages. They range from 5–8 inches (13–20 cm) long and appear above stalks that rise to 18 inches (45 cm) tall. Native to South and Central America, some cattleyas bloom three times each year.

Cattleya grows from rhizomes that stretch along the surface of the soil. The root system develops on the underside and the stems develop from the top. The swollen lower part of the stem is called the pseudobulb. The genus is divided into two categories: the labiate plants, which have single leaves growing from each pseudobulb; and the bifoliates, which have flower spikes rising between paired leaves from the pseudobulbs.

In the labiate group, which tends to be larger than the other, *C. labiata* itself bears ruffle-lipped flowers in the fall varying in color from deep mauve to rose to white, often with yellow throats. *C. trianae* produces flowers that grow to 9 inches (23 cm) wide and range from deep purple to white, blooming from late fall through the winter. *C. mossiae* is similar in color, but its flowers are slightly smaller than *C. trianae*, growing to 8 inches (20 cm) wide and blooming in spring. *C. gaskelliana* has deep amethyst-purple flowers, suffused with white, which bloom in summer.

The bifoliate group includes *C. loddigesii*, which grows 12 inches (30 cm) tall with rosy-lilac flowers blooming in late summer and early fall. *C. aclandiae* has yellowish-green flowers

with contrasting deep purple markings. *C. aurantiaca* includes a number of small selections that are suitable for growing in terrariums. 'Gwen Turner' with its small, brilliant, orange-red flowers, is a good choice.

General care: Cattleya needs bright light, but it should be protected from the hottest mid-day sun. Night temperatures should not fall below 50°F (10°C) with warmer temperatures during the day. It thrives in humid atmospheres, but its potting mixture should be allowed to almost dry out between good soakings. Plant in commercially available orchid mix and feed monthly with orchid fertilizer or other high nitrogen mix during the active growing season. After flowering, reduce watering and feeding until the new growth cycle begins.

Propagation: Propagation is by division of the rhizomes. Cultivation techniques are quite complicated. Check with a specialized source if you have an interest in propagating your own.

Pests and diseases: Generally trouble-free.

*Chamaedorea elegans (**behind**) (see p. 136) and Nephrolepis exaltata or the ladder fern (see p. 148)*

CEROPEGIA

The rosary vine is a charming, easy-to-care-for house plant. Its delicate appearance belies its ability to endure the dry, poorly lit conditions of many dwelling spaces. Ideal for a hanging pot or basket, ceropegia is a small succulent whose trailing stems grow quickly to 4 ft (1.2 m) or more. *C. woodii* has tiny, fleshy, speckled gray-green, heart-shaped leaves that grow on wiry, trailing stems. Tubular purple and pink flowers appear in late summer. *C. sandersonii* is a climber rather than a trailer, and it is suitable for a small trellis.

General care: Ceropegia will tolerate shady conditions, but it prefers a well-lit location out of mid-day sun. Pot in humus-rich potting soil with extra sand added for good drainage. Water sparingly, especially in winter, and keep in temperatures of 60–70°F (15–21°C). Pinch back stems severely to encourage new growth.

Propagation: Small corms develop in the angle formed by the stem and leaves. These may be removed and planted in a pot filled with peat moss and sand. Leave the tops of the corms above the soil level, water carefully, and they will quickly root. Propagation is also by cuttings or from seed sown in early spring.

Pests and diseases: Watch for mites.

CHAMAEDOREA ELEGANS

Also called *Neanthe bella* or parlor palm, this is a compact palm that takes some time to reach 2 ft (60 cm) in height and grows taller only slowly. It is one of the easiest palms to cultivate.

General care: Parlor palms prefer a semi-shaded position away from direct light, which turns the leaves pale. Maintain a minimum temperature of about 65°F (18°C) in spring and summer and spray once or twice a day with a mist of tepid water to increase humidity. In winter

it prefers to be kept cooler, at 45–50°F (7–10°C). Let the soil dry out between waterings. Feed about once a month during the growing period (April–September).

Chamaedorea sometimes produces a flower spike, which can be snipped off if you do not like the look of it. The flowers that form look like small yellow blobs. If you are lucky, tiny pea-like fruits may set, and these can be used for propagation.

Flowers are unlikely to appear before the plant is 3–4 years old.

Propagation: You can buy seeds or save your own if you have a plant that flowers. Sow in a seed tray filled with seeding mixture and then cover with a polythene bag. The seeds need a temperature of at least 70°F (21°C) to germinate and even then they may take 3–6 months to grow.

Pests and diseases: Generally trouble-free, but red spider mites, mealy bugs, root mealy bugs and scale insects are occasional problems; red spider mites are the most damaging to this plant.

CHLOROPHYTUM

Chlorophytum has long been known as the spider plant. It

Chlorophytum, Cissus antarctica and (**front**) *Begonia rex* (see p. 132)

Clivia miniata

has green and white striped leaves and reproduces itself by producing plantlets on the flowering stems – seed being seldom or never produced.

General care: Chlorophytum is very easy to keep and adapts well to various household conditions. Lots of light and a temperature of about 60°F (15°C) are best but by no means essential.

In early spring, shade the plant from the first scorching rays of the sun as these can brown the leaves. The plant adapts rapidly, however, and can soon tolerate direct sunlight for periods of the day.

Avoid overwatering and allow the plant to become almost dry between waterings. If the leaf tips turn brown, simply snip them off with a pair of scissors.

Propagation: The plantlets on the flowering stems can easily be used as a ready means of propagation. Simply look for the start of the first roots which appear even before the plantlet is removed from its parent. When these are evident, cut off the plantlet and pot in a 3½ inch (9 cm) pot of potting soil. Cut back the flowering stems to the base of the parent to keep the original plant looking tidy.

Pests and diseases: Generally trouble-free.

CISSUS ANTARCTICA
Sometimes referred to as the kangaroo vine, this cissus has a very similar habit to the rhoicissus. The leaf shape is a pointed oval with a serrated but not sharp edge.

General care: An indoor temperature of 60–65°F (15–18°C) is best, although 55°F (13°C) is adequate. A reasonably light position is favored. Too much direct sunlight will bleach the color out of the leaves. Do not keep the plant in a dry atmosphere as dehydration causes leaf tips and edges to turn brown.

The cissus is a good climbing plant, but it may become a little straggly. If this happens, trim back to keep it in shape.

Propagation: Use stem cuttings produced when pruning the plant. Cut them into sections each with 3–4 leaves, retaining about 1½ inches (4 cm) of stem below the bottom leaf. Dip this end into hormone rooting powder and insert into potting soil. Several cuttings can go in one pot – about 5 to a 3 ½ inch (9 cm) pot is perfectly all right. Cover the cuttings with a polythene bag until they have rooted.

Pests and diseases: Mealy bugs and aphids may attack.

CLIVIA
An old-fashioned parlor plant, the kaffir lily has handsome, strap-like foliage and striking, bright orange, trumpet-shaped flowers, making it a good year-round choice for house plant collections. It is a relative of the amaryllis and a native of South Africa. Adult plants reach 2–3 ft (60–90 cm), and the flowers bloom in late winter to early spring. *C. miniata var.* 'Citrina' has pale yellow flowers.

General care: Plant in potting soil rich in humus and organic fertilizer. Water freely during the flowering season and feed weekly with mild liquid fertilizer. Reduce water during the winter and stop feeding. Kaffir lilies like moderate temperatures and a bright northeast or northwest position out of direct sunlight. The plant performs well when rootbound, but it needs to be divided every 3–4 years right after flowering.

Propagation: Propagate by dividing small plants that form at the base of the parent or from seed.

Pests and diseases: Watch for mites and scale insects.

CODIAEUM
C. variegatum pictum, popularly known as croton or Joseph's coat, is a wonderfully colorful foliage plant, but it is not the easiest house plant to cultivate. Its long, wavy, oval or lance-shaped foliage begins a deep green and matures into a rainbow of colors, including yellow, pink, red, bronze and purple, depending on the amount of sun it receives. When grown as a house plant, codiaeum reaches 2 ft (60 cm), although in the greenhouse it can grow to 5 ft (1.5 m) or more.

General care: Croton has an annoying habit of dropping its bottom leaves when conditions are not perfectly suitable. To grow it successfully, keep it out of drafts and cold rooms. Croton thrives in light, sunny sites with high humidity and lots of water. Feed every other week with liquid fertilizer during the summer growing season and spray the foliage frequently. Temperatures should remain relatively constant at 65°F (18°C). Plant in a loam-based, standard potting mix.

Propagation: Cuttings taken from the top of the plant will root in a peat and sand mixture. Take cuttings in the spring. They will root more readily in a propagator.

Pests and diseases: Croton is particularly susceptible to red spider mites. Keep the atmosphere moist to discourage an infestation.

Columnea (right) and Gardenia (see p. 143)

COLEUS

The flame nettle, *C. blumei*, together with its numerous varieties, has long been a popular pot plant with its brightly colored and patterned leaves. Named sorts can be obtained from nurserymen, but seed strains are good and available in varied forms and colors.

General care: A windowsill with half-day or dappled sun is best. Extra humidity is not essential. Use one of the standard all-peat potting soils and apply a standard liquid feed at intervals of 2–3 weeks once the plants are well rooted and growing strongly. Keep the soil just moist but not over-wet. Pinch out the tips of the plants when 4 inches (10 cm) tall to promote bushy plants. The long spikes of blue flowers are attractive but they drop and make a mess so it is usually recommended to pinch them out when young.

Propagation: Sow seeds in spring at about 65°F (18°C); transplant the seedlings into boxes and then pot the best-colored ones when they have 4–5 pairs of leaves. Take cuttings in late summer or spring in a propagating case at seed sowing temperatures. Each cutting should have two pairs of leaves and will root better if dipped in a hormone rooting powder.

Pests and diseases: Generally trouble-free.

COLUMNEA

Few trailing plants give flowers; of those that do, none is as beautiful as columnea, with its magnificent flame-red flowers streaked with yellow, projecting like trumpets from its long stem of tiny paired leaves.

General care: If you have a warm, reasonably well-lit bathroom or kitchen where the temperature is about 68°F (20°C) and there is sufficient ceiling space to hang a columnea, you will be delighted by the colorful display that it will give each year. A bathroom or kitchen is best because the columnea thrives in a relatively humid environment. Although the plant needs light, it should not have prolonged exposure to direct sunlight which will discolor and scorch the leaves.

While columnea likes a relatively moist atmosphere, too much water at the root is harmful. Reduce watering to the bare minimum over winter. In this season it can also tolerate a lower temperature – down to about 55°F (13°C). After this cooler period, columnea will gently break into a massive display of flowers down the lengths of the trails.

If the plant gets unmanageably long, simply trim back the trails to an acceptable length.

Propagation: Take cuttings and divide them into sections of 3–4 pairs of leaves, leaving approximately ½–¾ inch (1–2 cm) below the bottom pair. Dip the cuttings in hormone rooting powder and insert about 4 cuttings into a 3 inch (7.5 cm) pot of seeding mixture. Cover with a polythene bag to conserve moisture. When rooted, remove the bag and grow the cuttings on in the pot. Pot the plants, still together, into a larger pot the following year.

Pests and diseases: Occasionally mealy bugs and aphids may attack the flowers during spring and summer.

CROSSANDRA

A native of the East Indies, the firecracker plant is a beautiful choice for an indoor garden and is well worth the extra effort it requires. It rewards the gardener with salmon pink flowers borne on long spikes from spring through the autumn and grows to 12 inches (30 cm) high with glossy, dark green, gardenia-like leaves. *C. infundibuliformis* 'Mona Walhed' is the only variety commonly available.

General care: The firecracker plant needs good light with protection from strong midday sun. Moderate temperatures that do not fall below 60°F (15°C) and frequent watering with tepid water will encourage blooming. Overwatering will cause yellowing of the foliage, and water that is too cold will produce spotting on the lower leaves. Do not spray from overhead. Feed with diluted liquid fertilizer every 2 weeks throughout the year and plant in regular potting soil mixed equally with sand or vermiculite. It has a tendency to look straggly after 2 years, so prune in spring to shape the plant.

Propagation: Propagate from root cuttings that have at least two sets of healthy leaves. Dip in rooting hormone, place in rooting medium and supply bottom heat.

Pests and diseases: Generally trouble-free.

CYCLAMEN

Cyclamen must be one of the most popular flowering house plants, producing blooms of white, pink, salmon, mauve, red or lilac over a long period, from early autumn to summer.

The silver-leaved cyclamen is probably the best-known type. It is, however, the one most likely to suffer from the normal home environment. The mini-cyclamen is hardier and more tolerant of household conditions. As the name suggests, it is smaller and the leaves are less colorful than the silver-leaved strain, but its flowers are magnificent; some of them even have a slight scent.

General care: Unfortunately, cyclamen is not the easiest plant to care for. Warm, dry, airless conditions spell its rapid demise and induce the all-too-common sight of a plant that has collapsed, its leaves and flowers drooping around the pot. Cyclamen prefers cool, light, airy conditions with a temperature of about 55°F (13°C). It does not tolerate central heating. A cool bedroom windowsill or any other light position away from excessive heat is ideal.

Watering is best carried out from below to avoid the risk of botrytis setting in on the corm.

After flowering, the plant will gradually die back to its corm. It can be left for a few weeks to rest; during this period it should be kept on the dry side. After about a month, start to give water again. Once active growth commences, feed every 2 weeks with a tomato fertilizer to encourage flowering.

Propagation: Cyclamen is relatively easy to propagate from seed. You can either buy it or collect your own from the plant. When the flowers have been pollinated their petals fall off, leaving behind a globular capsule where the seeds ripen. When the receptacle has matured it splits open, exposing the seeds.

Sow seed in trays of seeding mixture. Cover with about ⅛ inch (3 mm) of soil and keep at about 65°F (18°C) until germination has occurred – usually about 6–8 weeks. When the seedlings are large enough to handle, carefully transplant them into separate pots and grow on, watering carefully.

Pests and diseases: Cyclamen is prone to botrytis (gray mold fungus).

CYPERUS

C. alternifolius, also called the umbrella plant, is related to the ancient Egyptian papyrus, the plant from which paper was originally manufactured. The umbrella plant is highly regarded in modern households for its graceful beauty and its adaptable nature. It loves water, as its natural habitat is marshland. Its common name alludes to the way the leaves curve out at the top of the stem.

C. alternifolius grows 3–5 ft (90 cm–1.5 m) high in a clump of stiff stems with narrow palm-like leaves that radiate from the top. *C. a. gracilis* is similar but grows to only about 16 inches (40 cm) in height. 'Alba Variegata' has white stripes along the leaves. *C. diffusus* reaches 3 ft (90 cm) and has a spreading habit. The most beautiful cyperus is *C. papyrus*, and it is also the most difficult to cultivate. It grows best in a greenhouse, attaining a height of 6 ft (1.8 m). It is the only member of the family to blossom readily, producing drooping, radiating blooms.

General care: Cyperus loves moisture, and it thrives if its pot stands in lime-free water. Mist frequently and add diluted fertilizer every other week. Plant in standard potting mix, enriched with peat moss and perlite. Place in a bright, but not directly sun-exposed, position where air circulation is good and temperatures range between 50–60°F (10–15°C).

Propagation: Cyperus propagates easily from cuttings or from dividing an overcrowded plant in spring. Cuttings can be rooted in soil or in water.

Pests and diseases: Watch for whitefly.

CYRTOMIUM

C. falcatum looks very much like the holly used to decorate the house at Christmas, but it is in fact a member of the fern family. The small leaves that make up the fronds are a dark, glossy green. The holly fern has a graceful, spreading habit and is among the easiest of ferns to grow in the house. It grows to a height and spread of 3 ft (90 cm), and the fronds measure 6 inches (15 cm) wide. 'Rochfordii' is more compact and will withstand dark corners.

General care: The holly fern will tolerate near-freezing temperatures. Water freely during the growing season, mist occasionally and feed monthly. During the winter, reduce the water supply, stop feeding and put in a cooler location. Pot in well-drained potting soil with a bit of humus. Cyrtomiums like to be root-bound. When repotting is necessary, do so in spring and cut the plants back to encourage new growth.

Propagation: Propagate by division of established plants.

Pests and diseases: Aphids, red spider mites and scale insects can be a problem. Do not use insecticides on cyrtomium as they damage the fronds. Treat infected plants with soap and water or nicotine sulphate if the condition is serious.

DIEFFENBACHIA

Best known as dumb-cane, this group of plants is grown for its large, paddle-shaped, boldly variegated leaves. When mature, the plant may produce an insignificant flower spike that looks like an arum lily. The sap of the plant is poisonous and care should therefore be taken when trimming any leaves on the plant. Do not have one if there are children about.

General care: Dieffenbachia likes a warm, humid environment with a temperature of about 68°F (20°C). As it prefers light shade, it is happiest in the middle of a room. Though watering is not so critical, dieffenbachia

Cyperus alternifolius

is best kept relatively moist in summer, somewhat drier in winter. Yellowing leaves should be cut off at the base before they rot. If the plant becomes too tall, with a long bare stem, cut it back to about 2 inches (5 cm) above soil level and it will break into growth again.

Propagation: Dieffenbachia sometimes produces offsets which can be removed from the parent plant and potted on. Alternatively, if you cut the plant back, divide the stem into 2 inch (5 cm) sections. Lay them on their sides in a tray of moist seeding mixture. Cover and keep at 70°F (21°C) until rooted. Remove the cover and allow to grow on until large enough to handle and pot.

Pests and diseases: Red spider mites and mealy bugs are the worst nuisances; root mealy bugs may inhibit growth.

DIZYGOTHECA
The lacy *D. elegantissima*, often called false aralia, has delicate, feathery foliage, arranged much like that of a palm. The leaves are rich, deep green on the top and rusty-red underneath. The long, arching branches grow to 3–5 ft (90 cm–1.5 m) or taller if their upright shoots are not pinched back. *D. veitchii* is shorter and wider with deeper green foliage.

General care: False aralias like bright, northern exposures and warm temperatures around 60°F (15°C). Plant in standard potting mix, fertilize every two weeks and spray daily from early spring through fall. Allow the soil to almost dry out between waterings. Place in a draft-free location.

Propagation: Propagate from seed sown in a propagator in spring or from cuttings.

Pests and diseases: Watch for aphids and mealy bugs.

DRACAENA
D. deremensis is one of the hardier species of this genus. The leaf color of the plant is attractive and the long, slender, pointed leaves are

beautifully patterned in parallel streaks of green, white and cream. *D. marginata* is less spectacular and bears narrow dark green leaves with red edges.

General care: A slightly shaded situation is best, but short periods of exposure to sunlight will be tolerated. Let the soil almost dry out between waterings. Because of their thick leaves, dracaenas can store water for quite a long time and can cope with being kept on the dry side. A temperature of around 65°F (18°C) is best, although plants will tolerate cooler conditions.

Propagation: Basal shoots or stem tips can be rooted as cuttings in a propagating case at 70°F (21°C). The leafless stems of cut-back leggy plants can also be used. Cut into pieces about 1 inch (2.5 cm) long. Lay these sections on their sides in a tray of seeding mixture. Rooting should take place within 8 weeks. Transplant when the young plants are large enough to handle and grow on in individual pots.

Pests and diseases: Mealy

bugs and root mealy bugs are the major pests; the former may be found tucked in the little niche at the base of the leaf stalk where it joins the main stem.

ECHEVERIA
This genus contains 150 succulent plants, some rosette-forming, others of shrubby appearance. They bear tubular flowers of white, yellow-orange or red. *Echeveria glauca*, with blue-gray leaves, is one of the most common varieties, and can be grown outside in summer.

General care: Echeveria is a tough little plant but it does have certain preferences. In summer it needs plenty of water; in winter it should be kept almost dry. The plant likes to spend summer outdoors in the sun and air. Bring it indoors in autumn and give it plenty of light, with a minimum temperature of 41°F (5°C).

Propagation: Echeveria can be propagated quite easily from cuttings by gently pulling off a leaf and obliquely inserting it in a mixture of

equal parts seeding mixture and sand. Use the same mixture to raise echeveria from seed.

Pests and diseases: Generally trouble-free, but mealy bugs and root mealy bugs may attack.

EPIPHYLLUM
Epiphyllum or orchid cactus is one of the most attractive of the flowering cacti. The beautiful flowers are borne on green, fleshy, flat-sided stems and vary in size from 2–6 inches (5–15 cm) across. They may be single or double, and colored white, yellow, pink, orange, red or lilac. Some of the flowers are fragrant.

General care: In winter, keep the plant relatively cool, down to 45°F (7°C), but never let it dry out. In spring and summer, maintain regular watering. Give a liquid feed every 2 weeks once the flower buds are visible in spring. The best position is one where the plant can enjoy plenty of light but not direct sun during midsummer.

Propagation: Epiphyllum can easily be propagated from stem cuttings taken in summer and inserted into pots of seeding mixture after they have been allowed to dry off for a few days. Alternatively, raise it from seed sown in spring in 4 parts seeding mixture and 1 part sand and germinate at 68°F (20°C). Transplant the seedlings when they are large enough to handle and pot.

Pests and diseases: Mealy bugs and root mealy bugs may attack; aphids occasionally infest the flowers. Spray with malathion or dimethoate.

EPISCIA
Episcia is a relative of African violet and gloxinia. Native to South America, its trailing form makes it perfect for hanging baskets. If pruned faithfully, it produces mounds of luxuriant foliage and dainty, attractive flowers which bloom from

Dracaena marginata

spring through autumn.

E. *cupreata*, the flame violet, is the best known. It has soft, copper-tinged leaves and tubular orange-red flowers. *E. dianthaflora* has furry green leaves and white flowers, and *E. lilacina* has bronze leaves and lavender flowers. Other varieties have blooms that range from white to red, including yellow.

General care: Episcia likes abundant moisture and high humidity, but avoid spraying the foliage directly. Situate in filtered light in warm conditions, ranging from 65–75°F (18–24°C). Blackened leaves signal that the temperature has dropped below the comfort zone. Plant in peat moss mixed with regular potting soil and add sand to help drainage. Feed every other week with diluted liquid fertilizer during the growing season. Pinch back to encourage branching and cut back after flowering to bring on new growth.

Propagation: Propagate from runners in a propagator with bottom heat of at least 70°F (21°C).

Pests and diseases: Watch for leaf miners and mealy bugs.

EUPHORBIA PULCHERRIMA

The 'flowers' of *Euphorbia pulcherrima*, known as poinsettia, are in fact modified leaves called bracts. The range of colors extends from white or cream through pink to the color which everyone knows, bright red. The flowers of euphorbia are the little pips in the center of the bracts.

General care: Euphorbia should be kept at about 65°F (18°C), well away from drafts. They like plenty of light but should be moved away from a window at night during winter when they are in color, for they are very sensitive to low and fluctuating temperatures. As the temperature drops, so do the leaves, followed by the bracts.

Care should also be taken with watering. Although

Exacum affine

they should not be allowed to dry out, they must not be overwatered or the roots will rot. After 'flowering', prune the plant in spring by removing one-third to one-half of the growth so that the plant will start to 'break'. As the new shoots grow, feed the plant every week with tomato fertilizer at half strength. If the plant starts to outgrow its pot, transfer it to a larger one.

At the end of September, do not allow the plant to be exposed to any artificial light after the hours of daylight, otherwise it will not form its colored bracts. Euphorbia by nature responds to the shortening autumn days by initiating flowers and bracts. Artificial light during the hours of darkness makes the plant behave as if it were still summer!

Propagation: Euphorbia can be propagated by taking basal shoots from cut-back plants as cuttings consisting of a shoot with 2 or 3 mature leaves. Dip this into hormone rooting powder and then into a small pot of equal parts peat and sand. Cover with a polythene bag and keep at around 70°F (21°C) until rooted. This normally takes 3–4 weeks.

When the roots are established, pot the plant into a larger container of potting soil.

Pests and diseases: Whitefly are more unsightly than harmful, but should not be left to get out of hand.

EXACUM

The sweetly fragrant Persian violet, *E. affine* is a charming annual for indoor growing. Its bluish-purple, gentian-like flowers provide color for 3–4 months. The plant should then be discarded and new ones started for the following year's blooming season. The summer-blooming flowers have prominent yellow stamens and appear among glossy green leaves. This compact annual grows between 8–12 inches (20–30 cm) tall. Selections include *E. a. atrocaeruleum*, deep lavender; 'Blithe Spirit', white, and 'Midget', true blue.

General care: Provide Persian violet with filtered light and warm temperatures ranging between 60–70°F (15–21°C). Very warm temperatures will result in a shorter blooming season. Water freely during the growing and flowering season and fertilize every other week. Plant in a mixture of regular potting soil

and peat moss with vermiculite added for drainage.

Propagation: Sow seed in early spring at 70°F (21°C). When the seedlings reach 2 inches (5 cm), transplant them in groups of three to 4 inch (10 cm) pots.

Pests and diseases: Generally trouble-free.

FATSIA JAPONICA

Also known as *Aralia sieboldii*, this Japanese shrub makes a very handsome and desirable foliage house plant for a cool or unheated room. Eventually growing to 3¼ ft (1 m) or more, it bears large, hand-shaped leathery leaves with a bright gloss.

General care: Dappled or partial shade provides the best conditions. Extra humidity is not essential. Use any of the approved potting soils and repot or top-dress annually. Keep the soil moist but not overwet.

Propagation: Stem tips or sucker shoots can be taken as cuttings in a propagating case in late summer, but purchased seed is easiest. Sow *Fatsia japonica* in spring and pot the seedlings singly once the first true leaf is well developed.

Pests and diseases: Generally trouble-free.

X FATSHEDERA

This useful foliage pot plant arose from the mating of *Fatsia japonica* with the Irish ivy *Hedera helix* var. *hibernica*. All the comments for fatsia apply here, but the leaves are smaller. If allowed to grow naturally, it becomes a loose, thin shrub which needs support. Frequent pinching back of the stem tip will make it bushy and self-supporting.

Propagation: Either by cuttings or by layering.

FICUS BENJAMINA

Ficus benjamina, weeping fig, is an elegant plant with cascading foliage that makes it particularly suitable as a single specimen plant rather than as part of a group display.

General care: Not as hardy as its sturdy relative the rubber plant, *Ficus benjamina* needs a stable temperature of around 68°F (20°C), although a steady 60°F (15°C) is adequate. The plant must be kept free from drafts. If it is subject to sudden chilling premature leaf drop rapidly ensues, leaving the plant looking like a skeleton. Give weeping figs a situation of semi-shade 3ft (90 cm) or so away from a window; direct sunlight may bleach the leaves. Allow the plant almost to dry out between waterings. A humid environment is beneficial but not essential.

Propagation: *Ficus benjamina* is very tricky to propagate. If you want to give it a try, take tip cuttings about 3–4 inches (7.5–10 cm) in length, dip them in hormone rooting powder and insert individually in a 2½ inch (6 cm) pot filled with seeding mixture. Keep at 70°F (21°C) and cover with a polythene bag to conserve moisture. When rooted, pot into a loam-based seeding mixture.

Pests and diseases: Mealy bugs and scale insects are the most likely problems.

FICUS ELASTICA

The rubber plant, as it is familiarly known, has become amazingly popular. Its thick, glossy, green leaves grow alternately up the stem of the plant, borne erect when young, drooping as they get older. Variegated forms are available with pink or cream tints on the margin. New leaves form inside a rosy-pink protective sheath, which is discarded when the young leaf unfurls.

General care: The rubber plant's reputation for durability has probably been overstated. Ideally, it should be grown in light shade at a temperature of about 65°F (18°C) away from drafts. Allow the soil almost to dry out between waterings; if it is kept too moist the lower leaves may fall, giving you 3 ft (1 m) of bare stem with 2–3 leaves at the top! To remove dust, clean the leaves with a cotton wool pad or soft cloth moistened with tepid water.

Propagation: Take stem-tip cuttings in spring, making them 4–6 inches (10–15 cm) long. Insert in pots of equal parts peat and sand and maintain a temperature of 70–75°F (21–24°C) until rooted.

Leaf bud cuttings are used commercially for propagation, but results for the amateur are not always successful so you are better off using stem cuttings.

Pests and diseases: Mealy bugs and scale insects are the main pests to watch for, though aphids may disfigure young leaves.

FITTONIA ARGYRO-NEURA

Perhaps better known as the snakeskin plant, this pretty species is delicately patterned in green with white veins. It is a low-growing plant, good for ground cover in mixed plantings or bottle gardens.

General care: If there is one thing the fittonia dislikes, apart from the cold, it is to be allowed to dry out. Keep it moist most of the time, at a temperature of about 65°F (18°C) in a well-lit situation away from direct sunlight. Avoid drafts and a

Ficus elastica

dry environment. Trim as necessary to maintain a compact plant during growth.

Propagation: The method of propagation is easy and usually successful. When the plant becomes rather leggy, cut off the straggling shoots and insert 5 of them in a 3½ inch (9 cm) pot of seedling mixture. Cover with a plastic bag until they have rooted. Remove the bag and let the plants grow on.

Pests and diseases: Generally trouble-free.

FREESIA

The deliciously fragrant, jewel-colored freesia is a tender, cormous plant that thrives in cool conditions and offers wonderful color at winter's end. Native to South Africa, freesia grows on slender, arching stems that reach 12–18 inches (30–45 cm) high. Tubular, 2 inch (5 cm) flowers grow in clusters, surrounded by lance-like foliage. New Dutch hybrids have double flowers. *F.* x *hybrida* includes 'Albatre', white; 'Buttercup', yellow-orange; 'Charmante', pink and apricot; 'Flambeau', bright scarlet; 'Maryon', lavender; and 'Princess Marijke', bronze, orange and yellow.

General care: Freesia needs shady, cool conditions of about 50–55°F (10–13°C) and evenly moist but not drenched soil until shoots appear. Plant in standard potting soil with sand added for good drainage. After the shoots emerge, move to a sunny window. Feed with a general fertilizer after flowering ends in the spring. After the foliage dies back, dry out and store in a cool spot until autumn.

Propagation: Plant freesia corms in fall, 2 inches (5 cm) deep with the pointed ends facing up. Group five or six corms in a 5 inch (13 cm) pot and keep cool until growth begins. Seeds planted in spring will flower the following year.

Pests and diseases: Watch for aphids.

GARDENIA

Gardenia is one of the most highly scented flowering plants, with magnificent creamy-white flowers and glossy dark leaves. A compact, bushy plant, it is lovely if you can master its rather demanding requirements.

General care: Gardenia likes a semi-shaded position away from direct sunlight and a temperature of about 68°F (20°C). It also requires humid conditions and a fairly acid soil. Watering with rainwater is beneficial, but if you cannot collect any, use boiled, cooled tap water. Boiling removes some of the calcium salts from hard water which gardenias dislike. Throughout spring and summer, water every two weeks with a half-strength solution of tomato fertilizer to help it produce good-quality flowers in profusion. An application or two of iron chelate during the flowering period will prevent chlorosis, a condition typified by yellow patches between the leaf veins. This is caused by an iron deficiency due to too much lime.

Propagation: It is difficult to propagate gardenia from cuttings, but worth a try. Take tip cuttings with 3–4 leaves and dip the base of the stems into hormone rooting powder. Insert the cuttings in individual pots containing 50–50 parts peat and sand. Cover each pot with a polythene bag and keep at about 70°F (21°C) until rooted. Reduce the temperature to 65°F (18°C) and keep the pots away from direct sunlight in light shade.

Pests and diseases: Red spider mites and mealy bugs occasionally attack. Aphids attack the flower buds and young growth.

Freesia x hybrida

GUZMANIA

A member of the bromeliad family, guzmania is favored for its brightly colored, petal-like bracts, which last for about 2 months. The strap-like leaves, which grow to 12–15 inches (30–38 cm) tall, form a water-holding cup. Guzmania is often used in combination with other plants in tubs to create a colorful display.

G. lingulata 'Minor' is the most commonly available variety. It has scarlet, orange and bright yellow bracts from which rather inconspicuous white flowers emerge, and leathery leaves that grow 12–18 inches (30–45 cm) long. *G. l. cardinalis* has scarlet-red bracts with yellowish-white flowers, and *G. monostachya* produces numerous bracts; the lower ones are white, striped with dark brown, and the uppers are orange to red with white flowers.

General care: Guzmania does best when planted in a clay pot. It thrives in humid conditions and needs frequent misting in the summer. Fill the pocket formed by the foliage with tepid water and keep the potting soil, which should be two-thirds peat moss, mixed with a bit of sand, damp but not dripping wet. Direct sun will burn the leaves of this sturdy-looking bromeliad, but it likes bright, indirect light. Feed monthly during the growing season with fish emulsion and keep temperatures between 60–70°F (15–21°C).

Propagation: Propagate by offsets that form at the base of the cup. When the leaves of the parent plant have withered, knock the plant from its pot and carefully cut the offset and roots from the

parent with a sharp knife. Pot the offset with its roots in potting soil and cover with plastic for a week to speed rooting.

Pests and diseases: Watch for aphids.

GYNURA

The velvet plant is a vigorous grower whose chief attraction is its leaves and stems, which are covered with fine purple hairs. The flowers, which bloom in the fall, smell very unpleasant and should be nipped in the bud. *G. aurantiaca* is an upright, bushy plant that grows to 3 ft (90 cm) tall and has lance-shaped, 6 inch (15 cm) long leaves. *G. sarmentosa* has a more delicate form with narrower leaves and a creeping habit. It can be trained as a vine if given a trellis to climb.

General care: Gynura tends to get spindly and needs frequent pruning to stimulate new, bushy growth. Situate out of direct sun in the summer, but if the plant receives too little light, it will lose its purple sheen. Water moderately, but be careful not to stain the leaves. Pot in regular potting mixture with some peat moss and perlite to improve drainage.

Propagation: The plant can be propagated easily from cuttings. It is wise to replace it every other year as its appearance fades quickly. Take 4 inch (10 cm) cuttings in spring, dip in rooting hormone and plant in a small pot of sand and peat moss. Keep covered with plastic for 3 weeks and transplant in regular potting mix.

Pests and diseases: Watch for aphids.

HEDERA CANARIENSIS

The Canary Island ivy is a magnificent species with large, deep green, glossy leaves of triangular outline. *H.c.* 'Gloire de Marengo' has the leaves irregularly bordered with cream.

General care: It likes sun or shade but dislikes being kept too warm. Keep it where the temperature will not

exceed 68°F (20°C). In rooms warmer than this, the atmosphere is likely to be too dry and the leaf tips and edges will turn brown. In winter the variegation tends to fade a little, but once light intensities increase in spring the brighter pigments return. Like all ivies, *Hedera canariensis* is a good climber or trailer. It is a useful plant for a porch or unheated room. Take care not to overwater this ivy, but let the soil become somewhat dry between waterings.

Propagation: Simply trim off any unwanted stems and cut them into pieces with 2–3 leaves on each. Leave about 1 inch (2.5 cm) of stem below the bottom leaf. Dip the cuttings in hormone rooting powder and put 5 of them into a 3½ inch (9 cm) pot of seeding mixture. Cover with a plastic bag to conserve moisture during rooting and remove the bag as soon as the plants start to grow.

Pests and diseases: Scale insects can cause severe damage by mottling the leaves. Aphids, mealy bugs and root mealy bugs can also be a problem.

HEDERA HELIX

The small-leaved English ivy produces an attractive climbing or trailing plant that can be grown outdoors as well as indoors. There are many variations with leaves of different shape, size and color.

General care: None of the ivies likes to be too warm. They prefer cool, even cold, light airy conditions, and are particularly happy in an unheated porch or room. In a warm, dry environment the leaves will dehydrate and eventually die. A temperature between 45–50°F (7–10°C) is adequate. Take care with watering, and allow the soil to become almost dry before rewatering. Most ivies that die have been overwatered.

Don't worry if any variegation fades in winter; in the spring, as light intensities increase, it will return. Trimming of wayward growth can be done at any time. If the plant begins to outgrow its home, you can always plant it outside, preferably in spring or early summer.

Propagation: When you trim the ivy cut the stems into pieces with 2–3 leaves, leaving about 1 inch (2.5 cm) of stem below the bottom leaf. Dip the bottom piece of stem in hormone rooting powder and insert about 5 cuttings in a 3 inch (7.5 cm) pot of seeding mixture. Cover with a plastic bag or sheeting until the cuttings have rooted. Remove the plastic and grow in the same pot.

Pests and diseases: Watch for aphids, red spider mites or mealy bugs.

HIPPEASTRUM

For most of the year hippeastrum has little to show other than its broad strap-like leaves. When it flowers, however, the display is dramatic. Each bulb produces one or more magnificent blooms that are especially welcome in the drab months of late winter when prepared bulbs are usually brought into flower. The natural flowering time is spring. The flowers, produced on 2 ft (60 cm) stems, can be more than 6 inches (15 cm) across and vary in color from white to pink and deep red.

General care: Plant the bulb in a 5–7 inch (13–18 cm) pot of loam-based mixture, leaving about half the bulb above the soil. In winter, give the plant as much light as possible and water moderately, but regularly. Give a weekly liquid feed and keep the plant warm, at around 65–68°F (18–20°C). Increase watering as the plant grows and eventually flowers.

After flowering, the leaves will grow more actively and the plant should continue to be fed at reduced strength.

Hedera canariensis

This will help to promote flower production for the following year. As the leaves start to wither, reduce watering and allow the plant to rest in a dry state for its dormant period during the autumn and early winter before starting into growth again in about early spring.

Propagation: Either offsets or seed can be used. Separate offsets from the main plant when starting it into growth and pot singly into 3½ inch (9 cm) pots, transferring them to the final pot as the bulb expands.

Sow seeds in trays of seeding mixture in spring, cover and keep at about 70°F (21°C). When they have germinated and are large enough to handle, transplant them separately and treat in the same way as offsets, although they will take at least 2 years to flower. Bulb offsets are produced less freely than seeds but will flower sooner.

Pests and diseases: Mealy bugs may attack.

HOWEIA (syn. Howea)

Howeia forsteriana, commonly called the kentia palm, is one of the most elegant palms, with leathery leaves and a height of 6 ft (2 m) or more.

General care: The kentia palm prefers a shady position away from drafts in a temperature of 55–65°F (13–18°C). Humidity and ventilation are important; in a stuffy, dry environment the fronds will dehydrate and the edges will turn brown. Although these can be trimmed off, this is only a cosmetic treatment. Some move must be made to increase the humidity, such as spraying the plant with a mist of tepid water twice a day. Do not be tempted to treat the fronds with a leaf-shine cleaning material as this can often cause serious damage. Wipe dust from the fronds with a cotton wool pad or soft cloth moistened with tepid water.

Propagation: It is not easy to propagate palms from seed but it is possible – with patience. Germination is

slow and erratic and may take 3–6 months. Sow the seeds in a tray of seeding mixture. Lightly cover and keep inside a plastic bag at about 75–80°F (24–26°C). When the seeds have germinated, pot them on singly.
Pests and diseases: Generally trouble-free.

HYPOCRYTA

A member of the gesneriad family, hypocryta bears unusual pouchy flowers in shades of yellow, orange and bright red. They are pinched at the tip in a pursed mouth like that of a goldfish. A relative of the African violet, *H. nummularia* has arching stems that grow 12–18 inches (30–45 cm) long and glossy oval leaves. Its trailing habit makes it a good candidate for hanging baskets. It flowers throughout the year, but stages its biggest display in summer. *H. stigillosa* has velvety, dark green leaves and orange-red flowers that bloom in winter and spring.
General care: Hypocryta needs constant warm temperatures of 65–70°F (18–21°C) during the summer and slightly cooler in the winter. Sudden changes in temperature or drafty locations cause growth to stop. Water moderately, but mist the plant often to give it the humidity it thrives on. Provide filtered light and pot in peat moss and ordinary garden soil with perlite or African violet mix added to increase mix. Fertilize every other month in spring and summer. Prune before new growth starts as flowers set on new growth.
Propagation: Propagate from cuttings. Cut a 2 inch (5 cm) piece of stem, dip it in rooting hormone and a fungicide and pot it in sterile soil. Cover with a plastic bag for 3 days and after 2 weeks transplant 6–8 cuttings to an 8-inch (20 cm) pot.
Pests and diseases: Susceptible to mealy bug and mite infestation.

HYPOESTES

The polka dot plant, a native

Hippeastrum

of Madagascar, owes its beauty to its handsome, pink-splashed foliage. It grows to 2 ft (60 cm) and has 2–3 inch (5–7.5 cm) oval leaves. Mature plants of *H. sanguinolenta*, the most popular variety, bear purple and white flowers. The plant has wiry stems and should be pinched back regularly to promote a bushy appearance. 'Splash' has larger spots than most selections.
General care: Always plant hypoestes in a loose, peaty soil mixture and feed every other week with mild, acid fertilizer. Situate in a well-lit spot out of direct sunlight with good ventilation. Water freely in the growing season with tepid water and spray often.
Propagation: Grow from seed sown in spring in a covered propagator in darkness. When the seedlings appear, remove the cover, bring them into the light and transplant them. Prop-

agation is also possible from stem tip cuttings.
Pests and diseases: Watch for scale insects.

IMPATIENS

Impatiens, popularly known as busy lizzie, is still one of the best-loved flowering house plants. While the familiar plain green-leaved type with pale-pink or rose-pink flowers holds its own, variegated varieties are now freely available.
General care: Easily maintained, impatiens needs little special treatment. Place the plant in a light situation, but not in direct sunlight behind glass. Do not allow the soil to dry out. During the main growing period, spring through summer, feed the plant once every 2–3 weeks with half-strength tomato fertilizer.

To prevent the plant becoming straggly, trim it occasionally or pinch back the growing points. This helps to keep it compact and

well-shaped. A more drastic pruning in early spring will ensure that the plant retains its good shape.
Propagation: Busy lizzie is very easy to propagate. Simply take a 3–4 inch (7.5–10 cm) cutting from a top shoot and root it in a pot of sandy soil or in a jar of water. In either case, pot as soon as rooted.
Pests and diseases: Aphids and whitefly are the most likely troublemakers; it may also be attacked by red spider mites.

MAMMILLARIA

Mammillaria is one of the most commonly grown genera of cacti – no fewer than 200 different species are known. They are covered with nipple-like tubercules that give the plant its name. These are arranged in whorls that spiral around the plant. *M. hahniana* and *M. zeilmanniana*, both of which bear red flowers in a ring at the top of the plant, are among the most popular. Other species have white, yellow or pink flowers.
General care: Mammillaria needs to be in full sun in order to flower. In summer, water generously without soaking; in winter, let the soil dry out and do not let the temperature drop below 45°F (7°C).
Propagation: In May and August offsets are produced which can be removed from the parent. Let them dry for a day and pot in a mixture of 50–50 soil and coarse sand. Alternatively, they can be raised in spring from seed sown in a similar mixture, lightly covered with sand and kept at 68°F (20°C) until germinated. When seedlings are large enough to handle, transplant them.
Pests and diseases: Mealy bugs and root mealy bugs may be a problem.

MARANTA LEUCONEURA

Maranta is sometimes known as prayer plant because of its nightly habit of raising its leaves together like praying hands. Maranta

Plain and variegated Impatiens

produces tiny, violet-pink flowers on a long slender stalk but is entirely grown for its decorative paddle-shaped leaves. M. l. 'Kerchoveana' is additionally called 'rabbit tracks', owing to the shape and positioning of the bronze-brown blotches. M. l. 'Erythrophylla' has leaves with a red herring-bone pattern.

General care: Maranta is not difficult to grow. It likes warm, humid conditions in semi-shade with a steady temperature of about 68°F (20°C). Give maranta a liquid feed every 2 weeks.

Propagation: Division of the main plant is recommended. Alternatively, take tip cuttings, inserting them in pots of equal parts peat and sand in a propagating case at 70°F (21°C). When rooted, pot into larger pots of loam-based potting soil.

Pests and diseases: Red spider mites, mealy bugs and root mealy bugs may occasionally cause trouble; if so, spray with malathion.

MEDINILLA

This exotic plant is exacting, but if the indoor gardener is willing to expend some extra effort to provide the proper conditions M. *magnifica* will live up to its name. It grows 3 ft (90 cm) tall and produces large, leathery leaves and pendulous plumes of pink bracts that burst forth with clusters of delicate pink flowers. The flower may reach 16 inches (40 cm) long.

General care: This plant needs lots of humidity. Spray and water freely with tepid water and feed with mild liquid fertilizer twice a month from late winter through fall. Plant in bromeliad or orchid mix and keep in a well-lit position out of direct sun.

Propagation: Grow plants from cuttings placed in a propagator and transplant to a mixture of sand and peat moss. Flowering is not likely to occur for 2–3 years.

Pests and diseases: Generally trouble-free.

MONSTERA DELICIOSA

Sometimes called Swiss cheese plant or Mexican breadfruit plant, monstera is an unusual species with slits and holes in its large, glossy, green leaves. It may reach 6 ft (2 m) or more in height. Its tentacle-like aerial roots are an unusual feature.

General care: Monstera adapts to most environments with little trouble. To get the best out of the plant, ensure that it enjoys a semi-shaded position where the atmosphere is relatively humid, as these two factors are important if the plant is to produce leaves of characteristic shape. In a bright, dry position it will revert to a small leaf without slits or holes. To remove dust, clean leaves occasionally with a cotton wool pad moistened with tepid water. If the aerial roots become too rampant, wind them around the plant to encourage them to grow back into the soil, or put them into damp sphagnum moss or moss peat. Plants over 2 ft (60 cm) need support; a 'moss pole' is ideal.

Propagation: Monstera may

Neoregelia carolinae 'Tricolor'

produce a side shoot that can be separated when it is 6 inches (15 cm) tall and potted in one of the all-peat potting mixes.

Pests and diseases: Generally trouble-free.

NEOREGELIA

Neoregelia is a magnificent bromeliad with glossy green strap-like leaves in rosettes with the bases forming a cup. In the form generally seen as a house plant, N. *carolinae* 'Tricolor', the leaves are bright rose-pink at their base and white-striped above. At flowering time, which tends to be spring, this color may radiate outwards from the center. Lilac-pink flowers appear just above the red leaf bases.

General care: Neoregelia is easy to keep because it is so adaptable. A lightly shaded situation away from direct sunlight is best with a temperature around 60–65°F (15–18°C), although temperatures down to 50°F (10°C) can be tolerated. The funnel should always be kept topped up with water, rainwater if you can provide it. In summer, water frequently without soaking; in winter, keep the soil just moist. After flowering, the plant will devote all of its energy to producing offsets and the old parent plant will gradually die.

Propagation: Let the offsets make roots while still attached to the parent plant.

Notocactus leninghausii

Sever them in summer and put them in individual 5 inch (13 cm) pots of equal parts sand and medium loam. Provide each plantlet with a supporting stake and do not plant too deeply. Water sparingly but keep the atmosphere relatively humid until a sound root formation has been made.

Pests and diseases: Generally trouble-free but root mealy bugs may occasionally attack. If they do, soak the root ball in malathion.

NEPHROLEPIS EXALTATA

Nephrolepis or ladder fern is one of the more common ferns grown as house plants. It has long, stately fronds of pale or bright green depending on variety and looks attractive on a plant stand or in a hanging basket.

General care: Nephrolepis prefers a semi-lit situation away from direct sunlight. A temperature of about 65°F (18°C) is ideal provided that the atmosphere is not too dry, for its thin fronds are susceptible to dehydration. It will, however, tolerate a minimum winter temperature of 50°F (10°C). Do not let the soil dry out as this can, at worst, cause the plant to die back, and at least exacerbate the problem of drying fronds. An acid soil is required and feeding every 2 weeks from mid-summer will give a good growth of fronds.

Propagation: Nephrolepis can be propagated from spores but it is easier to increase by division or by removing plantlets that form on the stolons (runners). The plantlets should be potted in a moist peaty soil in late spring or summer. They will establish quickly if kept moist and warm.

Pests and diseases: Generally trouble-free.

NIDULARIUM

A bromeliad originating in Brazil, the bird's nest bromeliad gets its name from the red, strap-like leaves in the center of the plant that makes a flattened rosette from which the flowers emerge. The outer leaves are shiny, bright green and measure from 18–24 inches (45–60 cm) across. Before the flowers bloom, which may be any time during the year, the center rosette deepens in hue. The flowers remain colorful for months. *N. fulgens* has small violet-blue flowers; *N. innocentii* has deep, olive green outer leaves and bears cream-colored flowers; and *N. regeliodes* bears orange flowers and features foliage blotched with darker green areas.

General care: Water the bird's nest bromeliad by filling the vase formed by the foliage and mist frequently. Provide a lightly shaded spot with constant temperatures between 60–70°F (15–21°C). Cold temperatures cause rotting, and too much sun turns the leaves yellow. Pot in bromeliad mix.

Propagation: Propagate by dividing the new plants that form at the base of the parent. See guzmania on page 143.

Pests and diseases: Watch for scale insects and thrips. If they occur, wash the plant with soap and water. Do not use pesticides.

NOTOCACTUS

The most commonly grown species of notocactus is *N. leninghausii*, also sometimes known as goldfinger cactus. It grows slowly to a magnificent thick column and produces yellow trumpet-shaped flowers at its top that may reach about 2 inches (5 cm) in diameter.

General care: Like most

cacti, notocactus likes full light. In winter keep it cool at a temperature of about 55°F (13°C) and let the soil dry. Summer temperatures of about 65°F (18°C) are best, and allow the soil to dry out between waterings.

Propagation: Seed is the only sure means of increase. Sow in spring at a temperature of at least 70°F (21°C). Large plants can be decapitated, the top being used as a cutting after several days of drying out. Mature plants sometimes produce basal shoots which can be treated as cuttings.

Pests and diseases: Mealy bugs and root mealy bugs.

OPUNTIA

Opuntia is better known as prickly pear or bunny ears. Its stems are like round or oval pads which are covered with fine bristles and require careful handling. There are many different species with flowers which vary in color from yellow to orange and red. One of the most suitable species for the home is *O. microdasys*. It is a plant to 2 ft (60 cm) or more which produces numerous pads dotted with tiny white or yellow spines.

General care: Opuntia is quite easy to grow. It requires a well-drained growing medium and, unlike many cacti, needs some water the whole year round – plenty in summer, enough to prevent the soil drying out in winter. If it becomes dry, brown spots appear on the pads. A minimum winter temperature of 45°F (7°C) is necessary. Repot opuntia annually or biennially in spring to maintain a healthy plant.

Propagation: The easiest way is to propagate from the pads in summer. Wear garden gloves and wrap a piece of coarse cloth or paper round the plant to protect your hands from the spines. Simply pull off a pad, let it dry out for 2–3 days and insert it in a pot of equal parts

Pellaea rotundifolia (**back**) and *Platycerium bifurcatum* (see p. 150)

peat and gritty sand. Keep the soil moist but not water-logged, otherwise the roots will rot.

Pests and diseases: Mealy bugs and root mealy bugs may attack.

PELLAEA ROTUNDIFOLIA

The fronds of the diminutive pellaea or button fern are composed of small circular leaflets or pinnae. Fronds up to 20 inches (50 cm) long form a low spreading mat as the fern grows.

General care: Unlike most ferns, pellaea is happy in a light environment, though not direct sunlight. It will grow well under the low intensity of fluorescent lighting. Pellaea ideally likes a temperature of about 65°F (18°C) and needs to be kept reasonably moist. It will not tolerate temperatures below 45°F (7°C).

Propagation: Like other ferns, propagation from spores is possible (see Asplenium) but division is easier and quicker.

Pests and diseases: Generally trouble-free.

PEPEROMIA MAGNOLII-FOLIA

Commonly known as desert privet, *Peperomia magnolii-folia* is a most attractive plant with oval waxy leaves. *P. m.* 'Variegata' has green and cream variegated leaves.

General care: Desert privet is exceptionally adaptable and is ideal for a beginner's collection. It will continue to thrive in a wide temperature range of 50–65°F (10–18°C). Light is important as it keeps the variegated colors bright. In a shady position the leaves will become dull and the variegation will be less bold.

As the thick fleshy leaves act as water storage reservoirs, it is advisable to keep the soil rather dry. Too much water will drown the roots and the plant will rot. Let the soil almost dry out between waterings.

Propagation: This is best achieved by rooting stem cuttings. When the plant becomes rather leggy and top-

heavy, cut it back to a more compact shape. Trim each cutting to a section about 2–3 inches (5–7.5 cm) long and insert cuttings into a 3½ inch (7.5 cm) pot of moist seeding mixture. Do not cover with any plastic, as the leaves can store enough water to stop the plant wilting and could rot if kept in a humid environment.

Pests and diseases: Aphids and red spider mites sometimes attack in spring and summer. Take prompt action to stop any damage.

PHILODENDRON SCANDENS

The heart-shaped leaves of *Philodendron scandens* have given it the appropriate popular name of sweetheart plant. The handsome plain green leaves and a climbing habit make it a good-looking specimen plant or background feature in mixed arrangements. It normally requires some form of support, but can be treated as a trailer.

General care: A semi-shaded position away from direct sunlight is ideal, with a temperature of about 65°F (18°C). The plant should be allowed almost to dry out between waterings; keep watering to a minimum during the winter months.

As the plant grows, it may become untidy. If so, cut back to maintain its shape, and use the trimmings to provide cuttings.

Propagation: Take stem cuttings with one leaf each and about 1 inch (2.5 cm) of stem below. If the tip of the shoot is used, make sure it has one mature leaf and about 1 inch

*Peperomia (**front right**). Also shown (see pp. 146–147) Maranta l. 'Erythrophylla' (**left background**), M. l. Kerchoveana' (**left foreground**) and Monstera deliciosa (**right background**)*

(2.5 cm) of stem below it. Dip the cuttings into hormone rooting powder and insert 3–5 in a 3½ inch (9 cm) pot of peat-based seeding mixture. Cover tightly with a plastic bag. When rooted, remove the bag and leave to grow, potting the plants together as they mature.

Pests and diseases: Generally trouble-free.

PHOENIX CANARIENSIS

Better known as the Canary Island date palm, *P. canariensis* is a plant of superb geometric form with gently cascading fronds radiating from the center. It tends to grow about 6 ft (2 m) high in the home, but can well exceed this in time.

General care: The leathery fronds of the date palm make it adaptable to the warm, dry environment of the home. Watering should be carried out when the soil is almost dry. Do not overwater. A temperature of about 65°F (18°C) is ideal, but the date palm will tolerate 50°F (10°C). Place the palm where it gets as much sun as possible, as in its homeland it grows in desert oases and so needs full light.

Propagation: Date palms can be propagated from seed (date stones) germinated in a tray filled with seeding mixture, enclosed in a plastic bag and kept at about 70°F (21°C). They will take up to 3 months to germinate. Each seedling can then be potted up in potting soil.

Pests and diseases: Red spider mites, mealy bugs, root mealy bugs and scale insects may occasionally attack stems and leaves.

PILEA CADIEREI
Sometimes known as aluminum plant, this pilea is naturally variegated in the wild, its oval leaves always being patterned with silver. It is an evergreen, shrubby perennial to 1½ ft (45 cm) tall, wider when mature.

General care: Provided the temperature does not fall below 50°F (10°C), this is one of the easiest and most good-tempered of house plants. The leaf coloring is best in partial shade.

Propagation: Very easy from 3 inch (7.5 cm) long tip cuttings inserted in equal parts peat and sand and put in a propagating case in summer.

Pests and diseases: Generally trouble-free.

PLATYCERIUM BIFUR-CATUM
The common stag's horn fern is a most extraordinary plant. It produces two totally different frond shapes: the spore-bearing antler-like green frond that gives the plant its name and the simple basal sterile frond which helps to secure the plant.

General care: Platycerium is fairly tough and quite content at a temperature of about 60°F (15°C), although happiest at about 65°F (18°C). Allow the soil to almost, but not quite, dry out between waterings. Take care not to overwater. Give the plant a lightly shaded situation. It can be grown in a mixture of sphagnum moss and potting soil in equal proportions.

Propagation: Stag's horn fern can be propagated from spores produced from velvety brown patches that appear on the underside of the frond tips. Collect the spores carefully and sprinkle lightly on the surface of a tray filled with a mixture of equal parts peat and loam-based seeding mixture. Enclose the pot within a plastic bag and keep moist at a temperature of about 70°F (21°C). When the spores have germinated and are large enough to handle, pot up singly. Mature plants produce offsets which can be detached when they have 2–3 fronds and grown on more quickly than sporlings.

Pests and diseases: Watch for scale insects.

POINSETTIA
See under Euphorbia pulcherrima

PTERIS ENSIFORMIS 'VICTORIAE'
This fern makes a most attractive pot plant for the home. Well-grown plants can exceed 1 ft (30 cm) in height and have a very erect

Philodendron scandens (see p. 149) Rhoicissus rhomboidea (see p. 152) and (front) Tradescantia (see p. 155)

Phoenix canariensis (see p. 149)

habit. The leaflets (pinnae) are narrowly strap-shaped with a broad median stripe of silvery-white.

General care: Pteris is susceptible to dehydration. It must be kept in at least moderately humid conditions; occasional spraying with a fine mist of tepid water helps. It prefers a temperature of around 68°F (20°C) and, in common with other ferns, prefers a semi-shaded position away from direct sunlight. The minimum temperature it will tolerate is 50°F (10°C).

Propagation: Pteris spores can be germinated in the same way as other ferns, but mature plants can be divided in spring, a quicker and more satisfactory method.

Pests and diseases: Generally trouble-free – which makes up for its rather exacting cultural requirements.

REBUTIA

Rebutia is a small cactus that regularly produces an amaz-ing number of flowers for its size. The low, flattened, globular stems seldom exceed 2½ inches (6 cm) in height, but in summer produce a mass of trumpet-like flowers from white to yellow-orange and brilliant red, all round the base of the stem. Recommended are: *R. deminuto* and *R. krainziana*, both of which are red-flowered, and *R. aureiflora*, which is orange-yellow.

General care: Rebutia is one of the easiest cacti to cultivate and is an ideal plant with which to start a collection. It is happy growing on windowsills in full light and is tolerant of varying conditions. A cool dry winter followed by a warmer and more moist spring and summer are the ideal conditions. The flowers close during the evening but reopen with the next day's light.

Propagation: Rebutia is easy to raise from seed, germinated in the usual way for cacti.

Pests and diseases: Mealy bugs and root mealy bugs are the main problems.

RHOICISSUS RHOMBOIDEA

Rhoicissus rhomboidea or grape ivy is an accommodating climbing plant with shiny green leaves composed of 3 leaflets of roughly diamond shape, the top half with well-spaced teeth. The slender stems climb by using tendrils. The grape ivy can be trained up a single trellis or support to grow about 3 ft (1 m) tall.

General care: Rhoicissus prefers a slightly shaded position away from sunlight – indeed, it is an ideal plant for a shady corner. If the plant receives too much sunlight, the leaves may take on a yellowish suffusion. Rhoicissus will happily grow at temperatures between 60–65°F (15–18°C). Allow the soil to become almost dry before rewatering; do not overwater. Prune to tidy the shape of the plant if necessary in late winter.

Propagation: Use prunings as stem and tip cuttings. Trim these to 3–4 inches (7.5–10 cm) in length. Remove the lower 1–2 leaves and dip the end into hormone rooting powder. Insert 5–7 cuttings in a 3½ inch (9 cm) pot, using a peat-based potting soil. Cover with a plastic bag to keep them moist. Once they have rooted, remove the bag and allow the plants to grow, potting singly later.

Pests and diseases: Generally trouble-free.

SAINTPAULIA

Saintpaulia or African violet is a very attractive little plant that forms a close rosette of fleshy, heart-shaped leaves and produces flowers in a wide range of colors. Most commonly known for its deep purple-blue flowers, it is also available in white, pink, wine-red, light blue, dark blue and even bi-colored and frilled forms.

General care: It prefers a temperature of about 68°F (20°C) away from drafts and direct sunlight. Humidity is also important; many people grow them well in kitchens or bathrooms. Humidity can also be increased by plunging the plant, still in its pot, into another larger pot filled with moist peat. It is best watered from below. Place the plant in a saucer of water and allow it to soak up what it requires within about 20 minutes before pouring away the surplus. Dust can be removed from the hairy leaves by spraying the plant with tepid water. This should always be done at room temperature and away from direct sunlight. Cold or direct sunlight are equally bad for saintpaulia. The plant's leaves will become disfigured if water is left on them while the plant is in either of these conditions.

A stubborn African violet can be coaxed into flower by a very simple technique.

Various shades of Saintpaulia

Keep the plant on the dry side for 6–8 weeks, watering only if it looks like drying out and dying. Gradually increase the water, and feed every 2 weeks with tomato fertilizer at half strength.

Propagation: It is very simple to propagate African violets from leaf cuttings. Select a semi-mature leaf and cut it off cleanly at the base of the leaf stalk close to the center of the plant. Cut back the leaf stalk to about 1½ inches (3–4 cm) and insert the stalk into a 2 inch (5 cm) pot of seeding mixture, leaving a small space between the base of the leaf and the soil surface. Cover the leaf with a polythene bag and be patient. Rooting may take 6–8 weeks and it may be as long again before a plantlet emerges from the base. Pot on the new plant into a 3½ in (9 cm) pot of potting soil.

Pests and diseases: Aphids and mildew sometimes attack during spring and summer; the latter is more difficult to control.

SANSEVIERIA
The sansevieria commonly known as mother-in-law's tongue is S. *trifasciata* 'Laurentii'. Its familiar upright green and yellow edged leaves grow up to 3 ft (1 m).

General care: Mother-in-law's tongue prefers a well-lit situation at a temperature of about 65°F (18°C); in winter the temperature should not drop below 50°F (10°C) and the compost should then be kept on the dry side. Allow the compost to dry out between waterings. Wet soil conditions lead to rotting.

Propagation: Sansevieria is easily propagated by cuttings. Cut a leaf into 2 inch (5 cm) sections and put 4–5 sections into a pot of moist potting compost. Make sure the cuttings are the right way up. A propagating case is not required. When rooted, pot each plantlet into a 3 inch (7.5 cm) pot of potting soil.

Propagation by division is relatively easy and is the only way to increase S. *t.* 'Laurentii'; leaf cuttings only produce the common

Saxifraga sarmentosa

species without the yellow margins. Water the plant very sparingly after separation.

Pests and diseases: Generally trouble-free.

SAXIFRAGA
The strawberry geranium, S. *sarmentosa*, is a delicate-looking hanging plant which forms plantlets on the ends of long stolons. It is covered with a dense mass of 4–6 inch (10–15 cm) round, reddish green leaves, lightly veined in red with purplish undersides. It grows to 12 inches (30 cm) and produces 12 inch (30 cm) flower stalks bearing clouds of tiny white flowers in the summer. S. *stolonifera tricolor* 'Magic Carpet' is smaller, with green and white foliage edged in pink with rose underneath.

General care: Place in a sunny position, shielded from the direct rays of midday sun, and let the soil dry out between waterings. The strawberry geranium likes cool temperatures, of 50–60°F (10–15°C). Pot in a mixture of equal parts of peat moss and sand to twice as much standard potting soil and feed monthly from spring to fall with diluted liquid fertilizer.

Propagation: Propagate by pegging down the plantlets in pots of moist peat moss. Sever from the parent plant once rooting has occurred.

Pests and diseases: Watch for mealy bugs and whitefly.

SCHEFFLERA
A wonderful, architectural-looking house plant, schefflera boasts a graceful and imposing form. It grows to 8 ft (2.4 m) high and 4–5 ft (1.2–1.5 m) across. The umbrella tree, as it is popularly known, has long, graceful green branches with 6–8 oval leaflets spread in a palmate pattern. S. *actinophylla* is the most common species. S. *arboricola* is a recently introduced dwarf variety with two named selections, 'Geisha Girl' and 'Hong Kong'; both have compact clusters of leaves growing on upright stems.

General care: The schefflera is not very fussy about its environment. It will tolerate a fair amount of shade, but it prefers filtered sunshine. Water moderately and clean the leaves regularly. Plant in standard potting soil with good drainage and feed twice a year with mild fertilizer.

Propagation: Sow seeds in a propagator in darkness. When they germinate, bring into the light and thin out the weaker seedlings. Pot the remaining ones in 4 inch (10 cm) pots.

Pests and diseases: Generally trouble-free.

SINNINGIA
Next to the African violet, S. *speciosa*, the florist's gloxinia, is the most popular member of the gesneriad family. It is loved for its velvety, bell-shaped flowers which come in shades of white, pink and violet and may reach 5 inches (13 cm) across; some are ruffled and striped. Gloxinia grows from 12–16 inches (30–41 cm) high. S. *eumorpha* is the type most commonly available from nurseries. It has white flowers tinged with purple and furry foliage. S. *discolor* has tubular lavender flowers. S. *pusilla* is a compact selection.

General care: Gloxinia prefers a light but shaded position and temperatures ranging from 60–75°F (15–24°C). Water freely in the summer from below to keep the water off the foliage and flowers. Spray daily in the summer, but do not let the spray hit the flowers. If the stems or buds rot, be sure that water is not left on the plant. Gradually reduce watering in the fall as the plant enters dormancy. Feed every month with mild, liquid fertilizer. Pot in African violet mix.

Propagation: Plant tubers in winter – one to a 6 inch (15 cm) pot – leaving a bit of the tuber above the soil. Flowering will occur the following autumn.

Pests and diseases: Watch for aphids.

SOLANUM

What makes winter cherry, S. pseudocapsicum, ornamental is not its flowers but a display of round, bright orange, cherry-like fruits in winter. The small white flowers of summer are insignificant. The plant may reach 18 inches (45 cm) in height and is fairly compact. Deep green foliage sets off the berries well. Although solanum is from the same family as the tomato and the potato, its fruits are poisonous.

General care: Solanum can be grown for more than one season, although most people dispose of them once the fruits have dropped. They are very easy to grow, provided there is plenty of light and the plants are not allowed to dry out, particularly when in flower or after fruit has set. During spring and summer, a temperature of about 60–65°F (15–18°C) is ideal; they may even be kept outside from late spring through the end of summer. Feeding with diluted tomato fertilizer throughout the growing season will help to encourage stocky growth and a good covering of flowers – hopefully followed by berries. Fruit set can be increased indoors by lightly misting the plant with tepid water or by tickling the flowers with an artist's paintbrush to pollinate them. During the winter months solanum will tolerate a temperature down to around 50°F (10°C).

Propagation: Sow seed in early spring in a seed tray of seeding mixture, cover and keep at 65–68°F (18–20°C). When the seedlings are large enough to handle, transplant and pot singly in 5 inch (13 cm) pots of potting soil.

Pests and diseases: Aphids and whitefly may attack.

SPATHIPHYLLUM

The spathe flower offers the indoor gardener both beautiful, graceful foliage and delicate, summer-blooming flowers. It looks like a white version of the Hawaiian anthurium, but is much easier to cultivate. It has glossy green, pointed leaves that grow 18 inches (45 cm) long. Tall stalks emerge from the center of the plant which develop into delicate, snowy white, jack-in-the-pulpit flowers. These stay attractive for as long as a month, and many blooms may appear at the same time.

'Clevelandii', which grows to 2 ft (60 cm), produces waxy 3–4 inch (7.5–10 cm) flowers that fade to light green. 'Mauna Loa', which grows to 3 ft (90 cm), has 4–6 inch (10–15 cm) flowers.

General care: Spathe flowers like shady, humid locations. Keep the soil moist, spray occasionally and feed every 2 weeks in spring and summer. Plant in a mixture of standard potting soil and sand enriched with peat.

Propagation: Propagate by division of mature plants.

Pests and diseases: Watch for mealy bugs. Be careful that insecticide does not get on the flowers.

STEPHANOTIS

Stephanotis is a climbing plant with thick, fleshy, green leaves and is usually grown on a hoop so that its scented, waxy white flowers can be displayed to best advantage.

General care: A temperature of 68°F (20°C) is ideal. A reasonably well-lit situation away from direct sun will provide conditions in which the plants will flourish.

Keep the plants on the dry side over the dormant winter period. During the active growing and flowering period, do not allow it to dry out. A monthly feed with half-strength tomato fertilizer promotes stocky growth.

Spathiphyllum

Tradescantia

Propagation: Grow more plants from stem cuttings taken from non-flowering side shoots in early summer. Dip 4 inch (10 cm) cuttings in hormone rooting powder and insert in a 3 inch (7.5 cm) pot of seeding mixture. If you keep them at about 65°F (18°C) they should root in a few weeks. Pot as necessary. **Pests and diseases:** Generally trouble-free.

STREPTOCARPUS
Popularly known as the Cape primrose, this plant bears pink, red, purple or lilac flowers. The mid-green leaves are broadly strap-shaped, thick-textured and rich green, providing a perfect background to the lovely summer blooms.
General care: While flowering in spring and summer, streptocarpus prefers a temperature of around 60–65°F (15–18°C) in a lightly shaded situation, away from direct sunlight. Do not allow the plants to dry out in summer but keep them fairly dry for the winter, maintaining a temperature of 50–55°F (10–13°C). From March onwards, as temperatures gradually rise again, water more frequently.
Propagation: Streptocarpus is easily propagated from seed or leaf cuttings. During spring and summer, sow seed in trays filled with seeding mixture and keep covered at about 70°F (21°C) until germinated. When the seedlings are large enough to handle, transplant them and pot them individually in 5 inch (13 cm) pots of potting soil.

Streptocarpus cuttings are worth trying for fun. Select a semi-mature leaf and cut it off cleanly. Using a sharp knife and a chopping board, lay the leaf flat on the board and cut it in half down the middle of the vein. Cut each half into pieces about 1 inch (2.5 cm) wide, cutting outwards from the main vein to the leaf edge. Insert at an oblique angle, barely covering the lower third, in seed trays filled with seeding mixture. Mist with tepid water several times a day, or cover with a plastic bag or plastic sheeting to keep water loss to a minimum. When the cuttings have rooted, pot singly in 3 inch (7.5 cm) pots of potting soil and grow on watering carefully.
Pests and diseases: Generally trouble-free.

TRADESCANTIA
Wandering Jew, *T. fluminensis*, is one of the commonest and easiest of all house plants. An attractive trailing foliage plant, it looks best in small hanging baskets, high on a shelf or in a pot fixed to the wall. The best forms are those with variegated leaves.
General care: Tradescantia is a most adaptable plant. It grows well in various environments, but is best in a well-lit position at a temperature between 50–60°F (10–15°C). Allow the compost almost to dry out between waterings. Apply any of the appropriate liquid feeds at 2 week intervals from spring to autumn. Trim the plant back when it looks straggly and bare stems are visible.
Propagation: Take cuttings from leading shoots, reducing them to about 2 inches (5 cm) in length. Insert 3–5 cuttings in a 3 inch (7.5 cm) pot filled with potting soil and keep moist, but not wet. Rooting is rapid; during spring and summer it may take 2–3 weeks. Once rooted, grow in the same pot.
Pests and diseases: Generally trouble-free.

VRIESIA SPLENDENS
V. splendens is a bromeliad similar in shape to the aechmea, but its leaves are more slender. Banded dark green and strap-like in shape, they form a funnel-shaped rosette that collects water at its base. When mature, the plant produces a long orange-red bracted flat-sided flower spike; from this the short-lived yellow flowers emerge.
General care: Vriesia adapts to a variety of indoor conditions. Although it will tolerate temperatures down to 50°F (10°C), around 65°F (18°C) is best, in a semi-shaded position away from direct sunlight. Use rainwater if possible, although tap water is perfectly adequate. Try to keep the soil just moist most of the time. When the flower spike dies, gently remove it from the funnel.

V. splendens is an epiphytic or tree-living bromeliad, using its host for support. Adventurous indoor gardeners will find that it adapts well to being grown attached to a branch bound with sphagnum moss in a plant arrangement like a miniature jungle.
Propagation: It is usually propagated from offsets in the same way as aechmea. Pot the offsets singly in 5 inch (13 cm) pots of lime-free soil.
Pests and diseases: Root mealy bugs are the most likely pests.

ZEBRINA
Also known as wandering Jew and additionally as inch plant, *Z. pendula* is frequently mistaken for *Tradescantia fluminensis*. The two are similar in appearance and closely allied botanically, but the flowers of zebrina have the bases of the petals united into a tube. The leaves are always purple beneath and on the upper surface are 2 silvery longitudinal bands.
General care, Propagation and **Pests and diseases** are as for Tradescantia.

VEGETABLES

With very few exceptions, good vegetables can only be produced under good conditions. They need to be grown in an open position with plenty of light and sunshine and will never flourish tucked away in dark corners, under the shadow of buildings or in the shade of trees. Nor will they do well in an exposed or drafty position (the wind funnels created between high buildings and gaps in garden fences are particularly lethal), and in such situations some kind of windbreak or shelter must be erected to protect the plants. The ideal garden windbreak is about 50 per cent permeable, so that it filters wind rather than stops it in its tracks. Lath and wattle fences are good, as are netted windbreaks made from special nylon windbreak materials. These have to be battened to posts, which must be very well anchored as they take a tremendous strain in high winds. A windbreak is effective for a distance two to six times its height – the further from the windbreak the less the effect.

By far the most important factor, however, is the soil. Vegetables must have fertile soil and the key to successful vegetable growing lies in building up soil fertility. There are many ways in which poor soil can be improved (see Back to Basics, page 10). Most vegetables do best on slightly acid soils, at a pH of around 6.5.

Garden planning

A vegetable garden can be almost any shape. Traditionally vegetables were grown in large plots in rigid rows, with plenty of space between the rows (see photograph on page 158). Today it is realized that vegetables can be grown much closer together, and very often, instead of being in rows, they are planted in 'blocks' or patches with equidistant spacing between them. This has the additional advantage that the plants form a 'canopy' over the ground which helps to suppress the weeds.

Growing vegetables at equidistant spacing lends itself to much smaller beds, which can be accommodated more easily in small modern gardens. Beds 3–4 ft (1.2 m) wide are very convenient, not least because they can be worked from the edge without treading on the soil – and the less the soil is compacted, the better its structure.

In small gardens where it is hard to find space for vegetables, a few can be grown in flower beds. Runner beans look very decorative growing up a trellis at the back of a border, while beets, chards, carrots and the 'Salad Bowl' types of lettuce look pretty growing among flowers. However, the soil must be rich enough to support them.

The choice of vegetable crops has to be determined largely by family requirements and available space. Few people aim to be self-sufficient, so where space is limited it is probably not worth growing maincrop potatoes or vegetables like cauliflower which require a large amount of space for long periods. Concentrate instead on salad crops, which are so much better picked fresh from the garden.

A big headache is arranging for a continuous supply without gluts and shortages. With the wide range of varieties available today, continuity is much easier to achieve. Wherever possible in the text, suggestions are made for successive sowings of suitable varieties with this in mind. With some vegetables, root crops such as parsnips for example, the whole year's supply can be obtained from one sowing. With others, such as lettuces, carrots, beets and cabbages, it is necessary to make several small sowings for a constant supply of the vegetable throughout the whole season.

Any interested vegetable grower would be well advised to invest in a cold greenhouse or an inexpensive 'walk in' polythene tunnel. This increases the scope enormously by making earlier sowings and later harvesting possible. On a smaller scale, frames can be put to excellent use to extend the season. A well-planned vegetable garden will provide produce throughout the year.

Rotation

It is sound gardening practice to avoid growing the same type of vegetable in the same piece of ground several years running. This is because certain soil pests and diseases, which attack members of the same botanical family will build up if they have constant access to their host plants. In practice, rotation is a problem in small gardens, but is easier when vegetables are grown in several small or narrow beds rather than a few large ones; there are more permutations to allow greater flexibility. Wherever possible, try to rotate over at least a 3–year cycle. The main family groups which should be grown together in one area and then moved on another year are: legumes (all the peas and beans); brassicas (all the cabbage family, including swedes, radishes and turnips); onions and leeks. Important crops like lettuces, potatoes and carrots should also be rotated (see the simple rotation system illustrated on page 158).

Seed selection

Most vegetables are raised from seed, either bought over the counter or from mail order seed houses, whose catalogs are a mine of information. Several developments in seed technology have been of particular help to gardeners, and these include:

F_1 hybrids: These are specially bred varieties that produce exceptionally vigorous and uniform crops. The seeds

ABOVE: *The traditional method of organizing a vegetable plot. The drawbacks are that space is wasted between the plants and the soil structure is damaged by constant treading.*

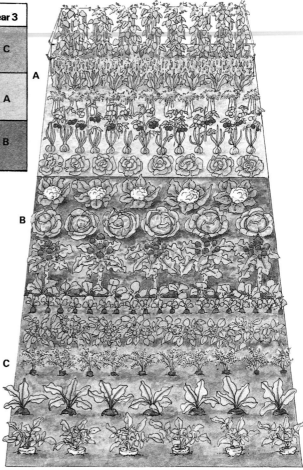

	Year 1	Year 2	Year 3
Plot 1	A	B	C
Plot 2	B	C	A
Plot 3	C	A	B

A simple rotation system: The garden is divided into three plots or areas, and the main vegetables grown are divided into three groups. Each group is grown in turn on each plot.
Group A: Legumes, onions and salad crops
Group B: Brassicas (plus radishes, swedes and turnips)
Group C: Root crops such as potatoes, carrots, beetroots and parsnips.

are more expensive than ordinary 'open pollinated' varieties, but are usually worth the extra cost.

Disease resistance: Several varieties (of tomatoes and cucumbers for example) have been bred with resistance to, or at least tolerance of, serious disease. These can be very useful.

Treated and dressed seed: Seed can be treated by the seedman to kill diseases that are normally carried on the seed (celery, for instance, can be treated against celery leaf spot). Seed can also be dressed with chemicals to combat soil diseases likely to attack after sowing. Corn-on-the-cob and pea seeds are often dressed to increase the chances of success with early outdoor sowings.

Pelleted seed: The seed is made into tiny balls with a protective coating which breaks down in the soil. The individual seeds can be handled very easily and spaced out accurately so that thinning is not required. The ground must be kept moist until the seeds germinate.

Foil packaging: Seeds packed in air-sealed foil packs keep fresh much longer than seeds in ordinary packets. Once the packets are opened, however, the seeds deteriorate normally.

Choosing a variety

With so many varieties to choose from today, there's bound to be some trial and error before you decide which ones are best for your conditions and requirements. A few outstanding varieties are mentioned in this book, but there are many others worth growing.

Keeping seeds

Seeds gradually lose their viability, or ability to germinate. In some cases (par-

snips, for instance), this happens much faster than in others (radishes, for example). Seeds will remain viable much longer if kept in cool, dry conditions, preferably in air-tight tins or jars. Never keep seeds in a damp shed or a hot kitchen.

Sowing outdoors

Outdoor sowings are either made directly into the ground where the plant is to grow or into a 'seed bed', which is an area set aside for raising plants; from there they are later transplanted into permanent positions. The main reason for sowing in a seed bed is to save space. While the seedling is developing in the seed bed, the ground it will eventually occupy can be used for another crop.

Preparing the ground

Whether sowing in a seed bed or in the growing site, the ground has to be prepared for sowing, a process known in both cases as 'making a seed bed'. A seed bed can be made satisfactorily only when the soil is in the right condition, neither so wet that the soil sticks to your feet, nor so dry that it is unworkable. In spring, especially on heavy soil, it is often a question of waiting until it dries out sufficiently. In very dry conditions

the soil may need to be watered before the seed bed can be made.

The purpose of a seed bed is to create a surface tilth where the soil is fine enough for seeds to germinate. The underlying soil needs to be firm, but not so consolidated that roots cannot penetrate.

Some soils can simply be raked down in spring and a fine tilth is created with no difficulty. More compacted soils may need to be forked over first, then raked, breaking down large clods with the back of the rake and raking off large stones and persistent earth lumps. Tread the soil lightly so that it is reasonably firm, and continue raking backwards and forwards until a good tilth is formed.

Seeds are normally sown in furrows. In a seed bed the furrows are close together, about 4–5 inches (10–13 cm) apart. Having prepared the seed bed, mark the position of a row with a garden line and make the furrow, which is really just a slit in the soil, with the point of a trowel or corner of a hoe. The depth of the furrow varies with the seed: most seeds are sown at a depth roughly two or three times their width. Place the seeds in the bottom of the furrow and use a rake to cover them with soil.

The golden rule of gardening is to sow

seed as thinly as possible. There is always a temptation to sow thickly in case germination is poor. In practice either soil conditions and seed are right and there will be a very high germination (and the resulting seedlings may be of poor quality because they are so crowded) or virtually none will germinate and one will have to sow again.

Either space the seed evenly along the furrow or, to save on thinning, sow 2–3 seeds together at 'stations' a few inches apart. Thin to one seedling at each station after germination. If your plants will eventually be grown, say, 6 inches (15 cm) apart, station sow about 3 inches (7.5 cm) apart. Fast growing seedlings like radishes can be intersown between the stations.

Thinning

Seedlings grow very rapidly and must never be allowed to become overcrowded. Thin them in stages, so that each just stands clear of its neighbor, until they are the required final distance apart. To avoid disturbing the remaining plants in the row seedlings can be nipped off at ground level, though in some cases, with lettuce for example, they can be eased out carefully and replanted elsewhere.

Sowing single seeds

Large seeds such as beans, peas, corn-on-the-cob, cucumbers and marrows can be sown by making individual holes with a pointed trowel.

Broadcasting

This is a rapid method of sowing used principally for seedling crops such as cress. Make the seed bed, then scatter the seeds thinly over the surface. Rake it over first in one direction, then at right angles. Cover the seed bed with a sheet of plastic or newspaper until the seeds have germinated. Never sow broadcast on soil known to be full of weed seed; it will be an impossible task separating the weed and vegetable seedlings. In such cases prepare the seed bed, leave it for a couple of weeks so that the main flush of weed seeds can germinate, hoe them off and then sow broadcast as described.

Sowing indoors

Half-hardy vegetables like tomatoes and peppers should be started indoors in colder climates, otherwise they would never mature in short summers. With other vegetables such as celery and lettuces, early crops or larger specimens can be obtained by sowing indoors. 'Indoors' implies sowing in a protected environment such as a greenhouse, in frames, or even on a windowsill. These early sowings are often made in an electric propagator which provides gentle 'bottom heat'.

Raising seedlings indoors is simplified by using commercially prepared sowing and potting soils, which are either soil- or peat-based. It is also possible to mix suitable soil.

Seeds are generally sown in seed trays or pots, but any container with drainage holes made in the bottom can be used. Fill it to within ¾ inch (2 cm) of the top with damp seeding mixture, firm it with the fingers, and level the surface with a block of wood. Sow the seeds thinly on the surface, spacing them out carefully if only a few plants are required. Cover them by sieving a little more of the mixture over the top, and level the surface once again. If the soil is dry, stand the seed tray in water to absorb moisture. Finally, cover it with a sheet of glass, or pop it into a plastic bag, to keep the surface moist until the seedlings germinate. Remove the glass or plastic for about half an hour a day for ventilation.

Once germinated, the seedlings must be in full light, but not direct sunlight. When they are large enough to handle, generally with about three true leaves, they need more room and richer soil. At this stage transplant into seed trays, or individually into small 2½ – 3 inch (6–8 cm) pots, filled with potting soil. Water the seedlings beforehand, then uproot them one by one with a small trowel, taking care not to damage the fine roots. Always hold them by their leaves. Make a hole in the soil large enough for the roots, put in the seedling, and firm the soil around it with a trowel. The seed leaves, the first tiny pair of leaves to develop on the stem, should be just above soil level. Space seedlings 1½ – 2 inches (4–5 cm) apart, and shield them from bright sunlight until established.

Hardening off

Before plants are moved into their final position outdoors, whether raised in pots or in seed trays, they must be gradually acclimatized to lower temperatures by 'hardening off'. This takes about 10 days. Start by increasing the ventilation, then move them outdoors during the day for increasingly longer periods, bringing them in at night, and finally leave them out at night. They are then ready for planting.

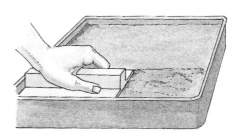

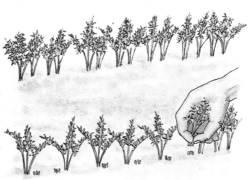

Thin by nipping off unwanted seedlings just above soil level; this method leaves the remaining seedlings undisturbed.

*Sowing indoors (**top to bottom**): Level the compost in the seed tray. Ensure that the seeds are well spaced out. Sift more compost over the seeds. Cover the seed tray with a pane of glass to germinate.*

159

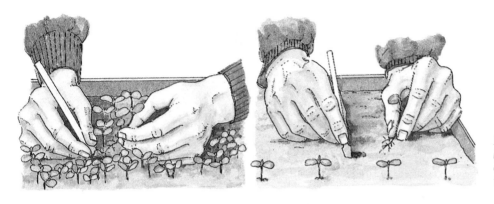

*Individually prick out crowded seedlings, (**far left**) and transfer them to rich compost to develop (**left**), holding them by their leaves to avoid damaging root hairs.*

Planting

Planting is inevitably something of a shock and everything has to be done to minimize the set-back and damage to the plant, especially to the root and delicate root hairs. In most cases the ground is prepared beforehand by forking it over (brassicas, however, can be put straight into un-dug ground). Remove any weeds and rake the surface smooth. The soil should be moist but not saturated; water lightly if it is dry. It is best to plant in the evening, or in overcast conditions.

It is most important that the plants being moved are watered well several hours beforehand, whether they are in a seed bed, in seed trays or in blocks. Then dig them up carefully with a trowel. Make a hole in the ground large enough to accommodate the roots and, holding the plant in one hand, fill in the soil around the roots, pressing it down with the fingers. Firm the soil around the stem, then give the leaves a tug. If the plant wobbles, it is not firm enough. If it seems necessary, water the plant afterwards.

Watering

Vegetables need moisture throughout their growth, but there are certain times when it is more important than others. Soils must be moist for seeds to germinate, for planting, and when fertilizers are being applied. For different groups of vegetables there are also 'critical periods', when shortage of water is very damaging. Wherever possible, try to ensure that plants are watered at these times.

The leafy vegetables – spinach, lettuces, brassicas, celery and so on – are thirsty plants, and benefit from heavy watering throughout their growing season, especially in dry summer months. A weekly rate of 2–3 gal/sq yd (11–16 liters/sq m) is sufficient. Their critical period is 10–20 days before maturity. If regular watering is impossible, concentrate on giving one very heavy watering, at twice the rate recommended above, during this period. The so-called 'fruiting' vegetables include peas, beans, tomatoes, cucumbers, marrows, and corn-on-the-cob. These are less demanding in the early stages, but once the flowers appear and the fruits start to form, they need heavy watering. Water them then at a weekly rate of 4 gal/sq yd (22 liters/sq m).

Root vegetables have a shorter critical period, but if the soil dries out root quality will be poor. When the plants are small, light watering may be needed in dry weather, at the rate of 1 gal/sq yd (5 liters/sq m) per row. Later in the season, when the roots are swelling, heavier watering at a bi-weekly rate of 3–4 gal/sq yd (16–22 liters/sq m) is recommended in dry weather.

Water penetrates the soil slowly, layer by layer, and it is much more useful to water occasionally, but heavily, rather than frequently but lightly. Surface watering simply evaporates before it reaches the plant's roots. Always water gently but thoroughly. Large droplets damage the soil surface and young plants, and splash mud up on to the leaves. Use a watering-can with a fine rose when watering seedlings and young plants.

Mulching

Mulching means covering the soil with a protective layer. This is generally some type of organic material, which will slowly rot into the soil, but over shorter periods plastic sheeting can be used. Mulching conserves moisture by preventing evaporation and prevents weeds from germinating. It also protects the soil surface from the damaging effects of heavy rain, and from compaction.

Many materials can be used for mulching. Their texture is important: they need to be fairly compact but not so compact that moisture and air cannot filter through to the soil. Home-made compost, leaf mold, lawn mowings which have been allowed to dry out first, well-rotted manure, straw and bracken are all suitable. Provided the plants are not completely swamped, the mulch can be anything up to 4 inches (10 cm) thick.

Ideally you should mulch when the soil is moist and warm. Never mulch when the soil is very dry, very wet, or very cold; it will simply remain that way, providing poor conditions for the plants. The best time to mulch is after planting, or when plants sown directly in the garden are several inches high.

Plastic mulches are useful in the short term, especially for summer crops, such as tomatoes and cucumbers. Either lay the film on the ground and cut cross-like slits through which the plants are planted, or plant first then gradually roll the film over, making slits and pulling the plants through. Anchor the edges of the film in vertical slits in the soil. The plants can be watered, when necessary, in the gaps around the stem.

Black plastic sheeting is most effective for preventing weed germination, while transparent and white sorts warm up the soil, the latter reflecting light up on to the plant.

Protected cropping

Cloches, frames, greenhouses, and low and 'walk in' polythene tunnels are all devices that can be used to give vegetables extra protection – 'protected cropping', to use the modern term (see also The Greenhouse, page 186).

Cloches are small units made in a variety of materials ranging from glass to plastic. Glass cloches are the most expensive but, breakages apart, are the most durable and give the best light transmission. They are, however, heavy to handle and a little awkward to erect. Of the many plastic materials, double-layered corrugated propylene provides excellent growing conditions, and plants do well in the somewhat diffuse light it creates.

Cloches are easily moved from one crop to another and are often placed end to end to cover a row. Their disadvantages are the labor involved in lifting them for watering, weeding, harvesting and ventilation, and that tall plants outgrow all but the largest cloches. Ventilation is essential in warm and close weather; if there is no built-in ventilation method, move cloches a few inches apart, so they are not too close.

Low plastic tunnels are cheaper than cloches and are used in much the same way. They consist of plastic film stretched over a series of low galvanized wire hoops. The film is held in place with fine wire or string stretched from side to side. The ends are anchored in the soil or tied to a stake (see illustration). The sides can be rolled up for watering and ventilation. The film usually needs replacing after two years.

Frames: Traditional frames were usually permanent fixtures, with brick sides and glass 'lights' or lids. Modern frames tend to be portable, and are constructed of wood, plastic material or aluminum and glass. They are fairly expensive for the amount of ground covered, and are best used for raising and hardening off plants, for summer crops or half-hardy vegetables such as cucumbers and peppers, and for winter salad crops.

Weed control

Weeds have to be controlled because they compete for nutrients in the soil, for moisture, and for light. There are two types: perennials and annuals. The perennials last from one year to the next by means of very deep roots, or by creeping stems and roots. Common examples are ground elder, chickweed, knotweed, clover and crabgrass. Once a garden is well established they pose little problem, but in the early stages they have to be dug out manually, making sure that no little pieces of root or stem are left in the soil, as they are very likely to regenerate. Chemical weedkillers may prove useful in clearing a weed-infested site initially. Suitable weedkillers include Treflan and Devrinal (which is

very effective against grasses). They can be applied with a watering-can. Always follow the manufacturer's instructions implicity. In some cases it is necessary to leave the ground for several weeks or months before it is safe to sow or plant.

Annuals germinate, flower and die at least once, maybe two or three times in a season, and are far more of a problem. Chickweed, crabgrass and annual meadow grass are most common. They seed prolifically, and because weed seeds often remain viable for many years, the proverbial one year's seeding really can mean 7 years of weeding. It is essential to prevent them going to seed. They are also best controlled by hand weeding or hoeing. Always hoe as shallowly as possible, to prevent damage to surface roots, and to cut down on the loss of moisture from the soil. In wet weather small weeds may re-root, so should be removed. In dry weather they can be left on the surface to wilt. Weeds that have gone to seed should be burned.

It is now known that the most competitive weeds in a vegetable garden are those between, rather than within, the rows – so concentrate on removing those first. For a crop sown directly in the ground, competition starts to become really serious 2–3 weeks after the crop germinates. Start weeding then, if not before. Raising plants indoors gives them a head start over weeds. Also, relatively close, equidistant spacing reduces the light reaching the soil, and is therefore an effective means of keeping down weeds – as is mulching. Using chemical weedkillers in an established vegetable garden is liable to damage plants, and is not generally recommended.

An organic mulch will generally improve the soil structure because it encourages worms. When applying the mulch, care should be taken not to swamp the plant.

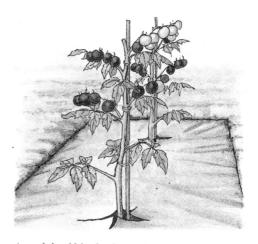

A mulch of black plastic is particularly effective for preventing weed germination.

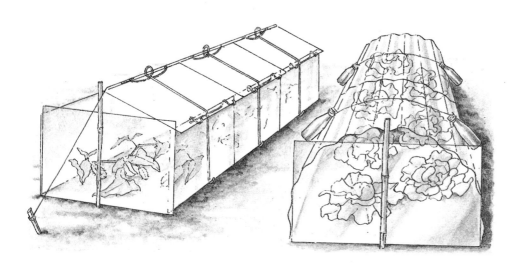

*Glass cloches (**left**) can be anchored by a system of string, 'eyes' and pegs, while plastic cloches (**right**) can be held down by*

water-filled plastic bottles attached to strings. The open ends of cloches must be covered to avoid drafts.

A-Z
VEGETABLES

ARTICHOKE, GLOBE

The globe artichoke is a gourmet's vegetable, and is also strikingly handsome with its beautiful silver foliage and thistle-like flowers. The edible parts are the fleshy bases of the scaly bracts enclosing the bud and the 'choke' beneath. Artichokes are perennial, but they start to deteriorate after their third season so it is wise to replace with new plants each year.

Cultivation: They need fertile, well-drained soil. Prepare the ground by digging in plenty of well-rotted manure or compost. A general fertilizer can be given before planting, or feed them with a seaweed-based fertilizer during growth. Choose an open but not too exposed position, as artichokes cannot stand severe winters, particularly if growing on heavy soil. They are recommended only for frost-free areas.

Plants are raised either by planting rooted suckers, known as offsets, or by seed. The former is the more reliable method of obtaining quality artichoke plants.

Either buy offsets in late winter or early spring, or take them from the outside edge of a mature established plant. Slice them off cleanly with a spade, making sure you have plenty of root attached. Plant them 2½ ft (75 cm) apart each way.

If using seed, sow indoors in late winter or outdoors in early spring, planting toward the end of spring. The quality will be variable, so build up the stock by taking offsets from the strongest plants in future years. During the growing season keep the plants weeded, mulched, and watered so that they do not dry out. The first heads should appear towards the end of the summer period.

In areas where the winters are not very mild, artichokes need some protection. Earth up the base of the stem in late autumn and protect the crowns with bracken, dead leaves, or straw. Remove the protective covering gradually in spring.

Pests and diseases: Aphids sometimes attack the developing flower-heads.

Harvesting: The artichokes are ready when the buds are nicely plump and the scales are still soft.

ARTICHOKE, JERUSALEM

Jerusalem artichokes are tasty, nutritious tubers, which can be baked or boiled like potatoes, or used to make an excellent winter soup. They are easily grown, and are one of the most suitable crops with which to break in heavy, previously uncultivated soil. They will tolerate a wide range of soils.

Jerusalem artichokes grow very tall, up to 10 ft (3 m), so can be planted 2–3 deep around the outside of a vegetable patch to act as a windbreak or can be used to screen off an unsightly feature.

Cultivation: The knobby tubers can be planted any time from late winter through the end of spring, about 4–6 inches (10–15 cm) deep and 1 ft (30 cm) apart. They are not always available in garden shops, but you can always buy a few from a greengrocer. Tubers the size of a hen's egg are best, but larger tubers can be cut into several pieces, provided each has a shoot. Once

Globe artichokes: the top head is ready for cutting

163

planted they require very little attention. In exposed gardens earth up the stems when the plants are about 1 ft (30 cm) high so that they are not rocked by winds. When the foliage dies off in autumn, cut the stems back to 2–3 inches (5–7.5 cm) from the ground.

Pests and diseases: Slugs may be a problem in some soils.

Harvesting: The tubers are extremely hardy and can be left in the ground all winter and lifted as required. Always keep back a few tubers for planting the following year, but to prevent them spreading, be sure you lift even the tiniest tubers and broken pieces.

ASPARAGUS

An asparagus bed is a luxury, permanently occupying a fair amount of ground in return for a short, but glorious, season.

Cultivation: A bed should last up to 20 years. Make it on an open site (not where asparagus has previously been grown), avoiding frost pockets. Asparagus will grow on a wide range of soils, but the site must be well drained. Traditionally it was grown on raised beds or ridges to ensure good drainage and long white stalks, but today it is usually grown on the flat. The variety 'Giant Mammoth' is recommended for heavy soils; 'Connover's Colossal' for light soils.

To prepare the bed, eliminate annual and perennial weeds, using weedkillers if necessary. Then dig in plenty of well-rotted manure or compost the autumn before planting. Very acid soils should be limed.

Asparagus can be raised from seed or purchased as 'crowns'. The quality from seed is more variable, and it takes a year longer to mature, but it can be quite satisfactory. Sow the seed several inches apart 1 inch (2.5 cm) deep in a seed bed in spring. Leave until the next spring, when the largest should be planted in the bed in the same way as bought crowns.

Long-podded broad bean plants laden with pods

If you are starting with asparagus crowns (which look rather like a cross between a spider and octopus!) buy one-year, rather than two- or three-year crowns. They become established much better. Dig a trench 1 ft (30 cm) wide and 8 inches (20 cm) deep, and for each plant make a mound 2–3 inches (5–7.5 cm) high in the bottom of the trench. Spread the crown on the mound, cover it with 2 inches (5 cm) of soil, and fill in the trench as the shoots grow. Asparagus can be grown in single rows, or in beds 2–3 rows wide. Average spacing is 1½ ft (45 cm) between plants.

Contrary to popular belief, there is no need to mulch or apply salt to the beds during the winter. However, they can be given a general fertil-izer in spring (preferably high in nitrogen and potash) or a seaweed-based fertilizer during growth.

Pests and diseases: Slugs can be a major problem in some gardens. The grubs and adults of the asparagus beetle – which has orange marks on a black body – attack stems and foliage. Spray with malathion.

Harvesting: Asparagus should not be cut until its third season – 2 years after planting. Using a sharp knife, cut the spears, 5–7 inches (13–18 cm) long, about 1 inch (2.5 cm) below ground. Once the bed is established, start cutting the asparagus in April and continue for 6 weeks in the first cutting seson and about 8 weeks in subsequent years.

BEANS

String, lima, soy, broad, run-ner: the term 'bean' covers such a wide variety of growth that it is useful to understand what they all have in common. They are all classified as legumes and they are all edible. For the home gardener, they are also a reliable and pleasurable crop.

What they do not have in common is their growth habit. Beans fall into two growth categories: bush, which are simply planted, and pole, which are vine-like and best cultivated on three stakes stuck in the ground and joined near the top as if you were building a teepee.

The breadth of the group is so great that the elements must be listed separately:

The common green bean, also known as the string or snap bean, is the most widely planted in home gardens. It grows either in bush or pole form.

Dwarf French beans

Lima beans are annuals, which also come in bush or pole varieties, but they do not produce as well in hot and dry climates.

Soy beans fall into the bush category. Their uses are widespread, but they require more space and time than other varieties.

The broad bean, also known as fava, is not popular in the United States, but it is easy to grow in almost all areas and it produces a tasty crop.

Runner beans are both pretty and tasty. Their vines flower annually and produce a crop that should be harvested while it is still young.

The entire family merits the consideration of any vegetable gardener. For more detailed information as to what will work best in your area you should consult your local nursery.

Cultivation: Plant out, after the danger of frost has passed, in a sunny location and fertile, loose soil. The bush varieties should be spaced 2–3 inches (5–7.5 cm) apart in rows that are 2–2½ ft (60–75 cm) apart. For the pole varieties, plant 6 ft (1.8 m) stakes 18 inches (45 cm) deep in the soil, leaving 4½ ft (1.3 m) above ground. Sow about six seeds around the base of each pole.

Pests and diseases: The different kinds of beans are susceptible to as many different kinds of predator and disease. Many of these depend on the climate in which the crop is being grown. Check with your local nurseryman to find out what protection to take for the variety you are interested in.

Harvesting: Most varieties will announce their own harvest date. Lima beans will produce bright, fresh, well-filled pods. Most of the varieties will offer several weeks of ripe crop. When they are firm, but not overly ripe, pick them. Freeze the surplus for later enjoyment.

BEETS

Beets can be pulled fresh from the garden from about the end of May until late autumn, and can then be either pickled or stored for the winter. There are flat, round, and long, tapered varieties in red, yellow and white forms.

Many varieties are liable to bolt (run to seed) rather than form roots if sown early in the year and/or subject to spells of cold weather. Fortunately, newer varieties such as 'Avonearly' and 'Boltardy' are bolt-resistant and are suitable for these early sowings.

Cultivation: Beets need rich, light soil. Very acid soils should be limed. If possible use ground manured for the previous crop.

The roots are best used when young and tender, before they become tough, so for a continuous supply of good quality beet it is advisable to make several sowings.

The first sowings can be made in spring under cloches, followed by unprotected sowings outdoors in early to mid-spring in both cases using bolt-resistant varieties. Make further sowings at monthly intervals until July using any variety. For winter storage, sow any of the round varieties, or 'Cheltenham Greentop', one of the long varieties, in late spring or early summer.

Beet should never be sown thickly, because the so-called seed is in fact a fruit containing several seeds, all of which may germinate. Single seeded, monogerm beet is sometimes available, and if so, is worth using. Sow seed ½–¾ inch (1–1½ cm) deep, and 1 inch (2.5 cm) apart, thinning later to the required distance. Rather surprisingly, early crops need the widest spacing. They can be as far apart as 3¼ inches (8 cm) between plants, in rows 8 inches (20 cm) apart. Main summer supplies and beet for winter storage can be 1 inch (2.5 cm) apart in rows 1 ft (30 cm) apart.

Beet needs to grow steadily, so the aim with any watering should be to prevent the soil drying out. If possible you should water at the rate of 2 gal/sq yd (11 liters/sq m) every 2–3 weeks in a dry season. A top-dressing of a general fertilizer might be necessary during the growing season if growth is poor.

Pests and diseases: Aphids can sometimes be troublesome.

Harvesting: Summer beets are pulled as required. For winter storage lift the roots carefully in late autumn and twist off the stems. Store them in a frost-free place in layers, in boxes of moist peat or sand, or in clamps outdoors. If you are unable to provide any of these conditions, you can try to stimulate them by using perforated polythene sacks.

BROCCOLI

Broccoli is something of a gourmet vegetable, attractive looking with a beautiful flavor. Moreover it is an excellent vegetable for freezing. It has several other merits: it grows fast, sometimes being ready less than 3 months from sowing; it can be planted very closely; and it requires a less fertile soil than most brassicas.

The best spears (heads) are obtained if broccoli can be sown directly in the ground, to avoid the check of transplanting. Sow 2–3 seeds together at the required distance apart, thinning to one in each position when the seedlings have germinated. Otherwise, sow in pots or peat blocks or, if there is no alternative, in a seed bed, transplanting very carefully while the plants are small.

The broccoli season lasts roughly from July to October if several sowings are made, but the plants are killed off by frost. Make the earliest sowings in early or mid-spring with the variety 'Express Corona'. Sowing can continue through spring into mid-summer using the varieties 'Express Corona', 'Green Comet', 'Green Duke', or 'Premium Crop'. These varieties all take different lengths of time to mature, so it is quite feasible to sow several of them at the same time to obtain continuity.

Cultivation: Unlike cabbage broccoli is very insensitive to planting distances, although the heaviest yields of good-quality spears are obtained by planting 6 inches (15 cm) apart in rows 1 ft (30 cm) apart. If the crop is grown for freezing it can be planted closer, say 8 inches (20 cm) apart in each direction. This has the effect of suppressing the sideshoots and making smaller terminal spears, all of which are ready at much the same time. Broccoli does poorly if checked, so make sure there is plenty of moisture, watering as suggested earlier for brassicas (page 16). It is beneficial to keep the soil mulched.

A somewhat different type of broccoli is the variety 'Romanesco'. It has large spears with a purplish tinge

Young summer beets

and an outstanding flavor. Sow it in spring, planting out 2 ft (60 cm) apart in summer. Harvest from July onwards.

Pests and diseases: As far as pests are concerned broccoli is susceptible to the normal run of brassica pests and diseases, but caterpillars are particularly troublesome. They conceal themselves in the crevices of the spears. Soak the vegetable in salted water for an hour or so before cooking to force them out.

Harvesting: Always cut the main, terminal spear of broccoli first, while it is still firm and compact. Smaller lateral spears will then develop so that picking can often continue over a fairly long period.

BROCCOLI, SPROUTING

Purple-sprouting broccoli is one of the major standbys of the late winter to spring period. It is very hardy and prolific. Three or four plants are quite sufficient for the average household. The slightly less common white form of sprouting broccoli is somewhat less hardy and less productive. There are early and late selections of both types, but no named varieties. See also Broccoli, above.

Cultivation: Seed should be sown in a seed bed or in soil or peat blocks from mid- to late spring, starting with the early varieties. Plant out firmly from early to mid-

A full stem of Brussels sprouts

summer, spacing the plants 2 ft (60 cm) apart each way. In good soil purple-sprouting plants can grow tall, so it is advisable to earth up the stems and stake the plants.

Pests and diseases: Sprouting broccoli is less prone to pests and diseases than most brassicas, the worst enemy being pigeons in winter. Clubroot, cabbage root fly and caterpillars can be a problem.

Harvesting: Snap off the flowering shoots when they are about 6 inches (15 cm) long, before the flowers open. Keep picking regularly. Sprouting broccoli is very suitable for freezing.

BRUSSELS SPROUTS

We associate Brussels sprouts with Christmas, but by sowing a succession of the modern F_1 varieties the season can now be extended from fall to spring. Like purple-sprouting broccoli, Brussels sprouts are among our hardiest vegetables, although they do suffer

damage in the most severe winters.

Cultivation: All varieties should be sown between early and mid-spring. They can either be sown under cloches or in a garden frame (this will produce the earliest crops), or in a seed bed outdoors.

From early to mid-spring sowing under cover, the following F_1 varieties should provide a continuous supply over a six-month period: 'Peer Gynt' (September to October); 'Valiant' (October to November); 'Perfect Line' or 'Achilles' (November to December); 'Rampart' (December to January); 'Fortress' (January to March). Of course you may want to select only one or two varieties to meet the household's requirements.

Plant in late spring and early summer in firm ground that has not been freshly manured. The standard spacing is 2 ft (60 cm) apart in each direction, a distance that encourages small, uniform sprouts to be ready over a relatively short period. However, if you prefer larger sprouts, maturing over a longer period, plant them up to 3 ft (90 cm) apart. Apart from watering soon after transplanting to help the seedlings to become established further watering is rarely required, except under drought conditions. This is because the wide spacing between plants means there is less competition for moisture.

Sprouts sometimes become loose or 'blown'. This may be caused by loose soil, by planting in freshly manured ground, or by giving too much nitrogen in the early stages of growth. Make sure the stems are earthed up or the plants staked and, if any extra feeding is done, late summer is the most suitable time.

Early varieties of Brussels sprouts, such as 'Peer Gynt', can be 'stopped', which means cutting out the top of the stem. This encourages the sprouts to button up sooner and to be more uniform in size, so giving earlier picking over a shorter season. It is particularly useful if you want all the sprouts to mature together and to be of an even size for freezing. Stop the plants when the lowest sprouts on the stem are about ½ inch (1 cm) in diameter. To be effective it must be done before the first frost – and it is only successful with early varieties.

Pests and diseases: Brussels sprouts are vulnerable to all the brassica problems, such as clubroot, caterpillars and cabbage root fly.

Harvesting: Pick the sprouts from the bottom of the stem upwards, and do not neglect the sprout 'top', which can develop almost into a miniature cabbage in spring and is a lovely vegetable in itself.

CABBAGE
There are many excellent modern cabbage varieties which, unlike the old-fashioned sorts, stand in good condition for several months once they have matured. This makes it feasible to cut fresh cabbages from your garden all year

round in many areas. Follow the sowing plan shown in the table for a continuous all-year-round supply of cabbages.

A neat patch of summer cabbages with uniform, firm heads

the ground and thin them out to the correct spacing. For soil conditions, planting, watering, and feeding, treat them as recommended for typical brassicas (see page 16). For practical purposes, cabbages are divided into spring (including 'spring greens'), summer, and winter types.

Spring cabbages are sown in late summer and planted in autumn. They can be allowed to form small heads in spring or can be harvested as looser, unhearted plants – spring greens. For headed cabbages, space the plants 12 inches (30 cm) apart each way. For spring greens arrange them closer, say 6 inches (15 cm) apart each way, or 4 inches (10 cm) apart in rows 1 ft (30 cm) apart. In this latter case you can use the second and third, fifth and sixth cabbages in the row first (and so on), leaving the remaining plants

Cultivation: All cabbages can either be sown on seed beds outdoors and transplanted, or sown in small pots. You can even sow them direct in

CABBAGES

When and how to sow	Suitable varieties	When to harvest
Spring cabbages Sow directly into the ground in early August, or into a seed bed for planting out in September	'Harbinger', 'Avon Crest', 'Offenham' selections	March to May
Early summer cabbages Sow in heat in late February in blocks or pots, planting out in mid-April	'Hispi', 'Marner Allfruh'	May to June
Mid-summer cabbages Sow in a garden frame in late March, planting out in late May	In order of maturity: 'Hispi', 'Marner Allfruh', 'Stonehead', 'Market Topper', 'Minicole'	July to September
Late summer cabbages Sow outside early May, planting June	'Stonehead'	September to November
Early winter and/or storage Sow outside late April, planting in early June	'Hidena', 'Jupiter'	November to December
Hardy winter cabbages Sow outside mid-May, planting towards the end of June	'Avon Coronet', 'Celtic', 'Celsa', 'Aquarius'	December to February

1 ft (30 cm) apart to heart up. Varieties such as 'Durham Early' and 'Avon Crest' are particularly suitable for use as spring greens.

Spring cabbages should be earthed up during the winter, and given a feed in spring. Don't, however, feed them when they are planted out, otherwise they will be too 'soft' to withstand the winter. They will survive all but the most severe winters.

Summer cabbages are sown in spring. They are larger, and should be spaced 12–14 inches (30–35 cm) apart each way if you want cabbages with smallish heads, and up to 1½ ft (45 cm) apart for larger heads.

Winter cabbages come in several distinct types. The Dutch winter white types are excellent fresh or in coleslaw, though they are not very hardy. They can, however, be lifted in November and stored in an airy, frost-free shed, or even in a garden frame – in which case place them on wooden slats, and cover them with a thick layer of loose bracken or straw. Inspect them from time to time and gently rub off any outer leaves which show signs of rotting.

The hardier types, which can be left in the ground all winter, include the crinkly-leaved savoys, the flat, reddish 'January King' type, and newer hybrids between savoys and winter whites. Plant winter cabbage about 16 inches (40 cm) apart if you want small heads, 18 inches (45 cm) apart for medium sized and 20 inches (50 cm) apart for large heads.

Red cabbages are sown in early spring, planting out 2 ft (60 cm) apart in early summer. Lift and store any remaining heads in fall. Good varieties are 'Langendijker Red' and 'Ruby Ball'.

Pests and diseases: Cabbage root fly, mealy bugs, aphids and cabbage white butterfly caterpillars are frequent pests. Clubroot is a disease that will seriously affect cabbage yields on infected land.

Harvesting: With the exception of a few modern varieties, spring and summer cabbages will stand for only a few weeks once mature before they start to 'bolt' or otherwise deteriorate. They should be eaten in their prime. If the ground is not required for another crop cut off the heads, leaving a few inches of stalk in the ground. Make a shallow cross, about ¼ inch (5 mm) deep, in the top of the stalk. Provided the ground is fertile and moist, a second crop of small leafy cabbages may be obtained.

Non-hardy winter cabbages must be cut before frost or, with appropriate varieties, lifted and stored before hard frost. Hardy varieties can be left in the ground until required.

CARROT

Carrots are fussy about soil. They will always do far better on rich, light, sandy soils, where the roots can expand without difficulty, than on heavy clay or stony soils. If you have heavy soil, work in as much organic matter as possible to improve it.

There are several different types of carrot. For early crops use the smaller finger-shaped carrots of the Amsterdam and Nantes types (try 'Amsterdam Colora' and 'Nantes Express'), or the little round carrots such as 'Early French Frame' and the selection 'Early French Frame – Rondo'. For the main summer supply and winter storage use the larger 'Chantenay', 'Berlicum' or 'Autumn King' types. Good varieties are 'Chantenay Red Cored', 'Berlicum-Berjo', and 'Autumn King-Vita Longa'.

Cultivation: For a continuous supply several sowings have to be made. Provided the soil is warm enough (carrots need a minimum soil temperature of 45°F (7°C) to germinate), make the first sowings in frames or under cloches in late winter or early spring. Follow this with unprotected outdoor sowings in spring. For both these sowings use early varieties; they will be ready by mid-summer.

For later summer use and winter storage, sow maincrop varieties from spring through mid-summer at roughly 4-week intervals. Finally, for a very late crop of small roots in winter, sow an early variety in late summer, cloching in fall.

Carrots should be sown very thinly (to minimize thinning), about ½ inch (1 cm) deep. The highest yields are obtained by growing them in rows about 6 inches (15 cm) apart. Early carrots, which should be encouraged to grow very fast, can be thinned to 3–4 inches (7.5–10 cm) apart. Maincrop carrots can be thinned to 1½ inches (3.5 cm) apart. Weed between the rows in the early stages; subsequently the natural canopy of leaves will help to prevent further weed growth.

Carrots will not grow well if the soil is allowed to dry out, and the roots are likely to split if there is heavy rain, or heavy watering, after a dry spell. Watering at the rate of about 3–4 gal/sq yd (22 liters/sq m) every 2–3 weeks will usually ensure steady growth.

Pests and diseases: Carrot fly is an almost universal problem with carrots, sometimes causing very poor crops. The flies are attracted by the smell of carrot foliage, and lay eggs which hatch into tiny grubs visible on the roots. There are no completely effective and harmless chemical remedies, but the following measures can be taken to minimize attack where the problem is serious.

Concentrate on early sowings (February and March), and on late sowings (June and July), which escape the worst attacks.

Sow thinly, and thin on calm, still evenings, nipping off surplus seedlings rather than pulling them out. Remove and burn the thinnings, or bury them deep in the compost heap to help put the flies off the scent. It is better to burn them if you possibly can.

Grow carrots in raised beds about 6 inches (15 cm) high, or in boxes, or under cloches, or in beds surrounded by wooden boards. These measures deter the flies because they only fly low, close to the ground.

Use the less leafy varieties

Early carrots pulled ready for use

such as the Amsterdam and Nantes types.

Lift maincrop varieties by October to prevent the late brood hatching.

Harvesting: Pull the carrots during the summer months as required. In mild areas on well-drained soils carrots can be left in the ground in winter, covered with about 6 inches (15 cm) of leaves or straw. Otherwise lift them carefully in autumn and twist off the stems. Store them in layers, in boxes of moist peat or sand, in a frost-free place.

CAULIFLOWER
There are cauliflower varieties for very season of the year, but as the winter and spring types (both previously known as winter broccoli) require a lot of space over a long period, people with smallish gardens are probably best to restrict themselves to early and mid-summer cauliflowers, and/or mini-cauliflowers.

Cultivation: There is no escaping the fact that good-quality cauliflowers can only be produced under good conditions. They must have rich soil, preferably on the slightly alkaline side. Very acid soil should be limed. The secret of success with cauliflowers is to try to encourage steady growth without checks of any kind. Plenty of water is a most important factor. To minimize the transplanting check, cauliflowers are best raised in small pots, or sown directly in the ground and thinned to the appropriate distance apart. If they have to be sown in a seed bed, plant them out as young as possible.

Cauliflower curds are very delicate and easily damaged by exposure to the elements. Summer cauliflowers can be protected from the sun, when nearing maturity, by half snapping a leaf over the head, and can be kept fresh for a few days until you are ready to pull them up. Winter and spring cauliflowers suffer most if they thaw out rapidly due to exposure to the sun after frost. This can be avoided by bending the stem over to the north and earthing it up on the southside.

Sowing times, correct planting distances and suitable varieties for the different seasons are given below.

Early summer cauliflowers: These are ready between mid-June and mid-July. Either sow them in a garden frame in fall, planting them outdoors in spring, or sow them in heat in mid-winter, harden them off, and plant them out in spring, 21 inches (53 cm) apart each way. Suitable varieties, in order of maturing, are 'Alpha', 'Mechelse Classic', and 'Dominant'.

Mid- and late summer cauliflowers: The mid-summer ones mature between mid-July and mid-August. They can be sown under cold glass in spring, planting out in late spring. Late summer cauliflowers, ready for use in late August and September, are sown in mid-spring and are planted out in early summer. Varieties 'Nevada' and 'Dok – Elgon' are suitable for both these crops, planted 21 inches (53 cm) apart each way.

Autumn cauliflowers: These mature between September and November, and are sown in late spring, planting out in early to mid-summer about 2 ft (60 cm) apart each way. Suitable varieties, in order of maturity, are 'Flora Blanca' and 'Barrier Reef'.

Winter cauliflowers: This type can only be grown in very mild areas, for use in winter and early spring. Sow them in late spring, planting out in mid-summer, 19 inches (48 cm) apart each way.

Spring cauliflowers: These over-wintering cauliflowers, maturing between March and late May, need hard conditions. Sow them in late spring, planting them out mid-summer. Suitable varieties, in order of maturity, are 'Angers No. 2 – Westmarsh Early', the 'Walcheren Winter' varieties 'Armado April', 'Markanta' and 'Birchington' and 'Angers No. 5'.

Mini-cauliflowers: Mini-cauliflowers are tiny curds, 1½–3½ inches (4–9 cm) in diameter, which make handy single portions and are good for freezing whole. They are obtained by growing early summer cauliflower varieties very close together, planted in square formation 6 inches (15 cm) apart in each direction. Sow in succession from early spring until mid-summer for a succession of crops from mid-summer through fall. These, of course, take up far less ground space, and mature much faster than normal-sized cauliflowers.

Pests and diseases: Clubroot is the most serious disease, and cauliflowers are vulnerable to the same pests as other brassicas. Caterpillars can hide in the curd.

Harvesting: Cut the curds as they are ready. If you have to store them, cover the curds with tissue paper and hang them upside down in a cool place.

CELERIAC
Celeriac is a member of the celery family and forms a large, rather knobby swollen bulb at the base of the stem. Although a little tricky to scrub clean, this makes an excellent winter vegetable. The leaves have a strong celery flavor and can be used, sparingly, as a celery substitute.

Cultivation: Celeriac, being a marshland plant, must have fertile, moisture-retentive soil, rich in organic matter. It also needs a long growing season if it is to reach a reasonable size. It is best sown indoors, in gentle heat, in late winter or early spring. Germination is often erratic, but once seedlings have germinated, transplant them and harden them off, ready for planting in the open in mid-spring through early summer.

Plant about 14 inches (35 cm) apart each way, taking care not to bury the crowns. The key to success is to water generously in dry weather, and keep the ground between the plants mulched to conserve moisture. Celeriac responds well to feeding with a seaweed-based fertilizer during the growing season. By mid-summer, the outer leaves can be removed, which exposes the crowns and is said to encourage them to swell. A promising new variety is Suttons 'Tellus'.

A large robust cauliflower with firm white curds

Pests and diseases: Celeriac is unlikely to be troubled by many pests, but leaf miners can tunnel and blister the leaves.

Harvesting: The crowns are ready for use from fall onwards. They are very hardy so can be left in the soil all winter. However, tuck a thick layer of straw or bracken between the plants to protect them from frost, and to make it easier to dig them out when the ground is frozen. They will normally remain in good conditon until spring, when they will run to seed.

CELERY

There are two types of celery. The traditional blanched, trench celery produces long, crunchy, white or colored stalks from fall to late winter. The more recently introduced 'self-blanching' types have shorter, greenish stems, which nevertheless have a good flavor. They are not hardy, but are ready between mid-summer and fall. They are easier to grow and require less space than traditional celery, which demands time, space and skill.

Good varieties of trench celery are 'Giant Pink', 'Giant White' and 'Giant Red' (reflecting the stalk color); reliable self-blanching varieties are 'Golden Self Blanching' and 'Lothom Self Blanching'. All of these are good both raw and cooked.

Cultivation: Celery requires moisture-retentive but well-drained rich soil, with plenty of organic matter dug in beforehand. Very acid soils should be limed. For trench celery prepare a trench the previous autumn if possible. Dig it 1 ft (30 cm) deep, and about 15 inches (37.5 cm) wide for a single row, 20 inches (50 cm) wide for a double row. Work a thick layer of well-rotted manure into the trench, then replace the bulk of the removed soil to within 4 inches (10 cm) of the top.

Celery has a high nitrogen requirement, so a nitrogenous fertilizer can be applied before planting and during

Self-blanching celery

growth; use a seaweed-based fertilizer during growth.

Sow seed in gentle heat indoors in early spring. Do not sow any earlier, as the seedlings may 'bolt' (run to seed) if subjected to a cold spell, or indeed any 'shocks'. For this reason it is worth sowing in small pots, thinning to one seedling in each. Sow very shallowly as the seed requires a certain amount of light to germinate and will fail if too deep.

Plant out in late spring or early summer after hardening off. Plant trench celery in single rows 9 inches (22.5 cm) apart, or in staggered double rows 10 inches (25 cm) apart. Plant self-blanching celery in block formation about 9 inches (22.5 cm) apart each way. In dry weather, when celery is growing, water it heavily at a weekly rate up to 4 gal/sq yd (22 liters/sq m).

Trench celery is earthed up in three stages, starting when the plants are about 1 ft (30 cm) high and repeating at three-weekly intervals until only the tips are visible. First tie the stems together just below the leaves, then pull earth up around the stalks to

a depth of about 3 inches (7.5 cm). Trench celery can also be grown on the flat and blanched by tying dark paper or wrapping black plastic around the stems.

Pests and diseases: Slugs and celery fly are the worst pests.

Harvesting: Cut the stems at ground level when required. Self-blanching celery is destroyed by hard frost. Trench celery may need protection with straw during the winter to keep it in good condition.

CHICORY, WITLOOF

Witloof or Belgian chicory is becoming increasingly popular; the bud-like, pale chicons make a pleasant winter salad and an equally good cooked vegetable. They are not difficult to grow, although the roots have to be forced in the dark to obtain the chicons. Very tight heads are obtained with the new varieties 'Crispa' and 'Normato', though the older 'Witloof' is still worth growing.

Cultivation: Chicory requires reasonably fertile, but not freshly manured, soil, in an open position. Sow the seed thinly outdoors in late spring in rows 1 ft (30 cm) apart. Thin in stages to 6 inches (15

cm) apart. The plants look like large dandelions. Keep them weeded but otherwise leave until autumn. In late fall dig up the roots and cut off the leaves about 1 inch (2.5 cm) above the crown. Reject any roots that are very fanged or very thin. To keep a household supplied throughout the winter, it is best to force a few roots at a time, say every 2 weeks. Store the bulk of the roots until required for forcing in layers in a box of moist peat or sand, in an outdoor shed. Forcing requires complete darkness and a little warmth. A simple method is to pot up 3 roots, closely together, in any soil in a 9 inch (22.5 cm) pot. Cover this with an up-turned pot of the same size, with aluminum foil over the drainage holes to exclude the light. Keep at a temperature of about 50°F (10°C) or a little higher. Provided the soil does not dry out, the chicons will develop in about 3 weeks.

Chicory roots can also be forced by planting them in greenhouse soil, and excluding light. This can be done by covering them with black plastic sheeting stretched over wire hoops and anchored into the soil on either side.

Pests and diseases: Generally trouble-free.

Harvesting: Once the chicons are ready keep them in the dark until they are used, as they become green and bitter on exposure to light. Cut them about 1 inch (2.5 cm) above the crown. If left in the pot or ground they often re-sprout to yield a second, smaller crop.

COLLARDS

Collards are grown and used much like cabbage, and are popular in the South for both summer and winter use. They do not form a true head but a large rosette of leaves, which may be blanched by tying them together. 'Hycrop Hybrid' is a mild, sweet-flavored plant that grows to about 15 inches (38 cm). 'Georgia' produces greens even under adverse conditions of heat and poor soil. It grows 2½–3 ft (76–90 cm) tall.

Cultivation: Collards prefer sandy or well-drained clay soils enriched with loam. Seed can be sown directly outdoors in early spring or in late summer for a fall crop. Mix in 4 pt (2.2 liters) of well-balanced fertilizer per 50 ft (15 m) of plants. Thin the plants to 6, 12, or 18 inches (15, 30 or 45 cm) depending on how they will be harvested. In areas of low rainfall, irrigate regularly.

Seeds can be started indoors in mid- to late winter, 5–7 weeks before setting outside. Collards will withstand a greater range of temperature than most vegetables grown in the South. Seed germinates in 4–9 days.

Pests and diseases: Insects that may cause problems are cabbage worms, aphids, harlequin bugs and root maggots. Diseases to watch out for are downy mildew and black leg disease.

Harvesting: Collards may be harvested in three different ways. The entire young plant may be cut off at ground level or the bottom leaves may be stripped off the plant periodically, leaving the bud to grow and produce more leaves. The last method is most popular with home gardeners since it entails making only one planting, and spring-planted collards may be continuously harvested throughout the summer and into winter. Immature plants may be harvested about 40 days and mature plants about 75 days after planting.

CORN

Corn-on-the-cob or sweetcorn is an increasingly popular vegetable but it is tender and needs a long, warm summer, so it becomes progressively harder to grow the further north one is. Early-maturing hybrid varieties such as 'Earliking', 'Kelvedon Sweetheart' and 'Northern Belle' are to be recommended.

Cultivation: Avoid exposed sites and very heavy or very

dry soil. Sweetcorn does best on well-drained, reasonably fertile soil, preferably manured for previous crop.

It cannnot be planted outside until there is no risk of frost, so is normally sown indoors for transplanting. However, the young plants dislike root disturbance, so where possible sow seed in pots of potting soil rather than in seed trays.

Sow about 1 inch (2.5 cm) deep in spring in gentle heat, sowing 2–3 seeds to each pot, thinning later to one seedling. Plant out, under cloches if possible, after hardening off. Sweetcorn should be grown in blocks rather than single rows, to assist with wind pollination, so space them 14 inches (35 cm) apart each way, several plants deep.

In the South seeds can be sown outdoors, preferably warming the soil first with cloches, or sowing 2–3 seeds at each 'station' under a jamjar or cloche, thinning to one seedling after germination. Seeds will not germinate until the soil temperature reaches 50°F (10°C), so it is generally unwise to sow outside until mid-spring.

Corn-on-the-cob is 'rocked' by the wind, so when the plants are 1–1½ ft (30–45 cm) high earth up the stems, much as one earths up potatoes, to a height of 2–3 inches (5–7.5 cm). Weed by hand if necessary, taking care not to disturb the shallow roots. Once the plants are flowering, water, if the weather is dry, at the rate of 4 gal/sq yd (22 liters/sq m) every few days. This increases the yield and improves the quality.

Pests and diseases: Generally trouble-free.

Harvesting: Expect only one or two cobs on each plant. They are ripe when the tassels are turning brown and the cobs are at a 45–degree angle to the stem and snap off easily. Press a fingernail into the kernel to see whether the juice is watery (under-ripe), 'doughy' (over-ripe), or milky (ripe). Harvest immediately, otherwise the sweetness is lost.

Corn with the cob ready for cutting

CRESS, MUSTARD and RAPE

Mustard and cress are traditionally grown on blotting paper indoors, but are also useful and very productive salad crops when grown in an unheated greenhouse or in the open ground, particularly in early spring and autumn. Rape, which has a milder flavor than mustard, is often used commercially as a mustard substitute. It makes an excellent salad crop and, if allowed to grow taller, can be cooked and used as 'greens'.

Cultivation: Very small patches, say 1–2 ft (30–60 cm) square, of these seedling crops will provide large quantities of salad material over several weeks. Sowings can be made in late winter and early spring, and again in fall, in unheated greenhouses, frames, or under cloches. The fall sowings will provide pickings late in the year and again the following spring. Sow outdoors from early to mid-spring, and in early fall. Mid-summer sowings may succeed, but

are likely to run to seed rapidly in hot weather. Prepare the soil, broadcast the seeds on the surface and cover with newspaper or plastic film to keep the soil moist until the seeds germinate.

Pests and diseases: Generally trouble-free, although 'damping off' (which prevents seeds from germinating or causes seedlings to wilt) may occur. Avoid by sowing in warm conditions in clean soil or by using seed dusted with a fungicide.

Harvesting: Start cutting the seedlings ½ inch (1 cm) above soil level when they are 2–3 inches (5–7.5 cm) high. If they are allowed to grow too high, they can become very hot-flavored.

CUCUMBER

There are two types of cucumber. The best quality are the greenhouse or frame cucumbers, which are long and smooth. The plants climb to considerable heights, and require warm, humid conditions and careful attention. Much more rugged are the outdoor 'ridge' cucumbers. These are

171

generally short and have prickly skins, though the improved varieties such as 'Burpless Tasty Green' and 'Burpee Hybrid' are longer and smoother. 'Perfection' is one of the best of the old ridge varieties. Good greenhouse varieties are 'Telegraph Improved', 'Butcher's Disease Resisting', and the all-female 'Femspot' and 'Landora'.

Gherkins are grown in exactly the same way as outdoor ridge cucumbers. Suitable varieties for gherkins are 'Venlo' and 'Condor'.

Cultivation: Cucumber roots appreciate very humus-rich soil. Prepare the ground beforehand by making a trench, or digging individual holes, about 1 ft (30 cm) deep and the same width, filling them with well-rotted strawy manure, covered with about 6 inches (15 cm) of soil.

Cucumber plants dislike transplanting, so they should either be sown directly in the garden, or in individual pots to minimize the shock. Outdoor cucumbers, which sprawl rather than climb, can either be grown on the flat, spaced 2–2½ ft (60–75 cm) apart, or trained up trellises or supports spaced about 18 inches (45 cm) apart. Sow cucumbers in mid-May in warmer areas, but wait till late May, or even June, in the colder climates. Sow 2–3 seeds together about ¾ inch (2 cm) deep, on their sides, and cover with a jamjar to assist germination. They can also be sown indoors in early spring, hardening off before planting out. Cloche protection in the early stages is beneficial.

To encourage fruiting, the old types of ridge cucumber are 'stopped' (the growing point nipped out), above the fifth leaf. The strongest 2–3 laterals are then selected and also stopped beyond the fifth leaf, others being removed. The Japanese varieties bear fruit on the main stem and only need to be stopped when they reach the top of the support.

Keep the cucumbers well watered and mulched, and feed occasionally with a general fertilizer during growth.

Sow greenhouse or frame cucumbers in late winter or early spring in a propagator at soil temperatures of at least 68°F (20°C). For early crops the greenhouse or frame must be heated, with night temperatures of at least 60°F (15°C).

Plant 18 inches (45 cm) apart, when the soil temperature reaches at least 60°F (15°C), and only in warm conditions; keep the greenhouse well ventilated in hot weather, but close it as soon as the temperature drops in the evening.

Cucumbers need to be tied to horizontal wire supports. Train them to the top of the wire then nip out the growing point; stop the laterals 2 leaves beyond a fruit.

With the older varieties it is necessary to remove the male flowers, as pollinated fruit is swollen and bitter. The female flowers are distinguished by a miniature cucumber visible behind the flower. With more recent 'all-female' varieties this is no longer necessary.

Pests and diseases: Red spider mites can be a problem; keeping the greenhouse atmosphere moist by syringing daily with water in hot weather will help to control them. Greenhouse cucumbers are subject to a number of diseases, so use disease-resistant varieties where possible.

Harvesting: Pick regularly to encourage further cropping.

EGGPLANT

Eggplants are among the most striking looking vegetables. The large pendulous fruits are normally a deep purple-black, but there are white forms such as the variety 'Easter Egg', which look uncommonly like hens' eggs.

Cultivation: Eggplants are demanding, so avoid poor, shallow soils. Dig in plenty of well-rotted manure or compost before planting, and make sure the plants have plenty of moisture throughout their growing season.

Sow seed in a greenhouse in gentle heat in mid- to late spring, provided that a minimum night temperature of 60°F (15°C) and day temperature of 65°F (18°C) can be maintained. When the seedlings are about 2 inches (5 cm) high, pot them up in 3 inch (7.5 cm) pots. Plant them in their permanent positions when the first flower truss is visible, generally April/May. Do not plant them outdoors until there is no risk of frost, from late winter to early June, depending on the region. Harden

Ridge cucumber

them off well beforehand.

Plant them about 17 inches (43 cm) apart. Eggplants can grow very large and top-heavy, so should either be staked or tied to some kind of support. To encourage bushy growth, nip out the growing point when the plant is about 15 inches (38 cm) high.

It is best to allow only four fruits to develop on each plant. From then on the plants can be fed with a tomato fertilizer approximately every 10 days.

Pests and diseases: Red spider mites and whitefly are liable to attack plants grown indoors.

Harvesting: Eggplants need a long season to mature, and are not normally ready until late summer. Pick them when they look plump and glossy. If frost threatens, uproot the plants and hang them indoors; fruits will keep for a few weeks on the plant.

ENDIVE

Endives are very useful salad plants all the year round, but especially in autumn, winter and spring. They are slightly bitter compared to lettuce, but this can be remedied by partial or complete blanching, or by shredding them fairly finely in salads. There are two distinct types: the broad-leaved or Batavian, and the curly-leaved, which has finely divided, attractive leaves.

Cultivation: Endives need an open situation and fertile, moisture-retentive soil. Sow in early spring for the summer crop, and through the summer for the winter crop. Sow either directly in the garden, or in a seed bed or in seed trays for transplanting. Sow about ½ inch (1 cm) deep in rows about 6 inches (15 cm) apart, thinning to 12 inches (30 cm) apart. The thinnings can be transplanted carefully to provide a succession.

Plants from the summer sowing can be transplanted into an unheated greenhouse or, alternatively, covered with cloches, for winter use. The plants are blanched when they are mature. The simplest method of partial blanching is to bunch up the leaves and tie them towards the top of the plant with raffia or an elastic band. This makes the central leaves whiter, and alleviates the bitterness. For complete blanching tie up the leaves when the plant is dry, then cover the plant with a box or plant pot with the drainage holes blocked to exclude light. Alternatively, plants can be lifted and planted in a darkened garden frame. They will be ready for use within 10–15 days. Use immediately otherwise they will start to rot.

Pests and diseases: Generally trouble-free.

Harvesting: Pick individual leaves as required or cut the whole head 1 inch (2.5 cm) above the stem. Leave the stump in the ground as endives will usually re-sprout over several months, which is most useful in winter and early spring.

FENNEL

Florence or sweet fennel is a beautiful, feathery-leaved plant grown for the swollen bulb at the base of the stem - though it may be admitted that in our climate it is sometimes reluctant to form the much-prized bulb. Fennel can be used cooked or raw, but the delicate flavor is most marked when eaten raw. Florence fennel should not be confused with the hardier, perennial fennel, which is grown as a herb.

Cultivation: Fennel likes much the same conditions as celery and, like celery, is liable to 'bolt' if subjected to spells of very cold or very dry weather or, because of its susceptibility to different day lengths, if sown too early in the year. Varieties least likely to 'bolt' are 'Perfection' and 'Zefa Fino'.

Although fennel can be grown on heavy soil, it does best on fertile, light, well-drained soil, requiring plenty of moisture through-

Florence fennel

out its growth. Work in plenty of well-rotted manure or compost before planting.

Seed can be sown ½ inch (1 cm) deep in small pots or peat blocks indoors, for planting out after hardening off. Make several sowings if a succession is required. The earliest sowings can be made in spring but, because of the likelihood of bolting, these are something of a gamble. The main sowings are made in early summer and again in late summer. These last can be planted into a cold greenhouse or frames to give a late autumn crop.

Plant out when seedlings are about 4–5 inches (10–12.5 cm) high, spacing the plants about 12 inches (30 cm) apart each way. Early plantings will benefit from cloche protection if the weather is cold or windy. Take precautions against slugs in the early stages, and keep the plants well watered and mulched. Feed them from time to time with a seaweed-based fertilizer. Although by no means essential, the bulb is traditionally blanched by earthing it up when it starts to swell. Pull earth up 2–3 inches (5–7.5 cm) around the base.

Pests and diseases: Generally trouble-free.

Harvesting: Depending on sowing times, the season can last from mid-summer through the end of fall. Cut the bulb about ¾ inch (2 cm) above the ground rather than uproot the plant. It will often throw out further small leafy shoots which are pleasant in salads or for flavoring cooked dishes.

KALE

The kales are especially valuable in the colder parts of the country because they are exceptionally hardy — though many people find them too coarse a vegetable.

There are broad-leaved and curly-leaved kales — the latter also known as Scotch kale and borecole. With the broad-leaved kales it is the young shoots, produced in spring, that are eaten. With the curly types, the leaves are eaten in winter and the shoots in spring. Kales tend to be rather large plants, but the dwarf varieties of curly kale, such as 'Dwarf Green Curled' and 'Frosty', are suitable for small gardens. The multi-colored 'ornamental' kales are beautiful plants, and add a wonderful touch of color to the winter garden. Contrary to general belief, they are edible — though not highly productive.

Cultivation: Kales tolerate poorer soils than most brassicas, though give their best in fertile soils. Sow them in spring in a seed bed, planting out firmly in summer — dwarf forms 15 inches (37.5 cm) apart, taller varieties 24–30 inches (60–75 cm) apart. These may need staking. Kales can be fed in spring to encourage the production of fresh shoots.

Pests and diseases: Kales are susceptible to the same problems as other brassicas, although they are less prone to clubroot. Caterpillars are usually the main problem.

Curly-leaved kale

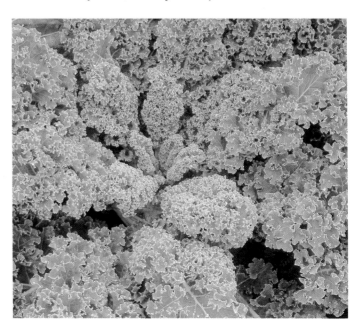

Purple variety of kohlrabi

Harvesting: Take only a few leaves at a time from any one plant, rather than stripping it. In spring snap off the shoots when they are 4–5 inches (10–12.5 cm) long; the plants will continue to grow and crop over several weeks.

KOHLRABI
Kohlrabi is an extraordinary looking vegetable – a ball-shaped, leafy swelling on a stem. Provided it is used young, kohlrabi has an unusual, delicate flavor, which is much appreciated in Europe where it is more widely grown.

Being one of the brassicas, it should be rotated with them in the garden. It does best in fertile, light, sandy soil, and is fast growing, being ready 6–8 weeks after sowing.

There are green- and purple-skinned forms of kohlrabi. As a general rule the more tender green varieties are sown until the beginning of summer, and the somewhat tougher purple varieties from mid- to late summer.

Cultivation: Kohlrabi can be sown in succession from late winter, in mild areas, until late summer. Either sow in seed trays and plant out when the seedlings are no more than 2 inches (5 cm) tall, or sow thinly in rows 12 inches (30 cm) apart, thinning as early as possible to about 9 inches (22.5 cm) between plants.

Pests and diseases: Seedlings may be attacked by flea beetle.

Harvesting: Use kohlrabi when it is between golf ball and tennis ball size: once they are larger they become tough and flavorless. Cook them without peeling, as much of the flavor lies just below the skin. They are excellent stuffed.

LEEK
The leek season can be spread from early fall all the way to the end of spring by selecting suitable varieties. Early varieties are long with pale foliage, while the later, hardier varieties are stockier and darker-leaved. The following are recommended varieties:

Earlies: 'Autumn Mammoth-Walton'.

Mid-season: 'Autumn Mammoth-Argenta'.

Late: 'Autumn Mammoth-Herwina' and 'Giant Winter-Catalina'.

Because leeks belong to the onion family, they should be rotated with onions. They require an open position and rich, well-prepared soil, with plenty of organic matter worked into it. This can be done shortly before planting. They also have a high nitrogen requirement, so apply a nitrogenous fertilizer before planting, or feed with a seaweed-based fertilizer during growth.

Cultivation: Leeks need a long growing season. The first sowings can be made indoors in gentle heat in late winter for planting out, after hardening off, in late spring. Make the first outdoor sowings in a seed bed or under cloches from early spring (provided the soil has warmed up) to the end of spring. Sow in furrows ¾ inch (2 cm) deep.

The main plantings are made in early summer, continuing through the end of summer. The ideal size for transplanting is about 8 inches (20 cm) tall; the larger the seedling the sooner it will mature, so plant in order of size along a row to make lifting convenient.

Water the seed bed thoroughly before lifting the seedlings, and trim off the tips of the leaves to prevent them dragging on the soil. Then make holes about 6 inches (15 cm) deep and drop the leek into the hole. The earth will fall back in naturally, so blanching the stem. Leeks can also be planted in a V-shaped furrow about 3 inches (7.5 cm) deep. Fill in the furrow as the plants grow to blanch the stem. The rows can be 10–12 inches (25–30 cm) apart, spacing the leeks 6 inches (15 cm) apart, or closer if you want smaller leeks.

Make sure the ground is moist after planting, watering daily (about a cupful for each plant) if necessary. Except in very dry weather, no further watering is required unless you want very large leeks.

Pests and diseases: Generally trouble-free, although downy mildew can be a problem in cool, damp seasons.

Harvesting: Lift leeks as required during autumn and winter, starting with the earlier varieties.

LETTUCE
With careful use of different varieties lettuces can be available most of the year in much of the country, though

Leeks planted in rows: they are ready for lifting in fall

it is not easy to produce good-quality lettuces in winter.

There are four main types: *Butterheads,* such as 'Unrivalled', have delicate leaves.

Crispheads, such as 'Webbs Wonderful' and 'Iceberg', have larger, crispier leaves but take about 3 weeks longer to mature.

Cos lettuces have conical heads and long, sweet, crisp leaves.

Loose-leaved ('Salad Bowl' type) lettuces are decorative and non-hearting, but can be picked over a long period.

A particularly sweet, crisp lettuce is 'Little Gem', usually described as a semicos. New lettuce varieties are continually appearing, many with useful resistance to diseases.

Lettuces must have fertile soil, an open position, and plenty of moisture throughout the growing season. Being a leafy crop, they also need plenty of nitrogen. Prepare the soil by working in plenty of well-rotted manure or compost. A base dressing of a general fertilizer can be . given before planting. Lettuces should be rotated to avoid the build-up of soil pests and diseases.

Cultivation: Apart from the 'Salad Bowl' type most lettuces stand for only a short time once they are mature, so frequent sowings must be made. You can sow them directly in the garden and thin to the correct distance apart, or in seed trays or a seed bed and transplant. Mid-summer sowings are generally made in the garden as lettuces transplant badly in hot weather. If the soil is dry at the time of sowing, water the furrow first, sow the seed, then cover it with dry soil. This slows evaporation and lowers the soil temperature, which assists germination in summer. If lettuces are raised in individual pots or peat blocks, which produce excellent plants, they can be transplanted at any time. Seedlings should be planted when they have about 5 leaves, with the seed leaves just above soil level. Small

LETTUCE

When and how to sow	Suitable varieties	When to harvest
Early spring sowing (under glass) Sow in cold greenhouses, in frames, or under cloches from mid-February in the South, early March in the North. Plant out in early April into frames, under cloches, or in a sheltered position outdoors.	*Loose-leaved:* 'Salad Bowl' *Butterheads:* 'Avondefiance', 'Unrivalled', 'Hilde II' *Cos:* 'Little Gem'	Late May and June
Summer sowing Make regular sowings between March and October. To ensure a continuous supply, make the next sowing as soon as the seedlings from the previous sowing have emerged.	*Loose-leaved:* 'Salad Bowl' *Butterheads:* 'Avondefiance', 'Continuity', 'Tom Thumb' *Crispheads:* 'Avoncrisp', 'Great Lakes', 'Minetto', 'Windermere' *Cos:* 'Little Gem'	Mid-June to mid-October
Autumn sowing (with winter protection or warmth) These need transplanting into frames, or cold or slightly heated greenhouses for a winter crop. Sow outdoors initially, and later under cover, from late August until October. Provide ventilation in winter to help prevent disease.	*Winter-maturing varieties:* 'Dandie', 'Kwiek', 'Ravel', 'Unrivalled'	November and December; February and March, depending on temperature
Autumn sowing (to over-winter) These hardy varieties can be over-wintered outdoors, or in frames or under cloches, as seedlings. Sow end August or early September, in the open, or under cloches, or in frames, thinning to about 3 inches (7.5 cm) apart in October, and to the final distance apart in spring. Alternatively, sow in soil or peat blocks. Over-winter in the blocks for planting out in spring.	*Butterheads:* 'Imperial Winter', 'Valdor' *Cos:* 'Lobjoits Green', 'Winter Density', 'Little Gem'	About May

varieties such as 'Little Gem', can be 9 inches (22.5 cm) apart; butterheads about 12 inches (30 cm) apart, and crispheads and cos up to 14 inches (35 cm) apart. For a reasonably constant supply of lettuce, follow the sowing plan (page 158).

Pests and diseases: Soil pests such as cutworms, leatherjackets, slugs and lettuce root aphid can cause serious losses, as can aphids. The most serious diseases are botrytis and downy mildew, which are worst in cold, damp weather.

Harvesting: Headed lettuces tend to bolt soon after they mature, especially in hot weather. Wherever possible they should be used in their prime. Make smaller but successive sowings if you have too many together.

Some types of lettuce will re-sprout if the heads are cut, leaving the stalks in the ground. This is particularly successful in spring with over-wintered varieties.

The 'Salad Bowl' types stand for several months without running to seed. The leaves can either be picked off individually as required, or harvested in one by cutting across the head, leaving about $\frac{3}{4}$ inch (2 cm) of leaf above the stalk. The stalk will throw out further leaves, so allowing a second harvesting a few weeks later, depending on the time of year and the weather.

OKRA

Okra is a member of the mallow family and is closely related to Chinese hibiscus and cotton. Grown extensively in home gardens in the South, it is commonly served as a main vegetable dish. It has about the same degree of hardiness as cucumbers and tomatoes and can be grown under the same conditions. The immature seed pods, produced over a relatively long period if harvested regularly, are the edible part of the plant. Okra varieties differ considerably in the size of the plants and the shape of the pods. The plants vary in height from 5–10 ft (1.5–3 m) after a few months

175

Early lettuce crop under cloches (see p. 174)

of growth. 'Clemson Spineless' is a medium-sized plant, about 5ft (1.5 m) tall, with straight, round pods. 'Louisiana Green Velvet' grows from 7–9 ft (2.1–2.7 m) tall with long, slender pods.

Cultivation: Any good garden soil should be sufficient, although sandy, loamy soil is ideal. Add manure or other organic matter and a general fertilizer before sowing seed. As okra is a warm weather species, don't plant until after the last frost. Soak the seed overnight in water to hasten germination and plant directly in the soil 1–1½ inches (2.5–3.5 cm) deep. After germination, thin the seedlings to 18 inches (45 cm) apart. Water freely.

Pests and diseases: Nematodes are the most serious pest and wilt can be a problem.

Harvesting: Cut off the pods with a knife or shears, carefully so that you don't injure

Okra (see p. 175)

the pods or the plants. Harvest before the pods become fibrous, usually when they are about 4 inches (10 cm) long. Refrigerate after harvest.

ONION

There are two main types of onion — bulb onions and green onions. With bulb onions the large, swollen bulbs are used fresh, or stored for winter. With green onions the young green leaf and shank, and sometimes the slightly swollen little white bulbs, are eaten — in salads or chopped for flavoring a recipe.

Bulb onions: These need a long growing season, and are either raised from sets, which are specially prepared miniature bulbs, or from seed. Sets give them a head start in life and are easier to grow, especially in poorer soils, but they have a tendency to bolt and only certain varieties are available, for example 'Ailsa Craig', 'Sturon' and 'Stuttgarter Giant', the last two being good keepers. Seed, although a little trickier to grow, works out cheaper and offers a far greater choice of variety. Recommended modern varieties are 'Rijnsburger Wijbo', and for storing 'Rijnsburger Balstora' and 'Hygro'. Good Japanese varieties for autumn sowing are 'Express Yellow', 'Imai Early Yellow' and 'Senshyu Semi-Globe Yellow'. 'Brunswick Blood Red' is a good red onion variety to choose.

Cultivation: Sets are planted from late winter until spring. Select small rather than large sets as they are less likely to bolt. Sets that have been 'heat treated' to discourage bolting are sometimes available: do not plant these until spring.

Make furrows about 1 inch (2.5 cm) deep and plant the sets so that their tips just appear above ground. They can be from 2–4 inches (5–10 cm) apart, the wider spacing giving larger bulbs, in rows about 9 inches (22.5 cm) apart. Birds sometimes tweak out the sets; if so, dig the sets out completely and replant, rather than push them back in. The rows can be protected with black cotton.

When using seed, prepare a seed bed with a finely raked surface about 10 days before sowing to allow it to 'settle'.

For a continuous year-round supply two sowings should be made, the first with standard varieties from late winter to spring, starting as soon as soil conditions allow. They can also be started indoors in gentle heat in late winter and planted out in early spring. These will mature in late summer, and the best 'keepers' will last until the following spring.

For supplies in the gap that follows in summer, use the Japanese varieties. Sow them in late summer. Although these cannot be stored for long, they are hardier and more reliable than the old autumn-sown varieties.

Sow onions very thinly about ½ inch (1 cm) deep, in rows about 10 inches (25 cm) apart. They should be thinned in stages, starting as

early as possible, until they are 2–4 inches (5–10 cm) apart, the wider spacing producing the largest onions. Use the thinnings as green onions.

Green onions: For a regular supply of these, start sowing under cloches in late winter and continue sowing at roughly bi-weekly intervals until summer, using the variety 'White Lisbon'. For very early supplies the following year sow 'White Lisbon-Winter Hardy' in mid-summer. Prepare the seed bed as for other onions but sow thinly, and 'thin' simply by pulling as required.

Pickling onions: Good varieties are 'Paris Silverskin', 'Barletta' and 'The Queen'. Sow the seed less than $\frac{3}{4}$ inch (2 cm) apart in rows 10 inches (25 cm) apart or in bands about 9 inches (22.5 cm) wide. No thinning is required as the competition will keep the bulbs small. They will succeed in poorer soils than bulb onions.

Pests and diseases: Onion fly is the most likely pest.

Harvesting: Onions to use fresh are pulled as required during the season. Onions for storage and pickling are lifted once the foliage has died back naturally. Don't bend them over, as this increases the chances of the onions sprouting in store. Bulbs for storage should be lifted and handled gently, and if possible dried off in the sun and wind outdoors, off the ground on upturned boxes. Dry them indoors if it is very wet. Store them for winter in a dry, frost-free place, either plaited in ropes or hung in nets. Never store thick-necked or diseased bulbs.

PARSNIP

Parsnips do best in deep, light, rich, stone-free soil, rather than in heavy soil. Improve the soil by working in plenty of well-rotted organic manure beforehand. It has always been suggested that manure causes parsnip roots to fork, but research has indicated that this is not so.

Cultivation: Grow parsnips in an open position. They need a long growing season, but will not germinate in cold soil. Sow outside from early spring (provided the soil has warmed up) until late spring. Only sow new seed, as parsnip seed loses viability very rapidly. Sow the large, flat seeds $\frac{1}{2}$–$\frac{3}{4}$ inch (1–2 cm) deep, in rows about 10 inches (25 cm) apart. To minimize thinning, sow 2–3 seeds in groups at 'stations' 5 inches (12.5 cm) apart, thinning to one per station once the seedlings start to show. Germination is often slow, so it is a good idea to sow a few radish seeds between the stations to mark the rows.

Parsnips can also be started off indoors. Sow seed in peat blocks or small pots in late winter. Transplant the seedlings outdoors, after hardening off, when they are no more than 2 inches (5 cm) high.

Keep the plants weeded, and water in dry weather at the rates suggested for beets (page 165).

Pests and diseases: Perhaps the most serious disease of parsnips is canker, especially on rich, organic soils. The tops of the roots blacken and crack, and eventually rot. If this is a problem on your soil, grow canker-resistant varieties 'White Gem' and 'Avonresister'.

Harvesting: The roots are ready by the beginning of fall and should be left in the soil until required, just pulling a little soil over the crowns to protect them. In low temperatures some of the starch in the roots is converted into sugar, making them sweeter. The foliage dies down completely so mark the end of the rows with sticks so that they can be found in snow.

PEA

Ordinary garden peas are shelled, and the green peas eaten. With the sugar or mange-tout peas, which are deservedly becoming increasingly popular, the

whole pod is eaten while the peas are still immature. The dual-purpose mange-tout variety 'Sugar Snap' can be eaten early as pods, or allowed to mature and shelled for peas.

In seed catalogs, peas are divided into 'earlies', 'second earlies', and 'maincrop' varieties, the difference between them being the time they take to mature. Earlies are ready in a minimum of 11 weeks, while maincrop varieties take up to 14 weeks. There are also round- and wrinkle-seeded types, the round being hardier and useful for very late and very early sowings, the wrinkle-seeded less hardy but sweeter and better-flavored. Peas vary in height from about 18 inches (45 cm) to 5ft (1.5 m), the taller types being less convenient but heavier yielding.

Good first early varieties are 'Feltham First', 'Early Onward', 'Hurst Beagle', 'Kelvedon Wonder', 'Little Marvel', and 'Meteor'. Good second earlies are 'Hurst Green Shaft', 'Onward', and 'Victory Freezer', while good maincrop varieties are 'Senator' and 'Lord Chancellor'.

Cultivation: Peas need an open site and well-worked, well-manured soil. If possible prepare a trench the previous autumn, digging it about one spade deep and 2 ft (60 cm) wide. Put in a good layer of manure or garden compost and mix it in well with soil from the trench. Otherwise, dig plenty of manure into the ground several months before sowing. Peas like coolish weather, so in mid-summer they can be grown in light shade.

Peas will not germinate in cold soil, so early sowings should be made under cloches. Alternatively, stake out the furrows and cover them with cloches to warm the soil, or simply expose them to the sun for a few hours before sowing. Peas can also be sown indoors in pots or blocks. There are several methods of sowing peas outdoors:

1. Make a flat-bottomed furrow about 9 inches (22.5 cm)

Bulb onions

Parsnips – best pulled as required

wide and 1½ inches (4 cm) deep, spacing the seeds 2 inches (5 cm) apart.
2. Sow in bands of three rows, each row 4 inches (10 cm) apart, the seeds also 4 inches (10 cm) apart. Allow 18 inches (45 cm) between the bands.
3. Sow in blocks or patches up to 3 ft (90 cm) wide, making the holes about 2 inches (5 cm) deep, spacing the seeds 2–3 inches (5–7.5 cm) apart.

Make the earliest sowings outdoors under cloches in late winter in a sheltered position, using an early variety.

Make the main summer sowings from spring until mid-summer, using second early and maincrop varieties. It is also worth trying to get a late autumn crop by sowing an early variety in mid-summer. In good summers this will pay off.

In mild parts of the country, hardy, over-wintering peas can be sown in fall to produce very early crops the following spring. Protect the

plants with cloches in severe weather.

It is important to support the peas as soon as any tendrils are visible. Small twigs are adequate for dwarf varieties, but taller varieties need longer twigs or some kind of pea netting. Water and mulch peas as suggested on page 161.

Pests and diseases: Mice can be a serious problem with early and late pea sowings. Birds also attack peas at all stages. Maggoty peas are caused by the pea moth. Spray with malathion one week after the flowers have opened.
Harvesting: Pick regularly to encourage further cropping. Mange-tout peas are ready when the immature peas can just be seen as bumps inside the pod.

POTATO

Potatoes take up a lot of space and are relatively cheap to buy, so if your garden is small it is probably only worth growing 'earlies', which are so superb when dug straight from the ground. They also escape some of the

pests and diseases that affect maincrop potatoes.

Potatoes should always be rotated over at least a 3 year cycle to avoid the build-up of soil pests and diseases, especially eelworm.

There is a confusing number of potato varieties to choose from, all with different characteristics. The following are particularly good:
Earlies: 'Maris Bard', 'Suttons Foremost'.
Second earlies: these take a little longer to mature – 'Red Craig's Royal', 'Wilja'.
Maincrop: these take longest to mature but give the heaviest yields – 'Desiree', 'King Edward', 'Pentland Squire'.

Potatoes need fertile soil with plenty of manure or compost in it, a good supply of nitrogen, and most important of all, plenty of moisture throughout growth. They will tolerate fairly acid soil.
Cultivation: Buy seed potatoes in late winter and start them into growth by 'chitting' or sprouting them. Stand them upright (the eyes uppermost), in shallow boxes or trays (egg trays are

ideal) in a cool room on a north-facing windowsill. Within about 6 weeks the potatoes will sprout: when the shoots are about ¾ inch (2 cm) long they can be planted, provided the soil and weather permit.

Earlies can be planted outdoors from early spring onwards, followed by second earlies and maincrops later in spring. Make a furrow or individual holes 4–5 inches (10–12.5 cm) deep, and plant the tubers upright. Both earlies and second earlies should be planted about 15 inches (37.5 cm) apart in rows 15–18 inches (37.5–45 cm) apart; maincrop potatoes should be spaced the same distance apart in rows 30 inches (75 cm) apart.

Early potatoes may need protection from frost. Either cover the leaves with newspaper if frost is forecast, or draw the earth up around the young growths.

As the plants grow, tubers near the surface are pushed

Regular picking promotes further cropping of peas

Potatoes may look robust, but harvest them carefully to avoid damaging their tubers

upwards and become greened, and therefore inedible. To prevent this, the plants should be earthed up when they are about 9 inches (22.5 cm) high. Pull earth up around the stems to a height of about 4–5 inches (10–12.5 cm).

Potatoes are sometimes grown under black plastic film to cut down weeding and avoid earthing up. If you try this, plant the tubers shallowly and anchor the plastic over them afterwards. When the leaves bulge up beneath the plastic, cut a slit and pull them through. Harvest the tubers by rolling back the plastic; they will be found virtually on the surface of the soil.

Potatoes are heavy feeders and drinkers. Unless the soil is very fertile, work a general fertilizer into the soil before planting and apply a nitrogenous top-dressing, or a liquid feed with a seaweed-based fertilizer, during the growing season.

In dry weather the yields

of early potatoes will be increased by watering roughly every two weeks at the rate of 3–4 gal/sq yd (16–22 liters/sq m). With maincrop potatoes the critical point is when the potatoes are the size of marbles. Give them one, very heavy, watering at 4–5 gal/sq yd (22–27 liters/sq m) at this stage.

Pests and diseases: In humid areas maincrop potatoes are often affected by blight, causing brown patches on the leaves. Eelworm causes weak and stunted plants. Where it is a problem, grow the new varieties that have resistance to the commonest types of eelworm: these include 'Pentland Javelin', 'Pentland Lustre', 'Pentland Meteor' and 'Maris Piper' (maincrop).

Harvesting: Lift early potatoes as required. Maincrop potatoes can be lifted for storage once the leaves have died down. Choose a warm day, spread them on the ground for an hour or so to dry, then store them in burlap sacks, or double-thickness paper sacks, in a frost-free room or shed. They must be kept dark. Cover the

sacks with extra matting or blankets if freezing conditions are expected.

RADISH

There are two sorts of radish: the familiar small summer radishes and the giant winter radishes which are used raw, sliced or grated, or cooked like turnips. The pods formed when radishes run to seed are also edible and very tasty.

Radishes do best in rich, light, well-drained, sandy soils, with adequate moisture during growth. Use soil manured for a previous crop and, if possible, rotate them with brassicas. The faster they are grown the better; slow-growing radishes become woody and unpleasantly hot.

Good summer varieties are 'Saxa', 'Saxerre', 'Robino', 'Ribella' and 'Cherry Belle' (all these can also be used for early sowings under cloches); and 'French Breakfast', 'Long White Icicle' and 'Red Prince' (which stands very well in summer). Good winter varieties are 'Black Spanish Round', 'China Rose' and 'Mino Early'.

Cultivation: Radishes develop so fast that they are frequently intersown in the same rows as slow-growing crops such as parsnips, or

used for intercropping. Summer sowings can be made in light shade. For a continuous supply make small, frequent sowings.

Earliest sowings of summer radishes can be made from late winter onwards under cloches or in frames, followed by outdoor sowings at roughly 10-day intervals. Make final sowings under cloches or in a cold greenhouse in late summer and fall.

Sow seed about ¾ inch (2 cm) deep in rows 6 inches (15 cm) apart, spacing the seeds about 1½ inches (4 cm) apart. This avoids the need to thin for, unless radishes are thinned very early, they fail to develop. If the soil is dry when sowing, water the furrow heavily beforehand. After sowing, cover the seed with dry soil.

During growth, water sufficiently to prevent the soil drying out but do not overwater, as this encourages leaf growth at the expense of root.

Winter radishes are sown in mid- to late summer in rows 10 inches (25 cm) apart. Sow very thinly, spacing the seeds 2 inches (5 cm) apart, thinning in stages to about 5 inches (12.5 cm) apart.

Pests and diseases: Radish seedlings are often attacked

Summer radishes

Rhubarb

by flea beetles.
Harvesting: Pull summer radishes as required. Winter radishes can be left in the soil, protected with straw or bracken. On very heavy soils they may be damaged by slugs: if so, store them in a shed in boxes of moist peat or sand. If you want radish pods, leave a plant in the ground to run to seed in spring. Pick the pods when green and crisp.

RHUBARB
Rhubarb thrives best in regions having cool, moist summers and winters cold enough to freeze the ground to a depth of 3–4 inches (7.5–10 cm). It is not adapted to most parts of the South, where temperatures exceed 75°F (24°C). It is a hardy perennial, producing its crop early in spring, largely from food that has been stored in the large fleshy crowns and roots of the plant during the preceding year.

Rhubarb is grown for its acid stalks, which are stewed for pies and vegetables. Both green- and red-stalked varieties are grown for home use. Green-stalked plants include 'Victoria', 'German Wine' and 'Sutton's Seedless'. Red-stalked selections include 'Ruby', 'Cherry Red' and 'Canada Red'. Rhubarb leaves should not be eaten as they contain oxalic acid.
Cultivation: Any deep, well-drained, fertile soil is suitable for rhubarb. Plow the soil to a depth of 12–16 inches (30–40 cm) and add rotted manure, leafmold and other organic compost material.

Rhubarb may be started from seed, but the seedlings vary considerably from parent plants. The usual method of starting plants is to obtain pieces of crowns from established plants in early spring. Dig the crowns and split them into pieces, with one large bud to each section of crown and root. Space the plants 2½–3 ft (75–90 cm) apart, placing the crown pieces at a depth at which the buds will not be more than 2 inches (5 cm) below the surface. Top dress the plants with a heavy application of organic matter in either early spring or late fall and water freely.

Pests and diseases: Generally trouble-free, with the exception of rhubarb curculio. Keep the planting area weed-free to control the beetle.
Harvesting: Remove seed-stalks as soon as they form. No leaf stems should be harvested before the second year and but few until the third. Food from the leaves is needed to enlarge the roots for the coming year's growth. Beginning with the third year, the harvest period may extend as long as 6 weeks or until the stalks become small, indicating that food supplies in the roots are becoming depleted. Don't remove more than two-thirds of the developed stalks from the plant at any one time. Pull only the large stalks, leaving the young ones to grow.

SEAKALE
Although considered an old-fashioned vegetable, the subtle, nutty flavor and crisp texture of blanched seakale stalks in spring is a treat. Seakale is perennial, and once established is productive for 8–10 years.
Cultivation: Prepare an open site by working in plenty of well-rotted manure or compost. Buy plants or rooted cuttings (thongs); alternatively, raise plants from seed or from your own thongs.

Sow fresh seed (old seed germinates poorly) in a seed bed in spring. Keep the ground moist until the seed germinates. Plant seedlings into their permanent position in autumn, 1 ft (30 cm) apart each way. Alternatively sow directly in the garden in rows 1ft (30 cm) apart, thinning to the same distance.

Thongs are obtained by lifting plants that are at least three years old in the autumn. Select roots of finger thickness and cut them into pieces 4–6 inches (10–15 cm) long. Trim them flat across the top and with a slanting cut across the bottom, so that you know which end is which! Store these upright in a box of moist sand until early spring when buds will have formed. Rub out weak buds, leaving one strong central bud, and plant the thongs outdoors in spring.

Water so that the ground does not dry out in the

Seakale is well worth growing for its delicate nutty flavor

summer. Allow the plants to grow undisturbed for their first two seasons, feeding them occasionally with a seaweed-based fertilizer. If they have many feeble shoots, thin them out to encourage stronger ones. In late autumn remove dead leaves from the base of the plant and cover the crowns with a little soil.

Pests and diseases: If club-root is in the ground, seakale is likely to be affected.

Harvesting: Plants are ready for blanching in their third season. The simplest method is to cover the plants in January with 1 ft (30 cm) high buckets or plant pots with the drainage hole blocked to exclude light. The whitened shoots can be cut in spring. Stop cutting in May and remove the buckets or pots so that they can continue to grow naturally.

Plants can be forced indoors for winter. Wait until the first frost then lift and pot up the crowns in peat, covering them with a flower pot to exclude the light. Bring them into a temperature of 60–70°F (16–21°C). After forcing the crown is exhausted, and if planted out again will take several years to recover.

SHALLOT
Shallots are a chunky-shaped type of onion, very much prized for pickling. They also make an excellent substitute for onions in early summer as they keep better than any other onions, remaining in good condition until summer. Single sets can multiply into clumps of up to 20 bulbs. There are both red- and yellow-skinned varieties.

Cultivation: Buy small, good-quality, virus-free sets: the ideal size is ¾ inch (2 cm) diameter (larger sets may 'bolt'). They can be planted in mid-winter in mild areas on well-drained soil, but elsewhere plant them as early in the year as soil conditions permit. Plant them like onion sets 6 inches (15 cm) apart in rows 10 inches (25 cm) apart.

Pests and diseases: Generally

Shallots suspended above the ground to dry

trouble-free.

Harvesting: Lift, dry and store as suggested for onions. Provided the stock remains healthy, keep back a few of your own bulbs for planting the following year, though it is probably wise to start afresh with bought sets every three years.

SPINACH
Spinach is very sensitive to day length, which is why it is apt to 'bolt' in the long days of summer. It does best in autumn, winter and early spring, when steadier growth allows several pickings.

Cultivation: For a summer supply frequent small sowings are advisable, as in general only one cut can be made before it runs to seed. In warm parts of the country the first sowing can be made under cloches in late winter, followed by outdoor sowings in spring. Make further sowings at 2–3 week intervals until mid–summer. For these summer sowings use

varieties such as 'Longstanding Round' and 'Sigmaleaf'. Sow ½–¾ inch (1–1.5 cm) deep, in rows 12 inches (30 cm) apart, thinning to 6 inches (15 cm) apart.

Winter spinach, which can be cropped from fall until late spring, is sown in late summer. Suitable varieties are 'Greenmarket' 'Sigmaleaf', and 'Broad Leaved Prickly'. In this case thin to 9 inches (22.5 cm) apart. The plants will be of a much better quality if they can be protected from the weather by covering them with cloches in fall. For spinach beet, see beets.

Pests and diseases: Generally trouble-free, but downy mildew can be a problem. Aphids may also attack.

Harvesting: Leaves can be eaten very small or allowed to grow larger. Pick them individually off the plant as required. The plants will make further growth, unless conditions cause them to 'bolt' instead.

SPINACH, NEW ZEALAND
This is a useful vegetable for

dry soils, and can be cropped regularly over a long period.

Cultivation: New Zealand spinach is a half-hardy vegetable. It must either be sown indoors in early spring, hardened off and planted out in late spring after risk of frost has passed or sown directly outdoors in late spring (or a little earlier under cloches). To assist germination soak the seed in water overnight before sowing. Space plants about 18 inches (45 cm) apart in each direction, allowing them room to sprawl over the ground. Although useful for dry, sunny corners, New Zealand spinach does equally well under normal conditions. It will continue growing until frost kills it and will often seed itself, reappearing the following year.

Pests and diseases: Generally trouble-free.

Harvesting: New Zealand spinach must be picked regularly, otherwise it becomes tough and forms knobby seedheads. Pick leaves as required or cut whole, young shoots from the base of the plant and strip off the leaves.

SQUASH
Squash covers a large group of plants which crop either in summer or winter. Winter species include hubbard, acorn and butternut squash, gourds and pumpkins. The summer species, zucchini and summer squash, require less space than the winter ones.

The entire family is sensitive to frost, but gardeners as far north as Canada can have success with the summer varieties.

Cultivation: For an earlier crop, sow the summer varieties indoors in early spring, transplanting to a sunny site only after the last frost has passed. In warmer climates, plant directly in the garden in early spring. Space plants 24–30 inches (60–75 cm) apart in rows 36 inches (90 cm) apart. Winter squash varieties, pumpkins and gourds should be planted

Spinach

in mid-summer and given plenty of room. Plant 36–40 inches (90–100 cm) apart in rows 6–8 ft (1.8–2.4 m) apart. They will overwhelm a small garden and should be included only in sites where their vines will not interfere with other crops. Both summer and winter varieties need plenty of sunshine and a heavy compost.

Pests and diseases: Squash borer requires applications of Marlate every 3–4 weeks.

Harvesting: The summer varieties should be picked while they are still a bit soft – about 6–8 weeks after sowing. Pumpkins and winter squash do best if they are left on the vine until the rind is hard. If they are to be stored for late winter use, they should be cut with 3 inches (7.5 cm) of stem attached to the crop. They should then be kept in a warm, dry place.

SWEDE or RUTABAGA

The large, rounded, usually yellow-fleshed roots of swedes are extremely hardy, very sweet-flavored and invaluable for winter. They belong to the brassica family, and therefore should be carefully rotated in the garden. Swedes do badly in very dry and very wet soils. They require light, fertile soil, limed if acid, and preferably manured for a previous crop.

Cultivation: It is only necessary to make one sowing of swedes, in spring. Sow seed ¾ inch (2 cm) deep, in rows 15–18 inches (37.5–45 cm) apart, thinning as early as possible to about 10 inches (25 cm).

In dry weather, water to prevent the soil drying out, but don't over-water, otherwise flavor will be lost.

Pests and diseases: Watch out for flea beetle attacks at the seedling stage. Mildew and clubroot can be real problems. If you've had these troubles, try the excellent new variety 'Marian', which has considerable resistance to both diseases.

Harvesting: Roots can be ready from fall through winter. Leave them in the ground until Christmas, when they should be lifted before they become woody. They can be stored in clamps outdoors, or layered in boxes of moist peat or sand and kept in a frost-free place.

SWEET POTATO

Sweet potatoes succeed best in the South, but they are grown in home gardens as far north as New York and Michigan. They may be cultivated anywhere with relatively warm temperatures and a frost-free period of 150 days. Sweet potatoes are a frequent holiday-meal vegetable, accompanying the Easter ham and Christmas turkey. 'Vardaman' and 'Vineless Puerto Rico' are ideal for limited-space gardens, and 'Centennial' results in a superior yield.

Cultivation: A well-drained, moderately deep sandy loam of medium fertility is best for sweet potatoes. Heavy clays and very deep, loose-textured soils encourage the formation of long stringy roots. For best results a moderate amount of fertilizer should be mixed well into the soil. In most climates it is necessary to start the plants indoors because the season is too short to produce a good crop. Cover the seed with 2 inches (5 cm) of sand or fine soil, such as leafmold. Transplant the seedlings outside when the soil is warm, 12 inches (30 cm) apart. Add fertilizer 3–4 weeks after transplanting. Sweet potatoes are quite drought-tolerant and will produce a fair crop under dry conditions, but ample moisture results in a better crop.

Pests and diseases: Generally trouble-free. Stem rot attacks certain varieties resulting in plant loss and yield reduction. Choose resistant varieties.

Harvesting: Dig up sweet potatoes a short time before frost. Be careful not to damage the roots. Let the roots dry for 2–3 hours, store in a warm room to cure for 10 days and then move to cool storage.

Sweet potatoes

SWISS CHARD

Swiss chard is a type of beet which has been developed for its tops instead of roots. Crop after crop of the outer leaves may be harvested without injuring the plant. A single planting will provide greens throughout the entire growing season. It will continue to flourish despite summer heat. Popular varieties include 'Vulcan', 'Lucullus', 'Fordhook Giant', 'Large White Rib' and 'Rhubarb'.

Cultivation: Chard thrives best in well-drained, reasonably fertile, neutral soil. It is sensitive to acidity. Sow in early spring as soon as the soil can be worked, covering seed ½ inch (1 cm) deep. Chard is a cool season crop and will withstand light frosts. It does best if planted 2–4 weeks before the last frost. For an early crop, sow in a greenhouse or coldframe and transplant seedlings outside after the danger of heavy frosts has passed.

Soil temperatures for successful seed germination range from 50–85°F (10–29°C) with a minimum of 40°F (4°C) and a maximum of 95°F (35°C). Adequate soil moisture is particularly important for seed germination and early plant growth. Irrigate during dry weather conditions. Thin the seedlings to 4–6 inches (10–15 cm) apart in rows 15–18 inches (38–45 cm) apart. For rapid and continuous growth, uniformly distribute 1 pt (500 ml) of complete fertilizer per 50 ft (15 m) of plantings.

Pests and diseases: Be on the lookout for cabbage worms, aphids, beet leaf miner and flea beetle. Wash aphids off with a fine spray of water. Crop rotation will reduce damage from leaf spot and

Swiss chard

Tall tomato plant varieties must be secured to stakes for support

other diseases.

Harvesting: Leaves and stems are ready to harvest about 50–60 days after planting. Cut off a few outer leaves about 1 inch (2.5 cm) above ground with a sharp knife. Continue harvesting throughout the summer and fall. New leaves will germinate from the central bud.

TOMATO

Tomatoes need a long season and warm conditions to do well. They can only be grown successfully outdoors in warmer climates; elsewhere they are best grown in frames or an unheated greenhouse. A heated greenhouse is only necessary for an exceptionally early crop.

There are numerous varieties, divided into tall, cordon types and dwarf, bush types. The former have to be 'side-shooted' and require staking, while the bush varieties sprawl on the ground.

Tomatoes should be rotated, and should not be grown near maincrop potatoes as they are easily infected with potato blight.

On the whole, the same varieties can be grown inside and out, though tall varieties, because they make more productive use of the space, are normally used for the greenhouse crop, while bush varieties are generally only grown outdoors. Reliable tall varieties are generally only grown outdoors.

Reliable tall varieties are 'Ailsa Craig', 'Alicante', 'Gardener's Delight' and 'Harbinger'. Reliable bush varieties are the F_1 hybrids 'Sleaford Abundance', 'Alfresco' and 'Pixie', which is a compact and heavy-fruited variety.

OUTDOOR TOMATOES
Cultivation: If possible grow tomatoes against a south-

facing wall or erect a windbreak or plastic film screen around them. They can also be grown outdoors in large pots or boxes (using a peat-based potting soil), or in growing bags.

Prepare the ground beforehand by working in plenty of well-rotted manure or compost, so that the soil is well-drained but moisture-retentive. A base dressing of a general fertilizer can be applied before planting.

Either raise plants yourself or buy some in, choosing stocky plants, preferably in individual pots.

If raising your own, sow in gentle heat indoors in a seeding mixture in early spring. Prick out the seedlings when they have 3 leaves into 4 inch (10 cm) pots, using a peat-based potting soil. After hardening off, plant outdoors in late spring, after any risk of frost. Plants should be about 8 inches (20 cm) high with the first flower truss showing. Protect them with cloches initially, if possible. Plant tall varieties about 15 inches (37.5 cm) apart, and bush varieties about 18 inches (45 cm) apart, though if planted a few inches closer they will usually give earlier, but slightly lower, yields.

Mulch plants with plastic to keep them clean, nip out the sideshoots of tall varieties, and 'stop' them, nipping off the growing point 2 leaves above a flowering truss, at mid- to late summer.

Tall varieties must be tied to 4 ft (1.2 m) stakes or horizontal wires attached to posts at either end of the row.

In well-prepared soil, outdoor varieties generally need no further feeding. In dry weather, water them about twice a week once they have started flowering at the rate of about 2 gal/sq yd (9 liters/sq m). Over-watering reduces the flavor. Tomatoes in pots or other containers will require more frequent watering and regular weekly feeding with a proprietary tomato fertilizer.

Pests and diseases: In wet seasons it may be necessary to spray against potato blight in summer, using a copper-based fungicide.

Harvesting: Fruits normally start to ripen by late summer. At the end of September hasten ripening by covering plants with cloches (cut tall varieties off their canes and lay them on the ground). Pull remaining plants by their roots before frost comes and hang them indoors, or in a greenhouse, to continue ripening.

GREENHOUSE TOMATOES

Cultivation: Tomatoes cannot be grown in the same greenhouse soil for more than 3 years as the soil becomes diseased. It then either has to be sterilized (which is difficult), or replaced. It is easier to grow tomatoes in pots, bags or boxes in fresh soil or potting soil, or to adopt a soil-less system such as ring culture.

Raise plants as for outdoor tomatoes, sowing in early spring and planting 5 or 6 weeks later. Tie the plants to canes or wire supports, or twist them up strings hung from the roof. Once the first truss has set, feed weekly with a high potash tomato fertilizer. Remove sideshoots from the plants and stop them after 7–8 trusses. Remove yellowing leaves from the base of the plant and keep the greenhouse well ventilated day and night to reduce the risk of disease.

Pests and diseases: Uneven watering may cause blossom-end rot, which produces sunken patches on the fruits.

Harvesting: Indoor tomatoes can be picked from mid-summer until late fall.

TURNIP

Provided the soil is reasonably fertile and there is plenty of moisture, turnips are among the fastest-maturing vegetables. They can be used fresh in spring and summer, or stored for winter use. When the plants are grown close together, leafy turnip tops can be used as greens.

The white-fleshed turnips are grown for summer use and should be pulled young and small, no more than 2 inches (5 cm) across. Good varieties are 'Purple Top Milan' and 'Snowball'. Best for winter use are the yellow-fleshed varieties, such as 'Golden Ball' and 'Manchester Market' ('Green Top Stone') which are hardier and slower-maturing.

Turnips are brassicas, so should be rotated accordingly (see page 158). They prefer ground that has been manured for a previous crop; if the soil is not very fertile, work in a general fertilizer before sowing.

Cultivation: For summer turnips make the first sowings under cloches in early spring, followed by sowings at monthly intervals until mid-summer, when the winter crop can be sown. The mid-summer sowings can be made in light shade, as turnips dislike intense heat.

Sow the seed about $\frac{3}{4}$ inch (2 cm) deep, the summer crop in rows 9 inches (22.5 cm) apart, the winter crop in rows 12 inches (30 cm) apart, and thin to 6 inches (15 cm) apart. As turnips grow so fast, it is important to thin as soon as the seedlings touch one another.

For turnip tops, sow winter varieties in late summer, or summer varieties in early spring, as soon as the soil has warmed up. Either sow a small broadcast patch or sow thinly in rows 6 inches (15 cm) apart, leaving them unthinned.

Pests and diseases: Flea beetle attacks can be a problem at the seedling stage. On ground infested with clubroot, turnips may be affected and their growth stunted.

Harvesting: Pull summer turnips from late spring onwards. Lift winter turnips around Christmas and twist off the stems. Store them in a frost-free place, layered in boxes of moist peat or sand, or in clamps outdoors. Turnip tops are cut 1 inch (2.5 cm) above ground level when the plants are about 6 inches (15 cm) high. The plants should re-sprout, so 2–3 cuts can be made.

White-fleshed turnips, pulled young and small

THE GREENHOUSE

Although gardening under glass can be a pursuit in itself, in this short section we look at a greenhouse as a useful adjunct to the garden as a whole. Its main uses in this aspect are threefold: as a nursery for raising young flower and vegetable plants, to over-winter half-hardy plants, and to extend the garden season of flowers, vegetables and fruit.

What sort of greenhouse?

Always buy the largest size that you can afford and have room for. Greenhouse gardening is apt to become compulsive and one always wishes a larger model had been chosen at the outset. The choice of size and design is now considerable and it is a matter of choosing what you fancy. It is worthwhile considering whether to have a greenhouse with a timber or an aluminum alloy frame. Alloy is very durable, requiring little or no maintenance, and the narrow glazing bars allow maximum light admission. However, metal is a better conductor of heat than wood and thus more heat is lost through an alloy than a timber structure. Aesthetically, red cedar wood, the best for greenhouses, fits in better with the garden scene and is almost as durable as alloy. Another point in favor of wood is the ease with which wire supports, benching and hanging baskets can be secured to it.

One further point to consider is ventilation. Almost without exception, custom-built greenhouses have all too few ventilators. For reasons discussed under 'Conserving heat', a confined space surrounded by glass quickly builds up heat when the sun shines. Between late spring and mid-autumn, temperatures can rise to lethal heights without ventilation. Ridge and side ventilators are essential, and there should be at least one or the other to every $6\frac{1}{2}$ ft (2 m) of length. If it means buying extra optional ventilators, then do so without hesitation. To use the greenhouse efficiently, make sure it has benching for both sides.

Siting

Although not obvious to the human eye, glass screens out a surprising amount of the sun's rays. For this and ancillary reasons the greenhouse should be sited in as sunny a position as possible. If it is to be kept frost-free or warmer and contain growing plants in winter, then its position in relation to the sun is even more important. Bear in mind that in northern climates the sun rises to only about 17° above the southern horizon in mid-winter and can easily be obscured

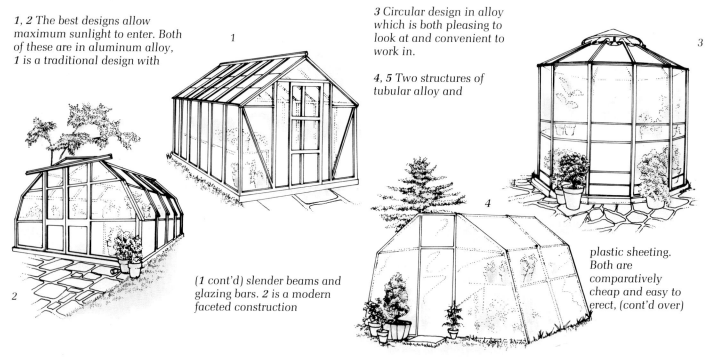

1, 2 The best designs allow maximum sunlight to enter. Both of these are in aluminum alloy, 1 is a traditional design with

(1 cont'd) slender beams and glazing bars. 2 is a modern faceted construction

3 Circular design in alloy which is both pleasing to look at and convenient to work in.

4, 5 Two structures of tubular alloy and

plastic sheeting. Both are comparatively cheap and easy to erect, (cont'd over)

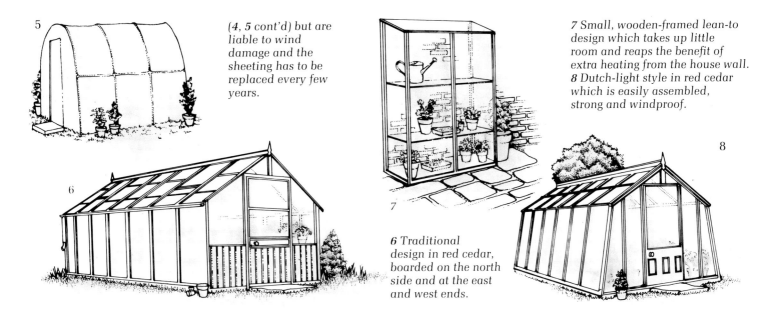

(4, 5 cont'd) but are liable to wind damage and the sheeting has to be replaced every few years.

7 Small, wooden-framed lean-to design which takes up little room and reaps the benefit of extra heating from the house wall. 8 Dutch-light style in red cedar which is easily assembled, strong and windproof.

6 Traditional design in red cedar, boarded on the north side and at the east and west ends.

by tall buildings and trees. For these reasons, align the long axis of your greenhouse east and west so that the long side faces south. If possible, provide some shelter from cold east and north winds – for example, by utilizing hedges, open weave fences or the plastic mesh sold as a wind-break. From a convenience point of view, choose a site as near to the house as possible. If you have a blank south-facing wall, seriously consider a lean-to greenhouse, ideally with a doorway directly into the home. Such a situation takes full advantage of the sun-warmed bricks of the house wall and, in winter, of the heat within the house. If artificial heating is contemplated, it can be easily taken from the house into the lean-to.

Heating
Artificial heat, although not essential, greatly increases the scope of a greenhouse. If half-hardy plants are to be over-wintered successfully, then just enough heat to keep out the frost is sufficient. If plants are to be grown during the cold months, e.g. salpiglossis in pots for a late spring display or winter-hearting lettuce, a night minimum temperature of 45°F (7°C) must be provided. About 50°F (10°C) is a suitable night minimum in spring for young bedding plants (e.g. begonia, lobelia, antirrhinum) raised from seed in a heated case in late winter. These heating levels are not high and are easily provided by one of the readily available, fairly inexpensive thermostatically controlled electric fan heaters.

Conserving heat
The sun's short-wave radiation passes easily through glass and warms all objects within the greenhouse. These objects re-radiate warmth as long-wave radiation, which cannot pass through glass, hence the rapid build-up of high heat in a closed greenhouse on a sunny day. This phenomenon is known as 'the greenhouse effect'. As soon as the sun sets or passes into shadow, heat is lost by conduction from framework and glass and the cracks around doors and vents. Artificially provided heat is lost in the same way. Heating costs can be reduced by using a heat conservation technique. Double-glazing with plastic sheeting so that there is a gap between it and the glass is fairly efficient, as is bubble glaze sheeting. Both reduce light intensity and are best not used on the south side.

Shading
During hot spells in summer even opening every ventilator and the door may not be enough to keep the temperature to manageable limits. When this happens, shading is the answer. The ideal is internal or external blinds, but they are expensive. The popular alternative is to use an appropriate shading compound which is painted or sprayed on the glass. Several are available; opt for one that rubs off easily when the weather dulls over and cools down.

Automation
For those who are away at work all day, there are automatic vent and blind operators. There are also various automatic watering systems, the easiest being sand trays kept wet by a refillable bottle or a header tank with a ballcock valve attached to the main water supply.

Cultivation
The essential activities of propagation, potting, watering and feeding are dealt with in the introduction to House Plants (page 122), with further points under Garden Flowers (page 16).

Maintenance
Keep the greenhouse as clean and uncluttered as possible. Wash the glass at least once a year each autumn and, if you live in an urban area, repeat at intervals in the winter. Smoke soon grimes up the glass and very seriously impairs light transmission. Spores of diseases and eggs of pests can lurk on wood and metal work so, ideally, empty the greenhouse once a year in late summer or early autumn and scrub the internal structure, including benching, with a sterilizing agent. This will lessen the all-too-willing attentions of pests and diseases.

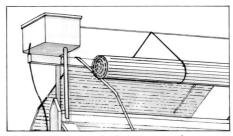

Roller blinds are the best type, either

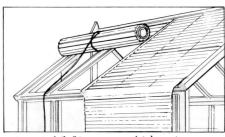

automated (left) or manual (above).

FRUIT

There is no reason why even the tiniest garden should not produce some sort of fruit for its owner. Most of the major crops are fairly adaptable in their demands, both for the available space and for the gardener's time. Some of the less usual fruits grow happily in deep shade, on peaty soils, in very cold gardens, in pots on the patio or terrace, in sunrooms and greenhouses, in conservatories or even on a moderately sunny windowsill or protected balcony.

Climate
All gardeners, whether in Maine, Miami, Kansas or California, should remember that local climate is far more important than mere latitude. For example, there are gardens in coastal parts of the Carolinas that will produce splendid crops of peaches, apricots and figs from wall-trained trees, yet a dozen miles inland even quince trees, reputed to be hardy, can be killed by the cold.

One of the best ways of finding out what will grow well in your area is to look at neighboring gardens, to contact – or, better still, join – a local gardening club, to ask at your local nursery or enquire of the nearest state experiment station listed in the regional section of this book (see page 214). You will discover which varieties and which crops do especially well in your area. It is best to seek local advice before ordering from a catalog or buying from a garden center. Supplement the information you get from books with other people's experience of actual conditions.

Whatever your location, however windy and cold, do not despair. There are excellent apple and pear varieties that will bear fruit in the coldest gardens; even wet mountain hillsides can provide strawberries and raspberries.

It is not possible to grow the major top fruits in a frost hollow. In such a garden, late spring frosts will ruin flowers and fruitlets and cold autumn nights will arrive far too early. In this situation, content yourself with growing late-flowering and early-ripening varieties of soft fruit only, and provide as much protection for it as you can.

The quality of the soil
Unless your soil is permanently waterlogged or completely dry, there will be some fruits that will grow for you. Having said this, most species are ideally suited by deep loamy soil with a pH of about 6.5. Dampish soils will produce excellent pears, plums and raspberries. Dryish soils suit many apples, peaches, nectarines and figs. Acid, peaty soils will produce blueberries and cranberries, but little else.

Fertilizers
Most of the soft fruits require a good diet. Apply garden compost, well-rotted manure or peat enriched with chemical fertilizer annually in winter. Strawberries, raspberries and currants need extra potash. Apply $\frac{1}{2}$ oz per sq yd (12 g per sq m) before planting out. Top fruits needing potash are apple and sweet cherry. Dress the soil in winter with potassium sulfate at 1 oz per sq yd (25 g per sq m).

If you cannot obtain manure, and do not have room to make a compost heap, feed the plants during the summer by watering them with suitable soluble fertilizers. Crops that need a diet rich in potash will like liquids of the type used for tomatoes. A general fertilizer will suit the rest.

Top fruits are worth cosseting for the first few years while they are establishing themselves. Pears, plums, peaches and nectarines all benefit from good dressings of well-rotted manure or compost, while apples prefer potash.

Supporting trained fruits
Top fruit and soft fruit grown as cordons, fans or espaliers need some sort of system to support them, whether free-standing or against a wall. The framework should be set up before the fruit is planted to avoid disturbing the bush or tree. What you need is a system of horizontal wires set about 18 inches (45 cm) apart. Use galvanized wire $\frac{1}{10}$ inch (2.5 mm) in diameter for permanence.

Against a wall, attach them to tensioning bolts with vine eyes set every $6\frac{1}{2}$ ft (2 m) along the length of the wires. In free-standing systems for fruit grown as screens or for espaliers in a fruit cage, the wires should be attached to strong timber posts. Use posts measuring 4 x 4 inches (10 x 10 cm) and treat them with fungicide. The end posts will need extra support at the base. Again, space the posts about 10 ft (3–4 m) apart.

Planting top fruit
The amount of trouble you take over planting, the first piece of work that you will have to do for your fruit, will affect most of your subsequent tasks. It is important, especially for top fruit, that the plant gets the best possible start in life so that even if you eventually have no time to devote to it you will still have a tree that will try to go on being productive. Fruit that gets a bad start may take years to become established.

If you have ordered plants from a distant nursery, they will arrive some time during the late autumn, or in winter, and will be bare-rooted; that is, most of the soil will have been shaken from their roots. Although most nurseries send out well-packed healthy material, open the package as soon as it arrives to check that the roots have not begun to dry out. If they have, soak the roots in water for a couple of hours.

If you cannot plant immediately be-

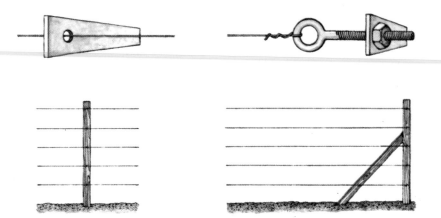

To support fruit, make a framework of horizontal wires threaded through vine eyes and attached to tensioning bolts.
In a free-standing support system, attach the wires to strong timber posts, with extra supports at the base of the end posts (left).

cause the soil is frozen hard or sodden and too wet to work, the trees should be stored until it is possible. Keep them in a shed, garage or cellar with the roots surrounded by moist peat. If the soil is fine for planting, but you do not have time to get the plants in the ground properly, simply dig a rough hole, put the roots in and cover them with enough soil to keep them firm. This process is known as 'heeling in'.

When weather conditions permit and you have enough time, dig a hole at the chosen site that will comfortably hold the roots when they are well spread out. If possible, fork a bucketful or two of compost or well-rotted manure into the soil at the bottom of the hole. Failing these, use a good handful of bonemeal. Mix some bonemeal or compost into the excavated soil.

Staking: All top fruits, whether bush or tree, need support for the first year or two while the root system becomes strong enough to provide sufficient anchorage for the leafy top. It would be heartbreaking to find new standards bent or snapped off at the graft, or bushes half rocked out of the ground by a summer gale, because they have not been staked.

Once you have excavated the planting hole and worked in some manure, place the stake in position. Square or round stakes are equally good, but they must be strong enough to do the job. Poles 2 inches (5 cm) in diameter or 2 x 2 inch (5 x 5 cm) stakes will be sufficient for the average standard tree. The length of the support depends on the length of the plant's stem. The top of the stake, when driven into the base of the planting hole, should be just below the first branch of the standard. Position the stake on the prevailing windward side of the tree, so that the tree generally pulls on the stake. On bushes, the stake inevitably stands among the branches. Secure the base and/or strong central branch firmly to the stake.

Filling in: Stand the young plant in the hole to ensure that the size is right. Spread the roots out evenly. Neatly trim off any that are broken or damaged. Put a spadeful or two of excavated soil over the roots and shake the plant gently to settle the soil between the main roots.

To get the planting level right, find the graft, which is usually visible as an oblique swelling on the stem, and make sure that it is several inches above the soil level. Sometimes it is possible to see where the old soil level was when the plant was in the nursery bed, in which case simply plant to the same depth.

Shovel in some more soil and shake again. Firm down with your feet. Continue until the hole is filled and the tree firmly planted.

Secure the tree to the stake. Strips of cloth make good ties, or stout twine threaded through a piece of hosepipe. Do not use nylon string or twine because it is so sharp that it will cut into the bark. A buffer of some sort between the tree and stake is useful.

Container-grown trees and bushes
These can be bought and planted at any time of year, using exactly the same method as for bare-rooted trees. Open up the lowest part of the root ball as much as you can before planting, paying attention to the coil of roots that often forms at the bottom of the bag or pot.

Once planted, if the weather is dry, water the young tree or bush copiously over the whole root area. Keep a close watch on the plant in the following months, especially in hot weather. It will take at least a season before there are sufficient new roots to let the tree fend for itself.

Soft fruits
These are planted in the same way as top fruit. Bush soft fruits are small when sold, and do not need staking. Strawberries are planted into a prepared bed (see p. 207).

Pruning
Pruning ensures that the tree or bush is kept within bounds, furnishes a supply of fruiting wood, and allows light and air to reach the ripening fruit. The method of pruning varies from species to species, and depends also on the form

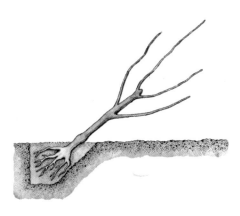

BELOW: *Heel in the fruit tree if you cannot plant it immediately.*

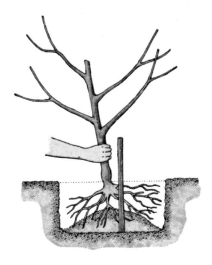

For permanent planting, position the stake before placing the tree in the ready-dug hole. Ensure that the roots are evenly spread (left). *After filling in, secure the tree to the stake and, ideally, place a buffer between them to prevent damage to the bark* (above).

FRUIT TREES: distances between plants

	APPLES		PEARS		PLUMS		CHERRIES	
	space between		space between		space between		space between	
	plants	rows	plants	rows	plants	rows	plants	rows
Center leader bush	semi-dwarfing rootstock 13–20	13–20			10–20	13–20	sweet 16–25	sweet 16–25
	dwarfing rootstock 6–16	10–20	6–20	13–20			sour 13–20	sour 13–20
Espalier	13–20	6	10–20	6				
Oblique cordon	3	6	3	6				
Fan		13–20		13–20		13–20	sweet 16–25	sour 13–20
Standard	20–33	20–33	20–33	20–33	20–25	20–25	sweet 15–30	

Distances (which are all in feet) between plants depend on the vigor of the variety: plants of a non-vigorous variety should be spaced according to the smaller of the recommended figures.

of plant that is required.

Almost every tree and bush fruit that we are dealing with produces flowers along shoots that were formed the previous season (second-year wood). In some fruits (group 1) that second-year wood will not go on to produce flowers in the third year (e.g. sour cherries, peaches). In other cases (group 2), flower buds continue to form in subsequent years, often on short side shoots called 'spurs'. Most apples, pears, plums and sweet cherries fall into this group.

It is nevertheless useful to think in terms of the spur when treating the first group of fruit types, where pruning has to ensure a constant supply of new wood. In general, this replacement wood can be thought of as very long spurs. 'Long spur' fruit includes raspberries and blackberries, vines, peaches and nectarines.

Most pruning takes place in winter. Remember that fruit against a wall will start to grow as soon as the sunlight begins to gain strength. Get all pruning done before winter spraying starts, and well before there is the slightest sign of the buds expanding. Chemicals used at that time will harm green tissue.

Do not prune plums or cherries in winter, as this can allow the entry of silver-leaf disease. Leave them until mid- to late summer.

Fruit forms

It is very important to understand what the basic differences are between the various forms of fruit tree that are available (see illustrations on page 193).
Maiden: A single shoot, usually one year's growth after grafting. If you have sufficient self-confidence to go on to produce the other forms of tree from a maiden, and the time to wait an extra year or two for a crop, you can take advantage of the fact that maidens are cheap to buy and very easy to establish in the garden. Prune in winter.
Cordon: A cordon is simply a maiden with side growths pruned back to form spurs. Some soft fruits, particularly currants and gooseberries, make good cordons, but these forms are most often used for the majority of apple and pear varieties, which easily form short spurs. They can be grown on wire frameworks or against walls.
Fans: Trees of fan shape are always grown against a wall or supporting framework. The maiden is cut back to 8– 12 inches (20–30 cm), and the two uppermost shoots that then develop are allowed to grow. They are tied into wires or canes to keep them in one plane, and the next year are themselves cut back and allowed to sprout two or three new shoots. The resultant 'spokes' are kept in the same plane, and are also trained along canes to keep them neat and straight. Fans take time and care to produce, and are expensive to buy.

Fans are suitable for vigorous types of fruit, especially plums, peaches, nectarines, figs and sour cherries. However, apples and pears can make splendid-looking fans, and because the spurs are so short, the structure shows up well.
Standards and half-standards: All side growths are pruned away and the leader allowed to grow to the required height – 6 ft (1.8 m) and 3 ft (90 cm) respectively. The growth point is then removed and the topmost three or four outward-facing branches that then develop are allowed to grow on.

Espalier: A well-trained and cared-for espalier looks marvelous in flower and fruit. Espaliers are more useful than fans, as they are easily trained to fill all available space. Each of the side branches can be extended as far as necessary.

The maiden is cut back to just above the height of the first wire, generally 18 inches (45 cm) above ground level. Three new shoots are allowed to form; the uppermost is allowed to grow vertically; generally the other two are allowed to grow out at a wide angle, tied to canes to keep them straight, and are carefully lowered to the horizontal in autumn.

The following season, the vertical shoot is cut back to the level of the second wire, and so on for as many subsequent years as there are wires.
Bushes: These vary in shape according to the natural habit of the fruit variety concerned and the needs of the gardener. Gooseberries and currants are most often grown in this way, but many of the top fruits are too. Bushes are useful as they are easier to tend.

Most top fruit bushes are produced by shortening a maiden to about 2 ft (60 cm) and letting a number of side shoots grow which are in turn cut back by half annually for the first few years.

With short-spur fruits it is an easy matter to grow the main structure of the bush, and then encourage and prune spurs in exactly the same way as for an espalier or fan. For long-spur types, allow the bush to build up a structure then remove fruited side shoots.
Soft fruit trees: These are naturally small and seldom outgrow their allotted space. Gooseberries and currants, which can be made to spur, are best

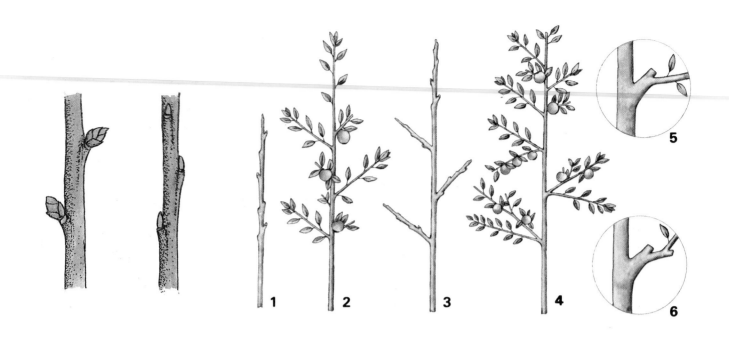

ABOVE: *Fruit buds (**left**) and wood buds (**right**). Never reduce wood buds to less than 4–5 per stem.*
ABOVE RIGHT: *Replacement shoot fruits (Group 1):*
1 1st winter, fruit and growth buds along previous summer's shoot.
2 1st summer, prune shoots next to fruits to 2–3 leaves, allowing some shoots to grow for next year's fruit.
3 2nd winter, as 1st winter.
4 2nd summer, as 1st summer, but allow 5–6 leaves beyond last fruit on each stem. Pinch out side growth to 2–3 leaves except for one near the base, which should be allowed to grow as a replacement fruiting shoot.
5 2nd summer, after harvest, cut out shoot at junction with replacement.
6 3rd summer.

treated in the same way as bush apples. When the main branches and the spurs become too congested, cut one or two branches out each year. Of the new, replacement shoots select the strongest and remove the others.

Currants should be cut to within 1–2 inches (2.5–5 cm) of the ground just after planting. The prunings can be used as cuttings to raise new plants. No further pruning should be necessary until the bush is several years old when, after harvesting, you should cut out between one-quarter and one-third of the branches at near ground level. This will encourage plenty of new growth, while keeping the bush open enough to ripen both fruit and new wood.

Dwarfing stocks

Most top fruits are sold in a grafted form, since this method of propagation ensures constant characters for each variety. It is possible to grow some from cuttings, and the resultant plants are often exceptionally vigorous.

Grafting is an ancient art. Before the Romans practiced it, it was known that the type of stock used affected the growth habit of the tree it supported. Over the ages, the selection of stocks became increasingly refined. Today, it is possible to buy most fruits on stocks that dwarf them to varying degrees.

When you buy a fruit tree, you are actually buying two plants, and you need to know what both of them are. If you have a small garden, and want bushes that remain in scale with it, check that the stocks will give you maximum dwarfing.

Most of the stocks, particularly for apples and pears, are known simply by code names. New sorts appear from time to time, so check with your supplier. Currently, Malling (M) is the most dwarfing stock for apples, followed by M26; M7 and MM106 are semi-dwarfing. Pears are usually Quince C (moderately dwarfing) or Quince A (semi-vigorous). Plums and their allies are usually on the semi-dwarfing St Julien A, though orchard trees may be on Myrobalan B. Sweet cherries are vigorous on Malling F12/1. The semi-dwarfing 'Colt' may sometimes be available, but is not always totally successful.

Pollination

Most fruits need pollination to take place before the crop can develop. The task is generally performed by bees, but for greenhouse crops you will need to do it by hand. You will also need to do it for certain fruits, such as apricots and some plums, planted against walls.

Hand pollination is an annual operation; however, other aspects of pollination need to be considered when planting many outdoor fruits. In many cases it is sufficient if pollen from one flower, or from other flowers on the same plant, is transferred to the stigma. Fruit formation ensues. Such plants are called 'self-fertile', and in the garden a single plant will produce a crop.

Other fruits, called 'self-sterile', can only be pollinated by pollen from a plant of another variety. To ensure a crop, two trees of different varieties, but which flower at the same time, must be grown.

Apples, pears, plums and sweet cherries have varieties which flower at different times in the spring. If you plant an early and a late sort, cross-pollination may not result because the flowers of one have faded before those of the other have opened. Varieties of these crops have been split into groups, all members of which flower at the same time. If possible, plant trees from the same group. The time of flowering is not related to ripening times, so you can still spread your crops over several weeks.

The shelter and warmth of a wall or glass encourage fruit trees to flower early. Peaches, nectarines and plums grown against a wall may all be in flower long before there are any bees around to pollinate them. You will have to do it yourself, using an artist's camelhair paint-brush.

To see if the time is right, have a look at the anthers of the open flowers. It is easy to see if they have split open, revealing white or yellowish pollen. Dab the brush into each open flower you can find, transferring the pollen as you

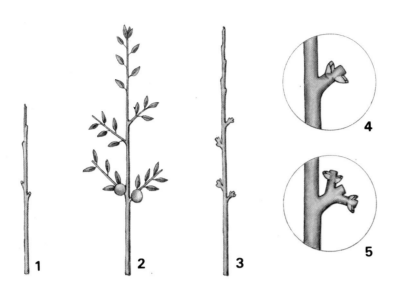

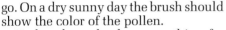

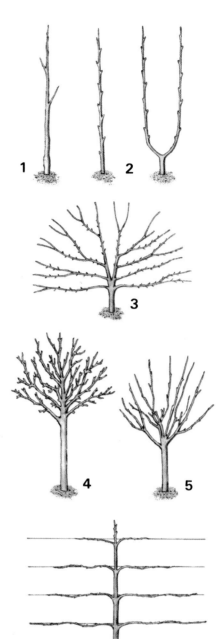

go. On a dry sunny day the brush should show the color of the pollen.

Under glass, do the same thing for peaches and nectarines. Strawberry plants being brought on early will need pollinating too, using the same method. The flower trusses of vines need tapping gently to shake the pollen on to the stigmas.

Harvesting

The time of ripening depends on the variety and season. If there is room for several varieties, choose some that ripen at different times to ensure an even supply.

Most fruits need to be picked as soon as they are ripe. Currants can be left on the bush for a week or two after they have reached their full color, provided they are protected from the birds.

Test pears and apples for ripeness by lifting each fruit gently from the branch in the palm of your hand. If it separates easily, harvest time has arrived. Remove the fruits carefully, as bruised or damaged specimens cannot be stored. If possible, harvest them into shallow baskets or boxes.

Storing fruit

A long-term storage place is necessary for winter varieties of apple and pear. It should be cool, though frost-free, and humid. A cellar, shaded garage or shed or cool pantry are ideal. In old kitchen gardens, sheds on the north side of the north wall were often used for fruit storage. In small modern houses, a cupboard in a little-used unheated room may suffice. The loft, and the cupboard under the stairs are usually so warm that the fruit will ripen too quickly.

Details on storing individual fruit

Spur-producing fruits (Group 2):
1 1st winter, growth buds only at the tip with fruit and growth buds mostly at the base of last summer's growth.
2 1st summer, prune side shoots so that 4–6 leaves remain.
3 2nd winter, prune side shoots to leave 2 buds, allowing the leading shoot to grow unless the space is filled; if so, treat the leading shoot as a spur and cut back.
4 2nd summer, allow only one bud to produce a growth shoot.
5 3rd winter, after summer and winter pruning a small spur is gradually built which will need radical shortening after several more years.

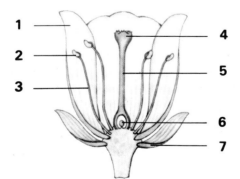

The parts of a flower: 1 petal or corolla; 2 anther and 3 filament, which form the stamen; 4 stamen; 5 style; 6 ovary; 7 sepals.

ABOVE: *Fruit forms – 1 maiden; 2 single and double cordons; 3 fan; 4 standard; 5 bush; 6 espalier.*

species are given at the end of each entry.

Unfruitfulness

If a fruit bush or tree that has been planted within the last couple of years displays plenty of healthy growth but no flower buds, one or more of the following factors may be in operation.

Some young top fruits, especially if on vigorous stocks, may take several years to reach flowering size. Seedling trees, ungrafted, can take many years.

Some types of apple, some soft fruits and most figs, will produce only leaves if they are fed heavily with nitrogenous manure. Stop mulching. If you are growing apples as bushes or standards with bare ground beneath, try sowing grass. This will compete for the available nitrogen, and reduce the speed of growth of the bushes or trees. Where possible, dress the soil with a potassium-rich fertilizer in winter.

Check your pruning methods. Check also the variety of fruit you are growing. Some pears and apples are tip-bearers, with flower buds borne at the end of last season's growth. If your plants cannot now be identified by type, try not pruning for a year and see if the situation remedies itself. Some apple varieties fruit so heavily that they only manage a crop every second season. Again, wait a year and see what happens.

If the plant is growing well, there are plenty of flowers but no fruit follows it may be that the plants were in flower very early, before there were any bees to effect pollination; this is most common in wall fruit. Next year, try hand pollination.

A bad season, because of late frosts or a long wet spell at flowering time, may cause unfruitfulness. If it can be done easily, try protecting plants from late frosts with netting, sacking or plastic sheeting draped over them.

Alternatively, it may be that there is no variety nearby that is suitable for cross-pollination. It is important to check carefully all your variety's pollination requirements.

Renovating neglected fruit

If you have taken over a run-down garden, many of the fruit bushes and trees may have become unproductive.

If you want to keep some of the old soft fruit, try cutting currants to within a few inches of the ground in winter and selecting the strongest of the new shoots the following summer, discarding the rest. Tangled gooseberries and currants can be heavily pruned, again in winter, so that only the best main branches are left. The final structure should be as open as possible so that new growth is not crowded.

Old top fruits are more of a problem. If you have neglected espaliers, fans or cordons, try cutting back to the original form, even if this means removing large branches.

Less neglected wall fruits will probably only need their spurs thinning out. Do this in winter, cutting them back to within a few inches of the main structure.

On overgrown bushes or standards, it is fairly easy to thin out the branches to give a suitable open structure.

A maturing crop of Bramleys

FRUIT

APPLE

The apple (*Malus domestica*) can form anything from a good-sized tree to a single cordon. As well as exhibiting variations in flavor, apple varieties ripen over a wide season. The earliest is available in mid-summer while the last to ripen is ready the following spring. If you have a small garden, or one in which there are many other fruits, it is probably best to plant late-season types, even if you have to store them.

Even if you only have room for cordons, plant as wide a range of apples as you can to give a number of different colors and tastes rather than an enormous quantity of one sort. The other advantage of planting several varieties is that you will avoid pollination problems. Nevertheless, make sure that those you choose all belong to the same pollination group.

Choosing varieties: Written descriptions of flavor and texture provide a basic guide. However, since different varieties do better in different parts of the country, the flavor varies too, and it is best, if you can, to taste the ones that grow in your locality to find out what you like.

If you are going to grow your plants in a heavily pruned form, avoid 'tip bearing' varieties like 'Worcester Pearmain'. Though these will form fruit spurs, young plants most often bear flower buds at the ends of last year's growths. In general, tip-bearers are best left to gardeners who can let them grow as bushes or half standards.

Most apple varieties prefer to be cross-pollinated; for some it is essential. 'Jonathan', 'Rome', 'Duchess', 'Wealthy', 'Golden Delicious', 'Yellow Newtown', 'Grimes' and 'Yellow Transparent' tend to be partly self-fruitful.

If you want to grow an unusual variety, check its pollination requirements with your supplier. Popular varieties of good flavor are available from nurseries.

Cultivation: The majority of apple varieties are remarkably easy to grow, being tolerant of a wide range of soils and climates. It is very easy

A good example of the impressive structure formed by a well-trained espalier.

'Discovery' apples ready for harvesting

to train apple trees into one of the artificial forms, and they can be used to make screens, low hedges, tunnels and arbors, as well as cordons and espaliers. For heavily pruned sorts, ensure that the trees are grafted on only a moderately dwarfing stock. For free-standing bushes in a small garden, the stock should be the most dwarfing of all.

Spacing is important, for there's no point in wasting space or in trying to cram too many trees into too small an area. Single cordons are best planted 2–3 ft (60–90 cm) apart. Espaliers need a minimum of 12 ft (4 m), but will appreciate more if you have room. So that you don't waste valuable wall space while the espaliers are maturing, put currants or gooseberries between the apples, and gradually grub them out as the espaliers expand. Bush trees need at least 6 ft (2 m) spacings if on dwarfing stock. In a proper orchard, standard trees need planting at least 20 ft (6.6 m) apart. The ground beneath wall fruit can also be planted up. Bulbs are a good idea because they are below ground level when you need

to spray the trees with tar oil.

The most important pruning takes place in winter, preferably in December or early January. This enables winter spraying to take place safely before the buds begin to expand.

For details of winter and summer pruning, see page 192.

Pests and diseases: The most troublesome pests are codling moth, apple redbug and, in the Northeast, apple sawfly, while the most common diseases are canker and scab.

Harvesting: Ripe apples will easily lift away from the branch. Early ripening sorts need to be eaten at once, otherwise they turn soft and mealy. Harvest such varieties a short time before they ripen and keep them for several days.

Apples for winter should be left on the branch as long as possible, though not into the season of hard frosts. Pick them carefully and place them with equal care into the basket or pail. Do not throw them in, or rot will set in where the fruit has been bruised and will spread fast. In the kitchen, wipe them over gently, wrap them in newspaper or appropriate fruit papers and pack them into boxes. It is also possible to keep the apples in poly-

thene bags with breathing holes punched into them. Allow 8–10 apples to a bag, and place them loosely and in a single layer in boxes. They must be stored somewhere cool and not too dry. A garage or well-shaded garden shed is excellent.

Over the subsequent weeks, check the fruit regularly for ripening. If more ripen than you can eat, remember that even wrinkled fruit cooks perfectly well.

Some North American varieties listed in order of ripening are:

Summer	Jonagold
Quinte	Empire
Yellow	Delicious
Transparent	Jonathan
Lodi	Winesap
Melba	
Duchess	
Early fall	Rome
Jerseymac	Stayman
Milton	Golden
Gravenstein	Delicious
Wealthy	York
Late fall	
McIntosh	
Cortland	
Spartan	

AVOCADO

The avocado is borne on vigorous growing, tender trees, which grow well in certain areas of the South-

west and Southeast. There are three basic types: Guatemalan, Mexican and West Indian. The West Indian variety is the most tender; it won't survive sub-freezing temperatures. The Guatemalan species will withstand temperatures as low as 25°F (−4°C), and the Mexican will tolerate temperatures as low as 20°F (−7°C). Most trees grow to 30 ft (9 m), and they fruit in cycles – heavy one year, light the next. Varieties that tend to be consistent producers are 'Bacon', 'Duke', 'Hass' and 'Topa Topa'.

Cultivation: Avocado trees need good drainage above all else. Roots tend to grow in the uppermost 2 ft (60 cm) of soil, so they should be watered frequently enough to keep that area moist but not soggy. The trees need an annual topdressing of balanced fertilizer in the acid soils of the Southeast; less feeding is needed in the West and Pacific Northwest unless deficiencies are noted. Avocados grow easily from seed, but seedling trees are generally of inferior quality and it's best to purchase young trees from local nurseries. The tops of the trees should not be shaded. Full sun results in better fruiting.

Pests and diseases: Avocado root rot is frequently a problem where trees are grown in wet soils. Watch out for verticillium also. Pests include mites and scale insects. Treat trees with evidence of chlorosis with iron chelate.

Harvesting: Avocados will not soften while still on the tree. It is difficult to know when green varieties are ready to be picked. Colored varieties may be gathered when the color change is complete. Let fruit ripen for 5–7 days at room temperature.

BLACKBERRY

In areas where they grow wild, blackberries are a summertime favorite of youngsters: a free snack-bar in the woods. Growing them in a garden takes more effort.

They are a biennial, producing fruit only in the second year, after which they must be discarded. The best varieties in the eastern states are 'Darrow' and 'Bailey'. On the West Coast, try 'Evergreen' and 'Thornless Evergreen'.

Cultivation: The best way to grow blackberries in quantity is on a wire framework of exactly the same sort as is used for espalier top fruit. The frame can be free-standing or attached to a wall, but in either case it needs to be sufficiently large to accommodate 2 years' canes. One wire supports canes from the right and left of each crown. If one plant only is required, it can be grown like a rambler rose up a start post 7 ft (2.2 m) tall.

Since the amount of fruit you get depends on the length of the canes grown the previous season, an annual mulch of manure is very beneficial.

If by chance you need more plants, or want to replace the ones you have, new ones are easily produced. Simply let a cane or two grow so that its tip touches the soil and in early fall keep it in place with a stone or a wire peg. It will soon take root. The following spring detach the new plant.

Pests and diseases: Diseases are rare and the worst pests are, not surprisingly, birds. Blackberry sawfly can occasionally be a nuisance.

Harvesting: Fruit for eating fresh or for wine-making needs to be as sweet as possible, so leave it on the plant for as long as you can. Fruit for jams, jellies and pies is better if picked a little earlier just as the berries turn black.

Avocados

BLUEBERRY

A longtime national favorite, bluberries thrive in areas with cool moist summers and acid soils. High-bush (*Vaccinium corymbosum*) varieties are among the most popular. They are branching deciduous shrubs 5 ft (1.5 m) or more high, with urn-shaped flowers and neat foliage that turns vivid red in autumn. The fruit is a delicious round black berry, heavily waxy-white bloomed like a grape, and in some varieties up to $\frac{3}{4}$ inch (2 cm) in diameter. They are borne in sprays of 8–10.

Of the enormous number of varieties, some of the more popular include 'Early Blue', 'Grover', 'Jersey' and 'Pemberton'. You will need to buy two sorts to ensure cross-pollination and a good yield.

Cultivation: If the soil in your area supports good ericas and rhododendrons, which belong to the same family as the blueberry, it is suitable for this crop. Blueberries need moist sandy or peaty soil with a pH between 4.3 and 4.8.

In suitable areas, high-bush plants are spaced with their centers 4 ft (1.2 m) apart. On acid sandy soils, give an annual mulch of compost or rotted manure at a barrel-load for 4 sq yd (3 sq m). On peaty soil, an annual dressing of general fertilizer at 2 oz/sq yd (50 g/sq m) will keep the plants cropping well.

Since blueberry bushes bear fruit on last season's wood, prune high-bush sorts lightly in the first few years, only taking out the weakest shoots. Later on, take out a few of the main branches each year, cutting them out at ground level to encourage strong new growth at the base. Each main shoot should last only 5–6 years before it is pruned out.

Blueberries are easy to propagate by taking cuttings in very early spring before the buds begin to expand. The cuttings should be about 8 inches (20 cm) long. Rub out any flower buds. Insert

A blackberry bush hung with ripening fruit (see p. 196)

the cuttings into sandy, moist soil in frames. Move the rooted plants to their final positions the following autumn.

Pests and diseases: Birds adore the berries.

Harvesting: Depending on the variety grown, fruit ripens from mid-summer onwards, when the full 'blue' color has developed.

CHERRY

There are three basic types of cherry: sweet, sour and duke.

Sweet cherries are derived from the wild cherry (*Prunus avium*). *P. cerasus* is the sour cherry. Duke cherries, which are worth growing if you can find them, are hybrids between these two. In small gardens the sour and duke types are the most useful as they are self-fertile. Because they will also fruit nicely in shade, they can be grown against north-facing walls. As they are less vigorous than the sweet types, they can be trained as fans.

Sweet cherries can be trained as fans but only on the largest walls. You may do better to grow them as bushes in a fruit cage; eventually they will need heavy pruning, but you will have had several years of risk-free cropping by then. Cherries also grow quite nicely in pots. Provided the plants have had an abbreviated winter, they can be brought into warmth in January and forced. By this means, garden owners may have cherries well ahead of the normal season. If growing sweet cherries, you'll need two varieties which must be hand pollinated with a tuft of fur or a camel hair brush. Try 'Bing', 'Hedelfingen', 'Lambert' or the self-fruitful 'Stella'. There are other delicious cherries to be had, many of which will happily accept pollen from the sour cherry.

Cultivation: Cherries do well on a variety of soils, as long as they are well fed. Apply a mulch of rotted manure or compost at least every other year, plus a light dressing of a potash-rich fertilizer.

If planting free-standing trees, bear in mind the difficulties of protecting the ripening fruit from birds. You are bound to lose the fruit on the upper branches, but it is possible to enclose the lower ones in large tubes of netting and thus manage to keep some of your crop. Otherwise, it might be worth trying some of the model hawks available.

If you want to try cherries against a wall, sweet varieties like south, west or east aspects. Once the basic branch structure has been built up, prune lateral shoots in summer to six leaves; prune again in early autumn to three buds. Do not prune in winter.

The best way to treat sour cherries is to cut out a certain amount of fruited wood each year and so encourage the production of new wood, while still keeping the tree within the bounds of the wall. Cherries can be grown as bushes in the fruit cage using the same methods.

Pests and diseases: Keep a constant check for the black, cherry aphids. Silver leaf disease can be a problem. Birds can take the flower buds and completely clear the trees of ripe fruit. Wall fruit is most easily protected, but take care to do it thoroughly. Birds find cherries very attractive and will find the tiniest chink that will let them into the fruit.

Harvesting: Once the color has developed to its maximum, keep tasting for the sort of sweetness you like. The stalks of sweet cherries come away from the branch very easily. Sour cherries require more care; pulling too hard can remove leaves, stem and all. Use small sharp scissors to cut the stalks. When harvested, eat the cherries at once; alternatively they may be bottled, soaked in brandy, or made into cherry wine.

CITRUS

Citrus includes lemon, lime and grapefruit as well as the kumquat and tangerine. These tender trees can be grown outdoors in zone 10 or

Ripe cherries ready to be picked

as indoor/outdoor container plants in any region. They are prized both for their zesty fruit and their ornamental value. Most standard citrus trees grow 20–30 ft (6–9 m) high; dwarfs grow to 4–10 ft (1.2–3 m).

Grapefruits like warmer summer temperatures than lemons and limes. Both seeded and seedless varieties are available. 'Duncan', 'Indian River' and 'Foster' are all well adapted to the warm regions of the Southeast. 'Marsh' is most prevalent in the humid regions of the Southwest.

Lemons are small trees which remain in active growth all year and are less cold-resistant than the tangerine and orange. 'Meyer', 'Eureka' and 'Lisbon' are all popular varieties.

Limes are also borne on small trees. 'Bears' is the best of the Tahitian type and 'Mexican' is the smaller, bartender's standard choice.

Blueberries can succeed well and are becoming increasingly popular.

'Nagami' is the most common kumquat. Kumquats are the most cold-tolerant of the citrus, and are very attractive when in bloom.

Cultivation: All types of citrus need fast-draining, sandy soil. They should be watered deeply every other week once established. Container-grown plants will need to be watered twice a week during warm weather. Trees should be fertilized three times throughout the year in late winter and early and late summer with a high-nitrogen formula. Citrus also benefit from feedings of iron chelates and zinc. Mulch with a 2–3 inch (5–7.5 cm) layer of sawdust, pebbles or gravel.

Pests and diseases: Watch for aphids, mites, scale insects and mealy bugs. Fungal diseases may be a problem when trees are grown in poorly drained soil. Take action at the first sign of attack by a pest or disease to prevent further damage.

Harvesting: Many citrus trees will fruit throughout the year. Pick when the fruit is deeply colored and store under refrigeration.

CURRANTS

Red, white and black currants were popular garden fruits many years ago, but they have fallen from favor for two reasons. Most importantly, growing them is forbidden in many areas. Because they can be hosts of the disease white pine blister rust, the U.S. Department of Agriculture has banned them from areas where white pine grows. If you are considering growing currants, be sure to check with your state experiment station to ascertain if they are allowed in your area. The various stations are listed in the regional guides beginning on page 214.

The second reason they are no longer frequently grown is that they are just too much trouble for the backyard gardener. Some of the least troublesome varieties are: Alpine currant, European blackcurrant (Northeast), clove currant (Midwest and Rockies) and winter currant (Pacific Northwest).

Cultivation: Currants do well in most soils, providing they are neither waterlogged nor overly dry. They produce early summer fruit in cooler climates or if grown in a shady spot in hot areas. The blackcurrants produce their best fruit in the second year, fading in later years. To ensure continual production, cut back the stems to 2 inches (5 cm) immediately after planting. This will encourage strong new basal shoots, and you can use the prunings as cuttings for new plants. All the currants require pruning once they are mature to let in light and air. The bushes should be planted about 6 ft (1.8 m) apart. This might look like too much space with new plants, but healthy currants will amply fill in the spaces.

Pests and diseases: Currant aphids infest the leaves, and birds steal the fruit.

Harvesting: It is easy to tell when currants are ready: pick one and taste it. You can leave ripe currants on the bush for a few days if you have no time to harvest, but beware of birds.

LEFT: *Oranges*

BELOW: *Ripe blackcurrants*

DAMSON PLUM

Botanically, damsons are varieties of *Prunus domestica insititia*, a sub-species of the common plum. Although variable in vigor, they form small trees usually under 20 ft (6 m) in height. Their flowers, which are small and white, are borne on naked twigs in early spring. The fruits are small, blackish purple outside, amber yellow within. The flesh is disappointing eaten raw, but a delectable and unique taste develops as soon as it is cooked.

The trees are happy in most soils and in the least sheltered of situations, but they prefer moderately cold winters. Damsons produce prodigious crops when well suited to the growing conditions.

Some varieties are self-fertile; others cross easily with other damsons or true plums. They are easily trained against west- or east-facing walls, either as fans or espaliers, though plums or

greengages better deserve the space. On a wall, damsons may need hand pollinating. 'French' produces an abundance of flavorful fruit, a bit smaller than other varieties. It is best used for making preserves. 'Reine Claude' is one of the best for the fruit bowl. 'Stanley' is an American variety that produces good fruit.

Cultivation: Although damsons can be grown in unpromising conditions, they will benefit from good soil and are best treated as plums.

Pests and diseases: As for plums.

Harvesting: Pick the fruit when it softens. As damsons are less sweet than most plums, birds and wasps are less of a problem. Picked fruit will store in a cool place for a week or two.

FIG

The fig (*Ficus carica*) is a deciduous tree with bold, handsome foliage; its unique fruit – green, purple or brown skinned – has flesh in various shades of dusky pink.

In warm parts of the country, a good single crop of figs can be had from freestanding plants. Elsewhere, the trees need the protection of a south-facing wall. For these there is always plenty of competition, but a dish of properly ripened figs is a strong inducement to find a space.

Under glass, even without much heat, most varieties of fig can be persuaded to give two crops, the first developing from young fruit buds that have withstood the winter, the second from fruit buds on the earliest part of the new growth. A much wider range of varieties can be grown as well, many with flavor far superior to the commoner kinds.

Outdoors, most figs, which are native to hot, dry Mediterranean countries, adapt to colder climates by producing masses of foliage and few mature fruits. They do best in the sun belt and southern parts of the Eastern seaboard. Most need to be planted in situations where there is a very restricted root run. Sunken brick boxes containing about 35 cu ft (1 cu m) of soil are the usual arrangements. The box has no bottom, but the lowest 9–12 inches (22.5–30 cm) is filled with coarse rubble or gravel which slows down the roots from exploring outside.

Figs also fruit well in large pots or tubs, though they need to stand somewhere sheltered. Large plants are easily toppled by a sudden summer gale.

The most frequently seen variety is 'Brown Turkey', unusual in that it does not need to have its roots cramped and can be planted in open ground. The fruit is not large or in the first rank for flavor. 'Adriatic' is one of the hardier varieties, which produces fruit along the East Coast.

Cultivation: Against a wall, or under glass, figs are best trained as fans. When the fan is full-grown, some of the major spokes need to be removed every few years to

'Brown Turkey' fig

ensure new growth, and so fruit, at the center. Alternatively, cuttings will root very easily, so overgrown and unproductive trees are quite simply replaced.

Do not leave figs grown outdoors to fend for themselves in winter. New wood may be killed by the cold, and you will lose the chance of fruit in the following summer. Provide some protection; the usual method with a fan is to untie the spokes, bunch them together, and cover them in a straw coat. Alternatively, cover with plastic sheeting.

Pests and diseases: Under glass, red spider can be a nuisance. Outdoors, birds are the main problem.

Harvesting: When the fruit ripens, the skin near the fruit's opening begins to split, revealing the juicy flesh. By that stage, the fig should come away from the branch easily.

Some people are slightly allergic to the skin of the fig. It is perfectly easy to remove this, starting at the split.

GOOSEBERRY

The gooseberry is another member of the *Ribes* family, as notorious as the James brothers. They are alternate hosts to the serious white pine blister rust, and the Department of Agriculture has outlawed their cultivation in areas where white

The damson will crop well in good conditions

pine grows. Check with your state experiment station, listed in the regional guide, before planting. The gooseberry is immensely variable – early or late, smooth or hairy, sweet or sour, soft or crisp (some sorts were used as salads in Elizabethan England) – and it comes in all sorts of colors, including green, yellow, red and white. They all make delicious desserts, jams, jellies and wines, and the sweet sorts are lovely eaten straight from the garden. Since dessert fruits do not travel well, they are less often seen at the supermarket.

The bushes make good hedges as most plants are quite spiny. They are easily trained against walls, where they are happy to face in any direction. All kinds are easily trained as cordons or fans. Even neglected plants fruit quite well, though they eventually become badly tangled and need savage thinning out every couple of years.

The best varieties are the red 'Poorman' and the green 'Downing'.

Cultivation: Gooseberries are fairly undemanding; they do well in most soils, but prefer well-drained loam. An annual or biennial mulch of manure or compost is helpful and keeps down weeds. Potash deficiency can show up as scorched leaf margins; use a potash-rich fertilizer, or apply a light dressing of sulfate of potash. About 1 oz (28 g) will suit a well-grown bush.

Clear out weak and twiggy growth that will not bear much fruit.

As the structure of the bush develops, encourage formation of fruiting spurs by cutting back laterals to 3 inches (7.5 cm). In summer, shorten laterals so that they have 5 leaves left.

Gooseberries make good single, double or triple cordons. Allow the leader or leaders to grow unchecked until they are as tall as you need. Winter-prune laterals to 3 buds, and in summer prune to 5 leaves.

If new bushes are required,

in autumn take cuttings of the summer's growth about 12 inches (30 cm) long. Remove all but the top 4 buds and insert so that about 6–7 inches (15–17.5 cm) is below ground. Set them in sandy soil in a partially shaded position. Transplant to a permanent site one year later.

Gooseberries will fruit quite well with no attention at all, though you will get a much higher yield if you find time to prune. Cut back the main growth shoots of young bushes by half each winter to encourage strong new growth. Varieties with a drooping habit of growth should be cut back to an upward-facing bud.

Pests and diseases: Birds are the worst menace; bullfinches peck out young buds in early spring and several species attack swelling fruits later in the season.

Gooseberry sawfly and magpie moth caterpillars can be a nuisance. In some seasons aphids can also be a problem. Watch out also for gooseberry mildew.

Harvesting: Once the berries have swollen to a reasonable size they can be picked for jams, jellies and sauces. They do not have to be harvested all at once. Those left on the bushes will ripen until they split.

Undamaged berries can be kept for a short time in the refrigerator.

GRAPE

Along with the growth of the U.S. wine industry has come a corresponding growth in the grape's popularity as a garden fruit. This is a delightful development, as the grape provides fine flavor whether ultimately served from fruitbowl or stemware.

Grapes fall into three major groups and, happily, at least one will thrive in all but the coldest areas of the country.

Vitis vinifera thrives in California, the Pacific Northwest and some areas of the East Coast. *V. labrusca* is less demanding. Its 'Concord' variety is widely grown across the Midwest and especially in the northeastern states. *V. rotundiflora* does well only in the warm southern states.

Vines can be grown as freestanding plants in vineyards, but most dessert grapes do best against a south-facing wall. In such a situation, grapes will fruit well quite far north, provided they are grown in a neighborhood where local conditions reduce the chances of a damaging early fall frost.

Many amateurs will achieve the best results in a greenhouse, whether there is room for one large pot, yielding perhaps a dozen good bunches, or for a full-sized vine, yielding hundreds. A slightly heated greenhouse would permit some of the choicer late-ripening grapes to be grown, particularly the various muscats, whose fine flavor repays the cost of heating in spring and autumn.

The choice of varieties now available is increasing, reflecting a renewed interest in the grape.

The most popular varieties from the Midwest to New England are: 'Concord', 'Niagara', 'Delaware' and 'Erie'. Varieties which will do well in the South include: 'Scuppernong', 'Thomas', 'Mish' and 'Flowers'. Varieties for California and the West Coast include: 'Thompson Seedless', 'Emperor' and 'Cardinal'.

Vines are ornamental in their own right. The leaves are handsome, the plants graceful, and the clusters of berries spectacular. For even more visual effect, choose from the varieties with particularly decorative leaves. The one called 'Purpurea' has deep purplish foliage which looks handsome when grown near some of the more refined and pale-colored clematis, and the leaves of 'Brandt' go a magnificent scarlet in autumn to set off the berries in a wonderful contrast of colors.

Cultivation: Vines are vigorous plants which must be pruned frequently and ruthlessly to avoid a picturesque but barren tangle.

Vines grown in pots can be treated in the same way as raspberries, with two canes allowed, one from last year to fruit, one of this year to grow. The old cane will attempt to grow too, but stop it by pinching out the main growing tip and all the side shoots 4–6 leaves after the flower truss if there is one, 2 if not. Allow only 1 shoot, the lowest, to grow and make

Ripe gooseberries take on a translucent quality

a new cane. In late autumn cut the fruited shoot back to 2 buds (easily visible), above the junction with next year's fruit cane. If both buds want to grow next spring, rub out the topmost one.

Grown against a wall, or in the greenhouse, a simple way to train a plant is to cut back the newly planted vine to 3–4 buds if you have glass to ground level, higher if not. Let 2 shoots develop, and train them horizontally along wires to right and left. Next year, allow buds to develop every 12 inches (30 cm) and train them vertically. You should now have a fork-shaped plant, with as many tines as you have room for. Thereafter, treat each cane as you would a potted plant. Take great care not to let vast amounts of foliage develop. Ripening grapes need sun and warmth for flavor, and the free movement of air is important, as the bunches of fruit are less likely to rot. Thin the leaves out if they become too dense.

The flowers will be opening by the beginning of summer. Outdoors, pollination is no problem. Indoors, the clusters need tapping gently with a cane to shake pollen on to the stigmas.

When the young fruitlets begin to form, the bunches must be thinned out by about half to leave the remainder room to develop. Equip yourself with a pair of scissors with long narrow blades. Surgical scissors are suitable in the absence of proper vine scissors. Snip away at each bunch to clear the fruitlets away from the center. In general, you can cut out whole bunchlets. Pay special attention to the top or 'shoulder' of each bunch.

Continue nipping out unwanted vegetative growth and when the berries are one-third their full size, have another look over each bunch. Once again, they will be congested. Using a twig, small spatula or an eraser-tipped pencil, lift up each branch of the bunch and snip out yet more fruit. Experience will tell you how much to cut out, but once more

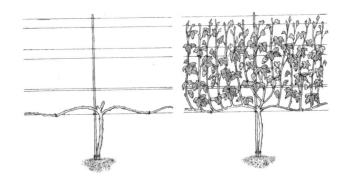

ABOVE: *Training a newly planted vine (**left**). Young grape fruitlets must be thinned out (**right**).*
LEFT: *Grapes ripening on a mature vine.*

about half the fruitlets should go. The aim is to get a well-filled bunch, but one in which each berry has room to swell, and in which air can freely circulate. Without this drastic thinning, the berries will be small and cramped.

In winter, prune back 'spurs' on espalier-trained vines to 1–2 buds. On vines trained raspberry-fashion, cut out the old canes and untie the newly grown ones so that they hang from the main trunk. This looks untidy, but makes sure that the buds break evenly along the cane and have equal vigor.

When the bunches are ripening under glass, keep the greenhouse vents open as much as possible when the weather is warm.

Pests and diseases: Under glass scale insect, mealy bug, red spider and whitefly can all be a nuisance. Outdoors, wasps, birds and mildew can spoil the crop.

Harvesting: Grapes will not be ripe until a week or more after the full color has developed.

Under glass, the fruit can be left on the vine more or less until it is needed. The last bunches should still be good well into fall if they were properly thinned and if the greenhouse has been kept dry. Keep examining the bunches for split or mildewed fruit and cut them out as soon as you see them, otherwise the rot will quickly spread.

LOGANBERRY and BOYSENBERRY

A number of species in the genus *Rubus*, both American and European, can be crossed with each other. The hybrids are all fairly modern, the loganberry (*Rubus* x *loganobaccus*) having arisen around 1880 in America. They are crosses between the raspberry and blackberry. The loganberry does not over-winter well in most parts of the country, but it thrives in the Pacific Northwest.

The hybrid berries all crop exceptionally well, which is the main reason for their success. The thornless hybrids are useful.

The fresh berries are colorful, sweet and abundant. They can be made into very good jams and jellies.

Cultivation: As might be expected, the culture of these hybrids resembles that of both parents. Since the canes are generally 6–8 ft (1.8–2.4 m) long, they can be trained up or along wires depending on the amount of space available.

Pests and diseases: The same as for raspberry and blackberry.

Harvesting: Pick the fruit when the full color has formed. Ripe berries are easily crushed, so go carefully when picking them.

NECTARINE
See next entry

PEACH

It is difficult to know why so few people grow their own peaches. The best suited climates for cultivation are the West Coast, the East Coast from Massachusetts to Florida and the states south and west of the Great Lakes. In these areas peaches crop heavily as free-standing trees, and they are fairly easy to manage against a wall, in a pot or under glass. The peach (*Prunus persica*) is a small deciduous tree with attractive pink flowers before the leaves in spring. The colorful fruits have a dense, fine, downy skin. The nectarine is a mutation of the peach with glossy, hairless fruits of an arguably richer flavor.

Cultivation: Peaches thrive in any well-drained soil. In general, it is best not to feed them too heavily or the foliage becomes too luxuriant, making pruning and training harder and keeping sunlight from the fruit.

On walls they are usually treated as fans, using the 'long spur' system (see pp. 191 and 193). Under glass, either grow them as bushes in large pots, using high-yielding varieties on dwarfing rootstock, or plant them out in cold greenhouse borders.

Peaches were traditionally grown in south-facing lean-to greenhouses, with the trees trained up the back wall. In modern free-standing greenhouses, it is possible to train the trees up the inside of the glass, attaching the branches to wire stretched along the main struts of the greenhouse. The main disadvantage is that the spurs and their replacements grow upwards and touch the glass. As a result, the leaves are scorched by hot sun.

If the greenhouse is large enough, it is simplest to plant the trees in the center. The main pruning, to keep them within bounds and allow you room to move, takes place in summer.

Good-sized nectarines ripening under glass

Peaches do not need winter heat. It is only necessary in early spring if you want to try to force an early crop of fruit.

Under glass, the flowers need hand-pollination. The trees are self-fertile. For tall plants in which the uppermost flowers are difficult to reach, try attaching the handle of the paintbrush to the end of a bamboo cane.

Do not let plants dry out in the early stages of fruit formation, otherwise the fruits open at the base and begin to rot. It is particularly important to keep potted specimens well watered.

Prune young side shoots – which are not needed to extend the tree or for replacement 'spurs' – to 4 leaves. It is essential to thin out young fruitlets. It is tempting not to do this, but the tree will only reward your negligence with small fruits of poor flavor, if any.

Peach varieties are available with different periods of ripening and flesh and skin color and flavor. In general, the white-fleshed sorts have the best flavor. 'Babcock' is a good one, and often seen. 'Rochester', later-ripening, is red-skinned but not of quite as good flavor. Recommended nectarines are 'Freedom' and 'Pioneer'. Always go for named varieties; seedlings do not come exactly true to type.

Pests and diseases: The main scourge of outdoor peaches is peach leaf curl disease. Birds, of course, attack the ripening fruit. Under glass, red spider can be troublesome.

Harvesting: Peaches are best picked in the morning. If anything more than the lightest tug is needed, leave the fruit on the branch – it is not ripe. Better still, let the peach fall off. Rig up netting beneath the tree to stop the fruit bruising itself on the ground or, under glass, pile crumbled newspaper beneath the branches.

Peaches only last at their peak for a day or two at the most. They can be kept longer in the refrigerator.

PEAR

The common pear (*Pyrus communis*) is basically a large deciduous tree with a profusion of white flowers in spring and leaves which can color brightly in autumn. It has a long history in cultivation, about 40 varieties being known in Roman times. Nowadays, pears are commonly grafted on to one of the quince stocks. This keeps them to a smaller size.

The fruit itself can be tricky to manage. Unlike apples, pears remain in eatable condition for a very short time. Unripe pears are too hard to eat, though they may be poached, preferably in red wine, but over-ripe ones are only fit for the compost heap.

That there are a large number of varieties with a corresponding range of flavors is not surprising in such an ancient and important crop. Pear varieties, like apples, may be either diploid or triploid. Diploid varieties, which include all commercial types grown in North America, have viable pollen and can pollinate one another with few exceptions. 'Seckel' and 'Bartlett' are incompatible.

Some choice selections include 'Anjou', 'Bartlett', 'Bosc', 'Flemish Beauty', 'Monterrey', 'Moonglow' and 'Winter Nelis'.

Cultivation: Pears on pear stocks will grow on a wide range of soils, even on those that would support no other fruit. On quince stocks, they need fertile garden soil, with plenty of moisture and nitrogen. Such trees need feeding every year with a good mulch of manure or compost. Since pears are quite as tractable as apples, they can be trained and pruned in exactly the same way. Ensure that wall fruits never lack moisture, for the ground at the base of old walls can be very free draining.

Many dessert pears ripen late in the season, so gardeners in colder regions should plant slightly less choice, early-maturing sorts. Do not despise old varieties with small fruits. 'Seckel' is old (mid-1700s), but the fruits are delicious, and it does well in cold, even shady, conditions. The cooking pears, too, make excellent winter eating, baked or stewed.

Pollination needs to be considered. Some varieties are fairly self-fertile, and so a single tree can be planted. 'Bartlett' is the usual one suggested, but there are others. Check with your supplier. In general, it is much better to

plant 2 trees of different varieties. As with apples, the crop is split into several pollination groups.

Although pears produce flowers in substantial bunches, it is best not to let them fruit in the same manner. Where possible, thin each cluster to one or two fruits. If you do not thin them out you will have large quantities of small fruits. Unlike peaches and nectarines, however, the flavor will not be impaired.

Pests and diseases: The worst disease is scab; it attacks some of the older varieties, but most of the newer varieties are resistant. Peach psylla is the most destructive insect in the East and is spreading rapidly to western regions. Birds are the worst pest.

Harvesting: When pears ripen depends on variety, locality, season and location in the garden, so experience

Even a modest-sized peach tree will yield a worthwhile crop of fruit.

is the surest guide. In general, pick fruit just before final ripening. Handle the fruit carefully, for although the flesh will still be hard, bruises at this stage may cause uneven ripening.

Store the picked fruit somewhere cool, keeping ones you want to eat soon somewhere warmer. Later-ripening varieties will take anything up to several months to become ripe. Since they need frequent checking, it is unwise to wrap and box them. Test them both by smell, and by gently pressing the fruit. You will soon become good at detecting fruit at the peak for eating. Unless you have somewhere cool to store the fruit, you may find that an entire crop has ripened more or less simultaneously. This is one reason why, if you have several varieties, they should be chosen with a spread of ripening times.

Cooking pears never soften. Most varieties can be used throughout the winter.

PLUM
Plums are popular with home gardeners throughout the country. The two main

Conference pears are self-fertile and will produce fruit from a single tree.

groups are European and Japanese. Native American plums are the hardiest and will thrive in the Great Plains area and in the Canadian prairie provinces. Plums are attractive when in flower, and look magnificent when the branches are loaded with fruit.

If you are prepared to plant something other than the reliable 'Green Gage', there are some delicious alternatives. One of the reasons why so many people plant 'Green Gage' is that, because it is self-fertile, only one tree is needed. There are other self-fertile varieties worth considering, particularly 'French Prune' and 'Damson'. The dessert plum 'Laroda' is self-sterile, and needs something to fertilize it.

Good-flavored Japanese varieties include 'Beauty', which fruits early in the season, and 'Duarte', which needs another Japanese type to cross-pollinate. 'Dakota 27' and 'Compass' are good hardy American varieties, but they are also self-sterile.
Cultivation: Plums are happy in most locations. Areas subject to late frosts are not suitable, however, as flower and

fruitlets can be damaged. Wall fruits are usually safe from frosts. Choose native American or hybrid varieties if you live in a cold climate. Allow at least 15 ft (4.6 m) of wall for a fan, and as much between plants if you are putting in dwarf bushes. It is preferable to buy maiden plants and do the initial pruning yourself. Remember to prune only between June and August, otherwise your plants may contract silver leaf disease.

Plums need plenty of nourishment, especially when they are young. Mulch annually with compost or rotted manure.

In a cold spring, fruits against a south wall may flower before the bees are around. Use a small soft-haired paintbrush to assist pollination. If you have planted varieties that need cross-pollination, pick a bunch of flowers from one plant and brush it against the flowers of the other (and vice versa).

Plums may crop very heavily. The fruits can be thinned, which will give you a smaller number of larger fruits. It may be necessary to ensure that the branches do

not break when fully laden by tying them to canes or poles as supports.

Pests and diseases: Aphids and birds are the commonest pests.

Harvesting: Plums may soften rather before they are sweet enough to eat. If you cannot keep the pests away, harvest the fruits as they soften and store them on a shelf in the kitchen, pantry or garage. You will lose a little of the flavor as the fruit subsequently ripens, which may take several days, or even a week. After ripening, the fruit will last on the shelf for about 10 days.

RASPBERRY

Several kinds of raspberry are native to the northern hemisphere, and many of them do well in the United States and southern Canada.

Well-grown rows, neatly tied and weighed down with lovely soft red fruit, look wonderful in the kitchen garden. Good dessert varieties are 'Taylor', 'Jewel', 'Canby' and 'Newburgh'. If you like unusual-looking fruit, try growing some of the yellow fruit sorts. They also have a subtly different flavor.

ABOVE: *Raspberries*
BELOW LEFT: *The 'Czar' plum is a self-fertile cooking variety.*

Autumn-fruiting varieties extend the season in favored districts. The flavor is slightly inferior to the summer-fruiting varieties.

Cultivation: The rootstock throws up shoots from below ground. They last two years; in the first they make growth, in the second they bear fruit. New roots or canes are planted 18 inches (45 cm) apart, with about 6 ft (1.8 m) between the rows if you have more than one. New canes are tied to a wire or string framework, either free-standing or against a wall. The simplest way of keeping the canes upright is to insert a 7 ft (2.1 m) bamboo stake every 6 ft (1.8 m) or so with horizontal strings 3 ft (90 cm) above ground level and, when the new growth needs more support, at 6 ft (1.8 m) above that again.

If the canes outgrow the

wires or strings, simply cut them off or tie them into the topmost support. Do not let them grow through the fruit cage roof. Pull out new shoots that interfere with the pathway between the rows of canes. As soon as fruiting has finished, cut out spent canes to give plenty of room and light to the new ones.

The autumn fruiting sorts are treated differently. They fruit on canes grown the same season. Fruiting stops in late autumn and the canes are cut down to within a couple of inches of the ground in late winter. The rootstocks tend to produce very large numbers of new shoots each spring, so pull out all thin, weak ones and any others not required.

All raspberries appreciate an annual mulch of compost, manure, or peat and artificial fertilizer. In either case keep the plants well watered, especially as the fruit is swelling.

Pests and diseases: Aphids

and raspberry beetles can be a major nuisance. Virus diseases, transmitted by both aphids and eelworm, are common and ineradicable.

Raspberries are so attractive to birds that you will be very lucky if you can harvest a respectable crop on canes grown outside a fruit cage.

Harvesting: Pick the fruit when it is fully colored and use as soon as possible.

STRAWBERRY

Strawberries are easily grown and speedily produce a crop. They are also easily propagated and maintained.

The large sorts now so widely grown are almost all hybrids (*Fragaria* x *ananassa*) between three American species. They started appearing in the mid-1700s, and are still the consuming passion of plant breeders. New varieties are bred for color, size, marketability, season of fruiting and disease resistance. Do not be persuaded to buy the latest variety by enthusiastic publicity. Buy or beg a few plants of as many varieties as you can, and see which you like best. There are great variations in flavor. Use only obviously healthy plants, the leaves of which are unblemished and well-colored. Different varieties of strawberry thrive under different climate conditions, so it is best to check at your local nursery to see which varieties will do best in your area.

Cultivation: Having settled on the variety or varieties you want, find out if virus-tested stocks are available. Rooted runners can be planted in the garden at any time of year. Runners planted by mid-summer, however, can be cropped the following summer; those planted at the end of summer should be given a year to build up a strong crown. To do this, remove most of the flowering shoots as soon as they appear.

Modern strawberries should be planted 15 inches (37.5 cm) apart, in rows 2½ ft (75 cm) apart, to give plenty of space for tending and

Standard strawberries

spreading out the developing sprays of fruit.

Ideally all runners should be removed during the growing season, unless you want to increase the number of plants. This leaves the strawberries in neat rows, and certainly makes life easier. In many gardens, however, the strawberry patch is allowed to become a jungle of new plants. If the ground was in good shape when the bed was formed, such tangles can be extremely fruitful for the next two seasons or so. After that, disease troubles generally build up, especially if the dead leaves are not removed each winter, and the plants become starved. You should then root as many runners as you need to restart the bed. Clear out the old plants at the end of the second or third crop. Manure the ground, add a handful of potash for each square yd/m of ground, and replant.

If you have time to keep the strawberries in neat rows, lightly mulch between the rows in early spring, using compost or rotted manure. Use about a spadeful for each crown, spreading

carefully to avoid burying the leaves and growth points. Replace the old plants with young ones every 3–4 years. Plants grown in rows can have their trusses of fruit placed on straw or even special fiber mats to keep them clean and less susceptible to disease – worth doing if you want top-quality fruit.

There are early, mid- and late-maturing strawberries. It is possible to speed up the production of any of them by using cloches. Glass ones give the earliest crop of all, but plastic ones, even if just of clear plastic sheeting, can be quite effective. Put the cloches in place as the days begin to lengthen. Once the flowers are open, allow plenty of air to circulate, especially on warm days. The flowers need full pollination if the fruit is to develop evenly, and if the cloches are closed the insects will not be able to get in. Later on, as the fruit swells, keep the cloches ventilated to prevent gray mold.

In the greenhouse, simply plant strawberries in open beds, or pot up vigorous plants in autumn.

A large pot of strawberries can look attractive on a patio.

Strawberry barrels or custom-made containers allow a small crop to grow when there is no room in the garden.

In order to have strawberries over a long period, you can grow perpetual fruiting types which produce a light crop throughout summer and early autumn.

Pests and diseases: Aphids and slugs are primary pests, gray mold (botrytis) and virus the main diseases.

Harvesting: The large fruit that ripens first is know as the 'king' and should be picked as soon as it turns a good red color. The other berries ripen quickly thereafter, so check the bed every day. Ripe fruit will store for several days if chilled.

STRAWBERRIES, ALPINE

Alpine strawberries have developed from the common European wild strawberry. The small fruits are slightly difficult to pick, but the flavor is marvelous.

The plants are usually runnerless, and are propagated by seed, or by teasing apart mature plants. If you sow in spring, you should have some fruit by the autumn. Protect the ripening fruit from birds with flapping plastic strips.

Several varieties are available. 'Baron Solemacher' is recommended; 'Alexandria' is superb. Particularly delicious are the white-fruited ones.

Planting strawberries: LEFT: *correct positioning, with the crown level with the soil.* CENTER: *incorrect – the crown is too high.* RIGHT: *incorrect – the crown is too low.* FAR RIGHT: *Superfluous strawberry runners should be removed.*

CULINARY HERBS

he use of plants to cure diseases and disorders of the body and to flavor food began in the ancient world; certainly they were valued by the Greeks and Romans. Culinary herbs seem to have reached a peak of popularity in Elizabethan times, but thereafter steadily declined until this century. At the present time they are again popular and very much 'the in-thing' in the modern kitchen. No doubt the current interest in foreign foods, most of which demand herbs, has been a primary factor, but reaction against the many artificial flavorings has also helped.

Since Roman times, and probably before, herbs have been grown in special beds and borders. This reached its greatest development in the Elizabethan period when specially designed and often intricately executed gardens were laid out, each bed edged with dwarf clipped hedges of box, rosemary or lavender. Herb gardens are again popular, though usually only on a small scale and without the clipped edging. Nicely done, they can be a decorative feature in their own right. The best basic design to work upon is a paved area near the house with small formal or informal beds let into it. This allows easy access for the cook and the not inconsiderable visual attractions of the herbs themselves to be admired from a house window.

Soil and site
As a surprisingly large percentage of the popular herbs come from southern Europe or the Mediterranean region, they need a sunny site sheltered from cold winds; the south or west side of the house, a wall or thick hedge are ideal. With the exception of mint, angelica and parsley, which thrive best in a moderately moist soil, all the other herbs listed here need a well-drained rooting medium which is not rich. Too rich a soil produces sappy growth of poor flavor and keeping quality. Where soils are heavy and liable to hang wet in winter or after heavy rain, create raised beds 4–6 inches (10–15 cm) high filled with a sandy medium. Alternatively, grow the herbs in pots or larger containers. A collection of herbs in a large container can make a pleasing, decorative and useful feature for the sunny corner of a patio. Herbs take well to pot culture and can be grown on window ledges both outside and in. Purchase perennial herbs in spring and plant or pot them using techniques described under Garden Flowers, page 16 and House plants, page 122.

Propagation
Herbs are easily raised from seed and division in spring, softwood cuttings in early summer, or semi-hardwood cuttings in late summer or early autumn. See under Garden Flowers, Annuals, page 16 and Propagation, page 19.

Harvesting and drying
Herbs grown for their young stems and foliage must be harvested before flowering, e.g. angelica, borage, chives, fennel and parsley. All are best used fresh, but the last three can be dried. A few herbs are grown for their seeds, e.g. dill and fennel. For these, the seed crop must be yellowing and starting to turn brown. Lift or cut the plants at ground level, tie in small bundles and hang head-downwards in a warm, dry place until the seeds fall easily when touched. Strip the seed and store in sealed opaque jars in a cool dry place. Bulbous herbs such as garlic are lifted when the leaves yellow, dried in the sun or in any dry place, then cleaned and hung up for use. The remaining herbs described below, though best used fresh, can be dried for winter use. Just as the plants come into flower, gather healthy sprays and space them out in trays kept in a warm airy place. An airing cupboard or the warming drawer of a stove are suitable provided there is adequate ventilation. A microwave oven completes the process in a few minutes. Do not mix herbs, otherwise the aromas will mingle. Turn the herbs once a day until they feel brittle to the touch. They should then be crumbled and stored in opaque jars, ideally in a cool, dark place.

Freezing
Tender-leaved herbs such as parsley, mint, chervil and chives retain more flavor if frozen. Blanch small sprays by dipping them in boiling water. Cool, drain, and then place small amounts in polythene bags and put them in the home freezer.

The culinary herbs listed below are the best known and most useful.

ANGELICA
Angelica archangelica
A robust, erect biennial or short-lived perennial which, if allowed to flower, reaches 6 ft (1.8 m) or more in height. It has handsome leaves divided into several leaflets and tiny greenish flowers in terminal, rayed clusters. Only young leaf and flower stalks are used for candying and adding to stewed apples or marmalade. Propagate by seed.

ANISE
Pimpinella anisum
A small annual plant which grows to 18 in (45 cm) in height and produces the seed well known in cooking and medicine. It has finely serrated leaves and tiny flowers. Although the seed is more commonly used, the young leaves can be used in salad. Propagate by seed only.

BASIL
Ocimum basilicum
his half-hardy annual, also known as sweet basil, can make a bushy, erect plant to 2 ft (60 cm) or more in height, with small, oblong leaves in pairs. The tiny tubular flowers are white. The clove-scented leaves must be used when young. Propagate by seed.

BAY
Laurus nobilis
Also known as sweet bay, this is the tree of heroes, the leaves being used to wreathe famous people in Grecian times. Although an almost hardy ever-green tree, it stands clipping well and can be easily rooted from cuttings so it is not necessary to provide a lot of room for its growth. The aromatic leaves are best used when newly matured. Propagate by semi-hardwood cuttings.

BORAGE
Borago officinalis
A decorative hardy annual up to 2 ft (60 cm) tall, but often less. It has large, rough, oval leaves smelling of cucumber and sprays of delightful sky blue starry flowers which can be candied and used to decorate cakes. Propagate by seed.

CARAWAY
Carum carvi
This hardy annual forms slim stems 2 ft (60 cm) or more in height, clad with ferny leaves and topped by flat heads of tiny white flowers. Its seeds are a favorite cake flavoring, but also try the young leaves chopped in soups and salads. Propagate by seed.

CHERVIL
Anthriscus cerefolium
Similar in overall appearance to cara-way, this biennial attains about 1½ ft (45 cm) and is grown for its parsley-flavored leaves. Propagate by seed.

CHIVES
Allium schoenoprasum
This densely tufted perennial has grassy, hollow leaves to 10 inches (25 cm) long with a delicate onion flavor. If allowed to develop, 1 inch (2.5 cm) wide globular heads of small rose-purple flowers top the foliage. Ideally, pinch out the flower spikes when small to promote more leaves, and use young leaves in preference to mature ones. Propagate by seed or division.

COMFREY
Symphytum officinale
A tall widespreading perennial which has coarse, rough leaves, blue or creamy white flowers and grows to 2–3 ft (60–90 cm) tall. It is a most useful plant in the garden as background. It is used as a medicinal herb and can be cooked like spinach or used in salad. Propagate by seed.

This bay tree is both practical and decorative

CORIANDER
Coriandrum sativum
An annual grown for its spicy, aromatic seeds. The plant however has an un-pleasant smell until the seeds ripen. Grow in full sun in a light rich soil, sowing the seeds in very early spring. Plants can be thinned to 4–6 in (10–15 cm) apart. When seeds have turned a light greyish brown cut down the plant and leave to dry for 2 or 3 days. When dry, shake out seeds and store. Cori-ander should be propagated by seed.

Chives, coriander and basil planted with lavender and screened at the back by Hemerocallis (see p. 46) and Phormium tenax.

CUMIN
Cuminum cyminum
A slender annual growing up to 1–2 ft (30–60 cm), the plant has long thin leaves and small pink or white flowers. Cumin is grown for its seed alone. Much used in Middle Eastern cooking. Propagate by seed.

DILL
Peucedanum graveolens
Much like fennel but with a single stem to 3 ft (90 cm) in height and of annual duration only, this herb is grown for its aniseed-flavored leaves and seeds. Propagate by seeds.

FENNEL
Foeniculum vulgare
This is a graceful clump-forming perennial. Its dark, almost blue-green, sweetly aromatic leaves are divided into numerous filaments and make a distinctive fish sauce. The flowering stems are best removed when young, unless seed is required. Allowed to grow, they rise 5–8 ft (1.5–2.5 m) tall and produce flattened heads of tiny yellowish flowers. Propagate by seed or division.

GARLIC
Allium sativum
The familiar white bulb of this plant is composed of several narrow bulblets known as cloves. The narrow leaves grow to 1½ ft (45 cm) tall. Sometimes, rounded heads of tiny, white, purple-tinged flowers are produced on stems above the leaves. Propagate by cloves.

HORSERADISH
Cochlearia armoracia syn. Armoracia rusticana
A hardy perennial with large floppy leaves growing from the base of the plant to a height of 2–3 ft (60–100 cm). The flowers are white on a single stem but do not appear every season. The large thick roots are used as a condiment to accompany roast beef and some oily smoked fish. Plant out young shoots, or bury pieces of root.

HYSSOP
Hyssopus officinalis
This hardy perennial grows up to 1½ ft (45 cm) in height. Technically it is a low shrub but it needs annual pruning to keep it low and compact. The narrow, aromatic leaves are in opposite pairs, and small tubular blue, pink or white flowers form showy erect spikes. Both leaves and flowers can be used to flavor stews and salads. Propagate by seed or semi-hardwood cuttings.

LOVAGE
Levisticum officinale
In leaf, this clump-forming perennial resembles celery. Allowed to grow, it sends up stems to 8 ft (2.5 m) tall which branch and bear yellowish flowers in umbels. Both seeds and leaves are used, the latter being nicest when blanched as for celery and used in salads. Propagate by seed.

LEMON BALM
Melissa officinalis
Sometimes simply known as balm, this is a widely clump-forming hardy perennial with pairs of corrugated lemon-scented oval leaves and clusters of small, tubular, white flowers which form leafy spikes. The leaves can be used fresh or dried. Propagate by division or seed.

LEMON THYME
Thymus citriodorus
see entry for thyme.

MARIGOLD
Calendula officinalis
As a herb, this is best known as pot marigold to distinguish it from tagetes. (See Garden Flowers section, page 31, for description.) The petals make a colorful garnish for a salad. A sunny site is best for this plant but it can tolerate some shade. Propagate by seed.

MARJORAM
Origanum majorana
Of the four different sorts of marjoram, this is the one commonly used for cooking. Usually listed as sweet or knotted marjoram, it is a shrubby-based half-hardy perennial grown as an annual from seed. It has slender stems about 1½ ft (45 cm) tall with pairs of elliptic leaves and loose clusters of small, hop-like (knotted) flower spikes bearing minute white or pinkish flowers. Its leaves are mainly used in meat dishes. Propagate by seed under glass.

MINT
Mentha
There are several different kinds of mint, all hardy perennials 2–3 ft (60–90 cm) tall, all of which can be invasive. They have opposite pairs of simple leaves and tiny, tubular, mauve flowers in terminal, often branched spikes. Common spearmint (*M. spicata*) is the form most usually grown, with smooth, bright green lance-shaped leaves. Apple mint (*M. suaveolens* syn. *M. rotundifolia*) has broadly oblong to rounded, white, hairy leaves. Peppermint (*M. x piperita*) yields the world's supply of peppermint oil. It is similar to spearmint (one of its parents) but is easily distinguished by its smell. Propagate by division.

NASTURTIUM
Tropaeolum majus
Better known in the flower garden (see Garden Flowers section, page 67), this plant yields seeds which are a substitute for true capers. The edible flowers and leaves can garnish salads. Propagate by seed.

PARSLEY
Petroselinum crispum
This very familiar hardy biennial, which can also be grown as an annual, forms a tufted rosette of finely cut leaves which are flat in the original species but in the best known varieties are 'crested' or mossy. If allowed to bloom it produces an erect branched stem to 1½ ft (45 cm) or more tall with tiny yellowish flowers in umbels. Parsley is a good plant for edging the herb garden, and ideal for container growing outside or indoors. Propagate by seed.

PURSLANE
Portulaca oleracea
An attractive tender annual with succulent leaves, small yellow flowers, and erect reddish stems, purslane grows up to 5 in (15 cm) high. It has a sharp clean flavor which is best used with other herbs. It is essentially a salad herb but the young shoots can be cooked as a vegetable. Purslane must be sown when all danger of frost has past in a sandy soil with a sunny aspect. Grow from seed.

ROSEMARY
Rosmarinus officinalis
A bushy evergreen shrub (see page 115) to 5 ft (1.5 m) or more tall, this herb is better known as an ornamental with its dark, almost needle-like leaves and lavender, sage-like flowers. The leaves go well with meat dishes. Propagate by hardwood or semi-hardwood cuttings.

RUE
Ruta graveolens
This evergreen shrub to 2 ft (60 cm) or more tall is primarily grown for its dissected blue-gray leaves and open clusters of yellow flowers with cupped petals. The very pungently smelling foliage can be used to flavor egg and fish dishes. Propagate by semi-hardwood cuttings or seed.

SAGE
Salvia officinalis
Like mint and parsley this is a very popular herb. It is an evergreen shrub to about 2 ft (60 cm) tall with finely wrinkled gray-green leaves and spikes of quite large, tubular, two-lipped blue-purple flowers. There are purple and variegated leaved varieties for the flower garden. Propagate by hardwood or semi-hardwood cuttings or seeds.

SALAD BURNET
Sanguisorba minor syn. *Poterium sanguisorba*
A clump-forming hardy perennial, attaining 2 ft (60 cm) or more in bloom. The long pinnate leaves are composed of 9–21 oval leaflets and have an almost fern-like quality. The oval greenish flower-heads are not showy but have a flower-arranging potential. The flowering stems are, however, best removed when young to promote more young leaves, which are used in salads and sauces. Propagate by division or seed.

SAVORY
Satureja
There are two kinds of savory, summer and winter. The latter (*S. montana*) is a hardy, wiry shrublet 6–12 inches (15–30 cm) tall with small narrow leaves and short spikes of small, pale purple flowers. Summer savory (*S. hortensis*) is a slender, erect hardy annual with similar but longer leaves and white to pale purple flowers. The leaves of both are used in fish, egg and salad dishes. Propagate by seed or semi-hardwood cuttings.

SORREL
Rumex acetosa
A low growing herb of the buckwheat family, sorrel has acid tasting leaves. It is commonly used in salads and in soups. Propagate by seed.

SWEET CICELY
Myrrhis odorata
A slow growing perennial which may reach a height of 2–5 ft (60–150 cm). It is a fragrant plant with a sweet anise flavor and can be used in salads or omelets. Propagate by seed.

TARRAGON
Artemisia dracunculus
This not quite fully hardy perennial forms wide clumps of erect stems to about 2 ft (60 cm) in height. The narrowly lance-shaped leaves are a grayish-green and an essential constituent of *fines herbes*. Small, greenish, bobble-like flower-heads may appear in good seasons. Propagate by cuttings.

THYME
Thymus
Several sorts of thyme have herbal uses, but the two most popular in the United States are common thyme (*T. vulgaris*) and mother-of-thyme (*T. serpyllum*). Common thyme produces hardy, wiry, spreading evergreen shrublets to 8 inches (20 cm) or more in height with tiny leaves and small pale purple to whitish flowers. Its leaves are gray-green, finely hairy and aromatic. Mother-of-thyme is a ground cover with rosy-purple flowers and very small, aromatic leaves. Propagate by division or cuttings.

REGIONAL GARDENING GUIDE

Our view of the earth from 100,000 miles in space shows a cloud-covered ball rotating in orbit. As we close in on this orbiting ball to look at North America, the continent below appears to be composed of a number of zones or belts. The mosaic effect of these belts is produced by vegetational regions of varying nature, some forest, some desert, some grassland. The differences are caused by natural variations in climate and topography that affect all natural growth. The contrast between the regions of the continent is more dramatic when we consider the golden autumn of New England, the tropical lushness of southern Florida and the sparse, arid regions of the Southwest.

Climate, more than any other factor, determines the success or failure of gardening efforts. North America has a vast range of climatic conditions which influence the kind of plants that will thrive in the region where you live. In this section we will discuss five geographic areas — the North, Northeast, Southeast, Northwest and Southwest — that share some climatic similarities, which the home gardener may use as a guide in his or her initial considerations of which plants to buy.

The first factor to take into account in plant selection is whether a particular variety can withstand the lowest temperatures likely to occur in your

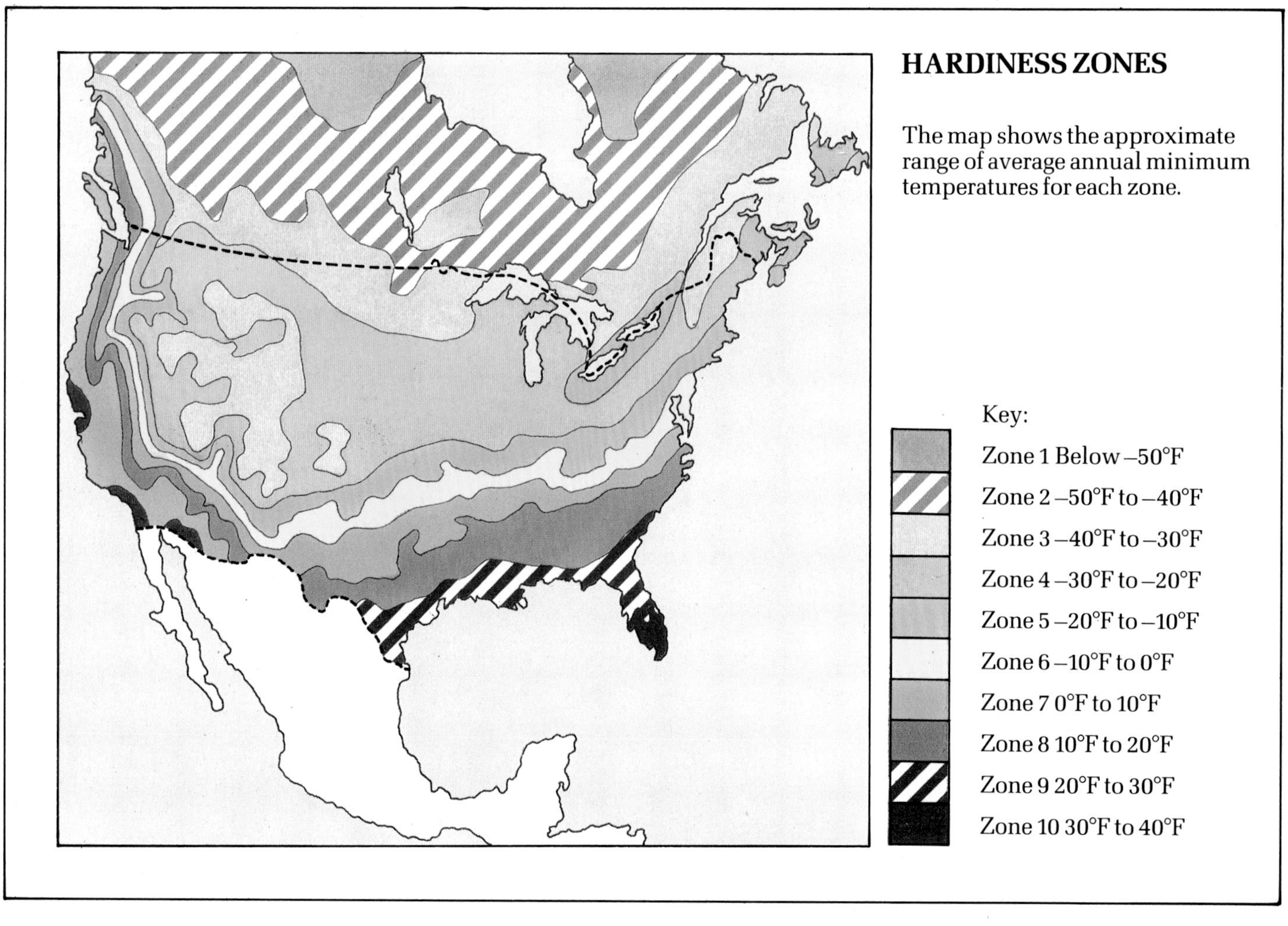

HARDINESS ZONES

The map shows the approximate range of average annual minimum temperatures for each zone.

Key:

Zone 1 Below −50°F

Zone 2 −50°F to −40°F

Zone 3 −40°F to −30°F

Zone 4 −30°F to −20°F

Zone 5 −20°F to −10°F

Zone 6 −10°F to 0°F

Zone 7 0°F to 10°F

Zone 8 10°F to 20°F

Zone 9 20°F to 30°F

Zone 10 30°F to 40°F

region. Temperature directly influences the rate of a plant's internal growing processes. The fastest growth will take place at the higher temperature limits of an individual plant's tolerance. If you're not familiar with local conditions, consult with local nurserymen or the local agricultural experimental station. The United States Department of Agriculture has devised a Hardiness Zone Map, based on average minimal night temperatures from weather stations throughout the continent, which is helpful in plant selection. This map separates the continent into ten different zones and is helpful in predicting the adaptability of plants to specific climates. The zone map is shown on the opposite page, and the zone references throughout the A-Z section of the book refer to this map. The lower number represents the coldest region in which the plant can survive and the higher number refers to the warmest region in which the plant will thrive. Some plants such as hardy bulbs and deciduous fruit trees actually need winter chilling and will lose vigor in a warm zone. No zones have been given for annuals or annual vegetables because they do not usually live through the winter.

These flowers thrive in zones 4 to 10.

The adaptability range for every plant is relatively fixed. Only by introducing new genes through the hybridization process can a parental line be changed with respect to its basic temperature tolerances.

Temperature is only one aspect of a region's total climate, however, and other factors are equally as important. Rainfall, sunshine, average cloud cover and growing season will also influence the performance of an individual plant. The zone hardiness ratings are helpful, but they do not conclusively determine whether a plant will thrive in a particular location. For example, many plants that will grow well in zone 9 in the Southeast will not tolerate the dry conditions on zone 9 in the Southwest.

Even without a relatively small climatic region, there are variations or microclimates that the home gardener needs to take into account when considering the purchase of a particular plant. Within and around the normal homesites, the local climate will vary quite a bit from the general statement for a given community. The house itself produces some dead shade during certain parts of the day. Also, there are many interactions between local temperature and moisture and the character of the soil.

By management, you can actually alter these microclimates through the plantings themselves and by use of mulches and other practices, such as those for water control. Through careful selection of the site you can modify air drainage, local wind currents, sun and shade, humidity, the water both on and within the soil, and soil temperature. The temperature is generally higher on the sunny side of walls — facing south and southwest — and near unshaded walks. Trees and shrubs can form buffers to protect tender plants from high winds. Tender plants can be covered with lightweight sheets, held down by stakes to avoid an anticipated late spring or early fall frost. So, although the hardiness values of various plants are fixed and will limit plant selection to some degree, there is much that the gardener can do to create an enviroment in which plants will thrive.

Agricultural experiment stations have been set up in each state, and they are an excellent source of information for the gardener. They issue bulletins and supply information on all phases of agriculture. Knowledgeable personnel are available to answer questions related to gardening under the conditions in your area. The addresses of these experiment stations are listed on pages 226–27.

THE NORTHWEST

The Northwest region, including British Columbia, has widely varied terrain. Although much of the region is mountainous and lies as far north as 49° latitude, there is also a large coastal region, influenced by the mild marine climate. The Pacific Northwest is famous for its beautiful gardens, and is one of the country's most ideal regions for horticulture.

The two principal climate types in the Northwest region are a marine climate west of the Cascade Mountains of Washington, Oregon and British Columbia and a continental climate east of the Cascades, through the northern Rocky Mountains and into the northern plains.

The marine climate is characterized by mild, wet winters and only moderately warm, dry summers. A considerable amount of summer cloudiness prevails. Winds can be a hazard in the Northwest, particularly on the coast; they lessen as the land extends into the inland valleys.

This area has a long frost-free season, but spring is frequently too cool and wet for early planting. Gardeners in this region benefit from getting a head start by beginning plants from seed in a greenhouse or propagator for transplanting outside later in the season. Vegetables should be limited to cool season types such as carrots and peas. Corn and tomatoes are practical only in certain warmer valleys. Gardeners in the Pacific Northwest can plant hardy annuals from early fall or from mid-February on.

In the continental area from the Cascade Mountains eastward to the northern prairie states, climate varies considerably due to elevation.

In the mountain valleys from Washington and Oregon eastward through the Rockies, gardening is usually successful at elevations at or below 1500 ft (457 m) above sea level.

Across the northern prairie states, gardening is done at even higher elevations because large amounts of sunshine and plains winds have a favorable influence on the spring climate. However, late frosts occur in the northernmost tier of states, and the frost-free season may be as little as 130 to 140 days in places.

From the Cascades eastward through the Rockies and into the northern plains rainfall is generally less than adequate for a garden, but water for irrigation is generally abundant, as is sunshine, making for fast growth.

The information in the table shows a large variation in rainfall and temperature from east to west in the Northwest region. The marine West Coast climate can be distinguished from the continental by the small temperature variation from summer to winter in Seattle and Corvallis as opposed to large variations in Spokane or Miles City. Also, the marine climate has much cooler summer months with a longer frost-free period than many of the continental climate localities; in other words the climate varies less than elsewhere.

The frost-free period in the table is the number of days from the last average date of 32°F (0°C) in spring to the average first occurrence of 32°F (0°C) in autumn.

Growing season length is influenced by elevation and slope of terrain. Higher elevations such as foothills – or higher plains areas as in western Nebraska and Kansas or eastern Colorado – have shorter growing seasons than lower valley regions like Boise or Yakima.

The growing season dictated by regional conditions is a controlling factor, but remember that it is possible to situate plants to take advantage of the microclimate of your site. Tender crops may be started earlier in spring if a gardening area slopes in such a way as to cause light night drainage winds, which are a frost preventative. South-sloping terrain generally warms more quickly in spring and may be less susceptible to frost; these conditions, and sunny locations, will give the warmest soil in spring to aid seed germination and promote a head start on the summer garden.

Large natural areas of water in the high plains and mountain regions have a mild climate in the immediate vicinity. Gardens which may not be possible a few miles away can be cultivated in these areas.

Seacoast Plantings
Gardens planted along shorelines present special challenges to the gardener. Salty ocean spray, strong winds, sandy soil and foggy weather demand careful plant selections. The plants listed under Seacoast Selections are proven performers in seashore conditions and will thrive in the sections of the Northwest that border the ocean as well as other coastal areas of the country.

Plant Selections

Shrubs and Climbing Plants
Abelia grandiflora
Akebia quinata
Buddleia alternifolia
Camellia
Campsis
Celastrus
Chaenomeles
Clematis
Clerodendrum
  trichotomum
Clethra ainifolia
Cornus
Cotoneaster
Cytisus
Daphne
Erica
Forsythia
Fuchsia
Garrya
Gaultheria
Hamamelis
Hebe

Hedera helix
Hydrangea petiolaris
Ilex altaclarensis
Kalmia latifolia
Kerria
Kolkwitzia
Lonicera
Mahonia aquifolium
Paeonia
Rhododendron
Rosa
Skimmia japonica
Spiraea
Syringa
Tamarix
Viburnum burkwoodii
Weigela florida
Wisteria sinensis
Perennials and Bulbs
Adonis
Aquilegia
Artemisia
Asclepias tuberosa
Aster

Astilbe
Bergenia
Brunnera macrophylla
Campanula
Chrysanthemum
Clarkia
Crocus
Delphinium
Dianthus plumarius
Dicentra
Digitalis
Echinops exaltus
Epimedium
Eranthis hyemalis
Gaillardia
Geum
Gypsophila
Helianthus
Hemerocallis
Heuchera
Hosta
Iris
Liatris
Lilium

Lupinus polyphyllus
Monarda
Narcissus
Nepeta
Papaver
Penstemon
Phlox
Platycodon
Primula
Rudbeckia
Salvia
Sidalcea candida

Seacoast Selections

Shrubs and vines
Acacia longifolia
Buddleia
Cistus
Clematis paniculata
Clethra alnifolia
Cytisus canariensis
Euonymus japonica
Genista

Hebe
Hibiscus syriacus
Ilex altaclarensis
Juniperus
Lonicera
Prunus maritima
Raphiolepsis
Rhododendron
  viscosum
Senecio laxifolius
Spiraea prunifolia
Tamarix
Thunbergia alata
Veronica prostrata
Wisteria sinensis
Perennials and Annuals
Achillea tomentosa
Aquilegia
Arabis
Armeria maritima
Artemisia stellerana
Astilbe
Aubrieta deltoidea

Aurinia saxatilis
Baptisia australis
Calendula
Centaurea cyanus
Chrysanthemum
  carinatum, frutescens
Clarkia
Dicentra spectabilis
Digitalis
Erigeron
Fritillaria
Hemerocallis
Geranium
Hosta
Lavandula angustifolia
Liriope spicata
Lychnis coronaria
Paeonia
Papaver
Phlox
Salvia
Schizanthus
Stachys
Verbena

Climatic Data for Representative Areas of the Northwest

City	Apr.	May	June	July	Aug.	Sept.	Oct.
Boise							
Temp. (F)	49.9	57.7	64.8	74.7	72.1	63.2	52.6
(C)	10.0	14.4	18.4	23.9	22.4	17.5	11.5
Prec. (in)	1.16	1.29	0.89	0.21	0.16	0.39	0.84
(cm)	2.95	3.28	2.26	0.53	0.41	0.99	2.13
Mean number of frost-free days = 171							
Bismarck							
Temp. (F)	43.0	55.4	64.5	72.2	69.8	58.7	46.2
(C)	6.2	13.1	18.2	22.5	21.1	14.9	7.9
Prec. (in)	1.22	1.97	3.40	2.19	1.73	1.19	0.85
(cm)	3.10	5.00	8.64	5.56	4.39	3.02	2.16
Mean number of frost-free days = 136							
Cheyenne							
Temp. (F)	42.6	52.9	63.0	70.0	67.7	58.6	47.5
(C)	5.9	11.7	17.4	21.3	20.0	14.9	8.7
Prec. (in)	1.57	2.52	2.41	1.82	1.45	1.03	0.95
(cm)	3.99	6.40	6.12	4.62	3.68	2.62	2.41
Mean number of frost-free days = 141							
Corvallis							
Temp. (F)	51.7	57.0	61.6	66.6	66.4	62.7	54.4
(C)	11.0	14.0	16.6	19.4	19.3	17.2	12.5
Prec. (in)	2.05	1.77	1.15	0.33	0.55	1.31	3.78
(cm)	5.21	4.50	2.92	0.84	1.40	3.33	9.60
Mean number of frost-free days = 210							
Denver							
Temp. (F)	47.5	56.3	66.4	72.8	71.3	62.7	51.5
(C)	8.7	13.6	19.3	22.8	22.0	17.2	10.9
Prec. (in)	2.05	2.20	1.64	1.36	1.43	1.08	1.01
(cm)	5.21	5.59	4.17	3.45	3.63	2.74	2.57
Mean number of frost-free days = 165							
Grand Island							
Temp. (F)	49.6	60.6	71.0	77.2	75.3	65.2	53.4
(C)	9.9	16.0	21.8	25.3	24.2	18.6	12.0
Prec. (in)	2.47	3.78	4.40	3.00	2.54	2.51	1.08
(cm)	6.27	9.60	11.2	7.62	6.45	6.38	2.74
Mean number of frost-free days = 160							
Helena							
Temp. (F)	43.3	52.9	59.5	68.4	66.2	56.0	45.6
(C)	6.3	11.7	15.4	20.4	19.2	13.4	7.6
Prec. (in)	0.83	1.56	2.23	1.03	0.89	0.95	0.66
(cm)	2.11	3.96	5.66	2.62	2.26	2.41	1.68
Mean number of frost-free days = 134							
Huron							
Temp. (F)	46.0	58.0	68.1	75.5	73.3	62.4	49.8
(C)	7.8	14.6	20.2	24.4	23.1	17.0	10.0
Prec. (in)	1.84	2.36	3.14	1.81	2.07	1.53	1.15
(cm)	4.67	5.99	7.97	4.59	5.25	3.88	2.92
Mean number of frost-free days = 149							
Miles City							
Temp. (F)	45.7	57.3	65.6	75.3	72.6	61.0	49.0
(C)	7.7	14.2	18.8	24.3	22.7	16.2	9.5
Prec. (in)	1.06	1.73	2.71	1.34	1.24	0.96	0.87
(cm)	2.69	4.39	6.88	3.40	3.14	2.43	2.20
Mean number of frost-free days = 150							

City	Apr.	May	June	July	Aug.	Sept.	Oct.
Minneapolis							
Temp. (F)	44.7	57.6	67.3	73.0	70.5	60.5	48.3
(C)	7.1	14.3	19.8	23.0	21.6	16.0	9.1
Prec. (in)	1.85	3.19	4.00	3.27	3.18	2.43	1.59
(cm)	4.69	8.10	10.2	8.30	8.67	6.17	4.03
Mean number of frost-free days = 166							
Pendleton							
Temp. (F)	52.0	59.6	65.8	73.6	71.9	64.2	53.7
(C)	11.2	14.5	18.9	23.3	22.3	18.0	12.1
Prec. (in)	1.09	1.12	1.17	0.22	0.28	0.63	1.18
(cm)	2.76	2.84	2.97	0.55	0.71	1.60	2.99
Mean number of frost-free days = 196							
Prince George, British Columbia							
Temp. (F)	54.1	63.8	70.1	74.8	74.2	65.3	51.8
(C)	12.2	17.6	21.1	23.7	23.4	18.5	11.0
Prec. (in)	0.84	1.32	2.13	1.64	1.92	2.02	2.04
(cm)	2.13	3.35	5.41	4.17	4.88	5.13	5.18
Mean number of frost-free days = 130							
Seattle							
Temp. (F)	51.3	57.4	62.2	66.7	65.6	60.5	52.6
(C)	10.8	14.2	16.9	19.4	18.8	16.0	11.5
Prec. (in)	2.15	1.58	1.43	0.66	0.81	1.83	3.50
(cm)	5.46	4.01	3.63	1.67	2.05	4.64	8.89
Mean number of frost-free days = 233							
Spokane							
Temp. (F)	47.3	56.2	61.9	70.5	68.0	60.9	49.1
(C)	8.6	13.6	16.7	21.6	20.2	16.2	9.6
Prec. (in)	0.19	1.21	1.49	0.38	0.41	0.75	1.57
(cm)	0.48	3.07	3.78	0.96	1.04	1.90	3.98
Mean number of frost-free days = 169							
Topeka							
Temp. (F)	54.5	63.8	73.8	79.2	77.6	69.0	57.9
(C)	12.6	17.8	23.4	26.4	25.5	20.7	14.5
Prec. (in)	3.50	4.32	4.54	3.25	4.66	3.44	2.56
(cm)	8.89	10.9	11.5	8.25	11.8	8.73	6.50
Mean number of frost-free days = 200							
Vancouver, British Columbia							
Temp. (F)	58.1	63.8	69.2	74.2	73.2	65.3	57.0
(C)	14.5	17.6	20.6	23.4	22.8	18.5	13.8
Prec. (in)	3.32	2.82	2.51	1.21	1.72	3.62	5.81
(cm)	8.43	7.16	6.38	3.07	4.37	9.19	14.8
Mean number of frost-free days = 233							
Yakima							
Temp. (F)	50.5	58.5	64.4	71.0	68.6	61.3	50.5
(C)	10.4	14.8	18.1	21.8	20.5	16.4	10.3
Prec. (in)	0.47	0.54	0.81	0.13	0.20	0.35	0.60
(cm)	1.19	1.37	2.05	0.33	0.50	0.88	1.52
Mean number of frost-free days = 177							

This colorful display is an example of what is possible in the Northwest.

THE SOUTHWEST

The Southwest region has many plant growth zones because of temperature and precipitation differences due to variations in elevation. Deciduous tree fruits with high chill requirements – such as apples, pears, peaches and cherries – are grown in the mountain valleys of Colorado, New Mexico, Arizona and California. Citrus is grown in selected low areas of Southern California and Arizona. Cultivation is carried on from below sea level to above 8500 feet (2575 m), over a range of 365 frost-free days to less than 60.

The Southwest has low rainfall, extremely low relative humidity (often as low as 4 percent), sunny days, high solar radiation, temperatures that are high during the day but drop as much as 50 degrees at night and periods of drying winds that are often hot during summer. Warm, sunny days in mid- and late winter are followed by freezing temperatures at night.

Because of limited water supply, many gardeners have installed 'drip' or 'trickle' irrigation systems that meter a very small amount of water to plants daily. These systems use only a quarter to a tenth the total amount of water applied by the conventional furrow and flood irrigation systems, but are more expensive to install. Mulching with plastic, straw or grass clippings is a common technique practiced by gardeners in the Southwest to conserve moisture.

The prevailing wind east of the Sierra Nevada Mountains is from the southwest and is very dry and strong – especially in the spring. Soil moisture is lost very rapidly, making frequent irrigation for young plants a necessity. Blowing sand that cuts off seedlings at ground level is a problem from early March to mid-May.

The exception to these general statements is the coastal area of California. Here the climate is dominated by the marine influence of the Pacific. In the northern part of the state, winters are cool and wet while summers are cool and foggy. In the South, temperatures are warmer but not hot, and the humidity is higher than areas just a few miles inland.

Soils vary in texture, but are, for the most part, alkaline. This alkalinity may present problems, especially to gardeners from humid regions. Adding organic matter plays an important part in soil management. It makes sandy soils retain more moisture, and also loosens up heavy or clay soils. Mulching with organic materials is also very useful. It helps fight weeds, conserves water and adds organic matter to the soil.

Plants for a Dry Climate

The desert areas of the Southwest challenge the gardener in many ways. Variations in elevation result in widely differing success with a variety of plants. The high desert of Arizona offers frequent freezing temperatures during the winter so that cold-weather perennials, deciduous fruits and flowering shrubs receive their winter chill period while summer temperatures remain below 100°F (38°C) for the most part. The low deserts of California and Arizona, on the other hand, are subtropical in nature. Temperatures rarely dip below freezing, and those of 100°F (38°C) or higher may persist for weeks at a time during the summer, making cultivations of many fruits and flowering shrubs impossible.

The desert areas all share low rainfall and dry, searing winds. The plants under Dry Climate Selections are well suited to the climate in most areas of the region.

Stachys grandiflora

Plant Selections

Shrubs and Climbing Plants
Abutilon
Antigonum
Brunfelsia
Buddleia asiatica
Callistemon
Camellia
Ceanothus
Chimonathus
Choisya
Cistus
Clerodendrum
Clytostoma
Cytisus
Distictis
Fatsia japonica
Fuchsia
Hardenbergia
Hibiscus rosa-sinensis
Hoya
Kadsura
Lagerstroemia
Ligustrum ovalifolium
Magnolia
Mahonia japonica
Mandevilla
Mina
Nandina domestica
Nerium oleander
Pandorea
Passiflora
Plumbago
Raphiolepis
Rosa
Trachelospermum
   jasminoides
Wisteria

Perennials and Bulbs
Achillea
Agapanthus
Alstroemeria
Aster
Bergenia
Brassica oleracea
Cerastium
Chrysanthemum
Convolvulus
Cuphea ignea
Demorphotheca
   sinuata
Dianthus
Digitalis
Gazania
Gerbera
Gladiolus
Helianthemum
Heliotropium
Hemerocallis
Iberis
Kniphofia
Lantana
Lavandula
   angustifolium
Liatris
Lupinus polyphyllus
Narcissus
Nierembergia
Oxalis
Papaver
Primula
Rudbeckia
Salvia
Silene
Stachys
Tigridia
Zantedeschia

Dry Climate Plant Selections

Shrubs and Climbing Plants
Abelia grandiflora
Antigonum
Bougainvillea
Buddleia
Callistemon
Campsis radicans
Cotoneaster
Euonymus
Lagerstroemia indica
Ligustrum
Lonicera japonica
Nandina domestica
Nerium oleander
Prunus caroliniana
Pyracantha
Rosa
Tamarix
Tecomaria capensis
Trachelospermum
   jasminoides
Wisteria

Perennials and Bulbs
Agave
Anemone
Baptisia
Centaurea cineraria
Euphorbia
Dianthus
Gaillardia
Gazania
Geum
Iris
Liatris
Limonium
Mesembryanthemum
   crystallinum
Mimulus
Sedum
Verbena

Climatic Data for Representative Areas of the Southwest

City	Apr.	May	June	July	Aug.	Sept.	Oct.
Albuquerque							
Temp. (F)	55.8	65.3	74.6	78.7	76.6	70.1	58.2
(C)	13.3	18.7	23.9	26.2	25.0	21.3	14.7
Prec. (in)	0.68	0.68	0.68	1.46	1.25	0.94	0.73
(cm)	1.73	1.73	1.73	3.71	3.18	2.39	1.85
Mean number of frost-free days = 198							
Denver							
Temp. (F)	47.5	56.3	66.4	72.8	71.3	62.7	51.5
(C)	8.7	13.6	19.3	22.8	22.0	17.2	11.0
Prec. (in)	2.05	2.20	1.64	1.36	1.43	1.08	1.01
(cm)	5.21	5.59	4.17	3.45	3.63	2.74	2.57
Mean number of frost-free days = 165							
Flagstaff							
Temp. (F)	42.1	50.1	58.2	65.6	63.6	57.5	47.0
(C)	5.7	10.1	14.7	18.8	17.7	14.3	8.4
Prec. (in)	1.28	0.74	0.52	3.11	3.03	1.69	1.48
(cm)	3.25	1.88	1.32	7.90	7.70	4.29	3.76
Mean number of frost-free days = 118							
Las Cruces							
Temp. (F)	60.0	68.0	76.9	80.0	78.1	71.7	61.2
(C)	15.7	20.2	25.1	26.9	25.8	22.2	16.3
Prec. (in)	0.25	0.34	0.58	1.58	1.79	1.21	0.70
(cm)	0.64	0.86	1.47	4.01	4.55	3.07	1.78
Mean number of frost-free days = 208							
Los Angeles							
Temp. (F)	58.8	61.9	64.5	68.5	69.5	68.7	65.2
(C)	15.0	16.7	18.2	20.4	21.0	20.6	18.6
Prec. (in)	0.97	0.38	0.09	0.00	0.01	0.20	0.54
(cm)	2.46	0.97	0.23	0.00	0.03	0.51	1.37
Mean number of frost-free days = 359							
Lubbock							
Temp. (F)	60.0	68.5	77.1	79.7	76.4	71.0	60.0
(C)	15.7	20.4	25.3	26.7	24.9	21.8	15.7
Prec. (in)	1.44	2.37	2.55	2.05	1.92	2.91	2.35
(cm)	3.66	6.02	6.48	5.21	4.88	7.39	5.97
Mean number of frost-free days = 205							

City	Apr.	May	June	July	Aug.	Sept.	Oct.
Phoenix							
Temp. (F)	67.7	76.3	84.6	91.2	89.1	83.8	72.2
(C)	20.0	24.8	29.5	33.2	32.0	29.0	22.5
Prec. (in)	0.43	0.12	0.08	1.00	0.93	0.71	0.44
(cm)	1.09	0.30	0.20	2.54	2.36	1.80	1.12
Mean number of frost-free days = 304							
Reno							
Temp. (F)	46.8	54.6	61.5	69.3	66.9	60.2	50.3
(C)	8.3	12.7	16.5	20.9	19.5	15.8	10.3
Prec. (in)	0.53	0.50	0.39	0.29	0.33	0.27	0.44
(cm)	1.35	1.27	0.99	0.74	0.84	0.69	1.12
Mean number of frost-free days = 155							
Sacramento							
Temp. (F)	59.6	65.3	71.3	75.9	74.9	72.5	64.5
(C)	15.5	18.7	22.0	24.6	24.0	22.7	18.2
Prec. (in)	1.04	0.54	0.16	0.00	0.00	0.30	0.80
(cm)	2.64	1.37	0.41	0.00	0.00	0.76	2.03
Mean number of frost-free days = 307							
Salt Lake City							
Temp. (F)	50.1	58.9	67.1	76.6	74.4	64.2	52.9
(C)	10.1	15.1	19.7	25.0	23.7	18.0	11.7
Prec. (in)	1.76	1.56	0.91	0.61	0.97	0.74	1.34
(cm)	4.47	3.96	2.31	1.55	2.46	1.88	3.40
Mean number of frost-free days = 202							
San Antonio							
Temp. (F)	69.6	76.0	82.2	84.7	83.7	79.3	70.5
(C)	21.1	24.6	28.1	29.5	29.0	26.5	21.6
Prec. (in)	3.25	3.50	2.58	2.30	1.64	2.86	2.33
(cm)	8.26	8.89	6.55	5.84	4.17	7.26	5.92
Mean number of frost-free days = 282							

This cactus garden is at Huntington Botanical Garden.

THE SOUTHEAST

The climate of the Southeast is primarily mild and humid, but there are a variety of conditions: arid plains in the West, forested mountains in the North, sub-tropical conditions in the Gulf states and tropical conditions in southern Florida. Compared with many areas of the country, the Southeast has a long growing season. With the exception of high elevation areas in North Carolina and Tennessee, there are at least 180 days without frost. This ranges to well over 300 days in south Florida and Texas.

Most regions of the Southeast receive about 50 inches (127 cm) of rain, although some areas in the mountains report as much as 80 inches (203 cm). Most of the rainy weather comes in late winter and early spring.

High rainfall and humidity, although needed for plant growth, also create gardening problems. The moist conditions are often ideal for many diseases of plant foliage that are not a problem in dryer areas.

The Southeast is known for its mild climate. Temperatures well below zero have been recorded, but these are usually of short duration. The biggest damage to gardens comes with late freezes in spring. In the lower South, high temperatures and humidity bring gardening activity to a virtual standstill in mid-summer. The heat and humidity of the Southeast create the conditions for the legendary Spanish moss, which often drapes old branches of southern live oak and other trees along the Gulf with dramatic hanging garlands of filmy gray growth.

The southeastern rim of these states is bordered by the Atlantic Ocean or the Gulf of Mexico. The elevation starts at sea level and rises as you go inland. In Alabama, for example, the elevation at Mobile is 11 ft (3.3 m); Montgomery, 169 ft (51 m); and Birmingham, 598 feet (182 m). In the mountains of North Carolina and Tennessee many areas are above 2000 feet (610 m).

Soils of the Southeast vary from lakeland sand to the heaviest prairie soils. With the abundant rainfall, they are subject to year-round erosion. They are rarely frozen for any length of time during winter, when much of the rain occurs. The light sandy soils are also subject to heavy leaching. Organic matter should be added frequently as it is dissipated rapidly by rainfall and high temperatures.

Mild temperatures and high humidity are ideal for a wide variety of plants and they also appeal to garden pests. Garden insects are more prevalent here than in other areas of the country, and more generations appear during a long growing season. One common pest in the region is the nematode. New gardeners in the region should have their soil tested for nematodes through the county extension office as a high percentage of old gardens are infested.

The climate is ideal for development of many plant diseases as well. Choose resistant varieties and familiarize yourself with fungicides to reduce diseases in your garden.

Tropical Plants

Heat, plentiful rain and humidity create conditions where tropical plants can flourish. Most American gardeners are limited to growing these in greenhouses, but residents in the Southeast area of zone 10 enjoy ideal year-round conditions for experimenting with lush, flamboyant tropicals. Since many of these are grown as house plants in the rest of the country, some of the following listings will be found under that heading in the A–Z section of the book.

Beaumontia grandiflora is a shrub which grows well in the Southeast.

Plant Selections

Shrubs and Climbing Plants

Abelia grandiflora, floribunda
Abutilon
Beaumontia
Brunfelsia
Callistemon
Camellia
Ceanothus
Chimonathus
Clematis hybrids
Clerodendrum fragrans
Cobaea
Cornus florida
Daphne
Erica
Erythina
Escallonia
Euonymus japonica
Forsythia
Fuchsia
Gelsemium
Hamamelis
Hibbertia
Hibiscus rosa-sinenis
Ilex crenata
Jasminum
Kadsura
Lagerstroemia indica
Lonicera brownii
Magnolia
Mandevilla
Nandina domestica

Nerium oleander
Parthenocissus henryana
Passiflora
Philadelphus
Photonia
Prunus laurocerasus
Raphiolepis indica
Rhododendron
Rosa
Spiraea
Tecomaria
Thunbergia
Viburnum farreri
Weigela florida
Wisteria sinensis

Perennials and Bulbs

Agapanthus
Anemone hybrida
Ceratostigma plumbaginoides
Chrysanthemum
Coreopsis grandiflora
Crocosmia
Cyclamen hederifolium
Dahlia
Filipendula palmata
Geranium
Hosta
Iris
Kniphofia hybrids
Liriope muscari
Stachys byzantina

Tropical Selections

Beaumontia grandiflora
Bougainvillea species
Brunfelsia
Callistemon
Clerodendrum
Clytostoma
Cobaea
Erythina
Gerbera hybrids
Hardenbergia
Hibbertia
Hibiscus rosa-sinensis
Hoya
Mandevilla
Mina
Monstera deliciosa
Pandorea
Plumbago
Pyrostegia
Schefflera actinophylla
Thunbergia

Climatic Data for Representative Areas of the Southeast

City	Apr.	May	June	July	Aug.	Sept.	Oct.
Atlanta							
Temp. (F)	61.1	69.1	75.6	78.0	77.5	72.3	62.4
(C)	16.3	20.8	24.4	25.7	25.5	22.6	17.0
Prec. (in)	4.61	3.71	3.67	4.90	3.54	3.15	2.50
(cm)	11.7	9.42	9.32	12.5	8.99	8.00	6.35
Mean number of frost-free days = 244							
Charlotte							
Temp. (F)	60.8	68.8	75.9	78.5	77.7	72.0	61.7
(C)	16.1	20.6	24.6	26.0	25.6	22.4	16.6
Prec. (in)	3.40	2.90	3.70	4.57	3.96	3.46	2.69
(cm)	8.64	7.37	9.40	11.6	10.1	8.79	6.83
Mean number of frost-free days = 239							
Columbia							
Temp. (F)	64.1	72.1	78.8	81.2	80.2	74.5	64.2
(C)	18.0	22.5	26.2	27.6	26.7	23.8	18.0
Prec. (in)	3.51	3.35	3.82	5.65	5.63	4.32	2.58
(cm)	8.92	8.51	9.70	14.4	14.3	10.9	6.55
Mean number of frost-free days = 252							
Dallas							
Temp. (F)	66.4	73.8	81.6	85.7	85.8	78.2	68.0
(C)	19.2	23.4	27.8	30.1	30.1	25.9	20.1
Prec. (in)	4.72	4.85	3.27	1.80	2.36	3.25	3.18
(cm)	11.9	12.3	8.31	4.57	5.99	8.26	8.08
Mean number of frost-free days = 249							
Houston							
Temp. (F)	69.4	75.8	81.1	83.3	83.4	79.2	70.9
(C)	20.9	24.6	27.6	28.7	28.8	26.4	21.8
Prec. (in)	3.54	5.10	4.52	4.12	4.35	4.65	4.05
(cm)	8.99	12.9	11.5	10.5	11.1	11.8	10.3
Mean number of frost-free days = 309							
Jacksonville							
Temp. (F)	68.1	74.3	79.2	81.0	81.0	78.2	70.5
(C)	20.1	23.7	26.4	27.5	27.5	25.9	21.6
Prec. (in)	3.07	3.22	6.27	7.35	7.89	7.83	4.54
(cm)	7.80	8.18	15.9	18.7	20.0	19.9	11.5
Mean number of frost-free days = 313							
Lexington							
Temp. (F)	55.3	64.7	73.0	76.2	75.0	68.6	57.8
(C)	13.1	18.3	23.0	24.8	24.1	20.5	14.5
Prec. (in)	3.87	4.16	4.31	4.83	3.40	2.65	2.12
(cm)	9.82	10.5	10.9	12.2	8.6	6.7	5.3
Mean number of frost-free days = 198							

City	Apr.	May	June	July	Aug.	Sept.	Oct.
Little Rock							
Temp. (F)	61.7	69.8	78.1	81.4	80.6	73.3	62.4
(C)	16.6	21.1	25.8	27.7	27.2	23.1	17.0
Prec. (in)	5.25	5.30	3.50	3.38	3.01	3.55	2.99
(cm)	9.83	13.5	12.4	8.59	7.65	9.02	7.59
Mean number of frost-free days = 244							
Miami							
Temp. (F)	75.0	78.0	81.0	82.3	82.9	81.7	77.8
(C)	24.1	25.7	27.5	28.2	28.5	27.8	25.6
Prec. (in)	3.60	6.12	9.00	6.91	6.72	8.74	8.18
(cm)	9.14	15.5	22.9	17.6	17.1	22.2	20.8
Mean number of frost-free days = 360							
Mobile							
Temp. (F)	67.9	74.8	80.3	81.6	81.5	77.5	68.9
(C)	20.1	24.0	27.1	27.8	27.8	25.5	20.6
Prec. (in)	5.59	4.52	6.09	8.86	6.93	6.59	2.55
(cm)	14.2	11.5	15.4	22.5	17.6	16.7	6.48
Mean number of frost-free days = 289							
Nashville							
Temp. (F)	60.1	68.5	76.6	79.6	78.5	72.0	60.9
(C)	15.7	20.4	25.0	26.7	26.0	22.5	16.1
Prec. (in)	4.11	4.10	3.38	3.83	3.24	3.09	2.16
(cm)	10.4	10.4	8.59	9.73	8.23	7.85	5.49
Mean number of frost-free days = 224							
New Orleans							
Temp. (F)	68.6	75.1	80.4	81.9	81.9	78.2	69.8
(C)	20.5	24.1	27.1	27.9	27.9	25.9	12.1
Prec. (in)	4.15	4.20	4.74	6.72	5.27	5.58	2.26
(cm)	10.5	10.6	12.0	17.1	13.4	14.2	5.74
Mean number of frost-free days = 302							
Richmond							
Temp. (F)	57.8	66.5	74.2	77.9	76.3	70.0	59.3
(C)	14.5	19.2	23.7	25.6	24.8	21.2	15.3
Prec. (in)	2.77	3.42	3.52	5.63	5.06	3.58	2.94
(cm)	7.04	8.69	8.94	14.3	12.8	9.09	7.47
Mean number of frost-free days = 220							
Tulsa							
Temp. (F)	60.8	68.8	77.3	82.1	81.4	73.3	62.9
(C)	16.1	20.6	25.4	28.1	27.7	23.1	17.3
Prec. (in)	4.17	5.11	4.69	3.51	2.95	4.07	3.22
(cm)	10.6	12.9	11.9	8.92	7.49	10.3	8.18
Mean number of frost-free days = 216							

A rock pool at Atlanta Botanical Garden, Piedmont Park.

THE NORTHEAST

Successful gardening can be carried out in every state in the Northeast if careful consideration is given to climate conditions. The region consists of Iowa, Missouri and states east of the Mississippi and from the Canadian border southward to, and including, Kentucky and Virginia. Two basic climate areas dominate this humid region, one with small temperature changes and another with moderate changes.

The small-temperature change area is primarily composed of all the Northeast region north of 40° latitude. This is a cold region, with hot summers (average above 71.6°F (22.1°C) and cold, long winters as in the New England states. The area is forested and has frozen soil and snow cover for several months in winter. Rainfall is adequate in all seasons.

The moderate-temperature change area comprises most of Illinois, Indiana, Kentucky, Ohio and the mid-Atlantic states. The climate is warm and rainy, and there is no distinct dry season. Winters are cool and short, with frozen soil and snow cover a month or less in duration. Weather in the summer growing season varies from hot in much of the area to cool, long summers in the Appalachian Highlands. Rainfall is adequate and sometimes abundant during the growing period. A maritime, equable climate exists at times along the Atlantic seaboard states.

Geographic features are favorable for gardening throughout the Northeast. Numerous streams provide a good drainage system. Swamps and high terrain areas are minimal in extent. Elevations range from 200–800 ft (61–244 m) above sea level in the eastern Great Plains and Great Lakes area to 0–200 ft (0–61 m) above sea level in the middle and north Atlantic states.

The Appalachian Highlands range from 2000 to 4000 ft (610–1219 m) above sea level and are 10 to 12 degrees cooler in summer because of elevation. Mountain valleys and high plateaus are usually problem areas in the Highlands due to cold air drainage and strong winds. The western slopes of the Appalachians are also cooler and cloudier during spring.

Areas within 20–30 miles (32–48 km) of the south and east shores of the major Great Lakes are very moderate, both in temperature and precipitation, during all seasons. Numerous lakes in this area provide some moderating effect. Spring and summer rainfall is minimal, but it increases in fall and winter. Temperatures are cooler for a longer time in spring, but warmth lasts into the fall.

Large, fertile flood plains are characteristic of river drainage systems throughout the Northeast. These areas have more water than is needed in late winter and spring.

Temperature and rainfall are important to success in gardening through all of the Northeast. Average temperatures and precipitation data are given in the table for representative cities in each state. Average monthly temperatures are used as a guide for planting and for determining the length of the growing season. The beginning and end of the latter for cool-season crops closely follows the time when average temperatures warm to 40°F (4°C) in spring and cool to 40°F (4°C) in fall. For warm-season crops an average temperature near 50°F (10°C) is used.

As a general rule, temperatures reach the level for safe planting of cool-season crops about March 15 in southernmost states of the Northeast region. The northward progression of safe planting dates is about 5 to 7 days later for each 100 miles (161 km). In southern mountainous areas, cool-season crop plantings can begin April 1. The planting season progresses northward 5 to 7 days later for each 100 miles (161 km).

Warm-season crops can safely be planted April 15 in southernmost states of the region. The season progresses northward with a delay of 5 to 7 days for every 100 miles (161 km). Mountainous areas need a delay of an additional 5 to 10 days, starting after April 20 in the South.

The average length of the frost-free growing period ranges from 180 to 234 days in the South and from 90 to 120 days in the northern and mountainous regions.

The growing season rainfall from March through October varies from 20 inches (51 cm) in the West to 40 inches (102 cm) in the South and East. Rainfall is the least in September through October and the greatest in June. Summer rainfall comes mainly from thunderstorm activity and is often poorly distributed during July and August. Dry, hot periods lasting 2–3 weeks are common during mid-summer throughout the Northeast. In these periods plants will need extra irrigation.

Extensive wet periods often occur in late May and June, while cool wet periods in April frequently delay spring planting. These wet periods produce seed rot and disease problems.

Climate effects must be considered in handling garden soils. Garden crops have a limited root system and require a continuous supply of nutrients and moisture. Excessive rainfall leaches out soluble nutrients, increases acidity, and causes aeration problems and poor root growth.

Climate and soil texture are important for soil warm-up in spring. Sandy soils warm earliest and have the widest daily variation. Heavy soils are cool in spring, warm slowly and hold heat longer in fall. Soil temperature at planting depth usually exceeds the air temperature by 5 to 10 degrees during the afternoon and cools to several degrees lower than the air temperature at night. Soil temperature variations are largest when the soil is dry and smallest when it is wet.

The direction of the slope of the garden area is important. Southeast, south and southwest sloping surfaces are warmer, receive more solar radiation and dry out faster. This may permit planting a week or more early. Gardens in low depression areas surrounded by high terrain are subject to cold air drainage and more frequent frost-freeze problems.

Freeze protection for garden plants is a necessity in the Northeast. In winter, perennials need protection from the freeze-thaw action of the soil and from extremely cold soil temperatures. Straw mulches are effective.

Soil freeze depths in the Northeast range from 2 inches (5 cm) to over 24 inches (61 cm), depending on snow cover. Root tissue damage develops at temperatures of 15° to 20°F (–9° to –7°C).

During spring, protecting plants with covers or by sprinkling on potential freeze nights pays dividends. Sprinkling is highly beneficial, particularly on dry, cool nights when evaporative cooling causes leaves to supercool. Sprinkling must begin a few degrees above freezing and continue until all ice has melted and the temperature is several degrees above freezing.

Rock and Slope Gardens

Rock gardens in the Northeast are often a graceful accommodation to sloping lots and rocky ledges. Unlike the formal English rock gardens, where expensive rocks are often purchased and carefully positioned, those in the Northeast are informal tapestries of miniature bulbs, annuals and perennials that lend color to sweeps of ground cover. Plants listed under Rock and Slope Selections are good choices.

Plant Selections

Shrubs and Vines
Akebia
Azalea
Calluna
Ceanothus americanus
Celastrus
Chaenomeles
Clethra ainifolia
Clematis
Clethra
Conifers
Cornus
Cotoneaster
Elaeagnus
Euonymus fortunei
Forsythia
Gaultheria
Hamamelis vernalis
Hydrangea petiolaris
Hypericum prolificum
Ilex
Kalmia latifolia
Kolkwitzia
Lathyrus latifolius

Lonicera sempervirens
Parthenocissus
   quinquefolia
Philadelphus
Pyracantha coccinea
Rhododendron
Rosa
Salix caprea
Spiraea
Syringa vulgaris
Viburnum
   rhytidophylla
Weigela

Perennials and Bulbs
Aconitum
Anchusa
Arabis aloida
Asclepias
Aster hybrids
Astilbe
Baptisia tinctoria
Brunnera macrophylla
Catananche caerulea
Chrysanthemum
Colchicum autumnale
Convallaria majalis
Coreopsis
Dianthus plumarius
Digitalis purpurea
Echinops exaltus
Epimedium rubrum,
   grandiflorum
Eranthis hyemalis
Filipendula vulgaris
Fritillaria
Gentiana
Gypsophila

Helianthus
Helleborus niger
Hemerocallis
Hosta
Iris
Liliuum
Lythrum salicaria
Monarda didyma
Muscari
Nepeta
Oxalis montana
Paeonia lactiflora
Physostegia
Primula veris
Rudbeckia
Salvia
Trollius
Veronica

Rock and Slope Plant Selection

Shrubs
Azalea
Berberis
Calluna
Daphne
Erica
Gaultheria
Hebe
Rhododendron

Perennials and Bulbs
Alyssum
Anemone blanda
Arabis albida
Aubrieta deltoidea
Chionodoxa luciliae
Crocus
Gentiana acaulis
Geranium cinereum
Geum
Helianthemum
Iberis saxatilis
Iris reticulata
Leucojum vernum
Linum alpinum
Myosotis alpestris
Narcissus
Polemonium
   caeruleum
Primula auricula
Scilla sibirica
Sedum
Silene acaulis
Tulipa

Climatic Data for Representative Areas of the Northeast

City	Apr.	May	June	July	Aug.	Sept.	Oct.
Albany							
Temp. (F)	46.2	57.9	67.3	72.1	70.0	61.6	50.8
(C)	8.0	14.5	19.8	22.5	21.3	16.6	10.5
Prec. (in)	2.77	3.47	3.25	3.49	3.07	3.58	2.77
(cm)	7.04	8.81	8.26	8.86	7.80	9.09	7.04
Mean number of frost-free days = 169							
Baltimore							
Temp. (F)	54.2	64.4	72.5	76.8	75.0	68.1	57.0
(C)	12.4	18.1	22.7	25.1	24.1	20.2	14.0
Prec. (in)	3.60	3.98	3.29	4.22	5.19	3.33	3.18
(cm)	9.14	10.1	8.36	10.7	13.2	8.46	8.08
Mean number of frost-free days = 234							
Boston							
Temp. (F)	47.9	58.8	67.8	73.7	71.7	65.3	55.0
(C)	9.0	15.0	20.0	23.3	22.2	18.6	12.9
Prec. (in)	3.77	3.34	3.48	2.88	3.66	3.46	3.14
(cm)	9.58	8.48	8.84	7.32	9.30	8.79	7.98
Mean number of frost-free days = 192							
Burlington							
Temp. (F)	41.2	53.8	64.2	69.0	66.7	58.4	47.6
(C)	5.1	12.2	18.0	20.7	19.4	14.8	8.7
Prec. (in)	2.63	2.99	3.49	3.85	3.37	3.31	2.97
(cm)	6.68	7.59	8.86	9.78	8.56	8.41	7.54
Mean number of frost-free days = 148							
Charleston							
Temp. (F)	55.3	64.8	72.0	74.9	73.8	68.2	57.3
(C)	13.0	18.4	22.4	24.0	23.4	20.3	14.2
Prec. (in)	3.68	3.71	3.69	5.67	3.95	2.92	2.58
(cm)	9.35	9.42	9.37	14.4	10.0	7.42	6.55
Mean number of frost-free days = 193							
Columbus							
Temp. (F)	50.8	61.5	70.8	74.8	73.2	65.9	54.2
(C)	10.5	16.5	21.7	23.9	23.1	18.9	12.4
Prec. (in)	3.49	4.00	4.16	3.93	2.86	2.65	2.11
(cm)	8.86	10.2	10.6	9.98	7.26	6.73	5.36
Mean number of frost-free days = 196							
Harrisburg							
Temp. (F)	51.8	62.7	71.3	76.2	74.1	66.9	55.7
(C)	11.1	17.2	22.0	24.7	23.6	19.5	13.2
Prec. (in)	3.02	3.90	3.42	3.51	3.65	2.82	2.97
(cm)	7.67	9.91	8.69	8.92	9.27	7.16	7.54
Mean number of frost-free days = 201							
Hartford							
Temp. (F)	48.5	59.9	68.7	73.4	71.2	63.3	53.0
(C)	9.2	15.6	20.5	23.2	22.0	17.5	11.8
Prec. (in)	3.73	3.41	3.70	3.61	4.01	3.65	3.18
(cm)	9.47	8.66	9.40	9.17	10.2	9.27	8.08
Mean number of frost-free days = 180							

City	Apr.	May	June	July	Aug.	Sept.	Oct.
Indianapolis							
Temp. (F)	50.8	61.4	71.1	75.2	73.7	66.5	55.4
(C)	10.5	16.4	21.9	24.1	23.3	19.3	13.1
Prec. (in)	3.74	3.99	4.62	3.50	3.03	3.24	2.62
(cm)	9.50	10.1	11.7	8.89	7.70	8.23	6.65
Mean number of frost-free days = 193							
Lansing							
Temp. (F)	45.7	57.1	67.4	71.7	70.2	62.0	51.3
(C)	7.6	14.1	19.8	22.2	21.3	16.8	10.8
Prec. (in)	2.87	3.73	3.34	2.58	3.05	2.60	2.50
(cm)	7.29	9.47	8.48	6.55	7.75	6.60	6.35
Mean number of frost-free days = 185							
Lexington							
Temp. (F)	54.4	64.5	73.6	77.4	76.0	69.3	58.1
(C)	12.5	18.2	23.3	25.4	24.6	20.9	14.6
Prec. (in)	4.04	3.85	4.72	3.98	3.21	2.80	2.28
(cm)	10.3	9.78	11.9	10.1	8.15	7.11	5.79
Mean number of frost-free days = 198							
Madison							
Temp. (F)	44.4	56.1	66.1	71.1	69.5	61.0	49.9
(C)	6.8	13.3	18.9	21.7	20.8	16.1	9.9
Prec. (in)	2.57	3.34	3.95	3.58	3.37	3.32	2.21
(cm)	6.58	8.48	10.0	9.09	8.56	8.43	5.61
Mean number of frost-free days = 177							
Portland							
Temp. (F)	42.5	53.0	62.1	68.1	66.8	58.7	48.6
(C)	5.9	11.8	16.9	20.2	19.5	15.0	9.3
Prec. (in)	3.73	3.41	3.18	2.86	2.42	3.52	3.20
(cm)	9.47	8.66	8.08	7.26	6.15	8.94	8.13
Mean number of frost-free days = 169							
Richmond							
Temp. (F)	58.1	67.0	75.1	78.1	76.0	70.2	58.7
(C)	14.6	19.6	24.1	25.8	24.6	21.3	14.9
Prec. (in)	3.15	3.72	3.75	5.61	5.54	3.65	3.00
(cm)	8.00	9.45	9.53	14.2	14.1	9.27	7.62
Mean number of frost-free days = 220							
Springfield							
Temp. (F)	53.4	63.9	74.0	78.0	75.2	67.6	56.7
(C)	11.9	17.8	23.5	25.7	24.1	19.9	13.8
Prec. (in)	3.59	3.88	4.45	3.49	2.74	2.93	2.91
(cm)	9.10	9.86	11.3	8.86	6.96	7.44	7.39
Mean number of frost-free days = 205							
Trenton							
Temp. (F)	51.7	62.3	71.0	76.0	73.9	67.1	56.8
(C)	11.0	17.0	21.8	24.6	23.5	20.0	13.9
Prec. (in)	3.21	3.62	3.60	4.18	4.77	3.50	2.84
(cm)	8.15	9.19	9.14	10.6	12.1	8.89	7.21
Mean number of frost-free days = 211							

THE NORTH

Zones 1 and 2 cover more than half the continent of North America. They include an area composed of a wide diversity of soil types, mean temperatures, frost-free periods, precipitation and snow cover. Home gardeners from Maine to the Yukon delight in cultivating a wide variety of plants, but choices narrow on the western prairie, with its scant rainfall, and in the northern territories, where the winters are severe.

Almost half of Canada is situated on a massive shield of Precambrian rocks hewed by a gigantic prehistoric glacier. It is very sparsely populated because of the harsh climate, which is unsuitable for any form of agriculture. This area is characterized by low winter temperatures, high levels of snowfall and long days of sunlight in the summer. With the exception of the Rockies and the ends of the Appalachian chain, most of the cold region is less than 1000 ft (305 m) above sea level and is of smooth or rolling contour. Except for the mountains, it is a glacial area with soil variations ranging from very heavy clays to gravel and rock. The soil ranges from extremely acid in the eastern areas to highly alkaline in the Great Plains areas of Manitoba. Precipitation varies from 40 inches (101 cm) in the eastern sections of Canada to 10 inches (25 cm) or less in the central West.

The warm maritime air of the Pacific makes the climate of British Columbia like that of the American Northwest, and gardeners should refer to that section for growing conditions. Winters are mild and summers warm, with rain falling all through the year but most heavily in winter.

Winter temperatures on the Atlantic shores of Canada are warmer than those in the interior of the continent, but the summer temperatures are kept lower than in the interior because of the cold Labrador current, which flows southwards close to the coast.

Much of the southern interior of Canada has a very continental climate with high summer temperatures. Because of the long days during the summer months, growth occurs more rapidly than might be expected during the relatively short growing season in the north. Many cool-season flowers such as peonies, sweet peas, delphiniums, chrysanthemums and begonias thrive on the region's cool, dewy nights and long, warm days.

Heavy snow cover provides a protective mulch in many areas, increasing the hardiness of the plants as much as a full zone. Perennials and low-growing shrubs covered with snow during the winter months may thrive in gardens where the hardiness zone would indicate they might not. In the western arid zones, perennials are extremely difficult to grow unless provided with a heavy mulch.

Perennials should be planted in late summer or early autumn. Annuals need to be given a head start indoors until the weather warms sufficiently outside. Coldframes can be used to extend the growing season. When the first autumn frosts arrive, cover the frame and open it during the warm part of the day so that the plant can complete its growing cycle.

The Indoor/Outdoor Garden

Gardening enthusiasts who live in northern climates can maximize their growing season and their gardens by planting perennials and shrubs in containers that can be moved outside in summer and enjoyed year round inside under controlled conditions. Many plants will thrive year after year with this dual identity provided they are given adequate fertilizer and root space as they mature.

Many attractive and functional containers are available in a wide variety of shapes and sizes to suit the growth habits of almost every plant. Materials range from traditional clay, wood and stone to metal, concrete and plastic.

Plants that will serve well outside in the summer and will winter over indoors are listed under Indoor/Outdoor Selections.

Plant Selections

Shrubs and Vines
Conifers
Gaultheria
Hypericum kalmianum
Potentilla fruticosa
Salix purpurea
Spiraea latifolia
Syringa prestoniae
Tamarix
Weigela
  middendorffiana

Perennials
Achillea
Aconitum carmichaelii
Allium
Alyssum montanum
Aquilegia vulgaris,
  formosa
Artemisia absinthium,
  stellerana
Aster
Baptisia australis
Bergenia cordifolia
Campanula glomerata

Cerastium tomentosum
Delphinium elatum
Dianthus var.
Dicentra spectabilis
Dictamnus albus
Filipendula rubra
Gaillardia
Gypsophila
Helianthus giganteus
Hemerocallis
Iberis saxatilis
Liatris scariosa
Muscari botryoides
Myosotis alpestris
Papaver orientale
Physalis alkekengi
Polemonium caeruleum
Polygonatum
  multiflorum
Pyrethrum roseum
Scabiosa caucasica
Scilla
Stachys grandiflora
Tulipa

Indoor/Outdoor Plant Selection

Shrubs
Abelia grandiflora
Abutilon
Azalea
Callistemon
Camellia japonica
Clerondendrum
  thomsonae
Daphne
Erica
Fuchsia
Hydrangea
Lagerstroemia speciosa
Nandina domestica
Nerium oleander
Rosa

Perennials
Agapanthus
Astilbe
Ceratostigma
Chrysanthemum
Clivia
Euphorbia
Gerbera jamesonii
Impatiens
Lantana
Pelargonium
Penstemon
Primula
Zantedeschia

Climatic Data for Representative Areas of the North

City	Apr.	May	June	July	Aug.	Sept.	Oct.	Annual
Edmonton								
Temp. (F)	52.2	64.3	70.3	74.1	72.2	62.1	52.1	
(C)	11.2	17.9	21.2	23.3	22.3	16.7	11.1	
Prec. (in)	0.94	1.91	3.13	3.31	2.32	1.30	0.78	13.69
(cm)	2.39	4.85	7.95	8.41	5.89	3.30	1.98	34.77
Ottawa								
Temp. (F)	51.2	65.8	76.1	81.2	77.2	68.1	53.8	
(C)	10.6	18.7	24.5	27.3	25.1	20.0	12.1	
Prec. (in)	2.73	2.52	3.49	3.44	2.62	3.24	2.88	20.92
(cm)	6.93	6.40	8.86	8.74	6.65	8.23	7.32	53.14
Quebec								
Temp. (F)	44.9	61.2	72.1	75.8	73.2	64.1	51.2	
(C)	7.1	16.2	22.2	24.3	22.8	17.8	10.6	
Prec. (in)	2.34	3.12	3.73	4.04	4.02	3.62	3.44	24.31
(cm)	5.94	7.92	9.47	10.3	10.2	9.19	8.47	61.75

City	Apr.	May	June	July	Aug.	Sept.	Oct.	Annual
Saskatoon								
Temp. (F)	49.1	63.8	71.3	77.3	75.2	63.3	51.1	
(C)	9.5	17.6	21.8	25.1	24.0	17.3	10.6	
Prec. (in)	0.74	1.42	2.63	2.41	1.92	1.52	0.94	11.58
(cm)	1.88	3.61	6.68	6.12	4.88	3.86	2.39	29.41
Toronto								
Temp. (F)	50.1	63.2	72.9	78.8	77.2	69.3	55.8	
(C)	10.0	17.3	22.7	26.0	25.1	20.7	13.2	
Prec. (in)	2.54	2.91	2.73	2.94	2.73	2.92	2.44	19.21
(cm)	6.45	7.39	6.93	7.47	6.93	7.42	6.20	48.79
Winnipeg								
Temp. (F)	48.1	65.0	74.1	79.3	76.2	65.3	51.2	
(C)	8.9	18.3	23.3	26.2	24.5	18.5	10.6	
Prec. (in)	1.42	2.32	3.13	3.14	2.52	2.32	1.52	16.37
(cm)	3.61	5.89	7.95	7.98	6.40	5.89	3.86	41.58

Agricultural Experiment Stations

NORTHWEST REGION

British Columbia
University of British Columbia
Vancouver
British Columbia
V6T 2Z7

Department of Agriculture
Parliament Building
Victoria
British Columbia
V8W 2W1

Colorado
Colorado State University
Extension – Experiment Station
Publications Office
Fort Collins
Colorado 80521

Idaho
University of Idaho
Agricultural Science Building
Moscow
Idaho 83843

Kansas
Kansas State University
Extension Horticulture
Waters Hall
Manhattan
Kansas 66502

Minnesota
University of Minnesota
Bulletin Room
Coffey Hall
St Paul
Minnesota 55108

Montana
Montana State University
Cooperative Extension Office
Bozeman
Montana 59717

Nebraska
University of Nebraska
Department of
Agricultural Communications
Lincoln
Nebraska 68583

North Dakota
North Dakota State University
Agricultural Experiment Station
University Station
Fargo
North Dakota 58105

Oregon
Oregon State University
Bulletin Mailing Service
Industrial Building
Corvallis
Oregon 97331

South Dakota
South Dakota State University
Bulletin Room
Extension Building
Brookings
South Dakota 57007

Washington
Washington State University
Bulletin Department
Cooperative Extension
Publications Building
Pullman
Washington 99164

Wyoming
University of Wyoming
Box 3354
University Station
Laramie
Wyoming 80271

SOUTHEAST REGION

Alabama
Auburn University
Alabama Cooperative
Extension Service
Auburn
Alabama 36830

Arkansas
University of Arkansas
Cooperative Extension Service
1201 McAlmont
P.O. Box 391
Little Rock
Arkansas 77203

Florida
University of Florida
Cooperative Extension Service
Gainesville
Florida 32601

Georgia
University of Georgia
Extension Editor
Athens
Georgia 30602

Kentucky
University of Kentucky
Bulletin Room
Experiment Station Building
Lexington
Kentucky 40506

Louisiana
Louisiana State University
Publications Librarian
Knapp Hall, Room 192
Baton Rouge
Louisiana 70803

Mississippi
Mississippi State University
Chief Clerk
Oxford
Mississippi 39762

North Carolina
North Carolina State University
Publications Office
Department of
Agricultural Information
Box 5037
Raleigh
North Carolina 27607

Oklahoma
Oklahoma State University
Central Mailing Service
Cooperative Extension Office
Stillwater
Oklahoma 74074

South Carolina
South Carolina School
of Agriculture
Clemson
South Carolina 29631

Tennessee
University of Tennessee
Agricultural Extension Service
P.O. Box 1071
Knoxville
Tennessee 37901

Texas
Agricultural and
Mechanical University
Texas Agricultural
Extension Service
College Station
Texas 77843

Virginia
Virginia Polytechnic Institute
Extension Division
Blacksburg
Virginia 24061

West Virginia
West Virginia University
2104 Agricultural
Sciences Building
Evansdale Campus
Morgantown
West Virginia 26506

NORTHEAST REGION

Connecticut
University of Connecticut
Cooperative Extension Service
College of Argriculture
and Natural Resources
Storrs
Connecticut 06268

Delaware
University of Delaware
Mailing Room
Agricultural Hall
Newark
Delaware 19711

Illinois
University of Illinois
Agricultural Science Building
123 Mumford Hall
Urbana
Illinois 61801

Indiana
Purdue University
Lafayette
Indiana 47907

Iowa
Iowa State University
Publications, Distribution
Printing and
Publications Building
Ames, Iowa 50010

Maine
University of Maine
Department of Public Information
PICS Building
Orono, Maine 04473

Maryland
University of Maryland
Information and Publications
College Park
Maryland 20742

Massachusetts
University of Massachusetts
Cooperative Extension
Service
Stockbridge Hall
Amherst,
Massachusetts 01002

Michigan
Michigan State University
Department of
Information Services
East Lansing
Michigan 48824

Missouri
University of Missouri
College of Agriculture
Extension Programs
214 Waters Hall
Columbia
Missouri 65201

New Hampshire
University of New Hampshire
Cooperative Extension Service
Plant Science Department
Durham
New Hampshire 03924

New Jersey
State University of New Jersey
New Brunswick
New Jersey 08903

New York
Cornell University
Ithaca, New York 14850

Ohio
Ohio State University
Extension Office of Information
2120 Fyffe Road
Columbus, Ohio 43210

Pennsylvania
Pennsylvania State University
Agricultural Mailing Room
Agricultural Administration
Building
University Park,
Pennsylvania 16802

Rhode Island
University of Rhode Island
Resource Information Service
24 Woodward Hall
Kingston
Rhode Island 02881

Vermont
University of Vermont
Publications Office
Morrill Hall
Burlington
Vermont 05401

Virginia
Virginia Polytechnic
Institute and State University
Extension Division
Blacksburg
Virginia 24061

West Virginia
West Virginia University
2104 Agricultural
Sciences Building
Evansdale Campus
Morgantown
West Virginia 26506

SOUTHWEST REGION
Arizona
University of Arizona
Cooperative Extension Service
Tucson, Arizona 85721

California
University of California
Agricultural Sciences Publications
1422 South 10th Street
Richmond
California 94804

Colorado
Colorado State University
Extension – Experiment Station
Publications Office
Fort Collins
Colorado 80523

Nevada
University of Nevada
Cooperative Extension Service
Reno, Nevada 89507

New Mexico
New Mexico State University
Department of
Agricultural Information
Drawer 3–A1
Las Cruces
New Mexico 88003

Utah
Utah State University
The Bulletin Room
Logan, Utah 84322

NORTH REGION
Alberta
University of Alberta
O.S. Longman Building
6906-116 Street
Edmonton,
Alberta T6G 2E1

Manitoba
University of Manitoba
Winnipeg, Manitoba
R3T 2N2

Nova Scotia
Nova Scotia Agricultural College
Truro,
Nova Scotia

Ontario
University of Guelph
Guelph,
Ontario N1G 2W1

Quebec
Université Laval
Cité Universitaire
Quebec,
Canada G1K 7P4

McGill University
P.O. 6070
Montreal,
Quebec H3C 3G1

Saskatchewan
University of Saskatchewan
Saskatoon,
Saskatchewan
S7N 0W0

CONTROLLING PESTS AND DISEASES

T he charts which follow cover all the pests and diseases mentioned in the various sections of this book. Although preventive measures are preferable, there are many chemicals for controlling pests. Read the labels carefully to see what is appropriate. Pest and disease conditions vary considerably from region to region and from year to year. It is best to check with your regional experiment station (listed in the regional chapters) to see what is appropriate for your area. Pyrethrins and other contact sprays such as malathion are sprayed directly on to the insects to kill them. Systemic insecticides such as orthene, disyston and dimethoate are absorbed into the plant, killing insects that subsequently feed on them. They cannot be washed off by rain and they do not harm ladybirds, bees or butterflies. Do not use them on edible plants unless the details specify that it is safe to do so.

Diseases spread rapidly in favorable conditions and are much harder to control, once established, than pest attacks, so any spraying either has to be done in anticipation of attacks, or as soon as the first symptoms are noticed. Even more than with pests, prevention is better than cure. Healthily grown plants, rotation, garden hygiene, and burning all diseased material are of paramount importance.

If you decide to use one of the recommended pesticides or fungicides, remember that some of them are highly poisonous and have unpleasant odors that linger in the confines of a greenhouse. Before purchasing, read the makers' instructions carefully. When making up for use, follow the instructions to the letter. Too great a concentration could damage the plant, one too weak probably will not kill the pest or disease. Wash out the sprayer immediately after the job is finished and never leave empty containers lying around once the fungicide or insecticide has been used up.

PEST	DESCRIPTION	CONTROL
Aphids	The color may vary from green to black, but all have matchhead-sized, long, soft bodies, with relatively long legs. They do not always have wings, in which case the plump body is conspicuous.	There are many aphid killers; malathion is popular, pyrethrum and rotenone are also good. Try dimethoate if you want a systemic insecticide.
Big bud mites	Only likely to affect blackcurrants. The buds become swollen — hence the common name. A tiny mite is responsible. Also known as blackcurrant gall mite.	Chemical control is difficult. Pick off affected buds. Regular spraying with benomyl (actually a fungicide) seems to give some control.
Birds	Certain birds, notably bullfinch, pigeon, sparrow, starling, blackbird, blue tit, jay, eat fruits and seeds and damage flowers, young leaves and buds.	Hanging strips of glittering foil or erecting scarecrows can be successful. Fruit must be netted and spring flowers and newly sown seeds strung with black cotton (not nylon thread, which can trap the legs of a bird).
Bryobia mites	Rather like a larger version of the red spider mite of greenhouse plants, this attacks the leaves of primroses and other primulas, various alpine plants, plus gooseberry, apple, pear and ivy, causing bronze-to-brown mottling, then shrivelling.	Spray with malathion as soon as the symptoms are seen and repeat once or twice later at weekly intervals.

Greenfly on a rose shoot

PEST	DESCRIPTION	CONTROL
Cabbage root flies	Although mainly a pest of cabbages, cauliflowers and Brussels sprouts, cabbage root fly also attack wallflowers. The plants will wilt and become stunted. If lifted, the small maggots will be seen eating the roots.	Not much can be done once the plants have been attacked. As a precaution dust the soil with diazinon when transplanting or thinning.
Capsid bugs	You are most likely to see the symptoms before you see the pest. It leaves small ragged holes in leaves, and flowers and leaves become deformed. The insects are up to $\frac{1}{4}$ inch (5mm) long, but very active and are likely to drop to the ground when you look for them. The color is usually green, but may be yellowish or brown.	A systemic insecticide such as dimethoate is particularly useful. For a non-systemic, try malathion.
Caterpillars	Too well known and too diverse to warrant description. The appearance obviously depends on the species, but it makes little difference to control.	Malathion and trichlorphon will achieve control. Rotenone – as a spray or dust – is also effective. You can try orthene.
Grubs	These are the larvae of various beetles which feed on roots and underground stems. Affected plants wilt and may die if too many roots are severed.	If grubs are known to be present, treat the soil with orthene, dursban or diazinon prior to planting.
Codling moths	A pest of apples. You are unlikely to notice the moths, but you will see the maggots inside the apples.	Spray with diazinon or methoxychlor just after the petals have dropped, and again three weeks later.
Cutworms	Caterpillars of certain moths, e.g. yellow underwing, heart and dart etc., live under the soil eating roots and stems at ground level or just below. These are yellowish, brownish or greenish fat caterpillars that roll up when discovered. Swift moth caterpillars are a dirty white and often wriggle when touched; they tend to live deeper in the soil. Affected plants wilt or grow very poorly and may die.	Keep the ground clear of weeds and if these pests are known to occur, treat the soil with orthene, dursban or diazinon prior to planting.
Earthworms	These familiar soil creatures are useful rather than harmful, but certain kinds make casts on the surface which can damage the edges of mower blades and look unsightly.	Use a solution of potassium permanganate or rotenone dust well watered in. This treatment brings the worms to the surface where they can be promptly swept off and disposed of. If a killer is required use chlordimeform.
Earwigs	Earwigs are usually about 1 inch (2.5 cm) long, brown in color, and with 'pincers' at the end of the body. Suspect them if plants, such as dahlias (but also many others), have ragged holes in the leaves or petals.	Set bait containing baygon. Traps should not be dismissed. An upturned flower pot on a cane, filled with straw, will attract them. You will have to empty the trap regularly and kill the earwigs.
Eelworms	Eelworms are microscopic. There are many kinds, and symptoms vary. The ones mentioned in this book are mainly bulb and stem eelworms, affecting plants such as hyacinths and narcissi. On these plants the neck of the bulb usually feels soft and if the bulb is cut across there will be dark rings of dead tissue. Growth is usually malformed or stunted.	There is no effective cure available to amateurs. Lift and burn affected plants, and do not replant the same kind of plants in that piece of ground.
Flea beetles	Flea beetles make small, usually round, holes in the leaves of seedlings, and occasionally older plants. The beetles are about $\frac{1}{8}$ inch (3 mm) long, and tend to jump.	Dust with diazinon or dursban.
Leafhoppers	It is not the leafhopper insect that you are likely to notice first, but the frothy 'cuckoo spit' that appears on plants from May onwards. It protects pale colored nymphs inside. The mature insects are up to $\frac{1}{4}$ inch (5 mm) long, and jump when disturbed.	Malathion should give control. You may need to use a forceful spray to remove the protective froth.
Leaf miners	The caterpillars of certain tiny moths and grubs of flies tunnel between the upper and lower leaf skins, creating pale sinuous tracks or brownish blotches, both of which are unsightly. Among plants commonly affected are chrysanthemum, lilac, laburnum and holly.	Remove and destroy infected leaves if there is only a small infestation. Use acephate controls on non-edible plants and diazinon on edible plants.
Leatherjackets	These grayish maggots of the cranefly are about 1 inch (2.5 cm) long, and are found feeding on the roots of plants, which may turn yellow and wilt, and even die.	Work diazinon into the soil around susceptible plants.

Blackfly

Capsid bug

Caterpillar

Codling moth damage

Mealy bugs on chrysanthemum

Red spider mites on tradescantia

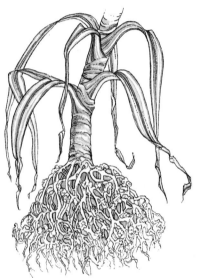

Root mealy bugs on dracaena

Scale insects on stephanotis

PEST	DESCRIPTION	CONTROL
Mealy bugs	Many house plants may be infected with one of various species of mealy bug. They are like large fat aphids with short legs, and are completely covered with white waxy filaments like wool. They suck sap and weaken plants. See also Root mealy bugs.	Brush with spray-strength solution of diazinon or malathion, or use dursban.
Narcissus flies	The bulbs produce yellowish, distorted leaves, and usually fail to flower. The maggot will be found inside the rotting tissue of the bulb.	It is best to lift and burn infected bulbs.
Raspberry beetles	The grubs of this tiny beetle feed in blackberries and loganberries, reducing their palatability.	Spray with malathion or rotenone.
Red spider mites	Several sorts of minute mites (known as 'red spider') attack a wide range of greenhouse plants and fruit trees outside. In the summer they may be either yellowish or greenish with or without red spots or entirely brownish-red. In autumn some sorts turn bright red. All suck sap and cause a yellowish mottling, followed by yellowing, browning and premature leaf fall. Established infestations are covered with a very fine webbing.	Spray with kelthane, orthene, dimethoate, diazinon or use dusting sulfur and repeat at weekly intervals until infestation is eliminated. Red spider can become resistant to insecticides and more than one type may have to be tried. To discourage breeding, spray daily with water.
Root mealy bugs	Very much like the common stem mealy bugs but living on roots, especially of succulents (including cacti) and other house plants. Plants fail to thrive, may wilt or yellow prematurely.	Soak the rootball with a spray solution of malathion or dimethoate.
Sawflies	These are the caterpillar-like grubs of a fly-like insect related to bees and wasps. Those on gooseberry and Solomons seal are the most conspicuous. The commonest sawfly on roses causes the leaflets to roll tightly, while apple sawfly feeds within developing apples and is often mistaken for codling moth.	Spray the conspicuous grubs with rotenone, malathion or trichlonphon. Leaf-rolling sawfly responds to dimethoate or diazinon. Apple sawfly must be sprayed with dimethoate or malathion the moment the petals fall.
Scale insects	Various species of scale insect can infect a wide range of house plants and those outside. The common brown scale insect occurs on shrub stems in sheltered sites and in greenhouses. It looks like a minute glossy brown tortoise and sucks sap, weakening the plant. This is one of the hard scales. Soft scales are oval and much flatter and soft to the touch. They are more likely to be on leaves or non-woody plants.	The tiny young scales are mobile and known as crawlers. They are easily killed. Late spring to early summer is their period of main activity on outside plants. Spray with malathion, diazinon or orthene. In the house crawlers may be active at any time, so try a systemic insecticide such as dimethoate or disyston, bearing in mind that some plants can be damaged by them.
Slugs and snails	Too well known to need description. There are several kinds of both slug and snail to be found in the garden. All respond to the same treatment.	Slug pellets based on metaldehyde or mesurol will protect plants reasonably well.
Thrips	These tiny insects are cylindrical in shape and usually under ⅛ inch (3 mm) in length. They have narrow, fringed wings and certain species swarm in summer when they are known as thunderflies. Not all species are pests, but those which are suck sap and cause pale mottling or silvering of leaves and flowers, which can also be crippled and die prematurely. Among garden plants likely to be attacked by various thrip species are onion, pea, gladiolus, rose, carnation and privet. Onion and privet thrip also attack a wide range of plants, particularly those grown indoors.	As soon as an attack is recognized, spray promptly with malathion, orthene, etc., and be prepared to repeat the treatment 2–3 weeks later.
Whiteflies	Small, white flies like minute moths. Not normally a problem outdoors, but may attack the plants that you take indoors or into the greenhouse for the winter.	A systemic insecticide such as dimethoate is effective. You can spray with non-persistent insecticides such as malathion, cygon or pyrethrum, but be prepared to repeat at intervals.
Wireworms	These are the grubs of various species of click beetle. The commonest sort is cylindrical with a tough yellow skin. It feeds on roots including those of carrot, beetroot and potato tubers.	If wireworms are known to be in the soil, apply dursban or diazinon prior to sowing or planting.

DISEASE	DESCRIPTION	CONTROL
Black spot	This very familiar fungal disease, which mainly affects hybrid roses, shows as dark brown to black blotches on the leaves. Further symptoms are premature leaf fall and weakening of the whole bush.	Spray with captan, benomyl or folpet when the leaves expand in spring. Repeat at 2-week intervals. Rake up and burn infected leaves in autumn as the fungus over-winters in this way. Where this disease is common, consider planting only disease-resistant varieties. Check the catalogs of rose specialists for varieties.
Blight of tomato and potato	One of the best known of all plant diseases, potato blight caused the Irish potato famine of the 1840s. Brownish black blotches appear towards the leaf tip then spread rapidly in damp weather leading to collapse and rapid rotting. Tomatoes are also susceptible to blight and show the same symptoms.	Immediately blight is recognized, spray or dust with zineb or maneb. If your area is attacked regularly, apply a preventative using the same substances, starting in early July and continuing at 10-day intervals.
Botrytis (gray mold)	As the common name suggests, the main symptom of this disease is a gray mold – usually on dead flowers or on fruit, but it can occur on leaves or stems. A cloud of dust-like spores may be released when the affected part is moved.	Remove any infected parts and destroy them. Then spray with benomyl or folpet, repeating at intervals if necessary.
Canker	Mainly on apples and some pears. Branchlets show sunken and cracked dead areas and some die-back occurs.	Cut out infected part, back to healthy wood. Check soil drainage (canker is worst in wet soils). Spray young trees with benomyl at leaf-fall.
Club-root	Although a problem of brassicas – such as cabbages and cauliflowers – it will also affect ornamentals such as wallflowers and stocks. Growth is poor and stunted and the roots are enlarged, often with unsightly swellings.	Treat the soil with vapam or terrachlor. For ornamental crops it is best to grow something different if you know the land is infected with club-root.
Damping off	This is a disease (which can be caused by several fungi) of seedlings. The seedlings collapse where they have rotted at soil level.	Use sterilized compost as a preventative measure whenever possible. Spray with thiram at weekly intervals.
Dollar spot, fusarium patch, red thread, ophiobolus patch	These are all fungal infections of lawn grass. Dollar spot causes 2–3 inch (5–7.5 cm) wide brown patches, and fusarium patch larger areas up to 1 ft (30 cm) across. Red thread causes even larger patches with the addition of red fungal threads. All are most common on fine lawn grasses, especially fescues. Ophiobolus patch creates bronzed or bleached areas of grass which die and leave bare, slightly depressed areas.	Immediately after mowing, apply benomyl or folpet. Improve aeration and fertility of the soil by feeding with general or special lawn fertilizer but avoid those with high nitrogen in autumn as they will create soft, disease-prone leaves.
Dry rot	Dry rot can affect a number of plants with bulbs or corms but gladioli are particularly vulnerable. The leaves turn brown and die; the corms show a number of small sunken lesions, or larger blackish areas.	Do not plant corms known to be infected; avoid replanting on infected ground. As a precaution soak the corms in a solution of benomyl or folpet for about half an hour before planting. (This is primarily a treatment for gladiolus corms, but it can be used for other cormous and bulbous plants.)
Fairy rings	Various soil-living fungi grow in a more or less circular fashion year by year. Liberation of nitrogenous substances as a result of a breakdown of organic matter by fungal threads causes the grass to grow extra-vigorously and a richer green.	Very difficult to eradicate, though certain rather poisonous mercurial compounds may be successful. Alternatively, dig out the turf for 2 ft (60 cm) beyond the ring, fork the soil and soak with a 1 in 50 solution of 40 percent formalin. Cover with plastic sheeting for 2 weeks, and 3–4 weeks later fill in with soil and re-seed or turf over.
Fireblight	Flowering shoots die, leaves look scorched and do not fall. All members of the rose family are at risk.	Cut out and burn diseased wood to a point 2 ft (60 cm) beyond visibly infected tissue.
Leaf spot	There are several leaf spots. They may vary from small, fairly regularly shaped spots to larger, irregular blotches. The colors vary from brown to black.	Spraying with benomyl or Bordeaux mixture is likely to achieve some control, but remove badly affected leaves and be prepared to repeat the treatment.

Whitefly on saintpaulia

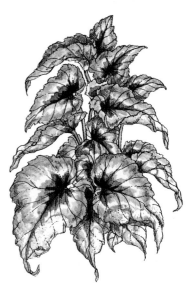

Botrytis on Begonia rex

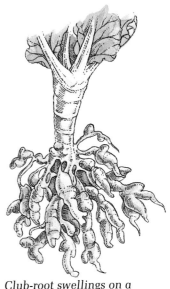

Club-root swellings on a cabbage plant

Powdery mildew

Downy mildew

Peach leaf curl

Scab on a ripe apple

DISEASE	DESCRIPTION	CONTROL
Mildew, downy	The plant becomes covered with a whitish or somewhat purplish growth. Easy to confuse with powdery mildew. If you wipe the growth off with a finger, downy mildew tends to leave the plant beneath rather yellow.	Mancozeb should give some control. Not easily controlled.
Mildew, powdery	The plants — particularly leaves and shoot tips — become covered with a white, powdery-looking growth. Infected parts may become distorted.	Try folpet, benomyl or sulfur. Be prepared to spray once every ten days to achieve control. If this does not work, it may be downy mildew — in which case try mancozeb.
Peach leaf curl	This is a distinctive disease; affected plants produce distorted leaves with ugly reddish blisters.	Collect and burn infected leaves as soon as you notice them. Spray with Bordeaux mixture after the leaves fall and again as the buds swell in late February or early March.
Rust	There are numerous rust diseases, but most produce brown or orange spots or pustules on the leaves.	Mancozeb should achieve some control, but you may have to persist with the treatment. Where rust-resistant varieties are available — as with antirrhinums — choose these if you have had trouble in previous years.
Scab	Scab is common on apples. Greenish-brown blotches appear on the leaves; cracked, corky spots on the fruit.	Folpet or benomyl sprayed every 10 days from bud-burst onwards should achieve control.
Silver leaf	Leaves at first silvered (not white), then brown and shrivelled. Shoots die. Plums, cherry, occasionally apricots, currants and apples and many other trees and shrubs can be attacked.	Cut out dead shoots or branches to 6 inches (15 cm) behind infection. Paint wound with fungicidal paint. Wash pruning tools after use. Do not prune very susceptible crops in winter.
Soft rot	Affects many different plants, including vegetables such as turnips and parsnips. Bulbs can become soft and slimy, with a bad smell.	There is little to be done about this disease except to destroy infected plants, and to make sure you plant a similar crop on different ground next time.
Tomato blight	Brown blotches appear on the leaves, dark brown streaks on the stems. Fruit tends to rot. See Blight.	Spray with mancozeb as a precaution in damp seasons once the first fruit has set. Repeat at 10-day intervals.
Tulip fire	Leaves and shoots are distorted and often withered. Flower buds usually fail to open.	Lift and destroy infected plants immediately. Do not plant suspect bulbs, and do not replant more tulips on infected land. If neighboring tulip bulbs seem unaffected, soak them in a benomyl solution for half an hour before replanting as a precaution.
Virus	There are many different viruses, and the symptoms vary with the disease and the plant. Suspect any plants that have distorted or stunted growth, or yellowish, mottled leaves that you canot put down to another problem.	Virus diseases cannot be cured, and leaving the plants risks spreading the infection. Lift and burn any suspect plant.
Wilt	As the name suggests, the most common sign of wilt (there are several kinds) is wilting leaves on the plant — though they may recover at night. If the stem is cut through some distance above ground level it will be discolored internally.	Try drenching the soil with benomyl or methyl bromide (made up as for a spray), and repeat the treatment. If this fails, uproot and burn the plant.

INDEX

ACKNOWLEDGEMENTS

The Publishers thank the following for providing the photographs in this book:

A–Z Botanical 65, 166 above; Pat Brindley 21; Camera Press 123; J. Allan Cash 181 above, 200 above; Bob Challiner 18; R.J. Corbin 14 below; Brian Furner 75; Garden Picture Library (Brian Carter) 30, 59, 97 below, 143, 218, (Derek Fell) 22, 25 above, 31, 40, 54, 56, 61, 66, 80, 82 above, 100, 103 below, 108, 112 above, 113 above, 119, 128, 131, 139, 141, 176, 183 below, 219, 220, (John Glover) 96, (Anthony Paul) 26 below, 49 above, (David Russell) 34, 63, 88, 105 below, 153, 154; Derek Gould 118, 137; Iris Hardwick 184 below; David Hoy 15; Andrew Lawson 134; Picturepoint 117; Harry Smith Collection 14 above, 78, 113 below, 197, 198, 204; Jessica Strang 221; EWA 151; Michael Warren/Horticultural Photos 83, 99, 110, 111.

The following photographs were taken specially for Octopus Picture Library:
Michael Boys 23 above, 24, 29, 33, 36 above, 37 above, 39 above, 41, 49 below, 82 below, 85 above, 91 below, 95, 97 above, 101 above & below, 102, 103 above, 105 above, 109 below, 177, 213, 223; Melvin Grey 144; Jerry Harpur 1, 2–3, 9, 13, 17, 23 below, 25 below, 26 above & below, 28, 35, 43 below, 45 above, 47, 50, 51 above & below, 52, 53, 57, 60, 85 below, 86, 90, 93

above, 98 above, 112 below, 115, 120 below, 121 below, 179 below, 194, 196, 200 below, 201 below, 202, 205 above & below, 207, 215, 217; Neil Holmes, 19, 81 above & below, 92, 93 below, 94, 106 above, 107, 109 above, 163, 164, 165, 166 below, 167, 168, 169, 170, 171, 172, 173 above & below, 174 above & below, 175, 178, 179 above, 180 above & below, 181 below, 182, 183 above, 184 above, 185, 199 above & below, 205 above, 206 below, 210; Margaret McLean 7; Roger Philips 124, 127, 129, 130, 132, 133, 135, 136, 138, 140, 142, 145, 146, 147 above & below, 148 above & below, 149, 150, 152 above & below; John Rigby 189; Paul Williams 157; George Wright 20, 32, 37 below, 38, 39 below, 42, 43 above, 44, 45 below, 46, 48, 55, 58, 67, 68 above & below, 71, 72, 74, 76, 79, 84, 87, 89, 91 above, 98 below, 104, 106 below, 114.

The Publishers thank the following for allowing their gardens to be photographed:
Mr & Mrs Martin Furniss, Cobblers, Crowborough, East Sussex; Mrs Aileen Mitchell, Dogginghurst, Essex; Mr Mark Rumary, Magnolia House, Saxmundham, Suffolk; Mrs Helen Schofield, Liss, Hampshire; Mr & Mrs J. Wright, Yew Tree Cottage, Liss, Hampshire.